DISCIPLESHIP

Towards an Understanding of Religious Life

Discipleship:
Towards an Understanding of Religious Life

JOHN M. LOZANO, C.M.F.

Translated by
BEATRICE WILCZYNSKI
from the original manuscript in Italian

Claret Center for Resources in Spirituality

RELIGIOUS LIFE SERIES
Volume Two
Chicago   Los Angeles   Manila
1980

Contents

Chapter II

Christian Vocations: Religious and Secular

Chapter III

 Religious Life: Dedication to God in the Church

Chapter IV

 The Charisms of Religious Life

Chapter V

✢ Celibacy for the Sake of the Kingdom

Chapter VI

The Religious Profession of Christian Poverty

Chapter IX

 The Religious Vow

Foreword

B y emphasizing the Church and the numerous ways by which it comes into being, Vatican II stimulated more intense reflection on the nature and ecclesial duties of religious life. The theology of the laity had been the preferred and cherished theme of prominent theologians before the Council, but the subject of religious life has returned to favor in current theology. It is enough to compare the sparse bibliography on this subject which existed before the Council with the abundance of articles, essays, and (to a lesser extent) books which have flooded religious houses during recent years. A rapid perusal of the bibliography at the end of this volume will prove instructive to the reader.

The reason for the change is obvious. By inviting religious communities to renew themselves in the spirit of the gospels, Vatican II led them to reflect on the meaning and value of this form of Christian life. It rapidly became evident that the centuries-old doctrinal synthesis on religious life could not support the new insights. The Council presented a new and richer image of the Church by stressing its inner and charismatic dimensions and by evaluating the role of the laity and of secularity. How easy it was, in the past, to speak of religious life as a state of perfection. It all seemed so clear with the ancient distinction between commandments and counsels. At first we religious were the "perfect ones," and later, the ones who publicly tended toward perfection. To reiterate these concepts today, after *Lumen Gentium,* would be highly problematical. Religious today must find a new explanation for their presence in the community of Jesus' disciples by penetrating deeply into the biblical Word and the Church's living tradition.

Many of us have set ourselves to reflect, to speak, and to write. The bibliography for this study clearly shows that many of the brief articles and essays are really testimonies from actual life, given by religious women and men in numerous popular reviews dedicated to the subject (e.g., *Sisters Today, Vida Religiosa, Vita Consecrata, Review for Religious, Vie des Communautés Religieuses,* etc.). These testimonies on various aspects of poverty, community life, prayer, and service, flowing out of group or personal experiences, deserve our respect. Professional theologians do well to listen to them. Theological reflection must pay attention to the movement of the Spirit, so long as discernment is employed.

There is also the area of popular handbooks and manuals, and of certain more-or-less theoretical studies which have helped many religious to understand the teachings of Vatican II in regard to their vocation. These writings have fulfilled their historical task despite their somewhat hasty composition. Without their heeding new exegetical insights and their going deeply enough into the history and theology of religious life, a kind of Scholastic summary becomes the only possibility for these authors. Monks (among them Fathers Leclercq and De Vogüé) continue to dust off their codices without being visibly influenced by the vast wealth of monastic theology.

But there is also a smaller group of theologians of religious life who are completing a laborious, in-depth study, taking into account exegetical conclusions, historical developments, and doctrinal variations. It would appear that this current research, begun by Karl Rahner and carried on by Fernando Sebastián, J. M. F. Tillard, L. Gutiérrez Vega, and Leonardo Boff, will make our time one of the richest periods for the theology of religious life.

This research has been preceded and accompanied by studies in the fields of history and literary criticism. By now we are rather well acquainted with the Pachomian environment (through Lefort and Bach), the Basilians (Gribomont) and their texts, the *Rule of the Master* and that of St. Benedict (De Vogüé), the theological, spiritual and literary traditions of Medieval monasticism (Leclercq), the early Franciscan movement (Esser), the Jesuit sources, etc.

This author intends to offer his own contribution to the research and reflection on religious life. Having spent several years teaching the theol-

ogy of religious life and the history of primitive monasticism in Rome's
Institute for Religious Life (Claretianum), at Loyola University, and at the
Catholic Theological Union in Chicago, he has wished to place the current
results of his work and study at the disposal of the public.

He offers this book in a spirit of service to those who are dedicated to the
same type of research and ministry, but above all to the many sisters and
brothers with whom he has had the joy of collaborating in chapters,
academic courses, and renewal programs.

In closing, the author feels the need to thank wholeheartedly his col-
leagues and brothers, Fathers Manuel Orge and Bruno Proietti, for their
suggestions in the bibliographical and exegetical fields, as well as Father
Bob Fath for his revision of the Italian text and of the English translation.

J.M.L.

EDITOR'S NOTE: At the end of several chapters of this study the reader will
find an excursus containing additional material on various themes treated in
the chapter to which it is appended. The author feels that the material in the
excursus is integral to the chapter, but may provide more detail than some
readers desire. Such readers may skip these excursuses without missing
any of the study's major themes.

B.F.

I

Discipleship

Describing the fundamental characteristics of religious life, Vatican II repeatedly stresses the *sequela Christi,* the following of Christ. In the Constitution on the Church, *Lumen Gentium,* it establishes a certain relationship between religious life and the following of Christ when it affirms "the religious state constitutes a closer imitation and an abiding reenactment in the Church of the form of life which the Son of God made his own when he came into the world . . . and which he propounded to the disciples who followed him."[1] Religious life finds in this phrase one of its meanings: an imitation of the type of life chosen by the Lord for himself and his disciples.

The decree *Perfectae Caritatis* is even more explicit. Its introduction reminds us that "from the very beginning of the Church there were men and women who set out to follow Christ with greater liberty, and to imitate him more closely."[2] In the following section discipleship becomes the very purpose for this kind of Christian life: "Before all else, religious life is ordered to the following of Christ by its members and to their becoming united with God."[3] This idea is repeated in two subsequent paragraphs in which the following of Jesus is presented as the special "profession" of religious,[4] or their particular vocation.[5] It is thus clear why the Council affirmed, from the very beginning of the second section of the decree, that discipleship is "the final norm of the religious life."[6]

For Vatican II the following of Christ constitutes one of the basic characteristics of religious life in the Church. Without fear of falsifying conciliar doctrine, we can also say it pertains to its deepest meaning. Even if the conciliar texts do not actually define discipleship, we can infer its meaning from the documents: a) an imitation of the Lord, not in a general ascetical sense, but in an actual reproduction of the type of life lived by Jesus and proposed by him to his disciples;[7] b) adherence to Jesus[8] and to his service.[9]

I. Historical Data

Are we facing an effort to renew the religious vocation by returning to its gospel sources? It is abundantly clear that the Council wanted to renew the spiritual life of religious by bringing it back to its "original inspiration" in the Gospel.[10] Yet for those who know the history of religious life it is also obvious that Vatican II did not introduce anything new on this point. The tendency to bring religious life back to the *sequela Christi* is one of the most ancient, yet constantly emerging, ideas in the course of history.

The tendency appears in the earliest and most important monastic texts. It is present in the second chapter of the *Vita Antonii* where St. Athanasius describes the birth of Anthony's vocation:

> Scarcely six months had passed since his parents' death, when, going to church, as was his custom, he thoughtfully reflected as he walked along how the Apostles, leaving all things, followed the Saviour, and how the faithful in the Acts of the Apostles, selling their possessions, brought the price of what they had sold and laid it at the Apostles' feet for distribution among the needy; and he considered how great was the hope laid up for them in heaven. Pondering on these things, he entered the church.
>
> It happened that the gospel was then being read and he heard the Lord saying to the rich man: "If thou wilt be perfect, go, sell what thou hast, and give to the poor, and thou shalt have treasure in heaven; and come, follow me."[11]

The importance of this account does not lie in its being the chronicle of an event that actually happened under given circumstances ninety years earlier. The *Vita Antonii,* the first Christian life of a saint, is a biography in the Hellenistic sense of the word: the description of a certain manner of life, motivated by certain ideals and offered as a model.[12] Athanasius intended to give a rule, as well as a treatise on spirituality, to the numerous anchorites who, often without any preparation, were dwelling in the deserts at that time. In the second chapter he is evidently quoting the main biblical passages that were cited in monastic circles as sources of inspiration for their lifestyle. These passages were, according to Athanasius: a) the gospel accounts of the calling of the Apostles; b) the summaries in Acts which speak of renunciation of one's goods in favor of the poor; c) the text of Mt. 19:21 ["If you wish to be perfect, go and sell what you own, give the money to the poor, then come, follow me"]; this Matthean test is originally and basically the story of a calling to discipleship;[13] and d) the summaries in Acts dealing with renunciation and solidarity with the poor.

Athanasius expresses a common opinion, not a personal one. Jerome, in his *Vita Hilarionis,* while recounting the calling of his subject, cites Mt. 19, the summaries in Acts, and Lk. 14:33 ("None of you can be my disciple unless he gives up his possessions").[14] The author of the lives of Hypatios and Cyriac, obviously inspired by the *Vita Antonii,* recounts that Hypatios discovered his vocation while he was in church listening to the reading of Mt. 19:19 ("everyone who has left house, brothers, sisters, father, mother . . . for my sake"), and Cyriac became aware of his calling when he heard the reading of Lk. 9:23 ("if anyone wants to be a follower of mine let him renounce himself, take up his cross every day and follow me").[15] The Abbot Pambo quotes both Mt. 19:21 ("go, sell what you own") and Lk. 9:23 in a similar context.[16]

This fact is noteworthy. In an effort to explain the original meaning of the monastic calling these authors amplify the account of the call to discipleship with certain texts (Lk. 9:23, 14:33) in which the conditions for the following of Christ are expressed in radical ways. For greater understanding we will call these gospel texts the sayings on discipleship. Similarly, Theodore calls the life of the followers of Pachomius an imitation of the Apostles in their renunciation of all things and their following of Christ,[17] while one of the authors of the Greek lives recalls that Pachomius made renunciation of all and the following of Christ the basis of his life.[18]

In the Latin cenobitical world the accent is placed on renunciation of goods as a necessary beginning for monastic life. But here also Mt. 19:21 is accompanied by other texts on conditions required in following the Lord. Cassian quotes the invitation to the rich man together with Lk. 9:62 ("once the hand is laid on the plough").[19]

In the *Rule of the Master* we find Mt. 19:21 quoted alone[20] and together with Lk. 14:33 ("none of you can be . . .").[21] The first Franciscan Rule of 1221 starts with Mt. 19:21 and continues with an anthology of texts on evangelical radicalism (Mt. 16:24, Lk. 14:16, Mt. 19:29),[22] while the second Rule quotes the invitation directed to the rich man together with Lk. 9:62.[23] It is well known that both St. Dominic[24] and St. Francis used the gospel rule for mission (Mt. 10, Lk. 10) as the fundamental text for their form of life,[25] following a tradition developed by the Medieval movements of the *Pauperes Christi*.

With individual variations the concept of the disciple who renounces all to follow Jesus in his life and ministry remains the model for all later institutes dedicated to evangelization. To mention only two examples, this model appears clearly in the process which led St. Ignatius of Loyola from meditation on the following of Christ, to the mystical grace in which he is associated with the Son, to the founding of the Company of Jesus.[26] The idea of the following of Christ is equally central in the vocation and spirit of the Claretians according to St. Anthony M. Claret.[27]

The fact that religious life arises primarily under the influence of the texts of the *sequela Christi* (call narratives and sayings which lay down the conditions for following Jesus) has ordinarily been expressed by calling it the *apostolic life*. This term refers to religious life inasmuch as it is born of the Gospel; i.e., it refers to the creative moment of the biblical inspiration. It seems that the first one to use this term was Theodore, a disciple of Pachomius, in the 4th century.[28] He was followed by Epiphanius[29] and by the historian Socrates.[30] In the West one finds the term in the *Ordo Monasterii*[31] and in St. Isidore of Seville.[32] From that time on, the term *vita apostolica* and the idea that religious imitate the life of the Apostles has appeared in a great number of texts pertaining to the vocation of monks, canons regular, and mendicants, as well as of modern institutes. Originally it meant that monks imitated the lifestyle of the disciples in renouncing all and following Jesus. Later, the term was used by monks, cenobites, and canons regular to indicate that all goods were held in common, in imitation of the apostolic community in Jerusalem. And yet, even then, the stories of the calling of the disciples and the texts giving the requirements for discipleship were often quoted in order to recall the original meaning of religious life.

In a third movement, among mendicant orders, the concept of apostolic life was again centered exclusively in the disciples' following of the historical Jesus, recalling how they left all, accompanied and served the Lord, obeyed the rules of mission, and were associated in the ministry of evangelization carried on by Jesus. The new concept of apostolic life was expressed very clearly and incisively by the author of the *Tractatus de approbatione ordinis Fratrum Praedicatorum:* "Vita apostolica est omnia propter Christum relinquere et, in paupertate ei serviendo, ipsum praedicare."[33] Service to the Kingdom through announcing the Gospel was thus reincorporated into the *sequela Christi.* This concept is certainly new when compared with the ordinary interpretation of the fourth through twelfth centuries, but, as we shall see, it corresponds to the calling and life situation of the disciples as shown in the Gospels.

The mendicants' interpretation subsists, though with some differences, in modern apostolic institutes in which ministry has a central position but poverty is equally important. This is clear in St. Ignatius of Loyola who, as Polanco wrote, wanted to imitate the "apostolic way."[34] St. Anthony M. Claret wrote to a friend, shortly after founding his congregation: "We are living a truly poor and apostolic life."[35]

II. The Following of Jesus in the New Testament

1. The Terms *To Follow* and *Disciple*

We have touched upon a fundamental concept of New Testament theology found in the Gospels: the *sequela Christi* defines the meaning of being a disciple of Jesus. That concept, expressed by the Greek verb *akolouthein* (to follow), is found in many Gospel texts. These texts may be classified into three groups:

A). A series of sayings on the conditions that must be met in order to be a disciple. Among these are:

1) One of the most ancient sayings that connects the condition of being a disciple with the destiny of Jesus is preserved in the double tradition of Mark and the Quelle, or Q Source (containing material common to Matthew and Luke): in Q, "Anyone who does not take up his cross and follow in my footsteps is not worthy of me" (Mt. 10:38), and, "Anyone who does not carry his cross and come after me cannot be my disciple"

(Lk. 14:27); in Mark, "If anyone wants to be a follower of mine, let him renounce himself and take up his cross and follow me" (Mk. 8:34). In regard to the Marcan text, compare Mt. 16:24 and Lk. 9:23 where Luke adds "(take up his cross) *every day.*"

2) A series of sayings from the Q source in which the disciple is invited to share the uprooted life of Jesus and to break all family ties. Two of these sayings are found in Mt. 8:18-22 and three in Lk. 9:57-62.

B). The accounts of the calling of the disciples: 1) the call of the first four disciples (Mk. 1:16-20, Mt. 4:18-22, Lk. 5:1-11); 2) the call of Levi-Matthew (Mk. 2:14, Mt. 9:9, Lk. 5:27-28); 3) the call of the rich man (Mk. 10:21, Mt. 19:21, Lk. 18:22); 4) the general description given by Peter of the disciples' response as opposed to the failure of the rich man (Mk. 10:28, Mt. 19:29, Lk. 18:28); 5) the two disciples of the Baptist who follow Jesus (Jn. 1:37-40) and Jesus' calling of Philip (Jn. 1:43).

C). A series of Johannine texts that express the relationship of believers with the Lord, e.g., Jn. 8:12 ("anyone who follows me will not be walking in the dark") and Jn. 10:4, 27 (the sheep who follow); cf. Rv. 14:4 (those who "follow the Lamb wherever he goes").

Eliminating the texts in which the term *akolouthein* has a purely material meaning (such as Mk. 5:37 and 11:9), the concept of following Christ in the Gospel undergoes the same semantic evolution as the term *mathētēs* (disciple) in the New Testament. The disciples were in the beginning, and in a strict sense remained, only those whom Jesus associated with his life and ministry (cf. Mk. 3:14). Later, in the central portion of Acts (6:1—21:16), the term is used to indicate post-resurrection Christians.[36] Within the actual limits of the gospel text the distinction between the pre- and post-resurrection meanings of the terms *to follow* and *disciple* is not definite. Moreover the Gospels take for granted the post-resurrection situation of their readers: the Gospels are directed to believers. In being so directed, discipleship is in an exclusively post-resurrection context (cf. especially the Johannine texts). Even narrative passages and sayings which originally referred to the disciples of the historical Jesus are meant to transmit a message to post-resurrection believers. As we shall see, the disciples of Jesus become prototypes of the Church. However, with the exception of the part of Acts already referred to, the term *disciple* is exclusively applied to the group that surrounded Jesus; the term *to follow* appears in this special context. This permits us to go beyond the redaction of the Gospels and to follow the process of their formation in order to establish the origin of discipleship in the historical reality of Jesus and his disciples.

2. The Group of the Disciples

The Gospels show us that the group of those who accepted the message of Jesus, who was announcing the Good News of the Kingdom and calling them to conversion (Mk. 1:14–15), establishes itself along a continuum of greater or lesser intensity of adherence to Jesus. There is the larger number of those who accept the message but remain in the same situation of home and work in which the Gospel found them, even though they are interiorly renewed by it. These believers appear above all in Galilee, but also in Samaria and Judea (Bethany) and even in the Decapolis (Mk. 5:18; Mt. 9:38; Lk. 19:2; Mt. 27:57; Lk. 10:38).

There is also a group of followers in a stricter sense: those who accompany Jesus in his missionary travels from Galilee to Jerusalem. The New Testament expressly names in this group the four who, according to the Synoptics, were called first (Simon, Andrew, James and John (Mk. 1:16–20); Levi, the son of Alphaeus (Mk. 2:14); Joseph, known as Barsabbas, and Matthias (Ac. 1:23); and also a group of women (Mary Magdalene; Johanna, the wife of Chusa; Susanna; and others) who provided for them out of their own resources (Lk. 8:1–3, cf. Mk. 15:40–41). At times this group must have been quite numerous. This will permit Luke to relate, besides the mission of the Twelve narrated in all three Synoptics (Mk. 6:7–13, Mt. 10:1, Lk. 9:1–6), the mission of the Seventy-Two (Lk. 10:1 ff). The Gospels place the Twelve within this larger group.[37]

Leaving aside the question of the relationship between the "Twelve" and the "disciples," which would not be useful for this study,[38] one could be tempted to introduce a distinction between two manners of following Jesus during his ministry. The distinction is not well founded. It attributes to the period of Jesus' ministry a concept of the disciple as a believer, and of the following as faith, a concept which appeared only later, in the apostolic Church.[39] It is significant that the term *disciple* is used in the Synoptics only to indicate a specific group of people who were with Jesus; the sayings on discipleship seem to have been originally directed to a limited group of followers. This permits us to go beyond the meaning the Synoptics gave to *disciples* and to understand the original meaning the word had on the lips of Jesus. To stop at the mere wording of the Gospels, or at the history of their textual tradition, is to refuse to follow a further indication that is suggested by the texts themselves.[40]

There is no difficulty in accepting the fact that Jesus should have had a group of disciples who lived with him and accompanied him in his ministry. In the ancient world every famous philosopher and rhetorician had his pupils. Under Hellenism, where every philosophy tended to become a form of spirituality, these pupils were also disciples. During Jesus' time there were the disciples of the rabbis, the *talmidîm* (even though the rabbinate had not yet been institutionalized as it was after the year 70), there were the followers of the eschatological prophet John the Baptist, and there were the followers of the apocalyptic prophets and those of the charismatic leaders of the Zealots (among whose disciples some were closer to their leader than others).

The problem arises when one seeks to understand the relationship uniting the disciples to Jesus by comparing their group with one of those we have just mentioned. Some years ago, following the lines traced by G. Kittel and K. H. Rengstorf in their two articles in the *Theological Dictionary of the New Testament*, the generally accepted view was that of A. Schulz,[41] who compared the ties which united Jesus and his disciples with those that bound the rabbis and their *talmidîm* (disciple-pupils), even though noteworthy differences were known to exist. More recently, especially following the criticism of M. Hengel,[42] the rabbi-*talmidîm* model has been abandoned. The Gospels in fact describe the relationship between the disciples and Jesus in terms that far transcend those describing the rabbis and their pupils: a) the initiative comes from Jesus and not from the pupil who is seeking a master; b) the attachment of the disciples to Jesus is founded on their acceptance of the Kingdom, which in turn leads them to some attachment to Jesus—it is not primarily the result of the recognition of a title of doctor earned through study (the term *to follow* thus has, in defining the relationship of the disciples to Jesus, a strong meaning not found when it relates to a rabbinical school); c) unlike the *talmidîm*, the disciples do not intend to become masters, and thus to succeed or surpass Jesus; they always remain disciples (Mt. 23:8).

Certainly Jesus did not limit himself to the announcement of the Kingdom. He instructed the multitudes, and above all his disciples.[43] Yet he was not, like a rabbi, a link in an exegetical chain, nor did he found his doctrine on tradition. He taught with his own decisive authority.

It is not necessary to show the differences between Jesus' disciples and those of the apocalyptic prophets or the leaders of the Zealot movement. These prophets and leaders recruited whole crowds and led them into the desert to show them the miracles of a new Exodus or to incite them against the Romans. The only point of contact between them and Jesus would seem to be the charismatic personal authority upon which the adherence was based.[44]

The Gospels compare the disciples of Jesus with those of John the Baptist. In this case, too, we are in the presence of extraordinary personal authority of charismatic origin. But it is impossible to reconstruct with any certainty the nature of the bonds that united the Baptist and his disciples. The Gospels bring out two differences which existed between John's group and the disciples of Jesus: the Baptist had taught some prayers to his followers (Lk. 11:1) and had prescribed some fasts (Lk. 5:33; Mk. 2:18 par.).

Prescinding from comparisons, let us try to understand the meaning that the following of Jesus had for his disciples. It is important to remember that Jesus was considered a prophet by his contemporaries (Mt. 21:46, Lk. 7:16). He himself formulated his mission in terms of both the Servant-Prophet who brings good news and healing, and the eschatological Prophet (cf. the close relationship between confessing Jesus and being accepted by the Son of Man in Mk. 8:38 and Lk. 12:8–9). The group of his disciples must have appeared as the group of the disciples of the Prophet. It is thus understandable that the story of the call of Elisha by Elijah (who becomes an eschatological figure) should have deeply influenced the shaping of stories relating the call of the disciples. In both accounts there is an element of extraordinary authority of charismatic origin which explains the special character of the disciples' relationship to Jesus.

Yet Jesus is more than just another prophet. Jesus neither places himself simply in the succession of the prophets of Israel nor is he considered as such by his disciples. He is the one who announces that the Kingdom is near, who shows with his signs that the Kingdom of God is already at hand and thus requires a radical conversion. In Mark the calling of the first four disciples is told immediately after a summary of the preaching of Jesus involving an eschatological announcement and a call to conversion: "The time has come, and the Kingdom of God is close at hand. Repent, and believe the Good News" (Mk. 1:14–15, 16–20). In this context the disciples appear not only as the first who accepted the Good News of the coming Kingdom, but also as those whom Jesus had called to take part in his life and ministry as evangelists of the Kingdom. "To follow Jesus" meant not only to accept his message, as many in the crowd had done, but to join Jesus in the eschatological proclamation. The essential element seems to have been faith in the nearness of the Kingdom. The following of Christ originally had this eschatological meaning.

The disciples' situation was therefore a radically new one, not only because the nearness of the Kingdom transcended the past and made the present of relative importance, but also because the authority of Jesus appeared to be unique ("but I say to you . . .") and to be founded on a unique relationship with God, whom he habitually called *Abba*. This implied an adherence to the person of Jesus, which became even stronger and more explicit.

To go beyond these data would be to venture upon the quicksand of discussions between exegetical schools. We do note, however, that M. Hengel limits himself too much by stressing the call as one to dedicate oneself to the ministry of proclaiming the Good News of exorcisms and of healing.[45] We have seen that even in Mark the first disciples are called to become fishers of men. Mark recounts the mission of the Twelve, to which Luke adds that of the seventy-two disciples. (While Hengel believes the former to be authentic,[46] P. Hoffman believes it to be a creation of Mark.[47]) So we see that even in the earliest accounts the disciples are shown to be associated in the actual ministry of Jesus. One thus wonders if the call to follow Jesus had only the purpose of providing him with heralds to announce the Kingdom. We have seen that faith in the eschatological message of Jesus entailed recognition of his unique mission and consequent adherence to him. The logion transmitted by Q (Mt. 10:38, Lk. 14:27) and by Mark (8:34 par.) warns the disciples of the possibility that their association with him might lead to crucifixion.

One may also ask whether it is permissible to exclude the fact that community life with Jesus, even though oriented toward evangelization, should have a special significance[48] when one knows that Jesus' eating and drinking with sinners was a foreshadowing of the eschatological community. Mark's affirmation in regard to the Twelve ("he called them to himself, to be with him and to send them to preach"—Mk. 3:13-14) is not necessarily a simple reflection of Mark's, as has sometimes been claimed. It may rather well show that their community life had special significance.

We may then conclude that the vocation to discipleship historically included a calling to place oneself at the service of the Kingdom with Jesus by means of evangelization, to be associated with him despite persecution, to participate in his uprooted manner of life, and (probably) to form a group together with him which would prophetically express, and actually initiate, the eschatological community.

3. The Sayings on Discipleship

A. The Texts

Gospel tradition is aware of a series of sayings attributed to Jesus on the conditions necessary for discipleship. R. Bultmann, separating these sayings from the "I" sayings formed in the post-resurrection community, sees no reason to assign them to the same phase and to deny their attribution to Jesus himself, even though subsequent redactions make it difficult to reconstruct the exact words of the Lord. Among later exegetes there is noteworthy agreement in attributing these sayings to Jesus himself, and in making their referent the group of disciples of the historical Jesus.[49] We may conclude that these logia represent the most ancient phase of the *sequela Christi* tradition.

In the first place we have a series of logia in Q which require a break in family ties and confront the disciples with the cross (Mt. 10:37-38, Lk. 14:26-27). Comparing the two versions one comes to the conclusion that the sayings were as follows: If anyone comes to me (Lk. 14:26) and does not hate father and mother, son and daughter, he or she cannot be my disciple. If anyone comes to me and does not take up the cross and follow me he or she cannot be my disciple.

Luke, who preserves some of the original traits better than Matthew, enlarges the scope of the text on renunciation of family ties by adding wife, brothers, and sisters, and makes the renunciation more radical by speaking of hatred of "his own life too" (cf. Mt. 10:39). The logion on the cross is transmitted by Mark in a secondary version ("let him renounce himself"—Mk. 8:34, Mt. 16:24, Lk. 9:23). Luke extends its meaning still further: "let him take up his cross every day."

A sequence of two texts from Q (Mt. 18:19-22, Lk. 9:57-60) proposes to those who want to follow Jesus the same kind of uprooted, itinerant life that he lived, forbidding the fulfillment of duties of piety that were sacred to the Jews (e.g., to bury one's father). The renunciation of family ties becomes, in this instance, a scandal for Jewish ethics. Luke continues with a saying that is exclusively his in which Jesus answers the man who wanted first to say goodbye to his relatives: "Once the hand is laid on the plough, no one who looks back is fit for the Kingdom of God" (Lk. 9:61-62).

In the three-fold Synoptic tradition, the story of the call of the rich man ends with the maxim: "I tell you solemnly, there is no one who has left house, brothers, sisters, mother, father, children, or land ... who will not receive a hundredfold." Mark preserves the primitive form of the saying and adds "and for the Gospel." Luke has "for the Kingdom of God" instead of "for me;" he adds "wife" after "house," and omits "land" among the objects of renunciation (Mk. 10:30, Mt. 19:29, Lk. 18:29). Luke also adds, in the manner of a personal conclusion to the sayings on renunciation: "So, in the same way, none of you can be my disciple unless he gives up all his possessions" (Lk. 14:33).

B. The Original Meaning of the Sayings

We are faced with a series of sayings attributed to the Lord which express stern requirements for becoming and remaining a disciple. Whoever wants to be his disciple ("if anyone comes to me ...") has to hate his or her own family, forego the duties of filial piety, take up the cross in Jesus' footsteps, and embrace a rootless, itinerant life like that of Jesus.

How can one explain the radical character of the requirements imposed by these sayings: "He who does not ... cannot be my disciple"? The saying about the cross can be understood in the light of the situation in Palestine at the time of Jesus. Even though Jesus did not try to surround himself with crowds, as the leaders of the Zealot movement did, the crowd often followed him. It was thus possible that the Romans could mistake him for one of the various pretender-Messiahs, or one of the organizers of resistance to the Empire, and that he would end up on the cross as they had. Whoever wanted to follow Jesus in his pilgrimage to Jerusalem to announce the advent of the Kingdom of God had to be ready to carry the cross or (as a saying common to all four evangelists states) "to lose his own life" (Mk. 8:35, Mt. 16:25, Lk. 9:24, Jn. 12:25-26). Faith in the Kingdom announced by Jesus required fidelity to the point of crucifixion and death.[50]

The meaning of Mt. 8:19 and Lk. 9:57 is even clearer. Whoever wants to follow Jesus as his disciple must embrace a style of life that is rootless, since it is itinerant or subject to persecution, just as Jesus' own was.

As for breaking with one's family, a radically literal interpretation becomes improbable when the saying is attributed to the historical Jesus and his disciples. Jesus had certainly renounced his family, remaining a celibate and leaving his relatives in order to form, together with his disciples, a family united by the will of God (Mk. 3:31-35 par.). And the disciples who followed had actually left their families behind them in order to embark on this adventure of announcing the Kingdom with him. But Jesus himself brought Peter back to his house (Mk. 1:29, Mt. 8:14-15, Lk. 4:38-39). Later Cephas, the other Apostles, and the brothers of Jesus appear with their wives (I Co. 9:5). How then can we justify the severity of the maxim regarding a break with relatives?

The "renunciation" of the family originally had an eschatological meaning in the preaching of Jesus and of his first disciples. Because the Kingdom of God is at hand it becomes necessary to leave behind everything that pertains to normal human living. We find ourselves in a radically new situation, the eschatological one, in which the important thing is to welcome the presence of the Kingdom and place oneself in its service; the manner of doing this is to follow Jesus.

No other reality, not even the sacred one of the family, can put conditions or limits on this loyalty. This fundamental meaning was strengthened by its connection with the prophetic-apocalyptic motive of the breaking of family ties during the tribulations of the last times (Mt. 7:6; Zc. 13:3; Enoch Eth. 99:5, 110:1-2). Jesus, who according to Mark had experienced some difficulties with his relatives (Mk. 3:20-21), declares that he has not come to bring peace but the sword in family surroundings (Mt. 10:34, Lk. 12:51-53). His eschatological discourse speaks of the suffering of mothers during the last days (Mt. 24:19). The concept of a fidelity that transcends all family pressures, based on the transcendent value of the Kingdom, must have taken on a particular coloring in the minds of the disciples insofar as they understood the imminent advent of the Kingdom as entailing the destruction of the old order of things.

C. The Meaning of the Sayings in Oral Tradition

In a study of his, G. Theissen[51] formulated an interesting hypothesis on the transmission of these sayings on discipleship. He starts with the assumption that, while the texts transmitted by writing preserve a fixed character, those transmitted orally tend to be modified in a manner that reflects the social situation of the group by which they are being preserved.

Thus the discipleship sayings, transmitted orally for some thirty years, express the *ethos* of people who have no fixed habitation and who take for granted a break with family ties. Theirs is a radicalism of itinerants. These sayings must have been preserved by a group that, contrary to the practice of ordinary believers, took them literally. That such charismatic wanderers did exist seems beyond doubt. The Didache mentions Christian pilgrims "who follow the rules of the Lord" (Did. XI:8). G. Kretschemer[52] showed the existence of such wandering charismatics in the Syrian tradition. E. Käsemann speaks of a primitive Palestinian mission of the prophetic type where the Q Source would have taken form.[53] It is above all from Q that the sayings on discipleship have reached us. It is also accepted that the rules in the sermon of mission developed into a codex for the first generation of itinerant missionaries.[54]

In this new context the discipleship sayings (referring to a rootless existence, a break with one's family, and the dangers to one's life) have been given a strictly literal interpretation. The labors and anguish of these people had to be counterbalanced by their expectation of the imminent return of the Son of Man (Mt. 10:23). The fundamental eschatological motive remained intact.

D. Call Narratives

When we come to the Gospels themselves, the discipleship teachings of Jesus do not reach us only through the sayings on discipleship. They are also concretely expressed in a series of texts that recount the call of some of the disciples. It would be well for us to turn our attention to these narratives before returning to the sayings regarding the following of Jesus.

We have seen that the concept of *following* in the New Testament is always connected with the historical Jesus. For this reason the term *to follow*, with its technical meaning, appears only in the Gospels (except for Rv. 14:4). Likewise, the term *disciple* appears very frequently (234 times) in the Gospels, and only in the central portion of Acts does it indicate post-resurrection believers in Christ rather than the disciple-companions of Jesus. Therefore the correlative concepts of *disciple* and *following* originally have a historical meaning.

It is true, however, that even if the Gospels use these terms to speak of those who accompanied Jesus, they are not simply narrating a chronicle but are offering a paradigm. The disciples become, in the Gospels, the prototypes of the post-resurrection Church. It has been pointed out that in Matthew *discipleship* and *following* evoke the image of the Church. In Luke "the disciples are a paradigm of the present Church."[55] This passing from a historical reality to a religious prototype is already discernible in Mark.[56] Another indication of this passing from history to a statement regarding the present is found in the increasing idealization which the narratives undergo from Mark to Matthew and Luke, and in comparing the Synoptic tradition to the independent tradition of John (Jn. 1:35-51).

Geographical and chronological details are so generalized in the Synoptics that it is clear the evangelists were not primarily interested in recounting an event but rather in transmitting a message to their readers. It is obvious that each evangelist inserts the following of Christ into his own theology.[57] However they all coincide in certain basic data. First they all emphasize the initiative taken by Jesus and his *exousia* (his singular authority). The events are narrated as if he had suddenly appeared in the lives of certain men and with a simple phrase, "follow me," had radically changed their existence. In Luke the impression of regal authority given by Jesus with this order is strengthened by the miraculous draught of fishes (Lk. 5:4-7), a narrative which appears in John's final appendix as a Paschal event in connection with Peter's mission (Jn. 21:4-7, 15-19).[58] The Synoptics do not mention any other human cause to explain the disciples' incorporation into the group. John, instead, tells of two disciples who followed Jesus after hearing the Baptist's testimony (Jn 1:35-39). One of them, Andrew, brought his brother Simon to Jesus (Jn. 1:40-42). From Bethsaida also came Philip, who was personally called by Jesus, and who in turn brought Nathanael with him.[59]

After having drawn attention to the initiative taken by Jesus, the Gospels emphasize the disciples' obedience: hearing Jesus' invitation, they immediately leave everything (Mk. 1:18) and follow him. Thus, in regard to the renunciation necessary for discipleship, there is also a process of idealization and radicalization in the Synoptics. In Mark and Matthew the first four who are called leave their nets, their boat, their father and the hired hands (Mk. 1:16-20, Mt. 4:18-22). Levi gets up from his desk (Mk. 2:14, Mt. 9:9). This means that Christ's call uprooted them from their profession and their families and gave a new direction to their lives. The change in profession is made clear by the explanatory sentence in the narrative of the call of the first four: "and I will make you fishers of men." In Luke, on the other hand, we find an all-inclusive and radical affirmation repeated in the two anecdotes of the fishermen and of the publican: "they left everything and followed him" (Lk 5:11, 28). This is exactly the same all-inclusive statement made by Peter in response to the rich man's failure (Mt. 19:27).

There is a definite convergence between the sayings on discipleship attributed to Jesus by oral tradition and these gospel narratives. Those who follow Jesus are his disciples, but discipleship demands the breaking with their families and the professional ties which held them up to that moment. We saw how Luke, who characterizes renunciation as "leaving everything," modifies the traditional sayings by including other objects of renunciation: house, wife, brothers and sisters. He concludes the section on discipleship with his reflection that no one can be a disciple "unless he gives up all his possessions" (Lk. 14:33). Renunciation of property is added to the breaking of family ties, on which the sayings insist. The same affirmation is to be found in the call of the rich man: "go and sell everything you own and give the money to the poor, then come, follow me" (Mk. 10:21 par.). Here also we have a call to discipleship, the only one in which Jesus does not limit himself to the order, "follow me," but commands the renunciation of all possessions.

We find here again, in a more acute form, the problem raised by the requirement of a break in family ties. Jesus never seems to have demanded renunciation of possessions. Levi, after having "left everything," prepares a banquet for the Lord in his own house (Lk. 5:29). The fishermen who left their boat later return to their boats and nets (Mk. 3:3; 4:1,36). The women who were following him assisted him with their own resources (Lk. 8:2-3). In the same way, not even the apostolic Church required the renunciation of property. It is then clear that neither Lk. 14:33 nor the call narratives, including that of the rich man, intend to impose certain definite acts of renunciation.

How then should we explain the radical character and the incisive style of the sayings on discipleship and the call narratives? We have seen how Mark recounts the calling of the first four (Mk. 1:16-20) just after having summarized Christ's announcement of the proximity of the Kingdom and his invitation to conversion and belief (Mk. 1:14-15). They appear, then, as prototypes of those who are converted and believe. This is even more evident in the call of Levi. The pericope of the calling is followed by the passage on the banquet with publicans and sinners (Mk. 2:13-17).[60]

K. Berger has cast a new light on this problem in his work, *Die Gesetz-*

esauslegung Jesu.[61] According to him these call narratives, formulated in the Judaeo-Hellenistic section of the Christian community, follow the model of the conversion (as the Hellenistic Jews conceived it) of a pagan to Judaism. Conversion to the living God of Israel involved a break with one's past social situation, with one's possessions, house and family. They considered, as a model of conversion, the command God gave to Abraham to leave all in order to embark on a pilgrimage (Gn. 12:1-9). The Masters in Israel did not require from the proselytes an actual break in family ties, nor the renunciation of their goods. They simply wanted to stress the unique character of the new covenant with God, before which every other relationship disappears, even while remaining. Applying this Hellenistic-Jewish model to Jews who became followers of Jesus, tradition intended to present attachment to Jesus as a radical conversion, not only on the part of the Gentiles, but also on the part of the Jews who, up to then, had observed the Law (Mt. 19:21). Jesus represented a *novum* in regard to the Mosaic dispensation also, inasmuch as the sovereignty of God which will manifest itself fully in the Parousia is already present in Jesus. The pre-resurrection disciples of Jesus have thus become the models of common Christian conversion.

In light of this parallel suggested by K. Berger we can give a more precise solution to the problem raised by the radical character of the renunciation of family and possessions required by the sayings (including Lk. 14:33) and the call narratives. It is not the case of a simple inclination to detachment that would become active when salvation is endangered.[62] What these texts want to convey is the unique, transcendent value of the Kingdom and of fidelity to Christ both as the focal point of the Christian's entire existence, and as the source of inspiration on which to model one's life, without allowing oneself to be influenced by any other existing thing. In the presence of Christ, at this depth of religious orientation, all other values disappear: not only economic realities, but also the more sacred ones of filial piety and family ties. It is not so much a question of a disposition of the spirit as of a lived orientation.

It is nevertheless true that beyond the sayings and narratives there loom the grave difficulties caused by family and wealth among Christians in the Apostolic Church, especially during persecutions. It is in such times that a basic orientation has to change into a radical, concrete renunciation in order to remain faithful to Christ and his Gospel. Yet Luke, pointing out that the disciple must carry the cross "every day," obviously intends to separate these texts from the narrow context of great crises in order to apply them to the problems which fidelity to Christ can pose in everyday life. It is then that renunciation must be shown in action.

III. Theological Reflection

1. Christian Discipleship

Having established a concept of the origin and meaning of the Gospel texts related to discipleship (sayings and narratives), we must now examine the role that the Word of God proclaimed in the Scriptures played in creating and inspiring religious life in the Church.

Obviously, the basis for our theological reflection must be the inspired Word and not the data offered us by the criticism of the history of traditions or of forms. These other data may, however, be useful in understanding the original context of the biblical texts and in helping us discern meanings attributed to them as simple reflections of subsequent history.[63]

In the Gospels the following of Christ has become the vocation of all believers, since the disciples of the historical Jesus became prototypes of the Church. There has been a re-reading of history in the light of post-resurrection experience. The gospel message therefore speaks of this discipleship extended to the whole Church. In the gospel message the following of Christ is the determining factor in Christian existence. The following is a total attachment to the person and message of Jesus. One encounters God revealing himself to us in Jesus as love and a saving will, and one joins him in serving the Kingdom. One accepts the Word of God that reaches us through Jesus (in his person, his life, his words) as the only norm of life. What is proposed to us is not a vaguely inspiring ideal but a very near and constantly urgent criterion. In other words, it is not a question of following Jesus with general readiness to prefer him in extreme situations of temptation or persecution. Understood merely as interior detachment, the message is weakened. The demands of discipleship follow us everywhere. It is difficult (impossible without divine help) for the human being to follow the Lord. Dietrich Bonhoeffer had the merit of remembering this.[64]

Vatican II took up again the central meaning of discipleship when, speaking of the common vocation of Christians to gospel perfection, it exhorts all to follow in the footsteps of Christ.[65] It reviews the relationship between the disciples and the Lord[66] and recalls the necessity of being ready to follow Jesus in the *Via Crucis* of persecutions that are never lacking to the Church.[67] In the context of this common calling, the Council speaks of numerous "counsels" Jesus proposed in the Gospel for the disciples' observance. These are the numerous concrete expressions which go beyond the Law (or, as Matthew indicates, beyond a minimal and literal interpretation of the Law) and which constitute discipleship.

Actual modes of life are simply ways and means to fulfill the arduous requirements of discipleship.[68] They correspond, says the Council echoing St. Paul, to the various charisms.[69] To avoid fatally misunderstanding Christian life, one must conclude that if, in relation to this common discipleship as the Gospels describe it, the actual modes of existence are simply means, then they are of secondary and relative importance. One runs the risk of both obscuring the reality of the Christian vocation and rendering poor service to religious life when one identifies discipleship with celibacy, the renunciation of property, and membership in a religious community. These are all aspects of one concrete form of following Christ, and are thus secondary to the following itself. We are certainly not permitted to put so much stress on embracing "the rule of life of the Lord," with its celibacy and uprootedness, when Jesus himself, by including married men among his Apostles, evidently did not place such overriding importance on this specific mode of life.

It often happens in religious life that one tends to use the concept of discipleship solely or principally to mean imitation of the lifestyle followed by Christ. When one does this without starting from the universal vocation to follow Christ, with all its consequences, one is in danger of relegating the following to religious alone, or to make religious ideal and privileged disciples. By so doing one departs from the Gospel and gives warrant to the objections of the Reformation churches so vigorously voiced by D. Bonhoeffer.[70]

2. The Origin of Religious Life as a Form of Discipleship

It is a historical fact that the founders of various forms of religious life, beginning with the great anchorite St. Anthony, intended primarily to embody, in a concrete lifestyle, the requirements of the following of Christ as they are expressed in the call narratives and the related sayings on discipleship.

Some raise the problem of whether the founders interpreted the biblical texts correctly. This problem is presented in a radical way by Protestant theology, which has often judged religious life to be a deviant phenomenon based on a re-reading of the Word of God with a gnostic or, more generally, a Hellenistic mindset. Among Catholics who accept religious life as an authentically Christian phenomenon, exegetes are ready to tell us that the interpretation of certain biblical texts commonly used in the history of religious life is erroneous. This applies to the theory of a state of perfection and to the distinction made between commandments (necessary for everyone's salvation) and counsels (the means to perfection), which certain people read in Mt. 19:16-22. We have no difficulty in accepting this opinion. We must add, however, that the category of "counsel" is foreign to the entire monastic tradition, which took every scriptural sentence as a commandment, not merely a counsel, of the Lord. Furthermore, the idea of a state of perfection can be abandoned without thereby undermining the nature of religious life. This concept was formulated to express a form of Christianity which literally and exactly implements what the sayings on discipleship and the call narratives express in the Gospels.

At this point, based on textual analysis, we might be tempted to suspect that religious life was born from a naive reading of the texts. While the sayings on discipleship and the call narratives do not intend to impose an actual and radical renunciation, the first monks and nuns would have interpreted them that way.

The same method of approaching the problem, by referring first to the biblical texts, appears in the apologetical vein among theologians of the religious life. There are those who want to make religious life absolutely originate from Scripture or, still better, from the earthly life of Jesus and supported by biblical data. Thus it is sometimes noted that there were different forms of following among the disciples of Jesus. There were many who accepted Christ's message but remained in the material situation in which the Word had reached them: among these were intimate friends of Jesus, such as Lazarus. Jesus called only a few to follow him in a special way. We must accept that this diversity of concrete ways of living out one's attachment to Christ is an undeniable fact; it illustrates the variety of forms of discipleship in the Church. But it is not possible to see here any foreshadowing of religious life in the strict sense. This is so principally because at least some of the disciples were married, and a complete break was not asked of any of them. Religious are Christians who want to embody the ideal of discipleship proposed by the Gospel, not to imitate the personal life of the historical disciples of Jesus. They are not followers of Peter or James; they want to be disciples of Jesus. If we then focus our attention on the gospel texts, we discover that the call narratives were included not to give a rule of life for a special group of Christians, but to be a source of inspiration for all believers.

Actually, behind all this careful steering between the historical group of the disciples and the Scriptures, there seems to be a false concept of the role of Scripture and of the relationship of religious life with Jesus. The problem of the origin of religious life should be put in a different way.

Religious life is a fact in the Church. It must then find its origin in the community of believers born from the death and resurrection of the Lord. Some disciples of the Risen Christ feel called to embody in a special way the particular requirements of the *sequela Christi* by embracing a celibate type of life lived either in solitude or community. These are the data that circumscribe the phenomenon. If this call is authentically divine, and not the exclusive result of a certain cultural conditioning, it comes from the Risen Lord, and thus must be considered one of the vocational charisms which the Lord distributes among the members of the Church for the welfare of the entire community (Rm. 12:4-8, I Co. 12:4-11). It must therefore have a Paschal and pneumatic origin.

Sacred Scripture states explicitly that such a vocation is an authentic calling from the Risen Christ when St. Paul defines celibacy as a charism. This was, in fact, Paul's own charism in regard to his lifestyle (I Co. 7:7): having been called to announce the Gospel to the Gentiles, he felt himself vowed to an uprooted life which he could not share with a woman. So while other Apostles, the brothers of the Lord, and Cephas had a Christian woman with them, he denies himself this right. While the others are provided for by the churches, he and Barnabas live from the work of their own hands (I Co. 9:5-7). As we shall see, celibacy is the radical and characteristic trait of religious life. The other characteristics originate from it and insert themselves into it. If one wants to speak of renunciation of property, done in order to express Christian community, it certainly appears in the New Testament as a definitely voluntary choice (Ac. 5:4), but at the same time the Levite Joseph Barnabas, who felt moved to do it, is remembered

(Ac. 4:36–37). Probably his and other similar cases prompted Luke or his source to attribute the common possession of goods to the whole primitive community of believers immediately after Pentecost (Ac. 2:44–45, 4:32–35).

Thus, even before the composition of the Gospels, some believers felt called to an exclusive dedication to "the things of the Lord," meaning by this expression (in the case of Paul and other itinerant missionaries) the preaching of the Gospel. They felt themselves moved to embrace certain traits of the historical Christ's life. Paul is celibate like Jesus; he and other missionaries lead a rootless life in service to the Gospel. It is clear in their case that their life was inspired not by a more-or-less faithful reading of the Gospels (which had not yet been written!) but by the impulse to adhere to the Lord and his interests. The origin of religious life (and more generally the following of Christ) is not traced to the sacred books, but to the very person of Jesus. One gives oneself to the Risen Lord and "his affairs" (the service of the Church) following an impulse of the Spirit. We cannot tell to what extent those apostles and prophets were aware of thus embracing the lifestyle of the historical Jesus. The idea of imitating Christ, which is only sketched on the ethical level in the New Testament, is not extended there to embracing his lifestyle also. Yet the first Christians repeated the logion with which Jesus, using his own life as an example, warned anyone who wanted to belong to his group about the type of existence that awaited them. On the other hand, Matthew and Luke ascribe to Jesus the rules of the apostolic mission followed by the first missionaries in Palestine (Mt. 10, Lk. 10). Later the Didache will speak of prophets who follow "the rules of life of the Lord."[71]

What can only be intuited when one speaks of apostolic times can be proved when one speaks of religious. The Spirit of the Lord, in calling some Christians to dedicate themselves in an exclusive way (i.e., by radically renouncing every other obligation toward which life can be oriented), recalls for them the memory of Jesus through the inspired Word. The *memoria Jesu* that has been rendered living and present by the Holy Spirit through the Word acts as a stimulus and source of inspiration for them. It is in this pneumatic sense, through the action of the Spirit, that religious life is connected with the very existence of the historical Jesus.

3. Scripture, the Creative Word

From the discussion above one gathers that religious life does not descend from the Gospels in the sense that certain gospel texts have instituted it. The texts on the following of Christ do not require religious life, even though it is guided by these texts. Only regarding celibacy for the sake of the Kingdom do we have God's word through Paul, who calls it a charism: one of the various gifts of the Spirit by which Christians contribute in various ways to the common building up of the Church.

Even if religious life does not materially descend from the Gospels the Risen Lord creates it in the Church through the Scriptures. In the call which is heard by some of the disciples after the Resurrection, Scripture plays a basic two-fold role. First, it is the Word of the Risen Lord creating new forms of discipleship in his community. This is evident throughout the history of religious life. According to Athanasius, Anthony felt that the memory of the first disciples of Jesus and of the Christians of Jerusalem had been brought back to him by the Lord and that the reading of Mt. 19:21 had been directed at him.[72] Augustine gathered his brothers and sisters under an impulse that became explicit while he was reading the *Summaries of the Acts of the Church* of Jerusalem.[73] Francis of Assisi discovered in the sermon on mission the type of life to which he felt interiorly called.[74] Anthony Claret felt himself called to evangelization while reading the Bible, especially the text of Lk. 4:18, on the mission of Christ to evangelize the poor.[75]

Second, Scripture serves as a source of inspiration and as the criterion by which to judge the authenticity of these concrete forms of *sequela*. The founders and their followers are human beings subject to various cultural and social influences. They form their rule, create various types of communities, develop theologies, and even ideologies, at the service of their institutions. Divine initiative and human response are ever present in the Church. The human responses, however, do not belong to the moment of divine calling but to that of human answering. They are thus fully subject to critique by the revealed Word.

The critique of religious life by Scripture is seen time and again throughout history. One cannot deny the process of re-Christianization apparent in primitive monasticism, which was so deeply permeated with Hellenistic influences. On the basis of the Gospels, St. Basil rejected a form of anchoritism that held itself completely aloof from the community of believers.[76] In order to reform Latin monasticism during a critical period, St. Benedict placed in the abbot's hands an essential rule which began with the double precept of love, quotes the commandments, and reaffirms the inspirational principle of the *sequela,* proceeding for the most part by biblical quotations and allusions.[77] Later St. Francis and St. Clare sought a return to gospel sources.

We must add that any form of Christian life, including religious life, must be constantly criticized by the principle of the following of Christ. Each form is subject to deviations, ideological contamination, and phenomena of necrosis when certain traditions which arose as an expression of discipleship in a specific environment no longer express it. However, the criticism of traditions and forms of religious life cannot obscure the Christian significance of a life exclusively dedicated to the Lord and his interest.

4. The Life of the Church

What we have said so far is that, while we must have recourse to Scripture in judging religious life, we still cannot fully understand religious life as a phenomenon unless it is situated in the context of Church history. Christians who feel they are called by the Spirit to live their discipleship in a particular form of detachment in which Jesus has preceded them (as have, allowing for proper distances, Paul and the other missionaries) are members of a historical Church that has special needs. A. Harnack and D. Bonhoeffer represented primitive monasticism as a protest against the secularization of the Church after the peace of Constantine.[78] Let us rather say that, at the end of the age of martyrs, the first monks expressed the radical requirements of the Kingdom in relation to a community that was no longer called to heroism. It is significant that the discipleship texts which Origen applied to the martyrs[79] were the same ones which the first monks felt called them to voluntary renunciation. The deaths of the martyrs showed the meaning and implications of discipleship during the first centuries of the Church. In the post-Constantinian Church the monks carried on the same role through their lifestyle.[80] That the people recognized the monks as the successors to the martyrs can be seen in their being given the same titles (*miles Christi, athleta Christi*) and by some being buried together with a martyr.[81]

Later, the rule of mission deeply impressed Francis and Dominic, both concerned with the problem of evangelical poverty in a Church governed by powerful popes and shaken by the misery of many. In this actual ecclesial situation itinerant preachers practicing extreme poverty appear as a concrete and authentic form of discipleship. Among the forms of apostolic life starting with St. Dominic, religious life centers on evangelization or service to the poor, forms that were particularly necessary for the times. We can then conclude that religious life, inasmuch as it is a concrete form of practicing discipleship, is born from an impulse of the Spirit, under the inspiration of the Scriptures, as an answer to the needs of the Church. Biblical inspiration gives it its fundamental meaning, but its actual concrete form is subject to the special needs of the Church. Since the forms of religious life are oriented toward specific needs of the Church, it is clear that in the Church itself we find another criterion that casts light on our critical reevaluation of religious life.

5. In the Service of God's Kingdom

In the gospel texts on discipleship there is an important element to which the theology and practice of religious life must give attention if it is to remain faithful to its biblical inspiration. This element is the inseparable connection that exists between discipleship and the service of the Kingdom of God. Mark already suggests the connection when he places the call of the first four disciples directly after the summary of Jesus' preaching about the Kingdom and his invitation to conversion (Mk. 1:16–20 following Mk. 1:14–15). The Synoptics make the connection when they describe the disciples during the life of Jesus (Mk. 6:7–13; Mt. 10; Lk. 9:1–6, 10:1–20). Luke also expresses the relationship in the maxim with which he concludes the call of the rich man when Jesus speaks of the reward that is reserved for those who have left all "for the sake of the Kingdom of God" (Lk. 18:29). Matthew has, in the same context, "for the sake of my name" (Mt. 9:29) and Mark, "for my sake and the sake of the gospel" (Mk. 10:29). In Mt. 19:12, the voluntary eunuchs are such "for the sake of the Kingdom of heaven." We have already noted that the renunciation of the disciples is the consequence of their total dedication to the Kingdom. One is a disciple because, like Jesus and together with him, one has put oneself in the service of the Kingdom.

We are touching here on the central motive of the expectation and preaching of Jesus: the Kingdom of God. The Kingdom as the theme of Christ's preaching has been one of the subjects most intensely discussed by New Testament scholars ever since Albrecht Ritschl placed it in the center of theological consideration,[82] and especially since Johannes Weiss began the historic-exegetic research on the meaning this expression had for Jesus.[83] A. Schweitzer, C. H. Dodd, R. Bultmann, K. Barth, O. Cullmann, J. A. T. Robinson, and R. Schnackenburg are only a few of the main exegetes and theologians who have taken part in the discussion.[84] The subject has become actively debated again with the current rebirth of Christological studies, from Moltmann to Pannenberg, from Schillebeeckx to Küng. It is not possible or necessary to summarize here the development of the discussion between those who defend the idea that the Kingdom was a future reality for Jesus, and those according to whom the Kingdom was a generally present reality for him. The two extreme positions are abandoned today.[85]

For Jesus and his people the Kingdom was, dynamically, the free and definitive intervention by which God would break into history, destroying and creating anew, profoundly modifying the order of things in order to save his People. In Jesus the Kingdom appears as yet-to-come (it is the object of expectation and announcement), but it is also in some way present in his ministry. The Kingdom opposes itself to the dominion of Satan, and is accomplished by the divine victory over evil. The signs of its in-breaking are not to be sought in the stars, or in great natural or historical cataclysms. In this Jesus rejects the apocalyptic concept of history and revives that of the prophets. These signs, on the contrary, should be sought in the fact that evil is overcome by grace. This victory is accomplished within personal experience: in the liberation of the sons and daughters of God through forgiveness of sins, exorcism-healings, and table fellowship with the outcast.

After Jesus, the Church began to consider his death and resurrection and the consequent outpouring of the Spirit as the decisive event which makes the present a time of salvation. The Church continues to pray, "Thy Kingdom come," while at the same time announcing that salvation has been accomplished in Jesus.

A life inspired by the dedication of Jesus and his disciples to the Kingdom is certainly a life entirely projected toward the future. The biblical God, the God of both the Prophets and Jesus, reveals himself in the future. Seeing that no length of time exhausts the revelation of his grace, his promise is always about to be fulfilled. After the death and resurrection of Jesus we are still saved in hope (Rm. 8:24). Thus the eschatological expectation is also faith in the transcendence of God and his grace. Yet the disciples are not called merely to wait. They are called to place themselves in the service of the Kingdom, becoming personally involved in the dynamics of God's saving will, announcing it constantly, inviting all to conversion, and battling evil here and now. Through his disciples, Jesus continues to announce, to heal, to bring outcasts to share in the love of God, and to put God on their side. The Kingdom of God thus appears to be a utopia that generates both struggles against oppressive evil and actions benefiting the human race.

One must be careful not to impoverish the idea of the Kingdom by a narrow interpretation, reducing it merely to the ethical level. The Kingdom is transcendent grace. For this reason it will never be definitively present in our human history. It expresses itself in a religious relationship of an obedience in faith to the salvific will of God from which it derives its ethical content. The Kingdom is not a purely interior and individual reality, as the first erudite monks believed when they identified it with mystical experience.[86] But neither is it merely a social order, as W. Rauschenbush contended, attainable through political or social action.[87]

6. Religious Life Among Other Forms of Discipleship

After having tried to clarify the question of the origin of this special form of discipleship constituted by religious life in the Church, we must now approach a second question which is also important in understanding the true nature of this kind of Christian life: its special significance in contradistinction to other forms of discipleship.

In order to answer this question we must return again to the precise limits which define the phenomenon of religious life in the Church. It is born within the community as a form of discipleship expressed through celibacy and lived sometimes in solitude (anchoritism) but usually in community.

Both St. John Chrysostom[88] and St. Jerome[89] commenting on the discipleship texts, and St. Thomas Aquinas[90] applying them to religious life, have pointed out that in the Synoptics the call of the disciples appears as a two-stage process of leaving and following, the second of which constitutes discipleship. Modern exegesis also repeats that it is in the act of following that the gospel narratives of the call to discipleship reach their climax. The act of following (and not the antecedent renunciation) is the exclusive object of the call, "Follow me." The fact remains, though, that the following of Jesus preached by the narratives and sayings is such that it presupposes the renunciation of all else. The sayings of *sequela* could not be more specific.

It is thus evident that renunciation is a constitutive part of that Christian existence which the narratives and sayings want to present. Precisely for this reason the "conversion to Jesus renouncing all else" is a common trait of all disciples. On the basis of St. Basil's distinction[91] between baptismal conversion with its renunciation of sin, and the conversion of those who want to "lead a life that is faithful to the Gospel" (which will become the monastic *conversio*), it has often been presumed that Christian conversion in general (and consequently that of Christians in the world) is a moral conversion, a renunciation of sin, while that of religious consists in the renunciation of certain good things (the benefits of family and secular life) for the love of Christ. This idea is false in regard to ordinary Christian discipleship because it loses sight of the *sequela Christi* which is the soul of every Christian life.

Must we also recall that the discipleship texts were intended for all believers and not only for a portion of them? Here we are talking about Christianity itself, not about various vocations within the Church. These gospel texts are not opposing Christ to sin, but to things which are good and even "sacred," such as the family and one's own life. Still more, the idea that Christians, as such, renounce only sin loses sight of the original meaning of religious life. What Basil spoke of was precisely "a life that is faithful to the Gospel." The monks were only trying to be Christians.[92]

Thus, the *sequela Christi* brings with it, for all believers, renunciation that is not merely a break with sin, but a refusal to allow oneself to be ultimately determined by anything other than Christ. At this deep level of religious faith that creates a world vision and gives its own meaning to existence, attachment to Christ excludes every other tie or relationship. This is why the Gospels say that the Christian leaves everything in order to cling to the Lord alone. Many renunciations, even of legitimate things, result from this adherence: renunciations woven into every authentic Christian life.

What constitutes the renunciation proper to religious is the abandoning of certain ties characteristic of one definite type of life in order to create another that is exclusively oriented toward Christ. This exclusive orientation toward the Lord, which is produced in every Christian life when one turns toward the Lord in an attitude of faith and love not influenced by any other truth or value, is concretized in religious life. If all disciples must "hate" their families, professions, goods, and even their own lives, to follow Jesus, religious renounce forming their own family so that, through celibacy, Christ may become their family and profession. The relationship with Christ which the married Christian attains through the Sacrament, that is, through a human reality assumed in faith, the religious has without any mediation except the *Sacramentum Ecclesiae*.

7. Charisms and Forms of Testimony

No form of gospel discipleship is merely an attachment to Christ. Inasmuch as it is a form, a specific Christian vocation, it is also a charism of the Spirit for the general building up of the Church. The variety of lifestyles and ministries is not only the fruit of the abundance of Christian existence, it is also required by the numerous needs of the Church (cf. I Co. 12).

In trying to discover the individual meaning of the various forms of *sequela,* one must ask what their individual contribution to the community of believers is. Looking around we see a wide range of ecclesial ministries carried on by religious. We are not interested here in these ecclesial ministries because they can also be carried out by other Christians. We are interested instead in the specific contribution religious make to the upbuilding of the Church.

We immediately think of testimony. We must not be too hasty, however, since every form of *sequela Christi* implies its own testimony before the Church and the rest of the world. Like the Twelve who were prototypes of the new Israel, so also the other disciples are called by Jesus to be with him in announcing the Gospel (Mk. 3:14).

Lay Christians make their own contribution by living out their call to discipleship in the web of human relationships, thus incarnating the Church in the present world. Spouses, for example, incarnate their adherence to Christ in relation to this *sacramentum proximi* to which they have bound themselves in the Church. It is in the context of these relationships (matrimonial, professional, etc.) that they must face the often arduous requirements of discipleship. There resides the difficulty which is proper to Christian life in the secular world. Since faith in Christ animates these relationships, the incarnation of discipleship must transcend the secular. Discipleship requires even lay Christians to leave everything. Thus, in being in the world and yet not of the world, the lay Christian testifies to the Kingdom of God.

The special contribution made by religious life is instead a testimony, through the lifestyle itself (and not only through a succession of choices), to the unique value of adherence to Christ, a value in constant danger of being obscured. By institutionalizing renunciation, religious recall the *unum necessarium*. By giving up their families they recall to everyone that "whoever does not hate father and mother, and son and daughter, cannot be a disciple." The unique value of the Kingdom is here visibly expressed in a concrete lifestyle before the whole Church, as a humble service rendered to the community. Religious life thus tends to express visibly the eschatological orientation of Christian existence, its attitude of expectation. This was indeed the meaning of Jesus' own celibacy.

Consequently it appears to us that what constitutes religious life is this institutionalization and visible expression, in a style of life, of the common renunciation and adherence to Christ. Naturally there are special difficulties here also. Inasmuch as discipleship is not necessarily bound up with its forms, but goes beyond them, there is the danger of being satisfied with an institutionalized renunciation (which as such has relative value) and with a lifestyle emptied of its content. Celibacy may thus become the solitude of the bachelor, and the community may become a club and power group. There is no sense in leaving natural family ties only to substitute other social ties for them. One does not leave one's family and profession for a group and its work, but for the Gospel. Yet this danger lies in wait for every form of Christian life. Matrimony can degenerate from a relationship in the Spirit to a mere emotional and physical reality. Thus in marriage, and in secular life in general, it is also necessary to reexamine and renew one's form of life continuously, in light of the following of Christ. Discipleship is primarily a question of faith and love, with all its consequences.

8. Vocation and Obedience

One conclusion is implicit in all the preceding discussion: one chooses this or that form of *sequela* in simple obedience to the call of Christ. Jesus calls not only to discipleship, but also to a concrete form of following. Even today the Lord continues to call "those whom he chooses." The call has for its object celibacy, single life, or matrimony, religious life or

Christian life in the world. To choose religious life because it is more difficult would not only be a mental error but a presumption of the heart. To choose it for its ''greater perfection'' would be to exchange the person of Christ for a Hellenistic ideal. To choose marriage because one is in love with a certain person, or because one does not wish to renounce the conjugal expression of sexuality, means failing in the requirements of *sequela* and emptying matrimony, from the start, of its sacramental significance. Conversely, one chooses this or that form of *sequela* because one feels called to it by the Risen Lord, because one has received a certain charism. It is a question of Christian obedience. Other factors can only be indications through which one becomes aware of one's particular calling. There is thus a need for a process of discernment in prayer.

9. Religious or Secular: the Only Alternatives?

Up to now we have spoken only of simple categories: religious and lay, celibate and married. Canon Law necessarily speaks in this way.[93] Actually, life in the Spirit, like biological life, is difficult to classify in a few rigid categories.[94] Christian life, too, is graduated into a rich variety of diverse vocations, as we shall see in the next chapter.

Excursus: The Pericope of the Rich Man

(Mk. 10:17–31, Mt. 19:16–30, Lk. 18:18–30)

The pericope of the rich man who, having asked Jesus what he should do to obtain eternal life, was called to follow the Lord after renouncing his possessions but did not accept the call, has had, especially in its Matthean version, a doubly important role in history. First, Mt. 19:21 is one of the texts which has most often been quoted to explain the origin and meaning of religious life. Second, this same passage has been quoted as the basis for various common theories that are interconnected, even though they are not all necessarily found, in the same Fathers' and Doctors' writings: the theory that considers celibacy and poverty to be counsels of the Lord, as distinguished from his precepts (from Ambrose onward); the theory that there are two stages of Christian morality and spirituality, the precepts and the counsels (from the Judaeo-Christians of the second century on); the idea of the counsels as means to attain perfection and, consequently, the theory of religious life as a state of perfection (Scholasticism). Subsequently we will study each of these theories separately.

However, we must immediately note two things. First, one must not confuse the fact that Matthew 19 had an important influence on the birth of monasticism, and of other later forms of religious life, with the use to which it was put in defending certain theological points of view. For, although it is true that monks and nuns probably read the term "perfect" in the Hellenistic sense of an ethical perfection to be reached gradually, it is equally true that the category of "counsel" is totally foreign to them, and that their opinion on the relationship between monasticism and perfection differs in some ways from that which was expounded by Scholasticism. Second, we must note that the interpretation of Mt. 19:16-30, in the sense of a morality in two stages, commandments-counsels, is not found in the Fathers' commentaries on the Synoptics. It appears only when some of them, while expounding this theory, refer to Mt. 19 to corroborate it. It seems theologically significant to us to point this out.

1. The Pericope in Mark

This pericope is found in all three of the Synoptics; its oldest form is to be found in Mark. Analyzing the texts makes it apparent that some details were added by Mark when he was working over the traditional material which was also familiar to the other two Evangelists. Exegetes usually distinguish three units in this material, originally separate: a) the anecdote of the rich man: Mk. 10:17-22; b) the paragraph on the difficulty or impossibility of the rich entering the Kingdom of God: Mk. 10:23-27; c) the paragraph which describes Peter's reaction and ends with the logion on the disciples' reward: Mk. 10:28-31. At this moment we are only interested in the anecdote of the rich man.

As regards the anecdote, R. Bultmann considers it to be an imaginary scene developed by tradition in the form of a scholastic dialogue (*Schulgespräche*).[1] There are those who think that the story was formed in order to give support to the logion in Mk. 10:23: "How hard it is for those who have riches to enter the Kingdom of God!" and was therefore influenced by it.[2] Actually there is no reason that obliges us to follow these authors. We can very well agree with W. Zimmerli[3] that the story is backed by the memory of a historical event.

Dispensing with all exegetical subtleties on details of composition, which would not add anything significant to our discussion, we note that in Mark the anecdote is built of two clearly distinct parts. The first part consists in that scholastic dialogue to which R. Bultmann refers: a certain person approaches Jesus and asks him what he must do to obtain eternal life. This question was common in Judaism. One would ask a famous teacher what, according to his personal opinion, was essential in the Torah. This same question, in another form, was directed to Jesus in Mk. 12:28: "Which is first of all the commandments?" Jesus answers, in Mk. 10:19, with one of those lists of social duties which were traditional among the Jews from the times of the first prophets and which rarely, though it did in this case, resembled so closely the commandments of the second Table of the Law.[4] The inquirer referred to above affirms that he has observed these things from his youth, and Jesus looks on him with love. One should remember also that the scribe who questioned Jesus on the first commandment received his approval: "You are not far from the Kingdom!" (Mk. 12:34).

The second part of the literary unit is the narration of a call to discipleship. Having looked on him with love because of his goodness, Jesus decides to associate him with his ministry: *follow me* (Mk. 10:21), but the man declines the invitation because of his wealth.

In the second part of the anecdote the initiative is no longer that of the anonymous pious Jew but, as in all the call narratives, that of Jesus. W. Harnisch has stressed that this entire little narrative has its culmination and ultimate meaning in the call to the following of Christ.[5] Thus one understands why Jesus should say to his interlocutor: "There is one thing you lack." S. Légasse[6] insists a great deal on the *you,* and concludes that, while the first part of the pericope formulates a doctrine of universal importance (the commandments as the way to enter the Kingdom), the second is concerned with a personal vocation which may not be generalized. It is only this particular person who is called to leave all his possessions and follow the Lord. This conclusion, while it is true in regard to the historical event, leaves us somewhat perplexed when applied to the actual version because, in the composition of the Gospels, the call narratives are no longer concerned with stories of the past but with prototypes of Christian existence. Whatever is lacking to the rich man who questions Christ is, therefore, lacking to all, including those who keep the commandments. What is lacking is adherence to Christ through faith and obedience to the Gospel, expressed by the idea of *sequela* in its post-resurrection content. In the traditional pre-Markan material there is already a deep ideological unity in the whole anecdote: one enters into life by observing the commandments, but above all by following Christ and by cleaving to him.

W. Harnisch[7] pointed out the contrast between the *all* in the rich man's answer, "I have kept all these" (Mk. 10:20) and the "*one thing* you lack," in Jesus' reply (Mk. 10:21). The one thing lacking does not belong to the type of things observed by the rich man from his youth; it is of a completely different kind. It is precisely the question of following Jesus and entering with him into the *eschaton*. Without wanting to discuss here the Protestant preoccupation with the disjunction of faith and works, a preoccupation which appears in certain commentaries on this passage, it seems clear that already in Mark the story of the call of the rich man, while approving the observance of social duties in the prophetic tradition, contrasts the unique value of following Jesus.

For those who accept the probability of an actual historical background for the anecdote, there remains the problem of the form given it by the Synoptics, and consequently of the tradition before the vocation: "Go and sell everything you own and give the money to the poor, and you will have treasure in heaven; then come follow me" (Mk. 10:21). Although Jesus called others to follow him as disciples, who then left their families, work, and social situation to follow him, in no other case did Jesus ever command anyone to renounce (and much less, to so radically renounce) their possessions.

Two solutions are possible. First, the invitation could have been formulated in this way not by Jesus but by ecclesial tradition, to emphasize the two requirements of discipleship which, in the other call narratives, are expressed by an actual response ("and leaving . . . they followed"). In this case Jesus would simply have said: "Follow me!" Secondly, Jesus himself could instead, while calling the rich man to discipleship, have warned him of the consequences this would bring to his situation as a wealthy man. In this case radical renunciation would not be a condition for discipleship, but a possible consequence, as that of the cross announced in the famous logion.[8]

2. The Pericope in Luke

Luke follows essentially the same tradition as Mark, and by so doing forms a group from which, as we shall soon see, Matthew separates himself. The third Evangelist introduces not only some stylistic changes, but some significant details. We will list them, following S. Légasse's clear analysis.

The man who questions Jesus is a member of one of the leading families (*árchôn*: Lk. 18:18). It is probable that Luke has an early memory of him. In Lk. 18:22, there is a pleonastic form: "sell *everything* (*panta*) you have", while in Mark one finds only: "as much as" (*osa*). This pleonastic locution is frequently used in the New Testament, but one must remember how insistently Luke repeats *everything* when there is a question of the requirements of discipleship (Lk. 5:11; 5:28; 14:33). In the same verse 18:22, where Mark (10:21) says "give . . . to the poor" (*dòs*), Luke writes: "*distribute* . . . to the poor" (*diádo*). In Luke the use of the verb *diadomaï* is limited to the distribution of possessions to the poor in the Church, and is to be found again in the second summary of the Acts: "it was then distributed to any members who might be in need" (Ac. 4:35). Similarly, in Lk. 18:28, Peter states that he has renounced all he had (*tà ídia*), an adjective in the New Testament found again only in the second summary of the Acts (Ac. 4:32) in connection with ecclesial communion: "no one claimed for his own use anything *that he had,* as everything they owned was held in common." Finally, in Luke it is not the disciples who show surprise, but the listeners: "In that case . . . who can be saved?"

From this analysis one concludes that the distribution to the poor, which in Mark and Matthew appears as something secondary, in Luke acquires greater importance and ecclesial significance. Renunciation permits the birth of the ecclesial community.[9]

3. The Pericope in Matthew

In Matthew we are immediately faced with a novelty: the whole pericope appears unified. Whereas the material received from tradition and preserved by Mark and Luke is divided into two parts (the first introduced by the anonymous rich man's question, and the other by the observation and invitation of Jesus), Matthew fuses both into one literary unit. Here, in fact, it is the rich man who asks both what he should do and whether, having observed his social duties, there is still something lacking in him.

A second new element is the concluding addition to the list of social duties: "And you must love your neighbor as yourself" (Mt. 19:19) taken from Lv. 19:18. Matthew is here recalling that second commandment which Jesus added to the first (to love God with one's whole heart) in his answer to the Pharisees where he summarizes the whole Law in terms of love. Thus the answer of Jesus to the rich man in Matthew takes on connotations that are more explicitly Christian.

A third difference, and precisely the one which has made this passage noteworthy in the history of theology and of exegesis, is constituted by the words that are the prelude to the invitation: "If you wish to be perfect, go and sell . . ." We therefore find that we have two answers of Jesus that start with: "If you wish . . .": Mt. 19:17 ("If you wish to enter into life, keep the commandments . . .") and Mt. 19:21 ("If you wish to be perfect, go and sell . . ."). One is faced, then, with the question of the relationship between these two parts of the pericope.

Historically, the first step toward an interpretation that became common from the Middle Ages on was made by Origen, who interpreted perfection in a Hellenistic sense.[10] In Greek and in the Bible, *perfect* is that which lacks nothing. From this point of view the Greek *teleios* and the Hebrew *tam* coincide. The Greek, however, sees perfection as an ethico-spiritual state which the subject reaches progressively, through practice, or, in mystery religions, through rites accompanied by exercises. Thus Origen asks himself how it is possible for a person to become perfect by the very fact of having renounced his possessions. Would the roots of his vices be suddenly extirpated and his virtues intensified? No, he answers, but in poverty he will find an efficient means to reach perfection. From this moment on, the "If you wish to be perfect . . ." will always be read as: "If you want to reach perfection, start by renouncing your possessions." The first monks put this into practice literally.

Ambrose[11] and Jerome,[12] basing themselves on the fact that, in Matthew, Jesus introduces the call to renunciation and discipleship with the words "If you wish . . . ," have spoken of a *counsel* of poverty. But, as we will see, for Ambrose the counsel is the distinguishing mark of Christian morality, while the commandments would distinguish the Old Testament.

Later, following an exegesis which will become common to Scholasticism, the Judaeo-Christian distinction between commandments and that which goes beyond what is commanded was applied to this text, a differentiation connected with the rabbinical pair, *sadiq–hasid:* the first, or righteous, who keeps the commandments; the second, or pious who goes beyond. Thus one came to see in this text a double aspect: the first, which involves observing the commandments and leads to entrance into eternal life, and the second, which involves observing the counsels (that which is recommended above and beyond the precept) and leads to perfection.

We will put aside immediately the idea that the words "If you wish to be perfect... " imply a counsel, because the first answer starts in the same way: "If you wish to enter into life . . .". Let us then concentrate on Matthew's concept of perfection.

Matthew is the only evangelist to use the term *teleios* (perfect) and he does so on two occasions. The first time is in the Sermon on the Mount. At the end of the paragraph on loving one's enemies, where Luke says: "Be compassionate as your Father is compassionate" (Lk. 6:36), Matthew writes: "You must therefore be perfect just as your heavenly Father is perfect" (Mt. 5:48). In Matthew the call to perfection is, therefore, part of the Sermon on the Mount, and consequently represents the calling of every follower of Jesus. In view of this fact alone, we must exclude a vocation to perfection that is reserved to only a few Christians. The "perfection" to which all followers of Christ are called in the Sermon on the Mount consists in a generosity over and above (Mt. 5:47) that of publicans and gentiles (Mt. 5:20), and also a justice that exceeds the virtue of the scribes and Pharisees. The sect at Qumran also thought of itself as a group of perfect people and showed this by their observance of the numerous extra precepts which the community had formulated for itself. In Qumran a legalistic point of view predominated. In Matthew the over-and-above is not determined by quantity, but by intensity of quality. The Law as reinterpreted by Christ has requirements which go beyond the literal, or even the traditional, interpretation of the scribes. Consequently, those who accept this interpretation from Christ and seek to put it into practice are perfect.

Coming back to the anecdote of the call of the rich man, we find in Matthew a scholastic dialogue developed in three phases, each introduced by a question of the interlocutor. To the first question, "What good deed must I do to possess eternal life?" Jesus answers, "Keep the commandments." Thus, in Matthew, Jesus refers us to the Decalogue, the preeminent part of the Torah. The man presses him further, asking Jesus for his personal basic summary of the Law: ''Which?'' Jesus answers by quoting some precepts from the second Table and adding, as a definitive conclusion, ''You must love your neighbor as yourself'' (Lv. 19:18). Thus we are already introduced to a Christian interpretation of the Law. The man then says, ''I have kept all these,'' and he asks: ''What more do I need to do?'' as if to say nothing more is lacking. But Jesus answers that, in fact, one thing remains to be done: to follow him, renouncing his possessions also.

S. Légasse notes that: 1) those who do what is good by observing the Law are already perfect according to the language of Jesus' time; 2) the rich man already observes the Law as interpreted by Christ, and is therefore already perfect according to Matthew (the Sermon on the Mount); and 3) the actual renunciation of possessions is never required by the Lord as a general doctrine, with the conclusion that the third part is not a general doctrine but a personal vocation: ''Go... sell... follow me.''[13]

We have already noted, however, in connection with Mark's version, that the call narratives are meant to define the vocation of the post-resurrection Christian. In this rich man who is questioning Jesus one can discern the post-resurrection Church: in this case the Judaeo-Christian Church of Matthew, which found its identity as a spiritual movement within the People of Israel in a fuller observance of the Law (Sermon on the Mount). Matthew is in agreement with this approach, both in the Sermon on the Mount and in the first two phases of this dialogue. But in Chapter 19 he adds that what ultimately defines the Christian, beyond the radical observance of the Law, is the following of Christ, with its consequences. Christ, the incarnation of the expectation of Israel, is the *quid novum* that defines the new situation of the Christian. One becomes perfect by accepting Christ's interpretation of the fullness of the Law, but above all by adhering to him. The first element, upon which the Judaeo-Christian mentality was inclined to focus, derived from the second.[14]

We are dealing, therefore, with two different things—even though they are closely connected in Matthew's mind—and not with a repetition of the same idea, as those exegetes affirm who want to identify discipleship with observance of the Law. In this text Matthew goes beyond the observance of the Law. Here Christian identity, as a religious relationship mediated by Christ, opens a passageway through the structure of Hebrew religiosity, in which the relationship with God is mediated by the Torah.

II

Christian Vocations: Religious and Secular

In Chapter I, after studying the kind of relationship that exists between religious life and Sacred Scriptures, we concluded that in the Gospels, and even in the life of Jesus as it can be reconstructed through the Gospels, the various practical situations in which the disciples met and sought to carry out the gospel message are not important. The important thing is fidelty to the gospel message, the basis for the Christian life. Jesus was a celibate; some of his disciples were also perhaps single, while the others were married. Although the greater part of them earned a frugal living, some were wealthy. Some were associated with him in his itinerant ministry; others remained in their homes. There was a variety of life situations, and no stress is put upon them. What counts is discipleship itself, not the concrete forms in which it is lived out.

I. The Phenomenon of Christian Variety

By the time the Gospels were composed (after A.D. 65) the Christian spirit had already begun to develop its manifold possibilities, thus giving rise to variations in the practical manner of fulfilling the Christian vocation and of belonging to the Church. Furthermore, in the churches of apostolic times, before the ministries were institutionalized, there was an even more surprising variety, so much so that exegetes find it difficult to understand the exact meaning of some of the terms used in regard to the various tasks carried out in the community. There were the Twelve, the Apostles, the Prophets, and Deacons (ministers) of the Judaeo-Hellenistic communities. In the churches founded by Paul, the variety of ministries and situations is such that the Apostle himself is not able to take them all into account. On the level of lifestyle there are the married and the single; among the latter are widows, virgins, and celibates. On the ministerial level there are apostles, prophets, evangelists, community administrators, teachers of the faith, those who are dedicated to works of mercy, etc. (1 Co. 12:8–18, 28–30; Rm. 12:6–18; Ep. 4:11).

This living variety in the Church led St. Paul to reflect on the various ministries and on the different lifestyles of celibates and married people. He shows himself equally sensitive to Christian unity and to this diversity. In order to explain the latter he uses certain important concepts: on God's part, that of a calling and of different gifts bestowed by the same Spirit; on the part of the community, that of ministries corresponding to various needs; on the part of the individual, that of obedience to a divine vocation. These concepts will guide us in our ensuing reflections.

It is evident that the importance of the common grace, on the one hand, and the mistaken idea he shared with all the first generation of Christians regarding the date of the *Parousia,* on the other, allowed the Apostle to attribute only a relative importance to various concrete situations. In the new dispensation it makes no difference whether one is a Jew or a gentile (1 Co. 7:19), or whether one is a slave or free, although the slave who has the opportunity to be emancipated should take advantage of it (1 Co. 7:21). Since the last days are approaching, spouses should live as if they were not married, and those who buy as if they had no possessions (1 Co. 7:29–31). Clearly it would only be the idea that the Church has a mission to accomplish throughout history that would permit a more exact evaluation of the different life situations of Christians and the more decisive classification of them as vocations. One must therefore consider the later history of the Church in order to understand the development of the theology of Christian vocation.

The facts are well known. Through gradual institutionalization, the ministries were reduced in number and arranged in a definite hierarchical order. Members of this hierarchy were then set apart from those who (to all appearances) carried on no ministry within the community. With the peace of Constantine, the process culminated in the assimilation of the political structures of the imperial court, which recognized an *ordo* and a *plebs*.[1] The wealth and variety of ministries suffered. But at the same time the ascetical movements which had thrived in the Church from the beginning of the second century climaxed wih the appearance of monasticism, proposing a Christian way of life differing from the one that had become common in the already-established Church.

This new type of Christian vocation had, before being accepted, to overcome certain misgivings it had aroused. The first two post-Biblical texts on the *casti* (celibates) show a fear that these might claim an ascetical superiority over the bishops (who were married).[2] Later Eustachius of Sebaste experienced difficulties with the bishops of Asia Minor. But monasticism was soon recognized, owing above all to the prestige of some of its heroes, such as Anthony, and to the intervention of some bishops, such as Athanasius.

The institutionalizing of the ministries, and of monasticism as well, brought about a two-fold differentiation of vocations in the Church: as regards ministries, the clergy and the laity; as regards lifestyles, religious and seculars. And on the one hand, the hierarchical structure of the Church, and on the other hand, the various forms of Christian life.[3]

Canon Law considers these two distinctions—between clergy and laity, religious and secular persons—as fundamental. It is obviously necessary for legislation to deal with large categories. It must consider large, established groups and cannot, nor should it, cover all the potentialities of Christian life. It is evident that there are common denominators within each large group; it is equally clear that when the actual life of the Church, or theological reflection upon it, are limited by these categories, the great riches of ecclesial reality are greatly reduced.

Indeed, the vitality of the Church is made possible by a periodic breaking of these barriers. On the one hand the Spirit creates new forms of ministry. The diaconate and minor orders of the ancient Church, which for centuries had been reduced to an artificial passing phase, have now been brought to life by the renewal of the permanent diaconate and by the recognition of numerous ministries. On the other hand the Spirit also now and again creates new forms of religious life which do not fit into canonical categories and which have to overcome certain obstacles before obtaining recognition: from conventual life, to apostolic institutes, to un-cloistered women, to institutes of common life, to secular institutes, and to initiatives that have not yet received a name. We can say that both Canon Law and theology always remain a few centuries behind the workings of the Spirit.

Christian richness appears more wonderful when one considers not merely the variety of ministries or of institutionalized lifestyles, but the total life of the Church. There are, certainly, ordained ministers and lay people, religious and seculars; but within these groups there is a great variety, and between the variations there are links, as in biological evolution. In regard to lifestyles, there are both the officially recognized religious and also those who, without seeking any official recognition, adopt celibacy for the sake of the Kingdom and dedicate themselves to the service of the community of the faithful. Among seculars there are both those who remain single and those who marry. Among the latter there are couples who feel called to broaden their matrimonial communion within a larger sphere (basic local communities, prayer groups), or to dedicate themselves to poverty, or to evangelization; and there are missionary couples, married deacons and their wives, etc. Who would dare place a definitive barrier to the grace of the Spirit?

Before reflecting on the characteristics belonging to religious life (a term we use in all its breadth), we should pause to examine theologically the origin and meaning of the variety of vocations to different forms of life. In doing so it will be very useful to recall, as a first step, the manner in which the relationships of religious and seculars, with their common Christian vocation and with each other, have been presented historically.

II. Historical Research

1. Within Monasticism

If we consult one of the first and most important sources on ancient monasticism, the *Vita Antonii* of St. Athanasius, we meet with a surprise. It does not refer to ''seculars'' in opposition to monks. St. Anthony considers himself as being part of the Christian people, even though he classifies the monks as a special group among them. Speaking of the demons, Anthony says: "if the evil spirits see each Christian (*pantas Christianoús*) and especially a monk (*málista*) laboring cheerfully and making progress, they will first attack and tempt...,"[4] and again: "If (the demons) had the power they would not allow any of us Christians to live."[5] When referring to Anthony's many visitors, the text speaks of "many people" who came, or of a "certain person" who came.[6] The visitors are not called "seculars," even though they were. To what should this attitude be ascribed? To the fact that the author of this biography was a bishop, who lived and worked among secular people? Or to the fact that, with St. Anthony, monasticism was just beginning, and the opposition of religious to seculars had not yet been established? Perhaps to both reasons.

We have stressed this because a definite opposition was soon to be established. The *Apophtegmata* are quite careful to contrast secular persons with monks. A monk who wore a short tunic was accused of being "secular" and was asked to leave, since that place was reserved for monks.[7] The two callings are already very clearly differentiated,[8] as well as their social duties: the monks protest because a tax collector wants to gather contributions from them, as if they were secular people.[9] This trend is accentuated in some Latin sources, such as the *Lives of the Fathers of the Jura*,[10] where reference is made to the people of the world (*saeculi homines*).[11] We know that the term *saeculum* as used in these *Lives* has somewhat negative connotations.

Judging from the *Apophtegmata,* the attitude of monks toward secular people, and their way of judging the latter, was not uniform. On the one hand it is said that a certain secular man, Evaristus, had surpassed a degree of virtue which had not yet been attained by two monks, and for this reason he is being included in the *Apophtegmata*. This is, however, the case of a secular man who not only shared his possessions with the poor, but who, since his wedding day, had never had contact with his wife.[12] Spyridion, a shepherd, was married and had a daughter; he later became a bishop. He also is included in the collection, with two of his sayings,[13] because of his sanctity. A monk is obliged to admit that St. Epiphanius, who never had gone to sleep harboring anything in his heart against anyone, had a better rule of life than his own, even though the bishop ate meat and he did not.[14] Are Spyridion and St. Epiphanius receiving favorable treatment because they were bishops? It would seem not. According to one of the apothegms, it was revealed to the great St. Anthony that there was a physician in the city who was similar to him (in virtue). He gave everything he could spare to the poor, and every day sang the Trisagion with the angels.[15] Also Count Longinus, a very charitable man, was gifted with charisms.[16] Even at that time, the subordinate and instrumental character of elements belonging to the monastic rule of life, from celibacy and poverty to the various forms of asceticism, was recognized. These elements were subordinate and instrumental in relation to certain fundamental virtues of Christianity—charity, above all. This is what Cassian wanted to say when he applied the Stoic category of *adiphora* (indifferent things)—which he translates as *media,* that is *nec bona nec mala* (neither good nor bad) in themselves—not only to celibacy and poverty, but also to fasting and vigils.[17]

There are, however, other passages in which the situation of the secular Christian is depicted in dark colors. Let us listen first to Mother Syncletica who said: "We who have chosen this way of life must obtain perfect temperance (*sophrosynen*); among secular persons (*kosmikois*), even when they seem to practice temperance it is mixed with intemperance, because they sin with all their other senses: their gaze is shameless and they laugh immediately."[18] And in an apothegm not included in Migne's edition: "Many hermits do what secular people do, and they are lost," a sentence in which the behavior of secular people seems to be identified with "bad behavior."[19] As usual the point of view of the *Master* (*The Rule of the Master*) is most pessimistic. His rule, in fact, warns the candidate to monastic life that "when he was a secular the devil did not tempt him, because he clearly was always doing the will of the one he was serving; but as soon as he would give himself to the fear of God in the service of Christ, leaving the allurements of the devil and the secular militia . . ." the devil would not leave him in peace.[20] Inasmuch as this warning is directed to all candidates to monasticism at the moment they are leaving secular life, we can conclude that, for the *Master,* secular life was synonymous with working for the devil and doing his will. There seems to be no room here for a Christian secular vocation.

How might one explain the negative image of seculars which monasticism, at least in some of its tendencies, was developing? One might perhaps point to the not-too-exemplary condition of the Church in the fourth century, when its recognition by the Empire had greatly lessened the cost of being a Christian and had given a position of prestige to the clergy. But it was probably due not so much to the general situation of the Church as to a defensive attitude. The monks felt tempted to adopt the easier aspects of secular life: certainly not the family or economic problems, or those pertaining to the education of children, but the manner of dress, the freedom to come and go into the city seeking diversion, etc. Since the secular attitude represented a temptation for them, they tended to consider it from a strictly negative point of view. One should note that this same phenomenon took place during recent centuries, under the influence of Jansenism. In the little treatises on religious spirituality, the "world" was then represented exclusively as an enemy to be avoided. It was not clear which world was being spoken of: the world that is hostile to the Gospel, or the world created by God and the object of the vocation of secular Christians.

2. In Monastic Theology: a Life Faithful to the Gospel

An examination of the way monks interpreted their manner of life in the Church involves some not too easily-resolved difficulties in understanding Christian secular life.

The first difficulty arises from the fact that the monks interpreted monasticism as the observance of the numerous precepts of the Lord contained in the Scriptures. We have seen how those things which the Fathers came to indicate as "counsels" were called "precepts" by the monks. This category was applied to all monastic asceticism, to constant prayer, and to the renunciation of possessions. Did the application of this category of "precept" to the special traits of the monastic vocation merely reflect the psychological fact that the monks felt their own obligation to practice them (in which case they would not be obligatory for all Christ's disciples), or that they considered them actual commandments binding for all?

The first interpretation is the one St. Gregory the Great will later adopt, distinguishing between universal precepts obligatory for all and the particular ones proposed to those who seek perfection.[21] In this interpretation, secular Christians have their own legitimate status in the Church, even though it is below that of the monks.

In the second interpretation it would be difficult, at least, to find a place for secular Christians, since they would be persons who had despised some of God's precepts. If one were to follow this tendency to the extreme, one would fall into an attitude similar to that of the messalians and the various encratite movements: one would make Christian life coincide, if not with continence (the monks knew that this was not a command of the Lord), then with the renunciation of possessions (which they called *praeceptum Domini*). From the positive way in which the *Vita Antonii* and some of the *Apophtegmata* regard Christians in the world, it is clear that such an attitude would have been rejected by the great orthodox monastic movement. We must therefore conclude that they were not concerned with the situation of secular Christians; but we should also add that their way of referring to their vocation as obedience to the Gospel precepts is, at least, misleading.

This manner of referring to monasticism as "the faithful observance of the Gospel" depends entirely on their way of considering the relationship between monastic life and Christian life. For us today religious life represents one of various Christian vocations. Even if those who remain attached to a concept of religious life as a state of perfection tend to see a sort of privileged position of religious life over the common vocation to holiness, it is clear that in the theology of Christian secular life now prevailing, and more generally in the context of present day ecclesiology, no one can escape the conclusion that religious life, like secular life, is basically a way of living a Christian life, and a means of fulfilling our common vocation.

For monastic theology, from the first hermits up to the Benedictines, monastic life was not *a* Christian vocation but *the* Christian vocation; the apex, one might say, of gospel living. Many facts make one aware of this: for example, Basil's constant reference, when formulating the rule of life for his brotherhood, to "living according to the Gospel," and not to a special form of Christian life; Chapter 4 of Benedict's *Rule*, in which, seeking to outline a practical rule for monastic living, he summarizes the Commandments and works of mercy, reechoes the Beatitudes, etc.;[22] the Shenoute formula of profession, in which the monks commit themselves to keeping the commandments;[23] and that of the Pseudo-Dionysius, which imitates the baptismal liturgy, even though the object of the promises is more specifically monastic (renunciation, and observance of the monastic rule of life).[24] The very concept of "conversion," which is so important in monastic theology, originates from the common Christian fact of baptismal conversion, and becomes more radical by being applied to the very lifestyle. We believe that the interpretation of the religious profession as being "a second baptism" belongs in this context.

There are some deep intuitions in this manner of considering the monastic vocation, especially that monasticism was straining toward the development of Christian life. What truly matters, in fact, are not the specific monastic traits, but the common Christian reality: a life completely oriented toward the will of God in faith and love, the effort toward constant prayer, the Beatitudes, etc. This is what matters, since the institutionalizing of religious life tends inevitably to defend institutions, and therefore looks at details rather than at the common gospel values. A second intuition confirms what we conclude from our analysis of the discipleship sayings and call narratives: that religious life consists solely in bringing the common requirements of the following of Christ to the level of a lifestyle, and institutionalizing its demands. The monks were right when they saw their lifestyle as a visible incarnation of the basic orientation of Christian living.

It remains true, however, that this manner of speaking may be misleading. How should one describe the situation of secular Christians? Are they only half-Christian, unable to live the Christian vocation in its fullness? As we shall see later there did not exist, at least until the eleventh century, a theology of the secular vocation (which was often described as a situation permitted to those who could do no better). In such a context it was easier to define monasticism as Christian life lived to its fullest extent, realizing at the same time that this might be interpreted in an inadequate way. Secondly, we must recognize that religious are such not because of their degree of faith, hope, and charity, nor of their attainment of the latter through an intense life of prayer, but because their life is lived entirely in the presence of God, in exclusive reference to him, through celibacy and the hermitic or cenobitical life. In this sense religious life is one of the possible Christian vocations, and a means of carrying out the common vocation. This is certainly a theological concept only recently developed, and it cannot, therefore, be attributed in its entirety to the Fathers or to ancient monasticism. But let us make two observations: 1) it is the only concept that prevents the confusion to which we referred above; 2) the concept typical of ancient monasticism was probably the result of anthropological and theological assumptions which have since been put aside by the common opinion of the Church.

3. St. Basil

The problem of the relationship between ascetical life and the Gospel imposes itself strongly when one reads the so-called *Regulae fusius* and *Regulae brevius* of St. Basil. These documents repeatedly refer to the lifestyle they propose as a "rule of life according to the Gospel,"[25] and as "a life according to the precepts of the Lord,"[26] while the life Basil and his companions led before is called "a life outside the precepts of Christ,"[27] or oftener "the common life," i.e., a life that is commonly followed.[28]

If Basil's *Asketikon* intended to propose a particular type of Christian vocation (monastic life), these texts would raise serious difficulties, because in that case only the monks would be faithful to the Gospel. Actually we know that Basil intended to place himself within an ascetical movement (that of Eustachius of Sebaste), and that he did not seek to create a different form of Christian life, but rather to bring all Christians to take the Gospel seriously. For this reason, in the *Asketikon,* relationships of the community with persons outside are accepted or rejected according to the spiritual quality of the individuals, and not according to whether they do or do not belong to an ascetical group. What counts is fidelity to a demanding Christian spirit. It is, however, true that the same *Asketikon* warns that it is impossible to keep God's commandments with a dissipated spirit, and therefore that "asceticism, according to the Gospel" requires the rejection of worldly preoccupations.[29] Basil repeats this immediately afterward: "life in the company of those who rashly scorn perfect observance of the precepts is dangerous,"[30] and consequently one must avoid it and form a brotherhood with those who are animated by the same ideals.[31] Later he adds that it is impossible (*adynaton*) to lead a "life according to the Gospel" unless one imitates the poverty of Christ by renouncing one's possessions.[32]

It is clear that the *Asketikon* is aiming directly at life's quality, and not at whether one is in the world (a category seldom used) or in a group of brothers or sisters outside of the earthly city. For this reason the passages that speak of those who scorn the precepts do not necessarily refer to secular persons as such, compared to the brethren. We have seen, however, that the *Asketikon* does declare that it is impossible to be faithful in the midst of those (in the cities) who despise the Gospel, and requires leaving them and renouncing one's possessions. This is equivalent to a rejection of what we now understand as secularity. Thus secular persons and "those who despise" come to be the same. Add to this the fact that the Basilian group assumes a promise of celibacy, and the problem is further complicated. The least one can say is, with Dom J. Gribomont, that some Basilian texts suffer from a certain ambiguity.[33] This results, too, from St. Basil's use of the term *kosmos* (world): usually in the New-Testament sense of a force that opposes

Christ, but at times very clearly in reference to "secular" occupations, without making any clear-cut distinction between the two uses.[34]

It seems to us, however, that these problems are to be found mostly in the large *Asketikon* (in the *Regulae fusius* and *brevius*). The small *Asketikon* translated by Rufinus has, instead of the prologue of the *Regulae fusius* with its admonitions to those Christians who do not keep the Lord's precepts,[35] another prologue which takes a very different point of view:

> We to whom the ministry of the word has been confided, must always be ready to instruct and help to perfect souls; we explain some things which regard the Lord's precepts to all, in the general assembly of the Church; others we comment upon more secretly to those who are more perfect, answering and interrogating those who so desire, on the faith and truth of the Gospel of Our Lord Jesus Christ, and on the rule of a perfect life (*de conversatione perfecta*) by which one can become a perfect and consummate man of God.[36]

Thus the precepts are taught to all Christians; the rule of life outlined in the *Asketikon* is, instead, directed toward those who want to become perfect. The question remains whether one may not become perfect without a rule that prescribes celibacy and the renunciation of possessions; but at least the other Christians are instructed in the Lord's commandments. The language is much more subtle. One should notice how, in the rest of the work, reference is more often made to doctrine and indications, rather than to precepts (which would be binding for all, according to the prologue of the *Regulae fusius*).[37]

4. Marriage and Virginity in the Fathers

We make no claim here to present an exhaustive study of this complex and delicate theme. We are only eager to show what consequences certain affirmations of the Fathers on marriage and virginity have on a possible interpretation of secularity as a Christian vocation. It is known that the Fathers insisted on affirming the lawfulness of marriage against all the denials of the Encratite and Manichean movements. They reiterated it often: "I do not therefore condemn marriage, but I prefer virginity to it."[38] As a matter of fact, whoever embraces marriage is *proposito minor,* that is, choosing an inferior situation.[39] However, in order to remain faithful to St. Paul in 1 Co. 7:7, St. Jerome declares that both marriage and virginity are *dona* (gifts), while still repeating that marriage is a lower gift.[40] Here again we find the traditional affirmation of the superiority of virginity.

This does not create a problem in regard to the possibility of a Christian secular vocation. The problem is caused, instead, by other statements that are not isolated. In the first place we find the repeated affirmation of Chrysostom that "marriage is necessary for the weak;"[41] that "he who, being able to preserve virginity, marries, does himself an injustice;"[42] that marriage is a condescension of God toward those whose virtue is only that of a child.[43] After these statements it is hard to see how Christian marriage can be a vocation. Can this vocation, in fact, be founded on a simple condescension granted to the weak, chosen only after having measured one's capacity for continence? Jerome thus shows marriage to be in opposition to spiritual life:

> What good is there in a situation which hinders prayer? Which does not allow one to receive the Body of Christ? While I fulfill the duties of a husband, I cannot fulfill those of a continent man. The Apostle himself, in another place (1 Th. 5), orders that one should pray always. If we are to pray always, it will never be possible to fulfill the obligations of marriage, because whenever I give my wife what I owe her, I will be unable to pray.[44]

And in another passage:

> We do not deny that among widows and married women there can be saints, but they are the ones who cease being wives and imitate the chastity of virgins within the bonds of marriage.[45]

Hence it seems impossible to reconcile marriage lived to the full and the spiritual life.

More decisive for an understanding of this opposition of the virgin (i.e. monk or nun) and the married person is the affirmation that marriage, although not a sin in itself, was the consequence of sin; in fact, Adam and Eve were virgins in Paradise, and had relations with each other only after they sinned. This affirmation, suggested by the Acts of Andrew in the second century,[46] is repeated by several Fathers.[47] We will consider it when we study the doctrine of the Fathers about virginity in Chapter V, on Celibacy.

5. Monks and Seculars in St. John Chrysostom

St. John Chrysostom represents a very different point of view from that of Basil. We have, of course, already read some passages of his *De Virginitate,* from which one can conclude that a true Christian vocation to marriage is impossible. But these texts do not express his entire thought, nor do they represent his best moments. They appear when he is comparing monks to secular people. First of all he insists on a universal vocation to perfection: "Everyone is called to perfection, and from this point of view there is no difference between clergymen and laypeople, between monks and those who live in the world. The manner only is different."[48] "It is a monstrous error to believe that the monk is obliged to live a more perfect life, while others can dispense themselves from it. . . . Secular people and monks have the duty of reaching the same pinnacle of perfection."[49] No Christian can, therefore, neglect any of the virtues.[50] The law of the Gospel is exacting for all: it is not enough to refrain from evil.[51] The Beatitudes are for everyone, and are not reserved only for the monks.[52] What then is the difference between seculars and monks? Only the lifestyle: "Nothing distinguishes the secular from the monk, other than the state of matrimony."[53] In some passages Chrysostom would seem to prefer that those who are dedicated to virtue should remain among other people: "I would like virtuous men to remain, for the most part, in the city, so that they might be like leaven among the others."[54]

As for the rest, one knows that Chrysostom's attitude changes according to the context and point of view, thus reflecting both the admiration and the apprehension of the bishops of his time toward the monastic movement. At times he accuses the monks of selfishness because they prefer their safety to helping their neighbor; at times he praises monasteries as lighthouses which illuminate those who are struggling in the sea of the world.[55]

6. From St. Gregory the Great to Jonas of Orleans

Chrysostom's attitude is unique. In fact, even when the bishops, having learned from their pastoral experience, showed a more positive attitude toward secular people, they still displayed a certain difficulty in understanding the secular Christian vocation. For instance, St. Gregory the Great made a clear distinction between the common precepts and those which pertain to monastic life, thus making possible a complete harmony of secular life with Christ's precepts.[56] In his considerations he often starts from the fact of being Christian.[57] He centers his attention on the various *ordines,* or groups of Christians, united by a common faith and charity, although having differing merits.[58] But the difficulty appears also in Gregory. According to him the special precepts, such as poverty, are dispensed to the more perfect (*perfectioribus*). One understands what he really means by this by reading his chapter on spouses and celibates in his *Regula Pastoralis:*

> The spirit of married Christians is, at the same time, weak and faithful (*et infirmus et fidelis*), because it does not succeed in despising fully all temporal things (*plene cuncta temporalia despicere non valet*), but at the same time it is able to unite itself to eternal values by desire. It lives meanwhile among the pleasures of the flesh, but is comforted by the food of celestial hope. In this way it possesses the things of this world for use during the journey, but hopes for the things of God when it shall have attained them. It cannot give in so completely to present occupations as to fall away from that for which it must vigorously hope.[59]

The tension between earthly occupations and an orientation toward the Father's glory in the life situation of the secular Church is well described. But the fact remains that if one remains a secular, it is because one is not able to despise all earthly things, and one has a weak, though faithful, spirit. There is no sign here of a true vocation to the secular life.

We would expect to find a more understanding way of stating the problem in Bishop Jonas of Orleans' *De institutione laicali.* In fact he dedicated this work to the moral and spiritual formation of secular people, whom he exhorts to persevere in a life of prayer,[60] and whose domestic tasks he calls "a pastoral ministry."[61] On Judgment Day, he says, the elect will be of two types: those who will sit in judgment together with the Lord, because they left everything to follow him; and the others who will be judged by the Lord because, not having left everything, they daily gave alms to Christ's poor.[62] But here again, the old idea of the weakness of secular Christians reemerges:

> Whoever, strengthened by divine help, is able (*valet*) to attain the heights of perfection by leaving everything for the sake of the apostolic (monastic) life will

not be judged in the judgment, but will be seated as a judge. Instead, whoever was not able (*nequit*) to reach the height of contemplative life will, if dedicated to the works of mercy in the active life, be separated from evil men on the day of judgment, and included among those to whom it will be said: 'Receive the Kingdom.'[63]

We already know this. The secular person is still one who does not succeed in renunciation. We can foresee no Christian secular vocation here either.

Urban II seems to have been of the same opinion when, in a 1092 Bull confirming the foundation of the Canons of Rettenbach, he stated that "from the beginning the Church has always offered two types of life to her children: one to aid the insufficiency of the weak, the other to bring to perfection the goodness of the strong." This affirmation was repeated by the papal legates in 1125, at the time of the first confirmation of the Premonstratensian Order.[64]

7. The State of Perfection

The universal attribution, beginning with the thirteenth century, of the category "state of perfection" exclusively to bishops as a *status perfectionis acquisitae*, and to religious as *status perfectionis acquirendae*, gives us an idea of the relationship between religious and secular life within Christianity. Leaving aside the historic development of the doctrine on the episcopacy as a state of perfection (already) attained, we must turn our attention to a development of thought which qualifies religious life as a state ordained for the attainment of evangelical perfection.

The history of this tendency in theological reflection begins as early as Origen. It is a result of injecting a Hellenistic note into the reading of Mt. 19:21. As we have seen, a Hellenistic interpretation is present, not when we define as perfect the state of those who lack nothing (since this is also the meaning of the Hebrew *tam*), but when we interpret perfection (*teleiosis*) as an ethico-spiritual state of the mind which can be reached only gradually. In Matthew's Gospel, the term *perfect* refers, both times it is used, to the existential situation created in the disciple by adherence to Jesus. One is perfect, that is, one is a disciple, when one accepts the radical interpretation of the Law given by Jesus, (Mt. 5:48) and leaves everything in order to follow him (Mt. 19:21). The invitation to the rich man is simply a call to discipleship.

Origen, interpreting *perfect* in the Greek sense, rightly asked how one might become perfect by simply renouncing one's possessions. Could a mere material renunciation cancel all defects rooted in the soul? He answered logically (from his point of view) that one does not automatically attain perfection by renunciation, but through it one gains an effective aid in tending toward perfection.[65] Origen's interpretation was almost inevitable because all masters of spirituality in the Hellenistic world (Neo-Platonists, Cynics, Neo-Pythagoreans, and Gnostics) pointed to the renunciation of possessions as a condition for dedication to philosophy and for advancement toward spiritual perfection.

Thus one came to distinguish two phases in the text which concerns us (Mt. 19:16-22). The first phase had to do with salvation, attained by observance of the commandments (Mt. 19:16-20); the second had to do with perfection, attained by discipleship and renunciation of possessions. We have already seen that such an interpretation is not feasible from an exegetical standpoint. Whatever relationship exists between the first and second part of the narrative, the call to discipleship is addressed to all Christians by Matthew.

The interpretation was, however, accepted. In fact, by opening the way of salvation to everyone through the observance of the commandments, but linking perfection to the renunciation of one's goods, the inclination of the Hellenistic world to distinguish between the masses and the elite of perfect ones (gnostics) was satisfied. At the same time the Church was not reduced, as the messalians and other rigorist movements desired, to an elite practicing celibacy and poverty. One could speak of a (broad?) way leading toward salvation, and a (narrow?) way leading toward perfection. St. Basil mirrors this tendency faithfully in the first version of his *Asketikon,* when he states that sin is renounced in the first confession (Baptism) by all Christians, and not only by "those who are in an advantageous state of life and are tending toward perfection." These, instead, renounce also the common (secular) life, their family and goods,[66] because these things "oppose the integrity of the Gospel and of salvation."[67]

It would be false and unfair to define the position of the Church, the Fathers, and the Middle Ages by referring only to this doctrinal tendency. We have seen that the monks were well aware that secular Christians could rival them in a life of perfection. Even St. John Chrysostom upheld the common call to perfection and the universal value of the Law of Christ expressed in the Beatitudes. While recognizing the influence exerted by

Origen's and Basil's point of view, we must affirm that the attitude of the Church was not univocal on this subject.

We previously found a second manner of presenting the relationship between religious life and perfection when we spoke of the Fathers' attitude toward virginity and marriage. Basil himself, in his prologue to the *Asketikon,* states that he teaches things regarding the commandments of the Lord to everyone publicly in the Church, while, "to those who are more perfect," he comments privately "on the rule of a perfect life . . . by which one can become . . . a consummate man of God."[68] His rules are therefore means for attaining perfection, but they take for granted a certain level of perfection already achieved. This same idea is repeated by Chrysostom (when speaking of virginity), by Gregory the Great, and by Jonas of Orleans: marriage is for those who are not able to remain continent, for "the weak," for those "who have the virtue of a child." The practice of religious life already presupposes a degree of perfection. We might say that we are dealing with a *status perfectionis acquisitae et acquirendae.*

St. Thomas presents the question in a different manner, taking the various data of biblical revelation more into account. Perfection consists essentially in loving God with one's whole heart, and one's neighbor as oneself. Perfection, therefore, is reached by observing the Law of Charity. St. Thomas is well aware that every Christian must strive toward charity, and that actually every Christian can attain it with God's grace.[69] This is not sufficient, however, to make of every state of Christian life a state directed toward the attainment of perfection. In fact a Christian is in a state of perfection, not because he has reached the interior perfection of charity, but for two reasons: 1) because he has made a public commitment to perfection;[70] 2) because, to this end, he has embraced certain means (the counsels) which are designed to remove the obstacles in the way of the attainment of charity.[71] We may then conclude that St. Thomas, faithful to his idea of a state of life as a permanent lifestyle embraced with a commitment, makes the concept of religious life as a state of perfection derive from the fact that its followers commit themselves publicly to it, and from the fact that this state consists in the profession of the counsels, means by which one more easily reaches perfection.

In regard to the first reason, St. Thomas affirms that "some fulfill that to which they have not bound themselves," meaning by this that some people can be perfect without having taken upon themselves the obligation of striving toward perfection (secular people). Undoubtedly the question of the relationship between religious life and perfection becomes much more precise and richer in gradations with St. Thomas. He resolves some difficulties we noted above, and yet there is a weakness in his thought on religious life as a state of perfection: the premise that secular Christians do not commit themselves publicly to perfection. Soon we will discuss this theme.

III. Theological Reflection

In the preceding historical research we examined various predominant currents of thought in the Patristic and Medieval Church on the relationships between two forms of Christian life, the religious and the secular. It is time to reflect on the various data which have emerged. So far these data can be reduced to two fundamental facts: first, the great variety of forms evangelical life assumes and in which being-Church is realized, and second, the reduction of these to two prototypal forms: the Christian religious, and the Christian secular.

1. Origin of the Variety

The Gospels, with their interest focused on Christian existence as such, do not give attention to the various forms in which this existence can, and must, be lived. The evangelists were concerned with the problem of leading all Christians to fulfill their common vocation. Limiting ourselves to the Gospels, we might draw the erroneous conclusion that God's Word is directed to the individual only as a personalized articulation of a common Christian essence. We would consequently be called to be Christians, that is, disciples; the rest would depend on external and accidental circumstances.

Actually this would suppose the concept of a relationship between God and the human person that does not correspond to Biblical descriptions. St. Paul, who repeatedly states that he is an Apostle by the will of God, and therefore in obedience to a calling (Rm. 1:1; 1 Co. 1:1; 2 Co. 1:1; Ga. 1:1;

Ep. 1:1, etc), did not believe that the divine will and vocation were limited to the Apostles. In fact he affirms that ''everybody has his own particular gifts from God, one with a gift for one thing, and another with a gift for the opposite'' (1 Co. 7:7). Biblical personalism is reflected here. God calls everyone by name, from Adam and Eve to Cain, from Abraham and Sarah to Isaiah, to Mary of Nazareth, to Simon, to Andrew, and to Paul. Would he concern himself only with the great figures in history? Not at all; each one of us is Adam, Cain, or Andrew. We have already heard Paul: all have their own gift from God. Theologically the person is constituted by this one Word directed to it, which unfolds the divine plan for it.

The fact that human beings can be different is simply the result of the greatness of human potentialities. Transferring this into the sphere of the Gospel, the fact that Christian being manifests itself in so many concrete forms depends on the infinite richness of the Spirit of Christ which pervades the Church. We noted this elsewhere when speaking of Christian forms of spirituality. We must repeat it here in discussing the multiform types of evangelical existence. Even if we place ourselves outside the point of view of faith, the fact remains clear: if Christianity developed so many forms throughout history, it is because these forms are enclosed in the Gospel message, as real possibilities.

The variety of concrete vocations thus finds its explanation in the one God, the one Lord, the one Spirit. ''There is a variety of gifts, but always the same Spirit; there are all sorts of services to be done, but always the same Lord; working in all sorts of different ways in different people, it is the same God who is working in all of them'' (1 Co. 12:4-6). However, St. Paul refers also to the one body, the Church, to explain the multiplicity of vocations (1 Co. 12:12 ff; Rm. 12:4-8). It is the Church, with its many needs, that requires the various services. Now, twenty centuries later, it is necessary to place these words spoken by the Lord through his Apostle in a historical perspective that Paul could not have had. The multiform types of Christian life which have appeared throughout history are the Spirit's answers to the specific needs of the community of believers: Monasticism in the Constantinian Church, Christ's Poor and the Mendicant Orders in the twelfth and thirteenth centuries, the numerous communities, especially of women, beginning with the seventeenth century, the basic communities in Latin America in the twentieth century, missionary couples, apostolic and prayer groups. We pointed out in the preceding chapter that the forms of discipleship are expressions of the historic journey of the Church.

2. The Common Orientation Toward the Church

In a theological discussion of the forms of Christian life, one must begin from this uncontested biblical premise: the various particular vocations are all directed toward the common building up of the Church. The ecclesiological element is therefore basic to an understanding of the variety of practical forms which Christian life can, and must, assume; they are created by the various needs of the Church. This is St. Paul's constant point of view in regard to the various charisms of the Spirit. Religious life, too, is a gift, granted by the Spirit to the community of believers, because they have need of it. In 1 Co. 7:7, St. Paul says that celibacy and marriage correspond to different gifts. Considering the strong ecclesial meaning of the term *charism* in St. Paul (cf. also Rm. 12:4-8), it is difficult not to conclude that the gifts that create matrimony and celibacy are also directed toward the Church. St. Jerome (the famous panegyrist of virginity, with his well-known points of exaggeration) interprets 1 Co. 7:7 as meaning that celibacy and marriage are themselves charisms.[72] They are, consequently, vocational gifts. One does not embrace celibacy nor marry only for oneself, but for God's Church, to whose life these gifts contribute in different ways. The conclusion is obvious. Basing oneself on the New Testament concept of charism as the origin of the various concrete situations in which Christians must live their discipleship, and keeping in mind the ecclesial meaning of this concept, it is erroneous to consider the forms of Christian life only, or predominantly, from the point of view of individual salvation or perfection. The variety must be explained, in the final analysis, in terms of the ecclesial community.

Thus we come to the strongly ecclesial interpretation St. Thomas Aquinas gives to "states of life." He, in fact, consistently bases the diversity of states of life on the concept of the welfare and perfection of the Church. The Church is basically perfect because Christ fills it with his gifts, but in a final sense it appears perfect when, thanks to these gifts, it manifests itself in a variety of lifestyles and ministries. These states of life, born as diverse participations in the fullness of grace communicated by Christ to his Church, are directed toward the welfare of the whole body.[73]

The actual lifestyles in the Church display and manifest the multiform potentialities of life in Christ exactly as the ministries do, though in a different manner. It is at this deep level of being that the various vocations to different lifestyles and ministries help the Church. They help it to express itself as a community animated by grace but never able to sufficiently realize all its possibilities. The catholicity of the Church also signifies precisely this. Historically, the community of disciples took shape neither as a priestly nor as a lay community, but as a ministerial one. It was not composed exclusively either of religious or of seculars, but of disciples. This was possible because Christian living does not begin from the human side, with our own decisions and deeds, but from the divine side with grace that transcends all else. So it becomes immediately evident how harmful the image of a monastic or clerical Church is to the correct interpretation of Christian being.

We have thus spoken of the Church as the end of the various forms of Christian existence and, consequently, as the ultimate reason for their multiplicity. Actually, though it is a mistake to enclose the theology of states of life within the narrow limits of individual salvation or perfection, it would be equally mistaken to omit all reference to these. The disjunction of community welfare and individual welfare is false. The human person is fulfilled in relationship with the other, and is oriented toward the community of persons. Biologically, psychologically, and spiritually, personal maturity and the gift of self to others involve each other. We must therefore speak of the lifestyles as ways leading to holiness.

3. The Universal Call to Holiness

The Gospels know only one class of Christians: the disciples of Christ. In the post-resurrection Church, ministries, then offices, and also life situations begin to be differentiated. But what is important is adherence to Christ and acceptance of the Gospel or, as St. Paul expresses it, being-in-Christ. The Sermon on the Mount is directed to everyone. The summary of the Law and the Prophets, as contained in the twofold precept of charity, is valid for all. All receive the Law of the Spirit within their hearts. The image of the disciple as a model of fidelity to Christ above all things is proposed to everyone.

Basing itself on the Lord's invitation "You must therefore be perfect just as your heavenly Father is perfect" (Mt. 5:48), on the common precepts of charity, and on the proclamation of the Beatitudes, ecclesiastical tradition has stressed that we are all called by God to holiness, that is, to the perfection of charity. This was stated by Origen[74] and by St. John Chrysostom (cf. texts quoted above), as also by Evagrius, in a work which had a great influence on spirituality.[75] Later St. Thomas repeated it, stating that the perfection of Christian life consists primarily and essentially in charity, the object of the two basic commandments.[76]

Vatican II officially reaffirmed the same doctrine in Chapter 5 of *Lumen Gentium:*

> The Lord Jesus, divine teacher and model of all perfection, preached holiness of life (of which he is the author and maker) to each and every one of his disciples without distinction: 'You therefore must be perfect, as your heavenly Father is perfect' (Mt. 5:48). . . . It is therefore quite clear that all Christians in any state or walk of life are called to the fullness of Christian life and to the perfection of love. . . .[77]

The holiness to which we are all called therefore consists in the fullness of Christian life and the perfection of charity. This is achieved by cooperating with grace in order to incarnate Christian discipleship, by modeling our person and life on Christ, by seeking to do the will of the Father as he did, and by dedicating ourselves to the glory of God and the service of our neighbor.

4. Convergent Ways

In regard to this twofold aspect of the Christian vocation, that of contributing to the upbuilding of the Church and that of attaining one's own fulfillment (which are closely interrelated), concrete lifestyles serve as ways and means. The Church offers a great variety of special vocations, some of which overlap in the same individual: the ministerial priesthood or the laity, religious life or life in the world, celibacy or marriage. Christians live their common vocation within their actual existential situation.

Christ's disciples follow one way or another in obedience to God's Word. Only by this does their state of life become a form of discipleship. In relation to their common calling to the perfection of charity, all particular vocations become ways and means. St. Thomas affirmed the purely instrumental character of the ''counsels,'' the charisms that define religious life: they are not in themselves Christian perfection, but they are the means by which to attain it.[78] The same should be said about marriage and the secular profession. The fact that most Christians are called to live their discipleship in the world means that they are called to attain the common perfection, not despite their secularity, but precisely through the fulfillment of their secular vocation. One's life in Christ grows by seeking the salvific will of the Father *hic et nunc* and fulfilling it. Communion with the will of the Father is the only source of holiness. Every form of Christian life is illumined and nourished by the Word and by the sacraments. Grace reaches all without distinction through these channels.

From this basic point of view there are no differences between the various forms of Christian living. St. John Chrysostom stressed this point. It is a question of convergent lines. In *Lumen Gentium,* Vatican II teaches that one attains Christian perfection not only in the many "forms and tasks of life," but also "according to (one's) own gifts.'"[79] The general vocation is specified by the various vocational gifts.

5. Partial Expressions of Being Church

If we compare individual special vocations with the general Christian vocation and spirit, they all appear as partial expressions of Christian life. We are not referring to personal communion with the Spirit, a union which varies in degree according to a greater or lesser fidelity to grace, but rather to the objective manner in which the various vocations realize and express the mystery of the Church. St. Thomas had already spoken of this in explaining the origin of the various states as all deriving from the inexhaustible fountainhead that is Christ:

> For even as in the order of natural things, perfection, which in God is simple and uniform, is not to be found in the created universe except in a multiform and manifold manner, so too, the fullness of grace, which is centered in Christ as head, flows forth to his members in various ways, for the perfecting of the body of the Church.[80]

Thus we add, just as neither man nor woman alone is a complete expression of the human being, but a different and complementary form of humanity, so too neither religious nor seculars exhaust all the potentialities of being-in-Christ. Multiplicity and variety necessarily suppose limitations. Only the Church in its totality is perfect. The description that Vatican II makes of the "various gifts" and the "various ways" assumes that they have an incomplete and complementary character. Incomplete expressions draw on each other.

This mutual completion between the forms of Christian life is accomplished in different ways. On the one hand, each brings its own contribution to the ecclesial community because, as a form of discipleship, it embodies a different way of being-in-Christ. On the other hand, each form depends on the others and acts as a corrective, because every Christian vocation tends to render absolute its own point of view of the world and the Church.

6. The Two Ways: Religious and Secular

Every lifestyle and every office has its way of being Church. While the difference between clergy and laity consists in a different manner of participating in the priesthood of Christ, and consequently a different relationship to worship and the ministries within the Church, the difference between religious and secular life (taking into account only the two prototypal forms) consists in a different way of carrying out our common Christian existence. They in fact represent lifestyles and are, therefore, two different ways of being-in-the-world and of relating to other human beings.

In obedience to their calling, secular Christians direct their efforts toward secular concerns. They ordinarily do this within the context of a web of intense interpersonal relationships, of family and of profession. Prescinding from St. Paul's discussion of the burden that such relationships place on people, we believe that we are faithfully following his insight when we understand his words in this deeper sense: the married Christian is concerned with things of the world, interpreting the term *world* in the positive sense of *creation:* "Be fruitful, multiply, fill the earth and conquer it" (Gn. 1:28). In the midst of, and collaborating with, others, secular Christians have the task of developing creation. In this concrete situation, the Word of God constantly reaches out to them, and they respond in faith, hope, and love. Secular Christians take up the values of the world, but at the same time they examine them critically and contribute to their formulation in the light received from the Word of God. They take them up on the level of love and duty, but at the same time transcend them. They are Christians, in fact, because they respond to the invitation to love God above all else, and to follow Christ.

Christian religious, on the other hand, are believers who, likewise obeying an individual calling, make of their relation with God (*re-ligio*) the sole criterion on which to construct their lives. Celibates are concerned with the Lord's affairs, and are intent on loving the Lord. For this reason they renounce the type of interpersonal relationships (marriage and parenthood) which make such a difference in a person's existence. Thus the total love of God with an undivided heart and the unique value of adherence to Christ by discipleship, both of which form the common vocation of a Christian, are expressed by religious on the level of a lifestyle, while their love of neighbor takes on a manifestly universal character. The family of a religious, like that of Jesus, is composed of all those who do the will of the Father: that is, of all his disciples.

This is obviously a vocation for a minority, since the Church is called to proceed with its journey through history by way of marriage and procreation, thus continuing to make the grace of the Incarnation shine forth. It is a vocation for a minority, as are all prophetic vocations. Through its exclusive commitment to Christ, and its renunciation of certain secular values, religious life "reveals more clearly to all believers the heavenly goods which are already present in this age, witnessing to the new and eternal life . . . and preluding our future resurrection and the glory of the heavenly kingdom."[81] It is essential that religious life should be a sign of transcendent grace. When we speak of celibacy we will see how one should interpret the "heavenly goods," the "new life," and the prelude to "our future resurrection." Christ and his grace are the heavenly goods; discipleship is the new life; and the resurrection is foreshadowed not because we will all be celibates in the Father's glory (Christ only said that we will not be married), but because marriage and earthly values become relative when compared with the grace of the Risen One and the presence of his glory among us. Religious life merely renders manifest this common and new being-in-Christ.

7. Orientation Toward the World

From what we have said one can understand the different ways of being-in-the-world, of being Church, which characterize the two types of Christian existence, secular and religious; but one can also perceive that they share a common orientation toward the world. In regard to these different manners of being in the world and in history, one clearly cannot speak of Christian secular life as a vocation of incarnation, except with added clarifications. Certainly the incarnation of grace within our human nature appears not only more visibly in secular life, but is accomplished in a more complete fashion, since the secular Christian fully assumes the tasks assigned to the human race by its Creator: procreation and dominion over creation, by marriage and work directed expressly toward making the world more human. But secular Christians, inasmuch as they are Christians animated by eschatological faith and hope, transcend mere temporalities (with which the sexual relationship and work are closely connected). Theirs is also an eschatological existence. St. Paul tells all Christians that they have a heavenly passport (Ph. 3:20). Secular Christians are entirely here and now, but not only here and now.

The eschatological orientation is expressed in a more thorough manner by Christian religious, who make Christ the sole and immediate goal of a relationship which defines their life and is its only profession. But even in them the incarnation is not absent. Theirs must be a fully human life, within time and in the world. E. Schillebeeckx has rightly stressed the fact, which is often overlooked, that celibacy can have a strictly human significance, because it is often chosen for motives that are human and not only for religious ones.[82] We add that celibacy chosen for religious motives, that is, religious life, also has its own orientation toward the world. As a type of Christian, and therefore human, existence it is a way of fulfilling oneself here and now, and thus must have its own earthly significance. In fact it is clear that the orientation toward the final consummation must progress through an orientation to this world.

Religious life contributes to the upbuilding of the (human) world, not only by the numerous social services which religious create, but in its being a type of human existence. It does this in two ways. On a strictly secular level it shows, by celibacy, that the human person is not necessarily bound to self-created structures, not even to the most immediate and natural ones, like the family. The unique value of the human person is thus affirmed. At the same time religious life shows that procreation is not the only way of contributing to the development of the human race. It is also possible to contribute to it by directing one's existence toward other types of equally human values. In the third place, through the charism of community life, which ordinarily completes that of celibacy, the existence of the individual opens up to a sense of communion which has been attained only gradually by the human race throughout its development.

So much for the purely secular level. On the specifically religious level, religious life contributes to the upbuilding of human existence in the world by revealing through faith, but also through celibacy undertaken for religious motives, the fundamental orientation of the world toward Christ. The world is journeying toward its final consummation, toward the Omega point so dear to Teilhard de Chardin.

It is clear that the idea of *fuga mundi* may be misleading. One rejects a certain manner of being in the world, but obviously one can never escape from the world. One remains always a human being and thus a being-in-the-world. The basic human vocation, shown by evolution which is backed by the creative action of God, cannot be suppressed. If it is the human prerogative to improve the world, religious life has its own way of improving it, namely by revealing its ultimate meaning.

8. "More . . . More . . ."

In reading the Vatican II texts that describe the nature of religious life, one is struck by their frequent use of comparatives. We read that religious desire to derive "still more abundant fruit" from the grace of Baptism, to consecrate themselves "in a more intimate way" to the service of God.[83] A bit later we are told that "the religious state of life, in bestowing greater freedom from the cares of earthly existence,... reveals more clearly... the heavenly goods which are already present in this age ... preluding our future resurrection...." It constitutes "a closer imitation ... of the form of life which the Son of God made his own...."[84] According to *Perfectae Caritatis,* religious are "men and women who set out to follow Christ with greater liberty, and to imitate him more closely."[85]

The Council's insistent use of comparatives is such that theologians must, of necessity, fix their attention upon it. One should note, however, that the comparatives in the Council texts refer to different aspects of the subject. On the one hand the consecration of religious is qualified as being "more thoroughgoing," in an evident comparison with the common baptismal consecration.[86] On the other hand religious life is said to constitute a closer imitation of Christ's way of life. At another level the greater liberty enjoyed by religious is pointed out to us[87] and, on a different plane, religious life is spoken of as the best expression of eschatological reality.[88] Some of these comparatives do not necessarily include the idea of a hierarchy of lifestyles because, on similar levels, one could say that secular life does more, or expresses better, this or that aspect of Christian living.

Much importance was placed, in the past, on a hierarchical order of forms of Christian life. One must remember the sort of elitist society which served as a background for this type of theology. It is well also to stress that several of the ideological premises on which this hierarchical order of states of life was founded are unacceptable today:

1. One cannot say that the original man and woman (that is, man and woman according to God) were virgins, and that marriage is part of the historical condition of fallen humanity.

2. We are not bound to adopt the spiritualist anthropology of the Fathers.

3. We cannot say that the Christian, as such, is bound to the observance of the precepts, while only a few Christians take upon themselves the observance of supererogatory commitments, since Christian ethics is constituted precisely by going beyond what is required.

4. We cannot say that while all are called to perfection, only a few commit themselves publicly to attain it.

5. We cannot limit the concept of vocation to religious life only, relegating the secular state to a condition that is merely the object of divine condescension toward the weak.

6. We can certainly say, with the Council, that religious life imitates more closely (in a material sense) the lifestyle embraced by Christ; but this does not establish an argument in favor of the superiority of religious life, because neither Jesus himself (who was surrounded by married men and women) nor the New Testament gives any importance to this fact.

By going to the root of the question it becomes clear that a hierarchical order of lifestyles is founded on the concept of a dichotomy between God and the world which is common to all Hellenistic spiritualities but has nothing to do with the Bible. All forms of Christian life are founded on a relationship with God, and all are oriented toward the world, although in different ways. We have already said enough about this.

Can we, therefore, dismiss the theme of a hierarchical order (as is often done at present)? Or should we declare that it is useless and impossible, as Dietrich Wiederkehr has done?[89] These two attitudes reveal the indifference and the uneasiness with which many Catholics, among them many religious, react to any comparison between Christian vocations that might seem to place one above the other. This is the consequence of many converging movements: in exegesis (the disciples in the Gospels); in theology (a reexamination of the questions of precepts-counsels, relationships with the world, secular values, reaffirmation of a common vocation to perfection); in spirituality (the lay and the secular), etc. We are also well aware that Vatican II has effectively contributed to strengthening this viewpoint.

Perhaps it might be better for us to analyze more closely the traditional data in regard to the comparison between celibacy-virginity and marriage. Clement of Alexandria seems to be the only early theologian to affirm that a married Christian who attains an undivided heart, that is, the unification of existence in God, is superior to the celibate who attains it by renouncing marriage.[90] It should be noted, however, that Clement is speaking of subjective merits. According to Jerome, Jovinian affirmed the superiority of marriage over celibacy.[91] The Fathers and Medieval Doctors unanimously sustain the opposite opinion.

In his study on religious life in the light of the Scriptures, *De votis monasticis* (1521), Martin Luther also took a stand on the comparative value of celibacy and marriage. He was anxious to show the unity of the Christian vocation and of a life born of the baptismal commitment. He therefore opposed the distinction which he abusively calls a state of perfection for the monastic elite, and a state of imperfection for the masses. In speaking of the greatness of the common vocation, he reechoes not only scriptural doctrine, but also the best witnesses of ecclesiastical tradition, such as Ambrose and Chrysostom. He also recognizes that "Jesus and Paul praise celibacy," but he explains,

> not because the chaste are more perfect than others because they are chaste, and not because they do not lust contrary to the commandment, but because they are free from the cares and tribulations of the flesh that Paul attributes to marriage, and may freely and without impediment dedicate themselves day and night to the word and faith. . . . Christ praises eunuchs, not because they castrate themselves, but because they do so for the sake of the Kingdom of heaven . . . for the Gospel.[92]

Luther makes a distinction here between celibacy as a lifestyle and continence in its material sense, which to us seems fully in harmony with the New Testament. What Paul praises is celibacy and not, like his Hellenistically-minded Christians, "not touching a woman." What Christ speaks of is the incapacity of marrying (both psychological and existential) caused by devotion to the Kingdom. Luther however, in his preoccupation over the fundamental principle of justification *sola fide,* and influenced by his reaction against the theology of a particular state of perfection, greatly limits the scope of God's Word on celibacy. He considers the latter as a human choice, founded on the convenience of having more freedom and time at one's disposal. He does not see that the common vocation is embodied in a variety of practical callings, and that celibacy can be a vocation from God (or, as St. Paul puts it, one of the Lord's charisms). This omission keeps him from seeing the ecclesial significance of marriage and celibacy as complementary forms of Christian life, and consequently from seeing that celibacy as such has its own full value in the Church.

The Council of Trent,[93] intervening in the controversy which had arisen on account of the Protestant Reformation's review of religious life, reiterated that "the marriage state is not to be preferred to that of virginity, and that to remain in virginity or celibacy is a better and more blessed thing than to contract marriage." The same doctrine was stressed by Pius XII in his encyclical *Sacra Virginitas.*[94] Vatican II repeats the traditional affirmation on "the greater excellence of virginity consecrated to Christ" in its decree on the training of priests,[95] while in *Lumen Gentium* it simply affirms that virginity and celibacy are states which have always been held in high esteem by the Church[96] and that the gift by which the Father creates virginity and celibacy excels among the numerous counsels proposed by the Lord in the Gospel.[97]

These are the data provided by tradition. Let us endeavor to understand their meaning. To do this we must, in the first place, make the distinction between the subjective and objective aspects of the question. Subjectively it is not only better, but it is also a duty, for Christians to choose the form of discipleship to which they feel called by the Word of God. In Chapter I, in speaking of the various forms of Christian life, we said that the only criterion of choice is obedience to our calling, not the consideration of whether the form is hypothetically more or less ideal. It is the person of Christ that matters, not a Greek ideal. To us it seems that the Council of Trent's words should be understood basically in this way. In fact one should note that, while the Council uses objective terms to deny that marriage is superior to celibacy (the matrimonial state is not to be placed above celibacy), when it speaks of celibacy it uses subjective terms: it is a better and more blessed thing to remain single than to marry (*melius et beatius manere in virginitate aut coelibatu quam iungi matrimonio*). It is a better and more blessed thing for those who are called to it. Let us put aside the question of whether this proposition is, or is not, evident today,[98] and state that it was not so in the context in which the Council was speaking, since Luther ignored the existence of a divine vocation to celibacy.

One might ask, however, in view of the evident premises of the past, whether the *melius* should not also be transferred to the objective sphere, thus establishing a hierarchical order of lifestyles. St. Thomas Aquinas,[99] echoing St. Augustine,[100] discovers the reason for the superiority of celibacy over marriage in the fact that celibacy is directed toward a good excelling that of marriage: marriage is directed toward the multiplication of the human race, while celibacy is directed toward a divine good and is spiritually fruitful. Aside from the question of St. Augustine's theology of marriage which conditions this conclusion, we suggest that this explanation raises a serious difficulty: are we not comparing celibacy, as a form of Christian life, with marriage in its purely human dimension? We know that it is not merely remaining free from the marriage bond that gives celibacy its value, but its being oriented in a special way toward the Lord. But is this not true also of Christian marriage? Marriage as a human reality is oriented toward the propagation of the human race and toward the mutual aid of the spouses. As a Christian reality consecrated by a sacrament, however, marriage is an ecclesial reality ordained for the growth of the Church (not only in the material sense, since parents are also the first catechists) and for the spiritual perfection of the spouses.

Perhaps it will be well, in this regard, to return to the use of the comparative degree by Vatican II. First, note that the comparatives were used after the statement that all forms of Christian life are ways and means serving the common vocation to holiness.[101] This implies a basic equality of the various Christian vocations which is far more decisive than the various degrees of "more . . . , more . . ." that could be distributed among them. We reached the same conclusion basing ourselves on the concept of discipleship and its various concrete forms. The special value of celibacy (and consequently of religious life) consists in its being a visible expression of the common vocation to love God with all one's heart or, in Christological terms, the common calling to follow Christ, abandoning all else.

It is important to note the Council affirms that religious life "reveals more clearly." The Council does not affirm, nor can we state, that religious life *fulfills* the condition of discipleship better, because discipleship does not consist in a lifestyle, but in faith, hope, and charity; religious life does, however, express this condition more visibly. Since, inasmuch as it is secular, Christian secular life deals with worldly concerns, it must reveal its eschatological orientation through its spirit, expressed and nourished by numerous and successive actions. A lifestyle created by renunciation, instead, expresses in its very essence the supreme value of the Kingdom. We must add, however, that Christian secular life as such is a better expression of the presence of grace overflowing into the world and becoming incarnate.

The Council adds to this consideration a reference to the traditional motive, inspired by St. Paul, of the greater spiritual liberty enjoyed by those who embrace celibacy for the sake of the Kingdom, because of its tendency toward unity of existence in God, which is our common vocation. This is precisely why Christian people have always considered monasticism as being, objectively, the more blessed (*beatius*) situation.

9. A State of Perfection?

We have developed above, on general lines, the history of the concept of a "state of perfection" as applied to religious life, understood to be a "form of life directed toward the attainment of perfection." Vatican II used this expression in the Constitution on the Liturgy before beginning a discussion connected with religious life.[102] However, in the texts which it later dedicated expressly to a presentation of the doctrine on religious life, the Council purposely avoided using this expression.

We said that affirming religious life to be a *status perfectionis acquirendae* is equivalent to saying that it is a state oriented inherently toward the attainment of Christian perfection. The theology of religious life, following St. Thomas, is well aware that perfection consists in the fullness of charity, and that this is the goal of every Christian life. It is also aware, together with St. Thomas, that some secular Christians actually reach perfection. There are some secular Christians whom the Church offers as models for all Christ's disciples. We have however noted that for St. Thomas and the theologians following him there are two reasons why religious life, in contradistinction to Christian life in the world, is in itself ordained for the attainment of perfection: 1) because in embracing religious life religious commit themselves publicly to strive toward perfection; and 2) because religious life includes the practice of the evangelical counsels, which are means for attaining the perfection of charity more easily.

In commenting on the first reason, St. Thomas refers to the perfection attained by seculars, affirming that ''some (persons) fulfill that to which they have not bound themselves''.[103] Only religious, therefore, and not seculars, commit themselves to strive for perfection. This statement leaves us perplexed. Sanctity is simply the development of baptismal grace. In asking for and receiving Baptism, one not only renounces sin (the preparatory renunciation of Baptism), but one makes the *propositum* of living the Gospel to the utmost. The *sequela Christi* is for everybody, as are the twofold precept of charity, and the Beatitudes. This commitment to live in openness to the grace of God, which calls us to progress toward maturity in Christ, is renewed in Confirmation and in the sacraments of Reconciliation and of the Eucharist. It is renewed particularly in the sacrament of Matrimony, a human reality which becomes sacramental through the relationship of faith between two believers. The religious profession is not, therefore, the only commitment to strive for the perfection of charity. From this point of view it can consist only in reemphasizing a common commitment.

In regard to the second reason, one should keep in mind the distinction St. Thomas himself makes between counsels as acts of virtue going beyond the minimum set by the commandments, and counsels as traits of life. At this point we must conclude that the counsels, as acts of virtue, belong irrevocably to the common Christian vocation. Ambrose and Chrysostom supported this, basing themselves on the Sermon on the Mount. Christian life is not defined by the minimum of the negative commandments, but by a calling to the maximum proposed in the two precepts of charity. One tends toward the maximum only insofar as one goes beyond the negative commandments, entering, that is, the sphere of what Ambrose calls the counsels. As traits of life (as charisms belonging to religious life) the counsels certainly *facilitate* the attainment of love with an undivided heart, that is, of perfection, inasmuch as they orient all of existence directly and exclusively toward God and give a universal scope to the love of neighbor. But it is also true that growth of life in Christ does not depend primarily on one's lifestyle, but on the sacraments. Marriage to a believer can also be an efficient means of growth in faith and charity.

In our opinion, the only firmly established fact in this discussion on the state of perfection is that the charisms of religious life have a way of facilitating growth toward perfection. This is not enough, though, to make religious life the only "state oriented toward the attainment of perfection." Since this statement can be misleading in reference to the common vocation to holiness and the connection that all forms of Christian life have with holiness, we can understand why the Council later abandoned it in the texts especially dedicated to religious life.

Excursus: The "World" in Religious Life

We think we have already made sufficiently clear what the relationship of religious life is with the world, that is, with humanity and its temporal and worldly tasks. Religious take upon themselves a form of human existence, celibacy, which has validity and meaning even in itself if it is chosen for justifiable human reasons. It acquires new significance when it is embraced in order to express that basic orientation of the world toward God and toward its fulfillment in Christ which is revealed by faith. One never renounces the world, but one carries it ahead toward its goal by renouncing certain human realities (marriage, parenthood).

The term "world" has, however, appeared very frequently during the course of religious life in partially different contexts. It will be useful to pause then and study briefly the development of the theology and practice of religious life in its relationship with the "world," seeking to clarify the precise meaning of this term in its various contexts. We will consider three aspects: 1) renunciation of the world, 2) despising the world, 3) separation from the world.

1. Renunciation of the World

At the very beginning of monasticism, *to renounce* and *to become a monk* became equivalent expressions. Before a public act of commitment to the monastic life was established in cenobitical circles, an act of renunciation was considered the beginning of a monk's career.[1] It is for this reason that John Cassian calls those who are still being trained *renuntiantes*[2] The equivalent Greek terms of *apotaxomenoi* and *apotaktitai* were used in reference to monks in general.[3]

In some cases "to make one's renouncement" meant to distribute one's goods.[4] This disappropriation, however, was the practical expression of a more general renunciation. The object of renunciation, in numerous texts, is the world: in the *Apophtegmata* the expression "to renounce the world" is synonymous with "to become a monk.'"[5] John Cassian often speaks of renouncing the world.[6] According to him the monk must be dead to the world from the moment he is clothed in the habit.[7] There is incompatibility between an orientation toward the world (or let us say, between a certain manner of being interested in the world) and monasticism.

The tradition continued in Latin monasticism, although the terminology changed. The *Vita Martini* and the *Lives of the Fathers of the Jura* speak of renouncing the (present) age.[8] In this tradition, therefore, it is the "age" (*saeculum*) which opposes monasticism, although there is also talk of "overcoming the world.'"[9] At times the world and the age are mentioned together as objects of renunciation[10] and of victory.[11] In the *Rule of the Master*, "world" (*mundus*) is always used in a positive sense (the created universe), whereas the "age" (*saeculum*) is spoken of as being in opposition to monasticism.[12] In St. Benedict's *Rule*, the *Master's* terminology disappears. The term *mundus* is never used as a noun, and *saeculum* is used in a more positive manner, so that it is applied also to the monk's life: *nostra vita in saeculo*, meaning "our life (including that of the monks) on this earth";[13] *secundum saeculum opera* is contrasted with *secundum Deum*[14] in order to indicate, with the first expression, work directed toward the sustenance of the physical body, and with the second, asceticism directed toward the sustenance of the soul "according to God.'"[15]

Examining more closely the context in which the terms *the world* and *this age* are to be found in monastic literature in order to understand the import of the required renunciation, we discover, first of all, a special insistence on contrasting them with the future age. They are often found in an eschatological context. The *age* which the monk renounces is contrasted with the *prize*,[16] or with heavenly riches.[17] It is together with this age that earthly glory will perish,[18] and from which one will pass to judgment[19] or to be with Christ.[20] Thus the realities of the age are transient,[21] having a low and earthly value.[22]

Cassian recalled that the monk must conduct himself as a pilgrim and an exile.[23] Thus he took up again a concept that was typical of Eastern monastic spirituality, *xeniteia*, the pilgrim's manner of existence, which the monk was supposed to make his own.[24] It meant that monks should live for the Lord alone, concerning themselves with his affairs, and unifying their lives in their search for him. They should radically exemplify the transitory character of earthly things.

Such broad terms as *the world* and *this age* had, naturally, to embrace the most varied connotations. This comes to light when masters of monastic spirituality speak of renunciation. St. Basil treated it in detail. According to him the renunciation prescribed by a "life according to the Gospel" does not consist specifically in renouncing the devil and his works. This is not proper to those "who are in a profitable life (spiritually) and tend toward perfection, because this renouncement was already made in their first confession (at Baptism)." What then should they renounce in order to penetrate into the dynamism of an existence straining toward perfection? According to Basil they should renounce their former life, their habits, the pleasures of this world, and also their families "according to the flesh." But above all they must renounce anything that may be an obstacle to their decision (*propositum*): parents and relatives and all material goods. Family and property are then the specific objects of renunciation. "To put it briefly, how can those for whom the world has been crucified for the love of Christ, and who are crucified for the world, become slaves of worldly concerns, when the Lord has commanded the renunciation even of one's own soul for the love of Him?"[25]

Cassian repeats almost the identical idea. According to the tradition of the Fathers and the authority of Scriptures, there are three monastic renouncements. The first one is material, having to do with the riches and good things of this earth. The second is moral, having to do with one's past life, its vices, and passions of the spirit and the flesh. The third is spiritual, consisting in detachment of the mind from all visible things in order to focus it on the contemplation of invisible realities.

Clearly, Cassian transposes his discussion from the objects of renunciation to the various levels on which the reunciation takes place: a purely physical leave-taking (the initial renouncement); a victory over persistent attachments to one's past; and an orientation of the spirit toward contemplation, even where there is no question of sin. In regard to the first manner, he quotes Gn. 12:1: "Leave your country, your family and your father's house." One must leave not only materially, but also in one's memory and attachments.[26] In his *Cenobitical Institutions,* the author connects the *world* both with the family[27] and with riches.[28]

In Chapter IV, when speaking of the charisms belonging to religious life, we shall see how ancient monastic tradition often tended to separate two types of renunciation from the other forms of self-denial required of the monks: namely the renunciation of family and that of possessions. St. Thomas Aquinas developed this tendency to the point of establishing a clear distinction between the renunciations that alter one's type of existence and those that do not bring about such a change.

To the third objection, that the religious is bound to embrace all the counsels, he answers: "There are some counsels such that if they be omitted, a man's whole life would be taken up by secular business; for instance if he have property of his own, or enter the married state."[29] Thus, in this tendency to focus on the renouncement of family and possessions as elements of the monastic vocation, we can see a specific expression of the renunciation of the world which characterizes the religious. Today we would affirm that the renouncement of secularity, which constitutes religious life as a form of Christian existence, consists in this and only in this.

But monasticism did not, and does not, speak in this way. Monks and nuns have an extremely dynamic concept of their life. The renunciation of family and material goods is only the starting point in their life. It is a physical (Cassian calls it a "bodily") fact from which one must advance, through progressive spiritual detachment, until one's whole existence has become unified in the search for God. The monk must think that in the world there exist only God and himself.[30] The world he renounces is human society[31] and the things that happen there. Since worldly conversations militate against a life concentrated only on God,[32] the Fathers recommend avoiding discourse on "anything concerning the world."[33] Thus we come back to the concept of *xeniteia,* defined as not even understanding the language of those who are concerned with things other than God,[34] precisely as happens to foreigners and travelers. Later, in the conclusion of this historical excursus, we will evaluate this attitude.

2. The *contemptus mundi*

Primitive monasticism was born and developed in a Hellenistic environment, dominated by a marked dualism between God and the world. Yet is is surprising to note that primitive monasticism never spoke of "despising the world." St. Anthony's attitude was clearly positive when he exhorted everyone "not to prefer any earthly reality to the love of

Christ.''[35] St. Benedict would adopt the same recommendation.[36] We are in the genuine Gospel tradition of discipleship; or, rather, the words of Anthony and Benedict do not reach the controversial tone of the Aramaic sayings on ''hating'' that which is not Christ, nor the incisive doctrinal formulation of the necessity of leaving everything in order to follow the Lord. They are speaking only of not placing anything before the love of Christ. While love and fidelity to Christ, as a transcendent value, are traits of every Christian life (St. Anthony impressed this on everyone, and St. Benedict spoke of it in connection with the Christian life of his monks), the monks express it by relinquishing all worldly values to follow the Lord. This is stated in the *Vita Martini:* ''We must leave the pleasures and the responsibilities of the world in order to be able to follow the Lord Jesus, free and unencumbered.''[37]

But to this practical renunciation which (we would say) is required by a special vocation, an evaluation of the world and its realities was added, showing these to be contrary to heavenly things. We have seen how the terms ''world'' and ''age'' are often used in an eschatological context by ancient monastic writers. In that context, the transitory character and the lesser value (*humilitas*) of earthly things is stressed. Thus Cassian speaks of contempt for all bodily pleasures, preferring heavenly rewards to them.[38] The expression *contemptus mundi* became so prevalent that it was even offered as the best summary of the attitude of monks, and more generally of religious, toward the world. Before generalizing about this, however, we must try to understand what Cassian means.

Following the well-known Stoic categories, Cassian affirmed that from the ethical point of view, the worldly realities which the monk abandons are, in themselves, *mediae,* neither good nor bad; or, as we should say today, objectively indifferent. Among these *mediae,* or indifferent realities, he lists marriage, work in the fields, wealth, and also solitude and all ascetical practices.[39] This means that he certainly does not consider either marriage or wealth as evil (nor as indispensably good), but at the same time he does not consider solitude and monastic asceticism as good things which must prevail absolutely. They are to be evaluated in their concrete orientation toward God; or, as we would say, in the context of a vocation. One must definitely take into account Cassian's evaluation of types of life when we hear him say that, in order to obtain purity of heart (the necessary condition for contemplation), one must despise (*contemnitur*) family, country, honor, riches, pleasures, and all the joys of the world.[40]

We may certainly disagree with Cassian in his transposing to Christian spirituality the requirements of Neo-Platonic and Cynic philosophers for dedication to philosophy, or for the attainment of contemplation—if by *contemplatio* we mean an act of mystical experience which is the fruit of perfect charity and the goal of every form of Christian life. Purity of heart results from the Word of God and from the sacraments, and therefore is not necessarily connected with any given situation in life. But though one may disagree with Cassian on this, it is necessary to admit that his *contemnere* means "to renounce." It is not a question of an abstract value judgment, but of a concrete choice. He does not use the term in a pejorative sense; this is confirmed by his use of it in the passage, "Having despised all things, and all the pleasures of the world, we are happy in this desolation (of the desert).'"[41]

We cannot enter here into the subsequent development of the doctrine of *contemptus mundi,* or into the broader question of the Church's attitude toward human values. The Platonism which influenced Fathers and Doctors prior to Scholasticism had considerable weight. Furthermore, the fact that Christian spirituality in the East as well as the West from the sixth to the sixteenth centuries was interpreted by religious whose writings exercised a considerable influence even later cannot be disregarded. The concept of *world* has traditionally had negative connotations among religious. Reading their texts, however, one becomes aware that religious were wont to express not a general value judgment on the "world," but rather a concrete one referring to their own vocation. In this context "the world," that is, certain secular values which form part of the vocation of the majority in the Church, was a source of temptation for religious. Their defensive attitude as they faced "all the joys of this world" is already apparent in Cassian, in the *Vita Martini,* and in the *Vitae Patrum Iurensium.*[42]

3. Withdrawal from the World

From the moment religious life appeared as a form of Christian life, the "world" referred to by teachings on the religious life was the human world: humanity engaged here and now in its twofold task of propagation and mastery over creation, involving earthly goals and the struggle to realize them. In reference to this "world," religious have not only spoken but have also acted, in a meaningful way, separating themselves materially from it. There has, however, been an obvious process (of development) in this theme of separation from the world. A history of Christian spirituality has been written under the title of *The Desert and the City*.[43] The two terms in the process are thus indicated.

A. Anchorites

For the anchorites the *fuga mundi* meant a material separation from the earthly city. In anchoritism renunciation was expressed in a concrete manner by withdrawal. In referring to one who had become a monk one simply said: "he retired" (*anachōrese*).[44] He "went out" (*exēlthon*) from the world.[45] In order to remind himself of his calling Arsenius often asked himself, "Arsenius, why have you left (*dió exelthes*)?"[46] In the *Lives of the Fathers of the Jura*, this is put in language reminiscent of the Gospel: "*Relictis urbibus, audituri in deserto sequimur Salvatorem*" (Having left the cities, we follow the Savior in order to listen to him in the desert).[47] For them God was to be found in material solitude. We know that, for the first anchorites, the separation between God and the world went so far as to include the whole human race in the world, in order to live in total solitude. Father Arsenius carried the *fuga hominum* (the flight from people) to such an extreme that one day he left his disciples secretly with the explanation that he could not live at the same time with God and with them.[48] This extreme isolation, which meant a flight not only from the world but also from the visible sacramental Church, was soon moderated by the presence of other anchorites belonging to the same colony. Then, as a remedy against the danger of distractions, there developed a spirituality of one's cell, of remaining within it, of retirement. The "cell" was then contrasted with the "world."[49] The silence of one's cell became the embodiment of *xeniteia*, of being pilgrims and strangers in the world.[50] Going out frequently to meet the brethren was a sign of being interested in something other than God: namely, the world.

B. Basil and Pachomius

St. Basil protests decisively against the anchorites' interpretation of a relation God-world, in which the second term, excluding only the first, takes in all human beings as such. He also insists that, in an existence completely dedicated to God, the *memoria Dei* (the constant remembrance of God) requires forsaking all the impediments, distractions, and occupations which fill ordinary (secular) life.[51] In order to free oneself from these, retirement is necessary, the *remota ac solitaria habitatio*[52] (*tó idiázein* not *tó anchorein*). However, for human and evangelical considerations, Basil rejects hermitic life and stresses, instead, the advantage of a life lived in common with those who share the same ideals. At this point, though, it is the whole community that must be separate from the earthly city. In fact, Basil organized his brotherhood on a family estate, together with some of his friends. This shows that the concept of relationships with the world had been modified.

Basil, who had begun his *Asketikon* by speaking of the two commandments of charity and of their interdependence,[53] could not logically accept the radical opposition of God and human beings as it had been lived in extreme but paradigmatic cases by some anchorites—even to the point of avoiding their fellow-monks. In him the disjunctive God-world is replaced by another: Gospel-world. It is not necessary to be separated from human beings as such, but from those "who scorn the perfect observance of the Gospel," because contact with them would cause contamination.[54] Thus a distinction is also made with respect to the brethren's contacts with their relatives: if "they live in a Godly manner" all the brethren should consider them as their own parents and brothers, and the Superiors should take care of them to avoid the individual brother's being involved in secular concerns. If, however, these relatives live an ordinary life, and scorn God's commandments, there should be nothing in common with them.[55] Thus the quality of individual lives has become the criterion for deciding relationships with the outside.

Later, after he had been consecrated bishop, Basil saw the question from a different point of view, for he called his brothers to care for pilgrims and the sick outside of their enclosure. At this point the neighbors' needs and evangelical charity, not the quality of people's lives, became the decisive factor.

Even before Macrina and St. Basil had initiated their "evangelical life" in Cappadocia, Pachomius and his disciples in Egypt had followed a course that, in some respects, was parallel. His group had started out from a semi-anchoritical spirituality, adding to it, however, strict organization and a common location. This led to the development of a spirituality in which fraternal relationships played a preponderant role, even becoming centripetal. In the beginning it was the question of a group open to the outside. Pachomius and his followers had settled in an abandoned village. Other people came to live there and Pachomius built a church where, on Saturdays, the brothers celebrated the Eucharist together with the seculars, while on Sundays a priest came to celebrate it for the brothers alone. Thus a balance was established between the internal needs of the community, wishing to express its inner union by means of its own eucharistic celebration, and its relationship with the other citizens. Later, however, as the number of the brethren grew, they had to leave and construct a "village" entirely for themselves. The cluster of houses was surrounded by a fence, and seclusion was established. The brothers were forbidden to leave it without permission, and priests and monks who visited the brothers could not enter the church during the community's prayers unless they had the abbot's permission. It was at this point that a mentality of opposition to those outside developed; the community became the "senate of the sons of Israel," that is, Israel in the desert, or the *collecta sanctorum,* the community of holy ones. It is evident that all this was due, in part, to a process of assimilation with surrounding monasticism, but above all to the tendency of consecrating the institution. Even their economic goods became "sacred," in contrast to the "carnal" goods of seculars.[56]

C. In the West: *monasterium* and *communitas*

In the Latin West the monastery, understood by this time as a cenoby, established itself as a school for divine service, far from the earthly city, and carrying on the divine service within its walls. An early text on monasticism, the *Rule of the Master,* required that everything necessary, including the garden, should be in the enclosure so that the brethren might have no need to go out and mix with secular people.[57] This rule was repeated by St. Benedict.[58] Why is this separation recommended? The *Rule of the Master* puts it this way: "The door should be always closed so that the brethren, being shut in with the Lord should, for the love of God, already be separated from the world and be living, in a certain sense, in heaven."[59] Thus the monastery appears here as a foreshadowing of heavenly life: one closes oneself in with the Lord. It is this that brings about the separation from the "age," evidently interpreted here as a concrete, earthly type of existence.

With the *Master* we are obviously in the context of a contemplative life. But there are also ascetical reasons for a physical separation from secular people. St. Benedict states it in a general way: running here and there is not good for the monks' souls.[60] The *Master* mentions the praises directed to monks by pious folk, which endanger humility, as well as the taunts of unbelievers.[61] St. Benedict suggests another reason: outside the monastery there is the risk of seeing and hearing things that are unsuitable.[62]

St. Augustine had started out with a monastic idea of community; thus, when he became bishop, he had to leave in order not to disturb his brothers with the pastoral and charitable relationships inherent in the episcopal office. But he then created another brotherhood of clerics who lived their Christian communion intensely, expressing it by holding their goods in common, but at the same time having ministerial relationships with the outside. The Augustinian *communitas* appeared before the faithful during the celebration of the liturgy, because it was formed by the bishop with his priests. Centuries later, as a consequence of the reform of the secular clergy, communities of clerics arose, following the Augustinian Rule (Canons Regular). Their communities were often located in cities, near the cathedral or the abbey church, and were thus continually in contact with the outside. However, the tension between a consecration to God and the ministry had not yet been solved doctrinally, and one often notes the phenomenon of these clerics leaving the cities in order to retire into solitude under the influence of monasticism.

D. Mendicant Orders and Apostolic Institutes

A fundamental change took place with the appearance of the first Institutes dedicated to works of charity (the "Hospitallers" and those dedicated to the redemption of prisoners), of the first Apostolic Institutes (evangelization: the Dominicans), and the mendicant form of life. The change was caused by two different factors.

First the mendicants, especially the Franciscans, proposed a new style of life which actually went back to the gospel ideals, sidestepping most of the structures that had been formed throughout the centuries. The "three counsels" as criteria for defining what is and what is not religious life began to emerge. Through them, religious life shows itself to be different from secular life. An integral part of this new evangelical life was communion with the poor, expressed by manual labor and, when necessary, by begging. This brought with it an uprooted life, without stability (one should note the importance of the concept of pilgrimage in the Franciscan Rule),[63] and constant relationships with seculars. The *conventus* (spontaneous groups of brethren) were situated inside the towns or in their immediate vicinity. There were even men and women (tertiaries) who followed the Rule of obedience to the Gospel within their own homes. There was a process of continuous osmosis here, even though a rapid institutionalizing of these *conventus,* and the construction of houses and churches led to greater stability and to more intense relationships within the community. Material isolation would never again be a criterion of religious life.

Second, the founding of charitable and preaching Institutes led to a rethinking of the doctrine on proper occupations for religious and on their relationships with the "world." In opposition to those who held that material separation and concerns pertaining only to worship were essential elements of the religious vocation, St. Thomas Aquinas broadened the concepts of "worship" and "divine service" to embrace anything that could be done as a result of one's dedication to God. The works of mercy and preaching thus became "divine service," and hence an integral part of the religious vocation. Religious might dedicate themselves to preaching,[64] but could also engage in secular affairs for reasons of charity (*ex caritate*),[65] and they could live off alms.[66] They might even bear arms to defend divine worship or public safety, and to relieve the poor and the oppressed.[67]

The fundamental elements of the theology of apostolic life were traced by St. Thomas Aquinas; but communities of regular clergy, of brothers, and of sisters, which came into being from the Catholic Reformation on, introduced their own type of very flexible inner relationships, including the suppression of the Office in choir and of other observances. These innovations permitted an intensification of relationships with the outer world for apostolic or charitable purposes. In order to obviate the risk that the environment might dissolve their religious identity, the apostolic religious counteracted it by: a) stressing spiritual asceticism such as detachment (Ignatian indifference), obedience, etc.; b) practicing a type of prayer in which forms of mental prayer predominate (e.g. meditation, examens) directed toward strengthening the interior life of the apostolic religious. What cannot be provided by the environment (as in monasticism) must be provided by one's own heart.

III

Religious Life: Dedication to God in the Church

In the first phase of our research into the meaning and value of religious life in the Church, we concentrated on the Christological moment in order to study its biblical roots. History showed us that the founders of various forms of religious life merely wanted to embrace new forms of discipleship in the post-resurrection Church. Discipleship is an evangelical category that has to do with Christ. In the Old Testament the idea of following Yahweh by means of justice appears only in a limited number of passages, always in a Deuteronomic context (Dt. 1:36; 13:5; 1 K. 14:8; 2 K. 23:3; 2 Ch. 34:31; cf. Jr. 2:2). The ordinary expression of obedience to Yahweh is "to walk in the Lord's ways": "Walk in the whole way that Yahweh has marked for you" (Dt. 5:33).[1]

Rabbinical interpretation shows a certain reluctance to speak of the following of Yahweh, probably because of Judaism's strong sense of divine transcendence. It tends therefore to interpret such expressions, occasionally found in the Bible, in the sense of an imitation of God, an idea which Philo gladly took hold of because it was in harmony with Hellenistic thought. Rather than applying to Jesus in the New Testament what was said of intercourse with God in the Old Testament, we are here dealing with a formula which clearly draws its historical origin from the group that followed Jesus during his ministry, and which has gradually grown in significance in the light of paschal faith.

Even in pre-resurrection experience the following of Jesus entailed a deep religious relationship which had its ultimate fulfillment in God. The first four disciples accepted Christ's announcement of the approaching Kingdom and followed him for this reason. This means that they encountered the salvific will of God in Jesus. In following Jesus their expectations were directed toward the Kingdom, even though their inherited Messianic hopes had misled them with respect to its method and times. The group of disciples was united by communion in the salvific will of the Father (Mk. 3:31–35 and par.; cf. Mt. 7:21). Those who say to Jesus: "Lord, Lord" (the ancient profession of faith) will not enter into the Kingdom (are not true disciples) but rather those who do the will of Jesus' Father who is in heaven (Mt. 7:21). Obviously the meaning of following as a cleaving to the salvific will of God becomes clearer the more one perceives the inseparable connection between Jesus and the Kingdom of God. If the apostolic Church spoke so much of following Jesus, while Jesus himself had prepared his disciples for the Kingdom and spoken of the Father, it is not only because of the historical necessity of making Christian identity clear in the midst of Judaism, but also because the Father's love shone transparently through the actions, words, and person of the Son. To follow Jesus is to accept the will of the Father who sent him.

The following of Christ, as seen in the context of New Testament Christology, is only a starting-point, not the point of arrival. Christ is in fact the mediator. His existence is a uniquely open one. Above all, Jesus lives in the presence of the Father. His life is one of complete dedication to his Father's concerns, nourished by a unique relationship with him. It is from Jesus' communion with God that the Gospel originated. To give oneself to Christ, and try to embody the Gospel, is precisely to open oneself to the mystery of the presence of God in Jesus. If religious life is discipleship, it is consequently the following of Jesus in his submission to the Father, in his communion with him. Thus the theme of religious life as "dedication to the divine service" is born.

Christ is also the Man-for-others, the Servant-Prophet who redeems us by his suffering, the Son in whom the Father's salvific love for all humanity is revealed. To give oneself to him, in the Christian sense, means to give oneself to others and become, in him, a man- or a woman-for-others as he was. Thus the ecclesial and ministerial meaning of religious life is born.

These are the two themes that we are about to examine in depth: religious life in relation to God, and religious life in relation to the Church and humanity.

I. The Service of God

1. In the History of Religious Life

In the history of the Church, monasticism and successive forms of religious life were first described, then doctrinally defined, as a type of existence characterized by dedication to God and by an exclusive orientation toward his service. The Middle Ages went so far as to define monasticism etymologically as a state of being *solus cum Solo*.

The best known of the early works on monastic spirituality, the *Vita Antonii* by St. Athanasius, establishes a complete identity between becoming a monk and consecrating oneself to God: "from the time Anthony became a monk and promised himself to God. . . ."[2] Mother Theodora, in an apophthegm not included in Migne, taught that the monks and nuns must live only for God.[3] Eucherius of Lyons (the purpose of monasticism is to give oneself to God[4]), and Cassian (monks have as their purpose the worship of God[5]) reecho this teaching. A monk's dedication to God is frequently called "the divine service." The purpose of the monastic life is to serve God,[6] and therefore monasticism is a *Dei famulatus*.[7] In the prologue to his *Rule* St. Benedict writes that he wants to establish a school for the Lord's service (*dominici schola servitii*[8]). Consequently the designation of "servant of God" was widely used in ancient times.[9]

St. Thomas Aquinas and St. Bonaventure, both members of religious orders which professed a new form of religious life differing from monasticism (the sole form of religious life until the twelfth century), carried over the concept of "divine service" into the new forms. St. Thomas reminds us that religion is the virtue by which one dedicates something to the service and worship of God.[10] It is therefore a common virtue, and cannot be limited to any particular vocation in the Church. Some Christians, however, call themselves "religious" because they bind themselves completely to the divine service, as if they were offering a holocaust to God.[11] St. Thomas insisted a great deal on the totality that marks the gift of self which the religious makes to God: *totaliter* (all-embracing),[12] *totam suam vitam*[13] (one's entire life).

According to St. Thomas, then, the distinguishing mark of religious life would be the totality of the gift to God. One is a religious, he explains on one occasion, not because of one's occupations (liturgy, prayer, or ministry), but by reason of the complete gift of self one has made to God. Then, sanctioning a theological thesis that was gaining ground in his time, St. Thomas considers that the totality of the gift is expressed in the profession (by means of vows) of the three "evangelical counsels." He does not deduce the necessity of professing the counsels directly from the concept of religious life as an all-embracing gift, but from the complementary concept of a state of perfection,[14] derived from the inherent intention of religious life.[15] It remains true though that the purpose of the counsels is to free life from secularism. Thus total dedication to God and the liberation of one's life from an orientation toward secular concerns go together.

Vatican II echoed these ideas of St. Thomas to a far greater extent than is apparent from the actual quotations. In *Lumen Gentium* the Council explained religious life thus:

> The Christian who pledges himself to this kind of life binds himself to the practice of the three evangelical counsels by vows or by other sacred ties of a similar nature. He consecrates himself wholly to God, his supreme love. In a new and special way he makes himself over to God, to serve and honor him. True, as a baptized Christian, he is dead to sin and dedicated to God; but he desires to derive still more abundant fruit from the grace of baptism. For this purpose he makes profession in the Church of the evangelical counsels. He does so for two reasons: first, in order to be set free from hindrances that could hold him back from loving God ardently and worshipping him perfectly, and secondly, in order to consecrate himself in a more thoroughgoing way to the service of God.[16]

The same idea appears again in the decree *Perfectae Caritatis,* section 5:

> The members of each institute should recall, first of all, that when they made professions of the evangelical counsels they were responding to a divine call, to the end that, not merely being dead to sin (cf. Rm. 6:11) but renouncing the world also, they might live for God alone. They have dedicated their whole lives to his service.[17]

These texts are of major importance in understanding what constitutes the very nature of religious life according to the Council. In fact Chapter VI of *Lumen Gentium,* after dealing in its first section (#43) with the phenomenon of religious life in the Church, intends in the next section to show the significance of this phenomenon. In the same way *Perfectae Caritatis,* having spoken of the phenomenon in the first section, and having treated in sections 2–4 of the principles governing renewal (which is the object of the decree) goes on, in section 5, to define the elements that are common to all forms of religious life, the essential elements from which renewal must draw its inspiration.

The Council texts raise various problems. We will put aside for now questions that have to do with a Christian interpretation of the vow, of the existence of the counsels and of their number and nature, of the idea of religious consecration and its relationship with baptismal consecration; these are themes to which we will return in subsequent chapters. What draws our attention at this moment is the affirmation that religious give themselves totally to God, whom they love above all else, so as to have a new and special title to serve and honor him.[18] This affirmation is repeated in the decree *Perfectae Caritatis:* "not merely being dead to sin, but renouncing the world also, they live for God alone. They have dedicated their whole lives to his service."[19] An echo of the thought of St. Thomas Aquinas is perceivable here, at least in regard to the *totality* of the consecration and the placing of *all* one's life at the service of God.

2. To Love God with One's Whole Heart

In answering the question of a Scribe, and entering discussions on the identity of the main commandment from which all others derive, Jesus repeated the Shema, which was so highly esteemed by pious Israelites: "Listen, Israel: Yahweh our God is the one Yahweh. You shall love Yahweh your God with your heart, with all your soul, with all your strength." But he then immediately added: "The second is this: You must love your neighbor as yourself," thus combining Dt. 6:5 and Lv. 19:18 (Mk. 12:28–31; cf. Lk. 10: 25–28, where the Scribe himself quotes the two commandments). In conclusion Matthew has: "On these two commandments hang the whole Law and the Prophets also" (Mt. 22:40).

This restatement of the first commandment by Jesus makes total love of God the first and central norm of the "law" for his disciples. The one God must be loved with unique love, with an undivided heart ("with all your heart"). Therefore all of life must be animated by this love of God. One should note, however, that from the biblical point of view the love of God does not exclude, but rather includes, everything that is good. The transcendent God of Israel does not make himself a rival to any other love.

Only idolatry, substituting a creature for God, is contrary to the first commandment (cf. Ex. 20:1-3). The pious Israelite marries in obedience to God (Gn. 1:28) and enjoys life and its good things with an intense religious feeling. Here we are far removed from Hellenistic dualism which considered God to be a rival of the world. Jesus stressed even more the inclusive character of the love of God, adding the second commandment of the love of neighbor. We come, therefore, to the same conclusion we reached in analyzing the concept of evangelical discipleship. It is the question of a deep orientation of one's entire existence toward God in an attitude of total love.

This is the law for Jesus' disciples. Obviously, when one speaks of love (of God and neighbor) the terms *law* and *commandments* take on a very special meaning, which is qualitatively different from their use when their referents are the prohibitions in the second part of the decalogue. St. Thomas Aquinas was well aware of this:[20] the disciple's perfection consists in loving God with all one's heart, and loving one's neighbor as oneself.

But there is a question as to whether St. Thomas allowed himself to be influenced by the Greek concept of perfection: not because, in quoting Aristotle, he equated perfection with totality (*tam* and *teleios* have the same meaning in the Bible) but because he considered perfection to be a goal that is reached gradually. Aquinas also noted, however, that "totality" of love can be understood in different ways.[21] We would say that it can, in the first place, be understood in the biblical sense of ordering all existence toward God, thus giving it a religious orientation in light of which all is seen and carried out. In this way one excludes not only sin[22] but also, more basically, an idolatrous orientation of life toward other good things. In the biblical sense (and in the *sequela Christi*) the perfection of love is not a goal but a starting point: only thus is one a believer and, in the New Testament, a disciple. In the Greek sense, totality of love is an intensity of affection, and thus a goal that, ordinarily, must be reached through gradual development.[23]

The first commandment of total love of God, restated by Jesus, becomes a vocation, the common vocation of his disciples. The orientation of all of life toward God becomes a distinctive characteristic and (translating the request into an anthropology which sees in the human being a process of transformation and growth) also an ultimate goal. The fact that Jesus associated the first commandment with a second one, requiring us to love our neighbors as ourselves, confirms still further the all-embracing character of love of God. One loves God and one obeys him by loving one's neighbor. In the Sermon on the Mount Jesus invites us to be "perfect" like our heavenly Father by generous love toward our neighbor. It is precisely love of neighbor that, in the Johannine tradition, becomes "the commandment" of the Lord (Jn. 15:12–13; cf. Jn. 3:23–24), the "new commandment" (Jn. 13:34; cf. 1 Jn. 2:3–11), and the distinguishing mark of his disciples (Jn. 13:35). It is a matter of obedience to God, but also of participation in the dynamics of his love toward humanity: God's love toward us shows its completeness when it reaches our neighbor through us (1 Jn. 2:5).

3. The Service of God as an Expression of Total Love

Being disciples of Jesus consists, then, in loving God with our whole heart, and loving our neighbor as ourselves. Guided by the example of Christ who died for us, we can also say that the *sequela Christi* requires that we love to the point of dedicating our lives to our brothers and sisters.

It is in this context that we must place religious life. As St. Thomas correctly insisted, it does not consist in greater love. The religious is not called to greater love, because all disciples are called to love with their whole heart. The religious is simply called to express the common vocation to a totality of love through a particular lifestyle. This explains why the term *totaliter,* which is so dear to St. Thomas in explaining not love but the gift of self, may be a source of confusion.

To be disciples of Jesus is to give oneself totally to God in Christ. The totality of the gift does not exclude the obligations of practical life. One gives oneself to God on a different level and in a different manner from that of giving oneself to one's spouse, children, or profession. But the characteristic of the religious is to express the totality of love, which is the common vocation, through celibacy and a life led either in solitude or in community, and to express it visibly in the Church and before all mankind. One should recall what has already been said about this in discussing discipleship; there is no need to repeat it here.[24]

From the very dawn of Christian monasticism, tradition characterized religious life as a life dedicated to the divine service. When we discussed the theme of traditional religious-secular relationships, we saw that representing monasticism as a life dedicated to the service of God often led to an unacceptable idea of secular life.

This manner of speaking may be misleading, for two reasons. First, there is the risk of mistakenly narrowing the concept of divine service. Second, there is the Hellenistic implication that it cannot be carried out except through a *fuga mundi* (an escape from the world). Since grave consequences might result from these two possible errors, involving the very concept of Christian living, we are obliged to dwell on these two themes.

To narrow the meaning of divine service by identifying it exclusively with the type of life led by religious would be contrary to the example of Jesus and to New Testament doctrine. Hans Küng wrote, rather precipitately, or perhaps in an attitude of deliberate challenge (for which we can be grateful to him) that Jesus was not a religious.[25] Certainly Christ's spirituality differed profoundly from that of the Essenes, but it differed also from that of John the Baptist: Christ was not isolated from the world, nor did he appear as a person closely bound by a rule, nor as an ascetic. The *Ecole française* was correct when it proclaimed him to be the "Religious of the Father." Through his celibacy and his single-hearted dedication to the proclamation and fulfillment of the Kingdom, his life was certainly the prototype of what we now call the religious life. But having said this one must make it quite clear that for him the service of the Father was not bound to any special lifestyle.

What Jesus preaches and requires is an ethico-spiritual quality of existence derived from faith and union with the will of the Father. We have already seen that, according to Mt. 7:21, one does not enter into the Kingdom because one calls Jesus, "Lord! Lord!," or because one preaches and works miracles, but because one does the will of the Father. Inasmuch as one seeks to accomplish the divine will in one's actual situation, one is a servant of the Lord. Not only celibacy, or a life dedicated to prayer, or ministries within the Church, but also marriage, having children, and working toward a society more worthy of children of God constitute divine service. Certainly celibacy is not a greater service to God than is marriage, nor is solitude a greater service than having children and educating them in the faith.

As for serving God according to the Gospel (a theme we will later go into more deeply), different lifestyles are simply concrete applications and means. It is not possible to claim for any one of them the exclusive right to the title "God's service."[26]

Still, the traditional affirmation that religious "dedicate themselves to the divine service" reflects experience, and has a valid meaning. It shows the awareness secular Christians have of the significance of religious life. The specific expression "servants and handmaids of God" or "of Christ," originally preceded the use of the abstract term that qualified religious life as divine service. This means that people considered religious to be bound in a special way to God. Monks and nuns were called servants and handmaids of God because their relationship with God showed in their lives in a tangible and characteristic way.

St. Thomas reminds us of this: the virtue of religion by which one recognizes and actively manifests one's (passive) bond with God, is a virtue proper to every believer. In this sense every Christian is a religious.[27] He says, however, that the term *religious* belongs *antonomastice*, in a strict sense, to certain Christians, because they bind themselves totally to the divine service, in the manner of a holocaust, not holding anything back for themselves.[28]

Following what has been said above, we conclude that certain Christians are called religious in a special way because they carry the bond with God which is everyone's vocation to the level of a visible lifestyle. Religion, the expression of the bond uniting us to God, becomes a concrete way of life with them. Thus we are only repeating, in the general context of religion, what we have already said in a specifically Christian context, speaking of the *sequela Christi*. It is not a question of living the *sequela* with all its requirements more intensely, but of incarnating it on the level of practical life. Specifically, then, the "total" gift of a religious to God is not of a subjective but of an objective nature. Subjectively one belongs totally to God in proportion to one's faith, hope, and love; here we are dealing with the Christian vocation in general. Objectively one belongs only to God inasmuch as one rejects all other bonds which might alter one's mode of existence. Dedication to God, in this case, is a public profession and a witness within the Church.

As concrete types of the Christian vocation, religious life and secular life are forms of existence. One must, therefore, consider their specific dedication to God and to his service from this objective standpoint. Nevertheless, the expression and carrying out of this objective bond with God is a means of growing in the awareness of one's personal relationship with Christ. Therefore, even though religious life is an objective form of life, it is at the service of life in the Spirit, nourished by faith, hope, and charity. Without this life in the Spirit, religious life becomes merely the facade of a house in ruins.

4. Serving God in the World

The second risk in identifying religious life with the service of God consists in linking the service of God with the *fuga mundi*. We spoke earlier of the relation between religious life and the world, and consequently between religious and lay people. But the theme of religious life as divine service obliges us, at this point, to recall certain truths.

We must definitely lay aside, in our theology of religious life, the concept of a rivalry between God and the material world which was so prevalent in Hellenism and which has so deeply influenced thought on religious life and its relationship to the world. The God of Israel, the God who reveals himself to us through Jesus, is certainly very different from the one whom the Gnostics—and in general all the spiritual leaders of pagan Hellenism—dreamed of. Far from being detached from the world and opposed to it, God manifests himself to us within history, and thus in the world. Our meeting with God takes place in the world, or, more exactly, in a meeting with the world. The Exodus and the ministry and death of Jesus are events in human history through which God reveals himself to us. To speak of Christ's death "under Pontius Pilate" is to refer to a definite human and historical event within which an experience of the divine unfolds for us.

E. Schillebeeckx reached the same conclusion, starting from a philosophy of the knowledge of God which he considers to be not only modern, but also typically Christian. He quotes St. Thomas Aquinas's affirmation that our ideas of God derive from our experience with things pertaining to the world and with the history of salvation.[29] He concludes that humanity together with the concrete world in which it lives, seen in their historical development, is the only *locus* for truth. God reveals himself through humanity, in the world, and within history. Thus God takes on a definite outline for us through this concrete experience of the world; to endeavor to abstract from it is equivalent to separating oneself from the living God of biblical revelation, and following an abstract concept of the Divinity.[30]

This remains valid in either direction: from God to us, and from us to God. It is only through an experience of the world and of humanity that the encounter with God is accomplished. We must remember that Jesus did not merely announce the Kingdom as coming in the future, but as being accomplished and in some way made present. We might say that it is awaited insofar as this world is raised up and opened toward its final perfection.

One can never leave the world (basically not even the first anchorites claimed to do this) but one can bring the world back to God, and one can carry it on toward the parousia. This has consequences for every type of Christian life: every form of discipleship must have meaning here and now, in the pilgrim Church and in a world that sighs in expectation. From these premises alone we can conclude that every form of service rendered to God is also service rendered to the world, to humanity, and to the Church. Shortly, when we speak of service to the Church as an essential element in religious life, we will be forced to come to the same conclusion from other points of view.

If we consider the attitude of Jesus himself, we realize that not all has been said if we limit ourselves simply to differentiating between the biblical God who comes to meet us in the world and the Hellenistic god who is in rivalry with the world. In Jesus, the love of God embraces the love of neighbor and of creation, just as in Judaism. But it would be wrong to conclude that his spirituality is narrowly secular, that it has no place for renunciation of earthly values. In examining the idea of discipleship we reached the opposite conclusion. How does one explain this?

We must realize that, although all dualisms of a static and ontological type (matter-spirit, world-God) are absent in Jesus, there is present, and even dominant in his spirit an eschatological type of dualism, dynamic and historical, such as had been developed by the apocalyptic currents of his time: i.e, the present in opposition to the Kingdom of God. Today one tends to reject the one-sided image of Jesus as an apocalyptic prophet which J. Weiss and A. Schweitzer popularized at the turn of the century.[31] But we are aware that the announcement of the impending Kingdom has a central place in Christ's teaching. He therefore uses a concept that was typical of the apocalyptics of his time, although he differs in his presentation of the history of salvation by using a method which is closer to that of the prophets of Israel. It is from this eschatological perspective that Jesus sets the Kingdom of God in opposition to all worldly values and human judgments, and hence requires a *metanoia,* a radical conversion.

Jesus lived entirely for the preparation and the announcement of the Kingdom, and he required complete renunciation from all his disciples. It is precisely this tension (and consequently this eschatological dualism) between the Kingdom and the human order that gives legitimacy to a non–secular Christian spirituality. One may serve the Kingdom, in certain vocations, through exclusive dedication to the announcement of the Kingdom and the consequent renunciations. To reject this possibility, basing oneself on the all-inclusive love of God, would be, in our opinion, to attach oneself exclusively to Genesis, ignoring an original and distinctive aspect of Christ's preaching.

5. Jesus, the Servant of Yahweh

We can glimpse the correct Christian interpretation of the service of God through the image of the Servant of Yahweh in the poems of Deutero-Isaiah (Is. 40–55) applied to Jesus by early apostolic preaching (Ac. 3:13, 26; 4:27,30). The narrative of Christ's baptism also refers to that image by quoting Is. 42:1 (Mk. 1:11; Mt. 3:17; Lk. 3:22). The poems of the Servant of Yahweh are quoted explicitly in various New Testament passages (Mt. 8:17; 12:18–21; Lk. 2:32; 22:37; Rm. 4:25, 15:21) and implicitly in a still-larger number of texts.[32]

In the Old Testament the Servant of Yahweh is, first of all, a person whom God himself has chosen (Is. 42:1) even before he was born (Is. 49:1). The Spirit descends upon him, anointing him and taking possession of him (Is. 42:1). The initiative, therefore, belongs to God. One does not become a servant of God through one's own choice nor (going beyond what we have already said) through one's own dedication to the divine service, but because one has been chosen by God for a particular task among his people. The theophany at baptism indicates a divine initiative in regard to Jesus, too, by quoting Is. 42:1, slightly altered in the Gospel text in order to present Jesus as the Son, not merely the Servant as in the poem (*ebed, pais*): "This is my Son, the Beloved; my favor rests on him. . . ." (Mt. 3:17; cf. Mk. 1:11, Lk. 3:22: "You are my Son . . ."). The dedication of self to the service of God entails grace and obedience to the gift received. Religious life begins with the grace of a calling, and finds its ultimate explanation in it.

Obviously, for the disciples of Jesus, all dedication to the service of God is a sharing in the service he rendered, and draws its inspiration from it. In the Old Testament God's servants were often the kings whom God had chosen and empowered with his Spirit so that they might save his people (2 S. 3:18; Hg. 2:23; Zc. 3:8; Ps. 89:4, 20 ff.), but more generally they were the prophets, who also were chosen and anointed by the Spirit so that they might speak in God's name to the people (Ex. 14:31; 1 K. 14:18; 18:36; 2 K. 9:7; 2 K. 17:13, etc.). In the poems of Deutero-Isaiah, the Servant of the Lord appears primarily as a prophet. His mission is to bring true justice (faith) to the nations (Is. 42:1,3), to lead Israel back to the Lord (Is. 49:5), to suffer, taking upon himself our sins (Is. 53:4-6), and to die for the justification of many (Is. 53:10-11). The explicit quotations of the poems of the Servant of Yahweh in the New Testament show Jesus to be the Servant inasmuch as he was called to proclaim true justice (Mt. 12:18), to heal many of their diseases (Mt. 8:17, 12:15-21), and to bring salvation to the people (Lk. 2:32), but above all because he gave his life for his brothers and sisters, dying for our sins (Lk. 22:37; Rm. 4:25). Dedication of self in suffering even unto death becomes, both in Is. 53 and in the New Testament, the vocation of God's servant and the means of salvation for the people.

Here, in the Lord's ministry and death—or rather in the ministry of Jesus culminating in his death—we have not only the source of inspiration for the divine service to which religious intend to consecrate themselves, but also a criterion by which the evangelical authenticity of that service can be judged. It also seems to us that certain fundamental concepts are implicit in the ministry and death of Christ.

First of all, Jesus not only takes up his service in obedience to the will of the Father (St. John's Gospel never tires of repeating this), but the service he renders to the Father consists in placing God on the side of those who are apparently far from him: the great mass of poor people condemned by the ecclesiastical establishment because they do not observe the Law and are therefore sinners, the publicans who are more or less rich but are excommunicated, the adulteresses and the prostitutes.

We cannot now enter into all the aspects of this question. We must limit ourselves to stating that, by continuing and deepening the prophets' preaching, Jesus offers an image of God that contrasts with the kingly and ritualistic image of the priests, and with the legalistic image of the Scribes and Essenes. The God whom Jesus brings close to us is not served with ritualistic ceremonies, nor with the observance of every traditional precept and taboo, nor even with asceticism. The Father of Our Lord Jesus is served in giving oneself completely to the redemption of the human race. One serves God by serving people. We should remember that even the Sabbath which—according to contemporary Judaism—was observed even by God and his angels in heaven, was placed by Jesus at the service of human beings. This, as constantly repeated in the Gospel of John, is the will of the One who sent Jesus.[33]

To avoid equivocation, the preceding statements may require some elucidation. In the first place it is not possible to imagine a spirituality and life more centered on God than is that of Jesus. It is his concern to obey the Father, to accept his mission, to love him with his whole heart and to serve him. But the obedience, the mission, the wholehearted love, and the service of the Father consist precisely in the redemption of his brothers and sisters.

In the second place, it would be false to conclude from this that prayer and fasting had no importance for Jesus. He prays in private, takes part in the public liturgy and, at least sometimes, fasts. What we must deduce is that the Father of Jesus is not served by prayer or worship or fasts that do not include the service of one's neighbor. Moreover one should not hastily conclude that in an evangelical spirituality there is no room for a life which takes prayer or worship as its own divine ministry, or for a life marked by asceticism. Even though Jesus was not himself a monk or an ascetic (we have, however, called him the religious of the Father) his spirituality leaves room for numerous variations; his spirit is multiform. The New Testament is a magnificent example of theological and spiritual pluralism, and Paul recommends to us respect for diverse spiritual forms and charisms. We must conclude, instead, that prayer, public worship, and asceticism are a redemptive ministry in Christianity, and that, in order to ascertain their spiritual authenticity, they should, in each separate case, be judged according to the distinguishing criterion of Christ's concept of divine service. Otherwise one runs the risk of developing a type of divine service that is utterly foreign to Jesus.

This biblical tradition on divine service is most enlightening. One is not God's servant because one is dedicated to his worship, but because one has been chosen by him to bring salvation to others through the Word, and above all through the gift of self, even to the point of dying for our neighbor's welfare. Christ's death on the cross shows, in a supreme way, how we can serve God: by dying for our sisters and brothers. One should add, as Luke does in the logion on carrying the cross, by dying (that is, by giving one's life) *every day*. We thus reach the ecclesial meaning of religious life as divine service.

This fact has not always been clearly understood. In primitive monasticism, whose strongly Christian inspiration appears to have been conditioned by Hellenistic presuppositions, there was too much insistence on the dichotomy between God and humanity. For instance Apa Arsenius, in seeking the way to salvation, thought that he heard God answering him: "flee from men."[34] Later he even abandoned his monastic brethren and explained: "God knows that I love you. But I cannot be with God and people at the same time. The heavenly choirs, which are composed of thousands, and tens of thousands, have only one will, whereas men and women have many wills. Therefore I cannot leave God in order to come to be with people."[35] Arsenius was Christian enough to understand that he had to love his neighbor: "God knows that I love you," so it was not lack of love that impelled him to flee. But he was unable to live both with God and with people, and gave as his reason the motive of an ascent from earthly pluralism, with its divisions, to celestial and divine unity, a motive that has clear Neoplatonic reminiscences. Probably, by his flight he was expressing his own particular vocation to prayer before God and on behalf of people, a completely legitimate calling. But if his words were to be understood as expressing a general principle, they would be in contradiction to Christ's example and his Incarnation. How is it possible not to be able to live both with God and with other people when God has definitively entered human history? Is not the God of Jesus the God who is on the side of his children, above all of those who are most in need of him, such as publicans and prostitutes? We have clear examples of solitude lived according to the Gospel in love of God and neighbor: in St. Teresa of Avila's fostering the evangelical life as an answer to divisions within the Church,[36] and in Thomas Merton's publishing his reflections on the war in Vietnam.[37]

II. Religious Life in the Church

Vatican II brought religious life back to the Church as its origin and its destination. This fact has not been sufficiently stressed in theological studies. A great deal has been said about the relationship between religious life and the Gospel. Efforts have been made to reunite religious life with the Jesus of history through the Scriptures. But one seems to neglect a fact that, although it does not need to be proved, should be thoroughly examined in its meaning: religious life is a typical phenomenon in the life of the Church. The conciliar documents begin by describing it as a phenomenon that appears in the history of the people of God.[38] The Church is therefore at the very source of religious life. The same Council then tells us that religious life is directed toward the life of the Church.[39] The Church as the origin and destination of religious life are two ideas that need to be examined thoroughly.

1. The Church: Origin of Religious Life

We must be aware of the point of view of Vatican II in speaking of the Church as the *ager dominicus,* the Lord's field, in which the seed of the Word brings forth religious life.[40] The image of the field that receives the seed is a feminine symbol. We thus find the motif of mother-Church made fruitful by the Spirit. When the Council speaks of the community of believers as the origin of religious life, it directs our attention first of all toward the inner dimensions of the Church, towards its interior dynamism as an adherence of faith, as an affirmation of hope, and as a transcending love of God. The decree *Perfectae Caritatis*[41] speaks, in fact, of the charisms received by various members, among which are the charisms proper to the religious life. We are therefore brought back to the Paschal mystery and to the experience of Pentecost.

The Spirit of the Risen Lord pours out his charisms within the *communio sanctorum,* and among these charisms are those which create religious life. The Church is already present wherever the Word is heard and followed; thus, if one listens to Christ's invitation in one's heart and decides to follow it, one is taking part in the full life of the Church even before carrying out the command. The importance of this affirmation becomes clear when one considers that religious institutes have often developed completely in the hearts of their Foundresses and Founders many years before taking a definite external form. The prolonged experience of the Spirit which led these Servants of God to seek for years the way in which they might serve was already a deeply ecclesial phenomenon.

Actually, in the earthly Church, the *communio Sanctorum* occurs in a historical community. And yet one often tries to understand various forms of religious life without fitting them into the period of Church history in which they were born, thus forgetting that they represent historical forms of one common discipleship, and as such can be understood only by starting from history.

It is not possible to explain the birth of primitive monasticism without seeing its relationship with the new situation of the Church midway between the third and fourth centuries: the end of the period of martyrs, the coming of official recognition, the establishment of the Church in cities, the transformation of the episcopacy. Similarly one cannot understand the initiatives taken by Benedict, by the Mendicant Orders, by Ignatius of Loyola, by Teresa of Avila, or by Louise de Marillac without fitting them into their times.

The various forms of religious life represent concrete answers to concrete needs of the ecclesial community. What first appears is a particular necessity within the Church: a renewal of fidelity to the Gospel, in Anthony and Basil; a crisis in monasticism, in Benedict; a return to the sources, with the decline of feudalism, in Francis; apostolic service to a Church that was torn asunder, and before whom new continents were opening up, in Ignatius; the sufferings of the poor, in countless Foundresses and Founders, etc. Through a specific need there emerges an awareness of a permanent service to which the Spirit is calling a group of men or women. The Spirit of the Lord acts by speaking within the heart, but also by speaking in history; his voice becomes perceptible through human experiences: through the encounter with a sick man on the streets of Granada, for St. John of God; through the discovery of prostitution, for Michelina of the Blessed Sacrament.

The interior thrust by which the Spirit of Jesus moves certain Christians to the *sequela Christi* transfers itself spontaneously to the visible plane of ecclesiastical society, as a sign and vehicle of the sharing of grace. A public mode of existence (already present among the anchorites in the desert before any institution had taken shape) and religious families (ecclesiastical institutes) are then born. This takes place through the recognition, granted by the Church and expressed by her ministers, of the specific lifestyle and groups centered in a common vocation.

It should be clear that ecclesiastical recognition is necessary only if one wants a public profession and an official institute. There is absolutely no need for official approval in order to live according to the Gospel, or to express the ordinary vocation to discipleship in a fundamental way by celibacy and poverty. This is a matter of the vocations and charisms which are dispensed by the Lord according to his will. There is not even need for permission to form a group of evangelical communion. The right of free association, which the Church recognizes as inherent in the human person, does not cease on the ecclesiastical level.[42] But it is natural for every group that is born in the Church to want to reveal its identity to the rest of the community, showing its participation in the Church's life both actively and passively. When there is the desire to constitute a social and public entity, it becomes necessary to have the approval of the ministers of the Church. In the beginning this approval was given without special juridical act, by maintaining relationships in which the bishops showed their esteem for the monks, while the monks recognized the bishops as shepherds of the Church.[43] Benedict, whose *Regula Monachorum* was certainly not approved by a formal act, asked the bishop, the abbots, and even ordinary Christians in the vicinity, to prevent the installation of an unworthy abbot elected by monks seeking an easy life.[44] Whatever happens in groups founded in order to live the *sequela Christi* is important for the entire community of believers.

Obviously, if a group wants to become a recognized institute, and asks for the approval of the Church, it will be necessary to sacrifice some freedom of initiative in order to fit into canonical categories and the framework of ecclesiastical society's laws. This sacrifice is made in return for the greater good of being able to live and work publicly for the Church. But this goes beyond the field of theology into that of law.

2. The Church: Destination of Religious Life

We have already seen, in passing, that religious life is directed toward the welfare of the entire ecclesial community. This direction is based, to start with, on an anthropology which considers man or woman as a social being, a being who grows within a community. Reaffirming this, Vatican II noted the interdependence between personal progress and the perfecting of society. Nobody grows only for oneself. In bettering oneself one tends to improve others, and in working for others one develops one's own power and capacities. Moreover, in speaking of Christian vocation and of its effect on the rest of the Church, one must also take into account the very nature of the Christian vocation and of the Church, a communion of faith and grace.

Unfortunately, this truth did not appear in the early manifestation of monasticism. Monks fled to the desert in search of their own salvation.[45] When bishops sought them out to ordain them priests or deacons, they did not say that in their monastic vocation they already had a way of contributing to the growth of the Church, but rather that, since they were not sure of their own salvation, they could not busy themselves with the salvation of others.

One finds this same concept in Gregory of Nazianzus, in his comparison of the active life of bishops with the contemplative life of monks: the monks are useful only to themselves, while shepherds of souls are useful to others.[46] Augustine echoes this same prejudice in linking contemplative life with *delectatio,* and the life engaged in pastoral activities and works of mercy with *necessitas.*[47] It should be noted, however, that according to Augustine one cannot be *otiosus* (contemplative) without thinking of the welfare of one's neighbor. This does not yet mean that contemplation is, in itself, fruitful for the Church, but that contemplatives must also think of others, give themselves also to the service of others.[48]

In the first hermits the influence of an individualistic anthropology is evident. The Hellenistic theory of different kinds of life is discernible in Gregory and Augustine. The idea of an influence exercised upon the rest of the Church is, however, implicit in the Basilian brotherhood, Macrina's sisterhood, and in the Benedictine monasteries, founded to promote a mode of life faithful to the Gospel. The monastery thus becomes a "school of the service of God." One should note, however, that the same erroneous point of view was still encountered in recent times when, in commenting on the two purposes assigned to Apostolic Institutes by many constitutions (personal sanctification and the salvation of others), personal sanctification was related to the religious life, while the ministry alone was related to the salvation of others.

To explain the bond between the religious life and the Church, Vatican II recalls the thought of St. Thomas and of St. Bonaventure, who spoke of the evangelical counsels as means for growing in charity.[49] Therefore Vatican II concludes that the counsels form a special bond with the Church and its mystery, implying that *caritas* is the very soul of the Church. The same Constitution, *Lumen Gentium,* also speaks of the prophetic witness that religious life carries on in the Church.[50]

It is obvious that all forms of Christian life are ways leading to evangelical perfection. All of them—celibacy for the sake of the Kingdom, or sacramental matrimony—are particular ways in living out the mystery of the Church. Every manner of living out discipleship in a concrete form belongs to the Church, which is the community of disciples; and, as we have seen, all forms bear a prophetic witness. We believe, however, that this is not a complete statement; an essential element is lacking for an understanding of the relationship between religious life and the Church.

In speaking of the Church as the source of religious life, we saw that its roots are born in the paschal mystery (the Church as *communio*), but that they pass through the visible dimension of ecclesiastical society. We must note the same thing in speaking of the Church as the destination of religious life: we are dealing not only with its being directed toward *caritas,* but also with its being directed toward that social and historical expression of *communio* which is the community of believers. The gift of self to God is accomplished not only *within* the Church, but also by means of a dedication *to* the Church.

The relationship with God, in Christianity, takes shape in a relationship with the Church. According to the Bible, the relationship with God is established within the community. At first it was the people who established this relationship. Later, with the deepening of an individual consciousness (Jeremiah, Ezekiel, and certain Psalms) the relationship with God became more personal, but it remained always within the setting of the people. The dimension of community is essential, and this is true both for Israel and for the Church.

In the New Testament there is something more: the relationship with God goes through Jesus. The disciples follow Jesus because they realize that in him they are meeting the decisive manifestation of the true God of Israel. In the Gospel according to John, which reflects Christian paschal experience, Jesus asks for faith in himself. The Christ-man serves as sacrament in our encounter with God. He is the Mediator. During his earthly life the sign of this encounter is immediate and tangible: ''Do you believe in me?'' With the lifting up of Jesus (Cross and Resurrection), Jesus becomes the Lord of Glory, and all power is given to him. He is the *Kyrios* through whom Yahweh exercises his kingship. But at this very point Jesus, the sign, is no longer visible. At this precise moment the Church, in which Christ in present, is born. Christ continues to be the one sign, and certainly the only Mediator, but he reaches us through the Word and the sacraments, that is, through the action of the community. It is within the Church that Christ's sacramentality and his mediation are carried out. Christ gives grace, and the Church (that is, our humanity) gives the visible sign. If therefore one meets God by following Christ, one follows Christ by giving oneself to the Church.

This is shown particularly in the sacraments, privileged moments of being Church. Intercourse with God is established through a relationship with the Church. In Baptism one becomes, in a new way, a child of God, but because one has been brought into the community by a rite of initiation. The Eucharist is communion with Christ, taking place in fraternal communion: the bread and the wine that we bring to the *mensa Domini* are, at first, our own bread and wine, signs of our brotherhood; and for this reason, through the action of the Church, they become the Body and Blood of Christ. The sacrament of reconciliation is reconciliation with God through reconciliation with the community. One can actually be justified by grace without the sacrament (contrition); the sacrament, however, is given when one is reconciled with the ecclesial community. In matrimony the partner becomes, at one and the same time, Christ and the Church: Christ as loving, Church as being loved.

The sacraments, as specific facts in Christian religion, serve to bring out one of its characteristic elements: that the relationship with God in Christianity is not a simple relationship with the Transcendent (which would find expression in flight and renunciation), but with the One who comes to meet us in history and in the community. Therefore the typical forms of Christian relationship with God follow a sacramental structure through the medium of the Church.

Every form of the following of Christ involves a particular dedication to the Church. Thus religious life, which is a visible expression of the renunciation required by discipleship, cannot be a renunciation of the Church; very much to the contrary. In its search for God religious life must reproduce that sacramental structure which is typical of the Christian religion. One gives oneself to God by giving oneself to the Church, that is, to people. In fact, as we shall see later, one cannot understand the religious vow historically or theologically except as a bond with God which is, at the same time, incorporation into an evangelical community. When religious life is led (as in the case of certain anchorites) apart from contact with the ecclesial community, separated in fact from its preaching and sacraments; or when, as often happened, one defines religious life only as a consecration to God, without any reference to the Church or the neighbor, one is following a dualistic course that is not Christian.

3. God and Human Beings

In the preceding paragraphs we have repeatedly used the same verb or the same noun in speaking of the relationship with God and the relationship with the Church: to give oneself to God, to give oneself to the Church; dedication to the service of God, dedication to the service of the Church. We were, in fact, eager to show that these are simply two phases of the same movement. In some cases we have distinguished between them, speaking of the following of Christ and of dedication to the Church, or of a meeting with God and of incorporation into the Church. The reason for this is that the two relationships have a very different character. One never follows Peter or Paul, that is, the Church, but only Christ (1 Co. 1:12-13, 3:4-15). And in the Creed we confess to believe *in* God, but to believe *about* the Church.

Religious life is religious because it is a relationship with God, a dedication to his service; not because it is a dedication to the service of humanity. It is the following of Christ, not the simple incorporation into the community, that gives it its fundamental meaning. One lives and dies for the Lord. This is shown in the preaching and sacraments of the Church: it is not the human word, or the human act of pouring water, or passing the chalice, but God's grace that justifies us. The word and the action are signs, but what counts is the reality which is indicated (and veiled) by the language of the Church. Yet grace does come to us through the human word and gesture, which are Word and Sacrament (gestures of Christ). We speak of receiving the eucharistic bread and wine, and we speak of receiving the Body and Blood of Christ. ''To receive'' signifies two different realities, one incarnate in the other. This is exactly what we mean to say when we speak of giving ourselves to Christ, and giving ourselves to the ecclesial community. The community is simply the water, the bread, the wine, in which Christ meets us and we meet him.

Earlier, when we analyzed the theology of the Servant of the Lord in Sacred Scripture, we saw that the Servant is what he is because he announces salvation to us and gives his life for us. Thus we find the same practical identity between dedication to the service of God and dedication of one's life to the welfare of one's brothers and sisters. Seeing that we are dealing here with a concept basic to the theology of religious life, it seems useful to dwell awhile on this theme.

III. The Worship and Service of God in the Church

Thus we see that religious life is intimately bound to the Church in two ways: a) by being born from the Church through a process that moves from within (the Spirit and its charisms) into the social reality of the Church; b) by being directed toward the Church, by means of a movement that passes through the sacramental level of the community of believers in order to reach the *communio sanctorum*. The worship and service of God, which is the purpose of religious life according to the traditional interpretation, is therefore a particular expression of the worship and service rendered to God by the entire Church, and must of necessity be considered from this point of view. We must consequently reflect on the precise meaning that the terms "worship" and "service" of God have in Christ's Church.

1. The Church: a Community of Worship and Mission

From the data in the first summary of Acts (2:42–47) the Church, from the very beginning, revealed itself as a liturgical community. Immediately after the Pentecost experience and Peter's first sermon in which he announces the Resurrection, Luke describes the life of the first believers as follows: "These remained faithful to the teaching of the apostles, to the brotherhood, to the breaking of bread and to the prayers" (2:42). "They went as a body to the Temple every day, but met in their houses for the breaking of the bread; they shared their food gladly and generously; they praised God. . . ." (2:46–47). Prayer in common, presided over by the Apostles, is mentioned on various occasions (1:14; 4:24–30; 6:4, etc.). Mention is also made of prayers offered on special occasions, such as for the election to some office in the Church (1:24; 6:6; 13:3; 14:23), the mission to the Samaritans (8:15), and the perseverance during persecution (4:24–30; 12:5,12). One can say that the primitive apostolic community began immediately to build up in itself the image of the heavenly Jerusalem, tending completely toward the glorification of the Father and of the Lamb (Rv. 5:8–14; 11:16–18; 19:4–8), or the announcement of Jesus, in John's Gospel, concerning the true worshipers in Spirit and truth (Jn. 4:23).

This Church, which considers itself a praying community, often expresses its worship in terms that are common to all religions: in divine praise, in supplication, and in thanksgiving. It is obvious that this group of Jews gathered together in the name of Jesus should have continued to use the prayers that are dear to Hebrew piety, the Shema and the Psalms, and to frequent the Temple. But at the same time this first apostolic Church expresses its relation of worship toward God in the breaking of the bread, in the Apostles' preaching, and in Baptism (Ac. 2:41). We already find here, in the initial group, the typical acts proper to Christian worship: the preaching of the Gospel, and the two basic sacraments of Baptism and the Eucharist.

The narratives of the Christian beginnings, however, reveal a second dimension that is likewise essential to the Church: that of being a mission community.[51] In the Gospels of Mark and Luke, each experience of the Resurrection is followed by its announcement (Mk. 16:9-20; Lk. 24:9, 33-35). In Matthew (Mt. 28:7,10) and John (Jn. 20:17) the impulse to announce the Good News originates in a command of the Risen One. All the Synoptics end with the mission of the Church to preach and baptize. Mission is therefore essential to the community of believers. Vatican II underscored this when it affirmed that the missionary nature of the Church derives from the mission of the Son and of the Holy Spirit.[52]

Thus the Church is centered in one event: the death and resurrection of Christ. It is called to announce this event and to bring us to participate in it. Hence its mission. It is very significant that the acts by which it fulfills its mission should be the same by which it expresses itself as a worshiping community: preaching and the sacraments. In Christianity, worship and mission are not two separate things; they are identical. The reason for this is that Christianity, before being a religion (a relationship between ourselves and God), is God's revelation, his salvific gift to us, a gift that culminates, and is definitely realized, in the Incarnation and in the Death and Resurrection of the Son. The Church is born as a participation in this action of God in Christ. Our first response, also a grace, consists in faith, and the Church's worship is essentially the sum of acts through which this grace is given and received: preaching and the sacraments. The Church's worship is a fulfillment of the paschal mystery, a gift of redemption to humanity. Worship and mission are already inseparably associated here.

But the Church is also destined to communicate this grace to those who are not yet its members. This is why the Church's typical worship consists in acts through which the grace of the Risen One is announced, offered, and given: in the preaching of the Gospel, in Baptism conferred on those who believe, and in the Eucharist. Christ offered the supreme liturgy by dying for us. Praise, glorification of the Father, and our salvation are identified therein. Jesus obeys the Father who wants the human race to be saved.

We have already noted that the Gospel according to John closely unites

Christ's obedience to the Father and his saving mission (Jn. 4:34–38; 5:30; 6:38–39). Let us now also recall what we said in studying the theology of the Servant of the Lord: Jesus is the Servant of Yahweh because he announces salvation to us. The worship of the Church participates in this action. Preaching and the sacraments fulfill, each in its own way, the worship consisting of the salvation of the human race, rendered by Jesus to the Father. Above all through the Eucharist, which is the sacramental reenactment of the Death and Resurrection of the Lord, the community glorifies the Father and brings its members to participate in salvation.

God is glorified when his will is fulfilled; and his will, as Jesus insistently repeats in the Gospel according to John, is that we should be saved. St. Augustine[53] and St. Thomas Aquinas have both pointed out that God does not draw any advantage from his glorification: "God seeks glory, not for His own sake, but for ours."[54] To glorify God, therefore, signifies to share in his glory, to be glorified ourselves by his love. Thus one must exclude from Christianity the idea of a worship and service of God that is directed toward him in his pure transcendence, without any reference to humanity. It should be clear, however, that the Church is purely and simply theocentric. As a human response it is entirely oriented toward God and his grace. But in opening itself to God it finds him, in his mercy, entirely open to the human race. The orientation of worship toward humanity has its source in its orientation towards God. Moreover the Church, before being a human response, is a divine initiative; it is a real, historical and social offer of grace, and as such it is sent to us.

2. Religious Life: Worship and Mission

What we commonly call religious life in Christ's Church is a type of Christian existence in which total dedication to God, the common vocation of all disciples, expresses itself by means of certain renunciations in a lifestyle. This is why Christian people began, at an early time, to call monks and nuns "servants and handmaids of God," and why such a life is understood to be directed in a special way toward the worship and service of God. We know, however, that this way of interpreting religious life is common to many beliefs: from certain Neoplatonic mystics, to certain Mohammedan sufis, to Taoism and, altering the concept of God, to Buddhism.

If one transfers this concept into the Christian sphere, it has to be reinterpreted according to the Christian idea of divine service. First because, as we have stated, all self-dedication to God in Christ implies a dedication to the Church, in accordance with the sacramental structure characteristic of the Christian religion. Second, it is necessary, in giving themselves to God, that religious meet a God who is entirely inclined toward humanity. We have already noted that every experience of the Resurrection, and of one's own salvation in Christ, involves a mission. One serves God by dedicating one's life to him for the redemption of one's neighbor. In view of the two motives listed above (the Church's presence in our journey toward God, and God who offers salvation to us), every form of divine service implies an ecclesial ministry. All religious life, is therefore, a form of ministerial existence.

Religious life fulfills its Christian vocation in the service of the Church, first of all and essentially, in its lifestyle. One follows Christ entirely for oneself, but in following him one helps the Church. To the extent one gives oneself positively to God in faith and love, one strengthens and enriches the Church as the Communion of Saints. One contributes also to its vitality through a specific witness, inasmuch as one affirms the transcendent value of the Kingdom by one's very lifestyle. It is therefore possible for persons and communities to exist whose specific vocation in the Church is precisely to serve it by externalizing the Gospel in a lifestyle marked by the following of Christ. This is St. Basil's concept of the religious life, the original concept of St. Francis of Assisi, and the concept that is typical of some modern communities, such as the Little Brothers and Sisters of Jesus. This, according to the more common interpretation, is also the charism of monasticism. One should note, however, that in the Franciscan movement and among the Little Brothers and Sisters, the fact of sharing, especially with the poor, is part of their charism. Their life is specifically one of sharing.

Generally, however, religious life assumes specific forms that correspond to a particular ministry in the Church, beyond the one rendered by the lifestyle itself. Some religious feel that the God to whom they are giving themselves calls them to a ministry of intercession for the Church and humanity. These are the so-called "contemplatives." Prayer, both alone and in community, private and liturgical, constitutes their *diakonia,* their service. This does not mean that they serve the Church only when they explicitly pray for it; they serve also with their prayers of adoration, praise, and thanksgiving. In praising God they open themselves to his love, and enrich themselves and the Communion of Saints. Mystical experience is also of help to the community. Thus one understands why interior life and a strong sense of the Church are interwoven in Carmel, as the examples of Teresa of Avila, Thérèse of Lisieux, and Elizabeth of the Trinity prove.

There are other Institutes which visibly participate in the Church's mission by an exterior ministry. Their members give themselves to Christ who calls them to preach the Gospel or to care for the poor. This would be incomprehensible in a dualistic concept of reality: religious life could only be contemplative, expressing itself ideally through anchoritism. One should remember how Pachomius replied to the words directed to him by an angel. After seven years of hermitic life he had forgotten his first image of Christianity as fraternal solidarity with those who suffer, and had been influenced by the movement of flight that was so strong in the Church of his time. At a certain juncture, however, he experienced a crisis in his vocation and began to question how it was possible for him to serve God. An angel came to his aid, inviting him to serve people. Pachomius answered angrily: "I want to serve God, and you tell me to serve men!" At that moment the original image of Christianity as solidarity, and the vow he had made to serve his neighbor, were reawakened in his memory, and he founded his community for the service of his brethren.[55] This anecdote reflects an extreme state of mind which was not unusual in the Hellenistic period but which has, for centuries, been untenable.

More common, however, is the opinion that the contemplative life is the ideal form of religious life because it is directed toward God alone, and that the apostolic life is a compromise dictated by necessity. This does not correspond to the nature of Christian religious life. First of all, as we have seen, there is no such thing as a Christian contemplative life that is not also dedication to the Church and to humanity. Secondly, the Church appears visibly, in all its completeness, in the apostolic life; for the Church consists not only in the experience of the Resurrection, but also in the irrepressible announcement of it. The Church which adores God, especially through religious who are vowed to prayer, adores and preaches through those who are vowed to the apostolate.

The external ministerial activities towards which various religious Institutes are directed may be of many sorts. It seems to us, however, that these can be reduced to two classifications: the apostolate and works of mercy. The apostolate, properly so-called, consists in every exterior activity directed toward arousing faith by transmitting the divine Word and nourishing it by means of the sacraments. Its purpose is to foster a life of faith. The ministry of the works of mercy, instead, is directed towards relieving our neighbor's sufferings, thus embodying Christ's love for the needy. Jesus himself combined the two ministries by preaching, feeding the crowds, and healing the sick. The ministry of charity is justified because it makes Christ's love present towards those who suffer physically and morally, even without reference to evangelization. Jesus freely healed even those who would later forget his message. Love of neighbor is already an *initium Ecclesiae*. Obviously the ecclesial reality is complete when, drawn by Christ's love for them as shown by his servants, those who suffer open themselves to him in faith, and celebrate the Eucharist together with them.

3. The Discussion in St. Thomas on the Active Life

The meaning and the value of a type of religious life specifically oriented towards an exterior ministerial activity in the service of the Church emerges, we believe, quite clearly from the preceding reflections. The question had already been discussed by St. Thomas in answer to those who, during his own lifetime, questioned the legitimacy of such forms of religious life. Aquinas treated this on several occasions in *Contra impugnantes Dei cultum* and in the *Summa*.

His first reason for justifying and explaining what he calls his active life (a religious life directed toward charitable works) is that religious life is such because of the total gift religious make of themselves to God and to God's service. He goes on to say that divine service is also carried out in the works of the active life by which one serves one's neighbor *propter Deum* (for the love of God.)[56] What is the meaning of that *propter Deum* which we have translated as "for the love of God"? He had already explained this in a prior work, the *Contra impugnantes Dei cultum:* "There are some religious orders founded to serve God in his members through activity, such as those consecrated to God to care for the sick, to ransom prisoners, and to perform the other works of mercy."[57] One serves God, therefore, by serving one's neighbor.

In another text St. Thomas more thoroughly examines a subject upon which he had already lightly touched: the importance of the dedication that characterizes religious life. Everything religious do must be referred to the radical act of dedication by which they have consecrated their entire lives to God. Hence one must fix one's attention not on what they do, but on the fact that they have given themselves to God to do anything required.[58] A life is religious not because of its material occupations, but because it is a lifestyle born from a dedication to God. One is not a religious because one prays more (a secular person may have a more intense prayer life), nor because one works harder (a secular person may work harder and better). One is a religious as a consequence of the dedication one has made to God of one's own person and life, excluding all other relationships that could legitimately define another type of Christian existence.

The opponents of the new forms of religious life also proceeded from a concept of religious life as an existence hinged on religion. How, they asked, could anyone be called a religious who dedicated himself or herself to works pertaining to the active life? The ancient distinction between the sacred and the profane was revived.

St. Thomas answered by affirming, first, that the virtue of religion includes not only acts of worship (in the sense of ritual), but also all those acts that have reference to the divine service. It is not only ritual offerings that belong to the virtue of religion. Everything that is done in the service of and for the honor of God pertains to that same virtue. Because of this, the entire life of whoever has consecrated it to the divine service is placed under the virtue of religion.[59] Basing ourselves on these words, we come to distinguish two separate concepts which were used, by his opponents, as if they were equivalent: the *cultus Dei* and the *servitium,* or *famulatus Dei.* The *cultus* (worship) would be limited to the liturgy and to prayer, while divine service would have a broader sense, including everything a religious does in view of his or her gift of self to God.[60] One should note that worship, according to its specific meaning, is a priestly activity; it is rooted in the baptismal or ministerial priesthood. On the other hand the priesthood (baptismal or ministerial) is directed towards worship. The service of God pertaining to religious life is born at a different level, a level not primarily of activities, but of lifestyle.

Secondly, St. Thomas answered the objection in a deeper way by broadening the meaning of the term *worship.* Desiring once again to prove the legitimacy of Institutes founded for charitable works, he writes:

Just as out of charity we love our neighbor for God's sake, so the services we render our neighbor redound to God, according to Mt. XXV:40, 'What you have done . . . to one of these My least brethren, you did it to Me.' Consequently those services which we render our neighbor, insofar as we refer them to God, are described as sacrifices, according to Heb. XIII: 16, 'Do not forget to do good and impart, for by such sacrifices God's favor is obtained.' And since it belongs properly to religion to offer sacrifices to God . . . it follows that certain religious orders are fittingly directed to the works of the active life.[61]

These words cast a clear light on our subject: the Christian concept of worship is not to be drawn from a distinction between the sacred and the profane, nor from a point of view which sees God and humanity in opposition, but from the inspired Word of God. Christ alone can decide what Christian worship consists in. In the Gospels the services rendered to one's neighbor are services rendered to Christ; they are, in a certain sense, liturgy. This is why the Letter to the Hebrews calls them "sacrifices that please God" (*hostias*). Obviously the service of the neighbor is, in a certain sense, liturgy (*sacrificia quaedam*) in proportion to its being born from the Eucharist, the sacramental celebration of sharing, and returning to it.

IV

The Charisms of Religious Life

Were it possible to question St. Paul on what constitutes the various forms of Christian life in the Church, he would no doubt indicate the various charisms bestowed by the one Spirit for the good of the entire Church. This, in fact, is his way of approaching the theme of the manifold vocations in the Church. He does this often, in referring to the various ministries (1 Co. 12:8–10, 28–30; Rm. 12:6–18) and later, to the various ecclesiastical offices (Ep. 4:11–12).[1] The diverse contributions Christians bring to the common building up of the Church are always explained by St. Paul as originating from the different gifts of the Spirit which complement each other.

Although it is true that the category of charism is quite broad in St. Paul, even when he uses it in a technical sense including transitory experiences of the Spirit, it is nonetheless true that the Apostle tends to identify charisms with permanent gifts that characterize a Christian's place in the Church. More and more it is a question of vocational gifts: "God has given the first place to apostles, the second to prophets, the third to teachers. . . ." (1 Co. 12:28), and the letter to the Ephesians echoes: "And to some his gift was that they should be apostles; to some prophets; to some evangelists; to some pastors and teachers. . . ." (Ep. 4:11). But it is not only a question of high and prestigious ecclesiastical offices: some have the gift of being good administrators of the church, and others dedicate themselves especially to works of mercy (Rm. 12:7–8).

Are we dealing only with gifts connected with various activities within the Church? No, why should we? St. Paul is, in fact, interested in linking the multiform variety of specific situations with their unity of origin (God, the Lord, the Spirit) and of object (the Church). Indeed, in 1 Co. 7:7, St. Paul refers to celibacy and matrimony as two lifestyles originating from different charisms given by the same God: ''I should like everyone to be like me (not bound by marriage: cf. 1 Co. 9:5) but everyone has his own particular gifts from God, one with a gift for one thing, and another with a gift for another.'' Here also the various existential situations of Christians are referred to as different gifts of God.

Beginning with the New Testament, the best way to find out what properly constitutes the essential elements of religious life in the Church is to establish which charisms make a Christian a religious, which gifts characterize religious life as a special lifestyle. In a certain line of traditional thought, which became characteristic of the Latin Church with Scholasticism, religious life has been identified with the category of ''counsels.'' This was inspired by the use St. Paul makes of the rabbinical distinction between what is prescribed and what is counseled (1 Co. 7:25). Here, however, St. Paul is speaking of ''directives'' received from the Lord, as distinguished from his own personal opinion. Later we will see how the concept of *consilium* is backed by certain profound intuitions, especially in St. Ambrose's interpretation. But its use in defining religious life probably raises more problems than it resolves. Furthermore, the category of ''counsel'' is systematically connected by St. Thomas with the concept of ''state of perfection,'' an extremely problematical concept which Vatican II put aside in texts expressly dedicated to religious life.

It seems that the best way to approach this theme is the one we suggested earlier, drawing our inspiration from St. Paul's manner of treating the subject of the various vocations in the one Church: to define religious life on the basis of the charisms, or vocational gifts, which Christian religious have in common. Charism is a concept which is biblical, and its use in the theology of religious life does not present the problems that the category of counsels does. Actually we are not presenting anything new; we are simply giving a central place, in our theological consideration of the religious life, to a category that was used from ancient times to characterize at least one of its typical elements: celibacy. In view of the Hellenistic tendency to overestimate continence and, in extreme cases, to make it obligatory (thereby condemning marriage), the Fathers had to insist that this was not a precept. In this context, however, Origen and St. Ambrose spoke of virginity as something that is offered to Christians by grace: "it is not imposed, it is proposed" (*non imponitur, proponitur*) wrote St. Ambrose;[2] "it is offered" (*virginitas offertur*), wrote Origen.[3] St. John Chrysostom went further: it is not a matter of an offering, in the sense of a proposal, but of a veritable gift of God granted to certain individuals. Chrysostom is influenced in this by the logion on eunuchs and the sentence which opens and closes it: "Inasmuch as it would have been burdensome to impose virginity with the force of law[4] he aroused their desire for it . . . he persuaded them to choose this type of life . . . he mentioned the eunuchs in order to encourage them. . . . (Celibacy) is given to those who wish (to accept it) . . . because, if it were only a gift from above. . . ."[5] Virginity is, therefore, a gift and a vocation (cf. "he aroused their desire for it," and "he persuaded them. . .").

Vatican II repeatedly used the category *consilium* in referring to the characteristic elements of religious life. Its reason for doing so is obvious; it was virtually obliged to it since, from the time of St. Thomas and St. Bonaventure, this category has become the only technical term in Western theology which refers to these constituent elements.[6] Nevertheless, Vatican II introduced some new elements. The first consists of its insertion of a reference to the counsels in Chapter V of *Lumen Gentium*, dedicated to the universal vocation to sanctity: "(Holiness in the Church) appears in a certain way of its own in the practice of the counsels which have been usually called 'evangelical'."[7] In the same chapter, speaking of the various ways and means of reaching the common sanctity, *Lumen Gentium* refers first of all to martyrdom, and goes on to say that holiness in the Church "is fostered in a special way by the manifold counsels which the Lord proposes to his disciples in the Gospel for them to observe," among which celibacy or virginity for the sake of the Kingdom is preeminent.[8] The second new element is the document's allusion to the exegetical problems raised by the term "evangelical counsel." For this reason Vatican II refers to "the counsels which have usually been called 'evangelical'."[9] As for their number, the Council speaks of "manifold counsels."

In the course of this chapter we will have to return to some of these problems. For the present we wish to emphasize that, although Vatican II generally refers to the distinguishing traits of religious life as "counsels," it also uses the term *donum,* the equivalent of the Greek *charisma.* It does so in the prologue of *Perfectae caritatis,*[10] in referring to the various forms of religious life, and later in referring to the various apostolic Institutes dedicated to various ministries within the Church.[11] In the prologue it expressly quotes Ep. 4:2, and in Section 8 refers to 1 Co. 12 and Rm. 12, thus quoting St. Paul's three classic texts on charisms. These two paragraphs, however, are not addressing the question of elements common to all forms of religious life.

Yet on two occasions the same Council, in explaining the nature of celibacy, also uses the category of *donum*, citing Mt. 19:11 and 1 Co. 7:7.[12] In fact, at the beginning of Chapter VI of *Lumen Gentium*, it extends the concept of *donum* to the three "evangelical counsels": "They therefore constitute a gift of God which the Church has received from her Lord and which by his grace she always safeguards."[13] Proceeding further it defines the role of the hierarchy in regard to the counsel-gifts with exactly the same terms it used in describing the attitude of pastors toward the charisms of the Spirit. According to Section 12 of *Lumen Gentium*, pastors are called by the Spirit to discern the authenticity of charisms and to regulate their use.[14] According to Section 43, bishops are called, under the inspiration of the Spirit, to interpret the counsel-gifts (not in order to discern their authenticity which has already been proved by the Church's life, but their meaning *hic et nunc*) and to regulate their practice.[15]

I. Historical Data

1. The Number of the Charisms of Religious life

We must ask at this point what the vocational gifts of the Spirit are that distinguish religious life as a form of Christian life directed toward the welfare of the entire ecclesial community.

The common doctrine in the Latin Church during the last seven centuries is well known, and was repeated by Vatican II which, in *Lumen Gentium*, introduced the theme of religious life by speaking of the evangelical counsels of consecrated chastity, poverty, and obedience,[16] and then referred to them as "the three aforementioned counsels."[17] This definition of religious life as a lifestyle characterized by the profession of the three "counsels" already appears in St. Thomas Aquinas. In his *Summa* he first speaks successively of poverty, perpetual continence, and obedience,[18] and then indicates, in the three related vows, the nature of religious life.[19]

Actually, when St. Thomas Aquinas affirmed this he was propounding a new doctrine. All monastic tradition had expressed itself in other terms. It is therefore useful to study theological developments on this theme.

A. In Descriptions of Monastic Life

Usually the Fathers and theologians of monasticism did not define monastic life; they described it, and mentioned traits which were apt to vary from one author to another. Gregory Nazianzus spoke of poverty, the condition of being like a pilgrim, of being despised, and of celibacy.[20] In the *Apophtegmata Patrum*, Abbot Andrew states that it is typical of the monk to leave his country, to be poor, and to suffer in silence,[21] while Abbot Poemen affirms that poverty, tribulation, anguish, and fasting are the instruments of solitary life.[22] For Abbot Elias the three typical virtues of monasticism are poverty, meekness, and abstinence,[23] while for Abbot John, monasticism consists entirely in suffering (*labor, komos*),[24] probably reflecting the idea that a monk or nun is one who denies oneself in all things (*qui sibi in omnibus vim facit*).[25]

This variety of traits shows that primitive monasticism did not consider certain traits as being more decisive than others in its manner of living a Christian life. For them a monk or nun was a Christian who lived in solitude entirely for the service of God; one, that is, who tried to accomplish the Word of God in one's own life and to live in God's presence in constant prayer. Yet, in the descriptions just cited, there are some significant concurrences. Poverty is present in all the enumerations. *Xeniteia* (being far from one's country and family, the uprooted existence of pilgrims) is mentioned on two occasions. The ascetic view of Christian living predominates: mortification of the body and the spirit through *enkrateia* (abstinence-continence), fasting, meekness, and the acceptance of the numerous sufferings that are the lot of those who want to remain faithful to the Gospel. It is noteworthy that poverty is often mentioned by the first monks, together with other forms of renunciation and causes of suffering. Celibacy is mentioned only once, and that by a bishop: Gregory Nazianzus. For the monks it was an integral part of *xeniteia*.

The cenobites, from Pachomius on, added community life as a special trait of their lifestyle which distinguished it from anchoritism; thus they began to develop a spirituality in which fraternal communion became of central importance. While, in Basil, monasticism is a matter of living according to the Gospel in all its breadth (fraternal communion being one of the aspects of evangelical life), the movement begun by Pachomius's followers culminates, in St. Augustine, in a theology of life dedicated to the divine service, whose central elements are communion of hearts and the sharing of goods.

B. In Monastic Treatises on Renunciation

If we pass from monastic descriptions to the texts which speak of the renouncements a monk must make in order to be what he is, two renouncements are constantly present: that of one's family, and that of one's goods. Perhaps the oldest text is to be found in the *Praecepta* of Pachomius, which direct that, before accepting a postulant, one should ascertain *"utrum possit renuntiare parentibus suis et propriam contemnere facultatem"*[26] (whether he is able to renounce his parents, and to scorn his possessions). In his chapter on renunciation St. Basil recalls the example of the Apostles who renounced their families and their possessions.[27] Evagrius Ponticus, in his *Tractatus ad Eulogium* defines the *xeniteia* of monks as a walking alone, leaving behind one's country, family, and wealth.[28] Finally, Cassian speaks of three renouncements: of wealth, of family, and of all visible things.[29]

That the concurrence, this time, should be almost complete is very significant. For the Fathers of primitive monasticism, monastic life is made possible by renouncing two types of possessions: the family and wealth. One must keep in mind the social context in which they spoke of renouncing their families. In the classical and Hellenistic worlds, marriage was not seen as the establishment of a new nuclear family, but as the continuation of the same patriarchal stock from which one had been born. The wife was brought into the house of one's parents to carry on the family by procreation. Celibacy, therefore, did not consist as it does today in renouncing the formation of one's own family, but in not continuing one's family— consequently renouncing it and leaving it. St. John Climacus shows this clearly when, speaking of leaving one's family as one of the most important aspects of *xeniteia,* he writes that a monk's "father" is the one who can forgive him his sins, his "mother" is compunction for his sins, the "wife" from whom he must never be separated is meditation on death, his "children" are the groans of his heart, his "servant" is his body, and his "friends" the legions of angels.[30]

C. In the Fathers

The Fathers outside monastic circles also linked celibacy and poverty. St. John Chrysostom unites poverty and celibacy in his commentary on I Co. 9:2.[31] St. Ambrose explains the category of *consilium* speaking fundamentally of virginity but, under the influence of Mt. 19:21, he sees poverty also as associated with it.[32] The same association is found in St. Augustine, in two different contexts. In *Contra Celsum,* he adds fasting,[33] thus reflecting the primitive ascetical idea of monasticism. In the *Enarratio in Ps. 103,* on the other hand, he injects his own idea by adding community. In this case, being a monk consists in "not marrying, not being engrossed in the care of one's children, not having a house of one's own, and entering into community life."[34] St. Bernard also lists celibacy and poverty as the two essential traits of a monastic vocation.[35]

D. In the History of Vows

In Chapter IX we shall discuss the history and theology of the vow. At present we will mention only the essential historical data which cast light on the question of the elements that characterize religious life. The Basilian *Asketikon* requires a profession of virginity by the adolescents who, having been educated by the brotherhood, want to continue in it.[36] St. Basil himself would have wished all his monks to make a public promise of virginity as the virgins were doing.[37]

The first one to establish a public ceremony of incorporation into the community, no longer through the reception of the habit but by binding oneself by certain promises, was the anonymous author of the *Rule of the Master* in Italy, during the first half of the sixth century. He asked, at that time, for a public promise of obedience.[38] A few years later St. Benedict included a promise of stability (which, according to the *Rule of the Master,* was supposed to be made by novices at the end of their novitiate, at least as a decision[39]); and St. Benedict added the promise of a *conversio morum:* a promise to live entirely for the Lord. Thus a triple obligation of Benedictine monasticism was born.[40]

E. Approaching the Triad of Poverty-Chastity-Obedience

If one reviews the texts we have quoted, one will notice that the distinguishing traits are often apt to be reduced to three. The texts of Abbot Andrew and Abbot Elias speak of three characteristics. Cassian also speaks of three in the passage mentioned above. Augustine refers to celibacy, poverty, and fasting in one text, and to celibacy, poverty, and community in the other. Later, in the twelfth century, Peter Comestor spoke of "*communis substantia, communis obedientia, communis delectio superna*" as traits of an apostolic life.[41]

It is significant, however, that in composing their triads none of the authors we have quoted associated obedience with celibacy and poverty. Only St. John Climacus in the seventh century does so, when he speaks of the renunciation of all things (poverty), of all persons and relatives (celibacy), and of one's own will through obedience.[42] Latin monasticism initiated the promise of obedience, but there was no explicit promise of celibacy or poverty. Poverty became effective upon the formal renunciation which was required for incorporation.

Only among the Canons Regular, that is, within the tradition of priestly communities born from a movement toward reform, were the vows of celibacy and of community of goods required, together with the vow of obedience. Thus a movement which applied the law of ecclesiastical celibacy more rigorously, and which favored community life for the clergy in order to protect that observance, reached its culmination. It seems that the first time the triad appeared was in the formula of profession pledged by Canons Regular in the Abbey of St. Geneviève in Paris in 1148.[43] It was adopted into the Trinitarian rule in 1198.[44] Perhaps following a suggestion by the Roman Curia, St. Francis included a reference to the triad in his revision of the first version of his rule which had spoken only of the *sequela Christi*. But whereas the Canons Regular spoke of *communio bonorum*, he spoke of poverty: *sine proprio*.[45] The triad, accompanied by the vow of stability, appears in the constitutions of the Dominican nuns of San Sisto in Rome. Finally, in the mid-thirteenth century, Innocent IV stated to the Poor Clares that obedience, poverty, and chastity are "*substantialia cuiuslibet religionis*" (essential elements of every religious Institute).[46] A short time later St. Thomas Aquinas inserted the triad into his theology of religious life as essential elements.[47]

2. The Charisms of Religious Life

We already have at hand a series of data gathered from the history of religious life which will help us understand what the characteristic elements of religious life as a particular form of Christian life really are, and which, according to St. Paul's language and point of view, can be called specific gifts of the religious vocation.

Throughout the various points of view we have encountered, two elements tend to recur with strong emphasis in the life of religious: celibacy and poverty. It is true that the first monks never actually used the term *celibacy*, but it is equally true that solitude or anchoritism was basic to their lifestyle. They were Christians who embraced solitude, went away (*anachorein*) from other human beings, and took upon themselves *xeniteia* in order to dedicate themselves entirely to the Lord's service. This is the fundamental meaning of celibacy. We can actually say that their life of solitude was a radical form of celibacy in which not only the family relationship was eliminated, but likewise all other social relationships. Monasticism, the life and condition of a hermit, essentially meant celibacy. In fact monks continued to call themselves monks even after they were no longer living alone but in a community of celibates.

Poverty as a characteristic of monasticism stands out very clearly in the lives of the fathers. In fact the public act by which they renounced the world and gave themselves to the service of God consisted in publicly renouncing their possessions and distributing them to the poor. Thus it is clear why the texts on monastic renunciation constantly demand the renunciation of one's family and possessions.

On the other hand, obedience is absent in the earliest manifestations of religious life and, precisely, in hermitic life, which the Fathers considered a prototype of monastic life, reserved for the perfect. The anchorites professed solitude. Once formed, they lived by themselves without any interpreter of the divine will except Scripture and their own conscience. The practice of obedience, roughly outlined in the desert by a willingness, now and then, to accept the teaching of another (always on one's own initiative), began to take actual shape within the first communities. It was, in fact, one of the fundamental aspects of community life, as we shall presently see. From these premises one conclusion emerges: that what we understand as religious obedience is a distinctive trait of one form of religious life, cenobitical life; it is therefore not common to all forms.

Should we conclude, then, that the charisms (or in the ordinary language of the last centuries, the "counsels") which create religious life are two: poverty and celibacy? The affirmation would be backed by a long tradition which goes, with slight variations, from Chrysostom and St. Ambrose to St. Bernard. We have already seen how, in the matter of the counsels, Chrysostom and St. Ambrose associate celibacy with poverty.[48] St. Augustine also speaks of them together, though he adds a third element to them, differing according to the case.[49] Even as late as the twelfth century St. Bernard applies the concept of counsel to celibacy, and immediately quotes Mt. 19:21 on poverty.[50] If we follow the line of tradition concerning renouncements typical of monks, we find that there is constant mention of the renunciation of family (celibacy) and of possessions (poverty).

The dyad (celibacy-poverty) is not only traditional (far more so than the triad that adds obedience), but clearly has an evangelical basis. The sayings on *sequela* insist on bringing out the unique value of adherence to Christ as compared to family ties (Mk. 3:31–35; Mt. 10:37) and material possessions (Mk. 10:21; Lk. 14:33). In fact one of the texts (Mk. 10:29 and par.) refers to the objects of both renunciations.

K. Rahner well expressed the meaning of several of Christ's warnings on the dangers of wealth when he considered them in relation to humanity's eschatological situation. God presents, in Jesus, the ultimate offer of salvation and forces us to make a final decision. Thus, according to the teaching of Jesus, a radically decisive situation has arisen in the *kairos,* the acceptable time which the life of Jesus represents for humanity. According to Jesus, the advent of the Kingdom of God in the sense defined above means that human wealth has become a danger and an obstacle in accepting the Kingdom of God in faith, so much so that it is easier for a camel to pass through the eye of a needle than for the rich to enter the Kingdom.[51] We should like to add here that the same original eschatological meaning applies to certain warnings of Jesus on the dangers of family ties (Mk. 13:12; Mt. 10:34–36; cf. Mt. 10:37; Lk. 12:51–53). The *sequela* texts and call narratives move from this eschatological context to affirm explicitly the supreme importance of adhering to Christ beyond every earthly good, and specifically beyond family ties and riches. Certainly it is not a question of these two renouncements alone. One saying speaks of total renunciation of self and of one's own life (Mt. 16:24-26 and par.). The Christian is therefore placed in a situation of suffering, like Jesus, in which the transcendent value of grace becomes visible. But it is likewise true that the logia put special stress on renouncing family ties and material goods as significant expressions of this situation.

Religious life consists in making visible, through one's very lifestyle, the common calling to follow Christ, and that eschatological situation which makes each Christian confront the Kingdom above and beyond all that is good in this world. Thus it is understandable that celibacy and poverty should become distinctive characteristics of religious life. St. Thomas Aquinas, speaking of the counsels characterizing religious life, the profession of which brings the Christian out of the secular condition, was able to list explicitly only celibacy and poverty.[52]

Thus we may conclude that celibacy and evangelical poverty belong to religious life inasmuch as it is a visible incarnation of *sequela* and the expression of the eschatological orientation of Christian existence. Is this fact sufficient to justify speaking of only two vocational charisms: celibacy and poverty? The answer is not as obvious as it might appear.

Going back to the New Testament, the term *charism* (a vocational gift which creates a particular type of Christian existence) was applied only to celibacy. The New Testament never speaks of the charism of poverty. Nor is the problem merely philological. In fact, celibacy and marriage correspond to different gifts, and create an either-or situation. Celibacy is not simply a (higher) degree of the chastity which pertains to Christian life as such and which must therefore exist in marriage, too. Celibacy is a different manner of directing one's existence, of relating to others, of being in communion with God and with one's neighbor. It therefore not only corresponds to a specifically different charism, but is the fundamental gift that creates religious life as a type of existence exclusively oriented toward the Lord and his service.

The question becomes much more complex with poverty. Considering it from a practical point of view we note a profound difference between celibacy and poverty. Whereas the former presupposes a radical suppression of one type of interpersonal relationship, and thus creates a different type of existence, poverty has to do with a relationship with material things. This relationship to possession can only be limited, not suppressed, since the human being survives only through the use, and therefore through the possession, of material things. In fact the process of civilization has been possible thanks to a process of dominion over the earth.

If we now turn our attention to the New Testament we find that, in the lives of Jesus and Paul, and in the latter's doctrine, celibacy results from a particular vocation in the context of evangelical life, while poverty is the common vocation of every disciple. Thus poverty presupposes an actual going beyond earthly goods, and a limitation of their use by simplicity and generosity. Fidelity to Christ (who calls to a specific ministry in the midst of temptations and persecutions) may require the practice of poverty through a total or partial sacrifice of one's material comfort. This was the case of the disciples who accompanied Jesus during his ministry, sharing the discomforts of his uprooted life. But in reconstructing the practice followed by Jesus it would seem that, at least generally, he did not require the renunciation of personal possessions. We spoke of this in the discussion of *sequela*. The important thing for Jesus was that one should seek the Kingdom, not whether one possessed material things.

Passing from the consideration of the practice adopted by Jesus during his ministry to the Gospel as preached by the post-resurrection Church, and specifically to the texts on *sequela* and the call narratives (including the call of the rich man, Mt. 19:21), we already know that these were not intended to create a particular type of Christian life, but to establish a fundamental orientation for the life of each disciple. In applying what we have said regarding the relationship between religious life and the Gospels, we must now conclude that religious, in reading these texts, felt themselves called to express a common element of the Christian vocation in a visible way.

Thus we come back to the history of religious life. This does not offer univocal facts either. The anchorites' poverty, which limited them to what was strictly necessary for survival but allowed them to administer their own revenues, differed only in degree from the poverty of Christian lay people. In fact it seems to us that a high degree of austerity and generosity is possible in secular life without its ceasing to be a life-in-the-world. The same can be said of the radical form of poverty practiced by some religious families; it is practiced also by some married Christians. So we must conclude that poverty alone is not sufficient to establish a particular type of Christian life. It enters only as a qualifying addition to celibacy. In our opinion, therefore, what constitutes a specifically different form of poverty is the community of goods. But this is obviously an aspect of life-in-common, as is obedience. For this reason we prefer to discuss the sharing of goods, as a special form of evangelical poverty, when we speak of community life.

3. From Celibacy to Solitude or to Life in Community

Keeping in mind what has been said, we cannot avoid one conclusion: celibacy constitutes the basic charism of religious life, the one that makes it possible. Those who, embracing celibacy, choose to direct their lives toward the Lord alone, not only on the religious level (the level of faith and love) where the Lord is supreme for all Christians, but also on the level of their lifestyle, are religious in the theological and spiritual sense. Theologically, whoever does thus in the midst of the world, outside any canonical institution, is already a religious. In this basic and essential sense the same is true for members of secular Institutes, as well as for anchorites and cenobites.

However, the basic charism of celibacy is rendered complete by a vocation to practice common evangelical poverty in a special way. The connection between celibacy and poverty is due to the eschatological orientation that celibacy imprints on religious life. There are other charisms too, that complement celibacy, bringing it to a more practical application. These are the gifts that create the various types of religious life. In the life of solitude, preserved in the Eastern Church and foreseen again in the Code of Canon Law now being revised, the charism of celibacy is completed and radicalized by a vocation to anchoritism. The hermit's profession is essentially celibacy and anchoritism. In cenobitical life, the charism of celibacy is completed by a vocation to community life. Although it is true that every Christian (even the hermit) is essentially a being-in-community who, as St. Basil rightly said, must express this community in some way, the religious who is called to a life of fellowship according to the Gospel is embracing a lifestyle clearly different from that which embodies Christian community in the context of family and social relationships. Celibacy and community complete and modify each other. The search for, and accomplishment of, the divine will in communion with one another (obedience) and the sharing of goods are essential aspects of this charism which calls to, and prepares for, discipleship in community. For the members of Secular Institutes, which do not require community life, the charism of celibacy is completed and differentiated by the vocation to remain within secular structures (with the exception of marriage).

II. The Nature of the Charisms of Religious Life

Trusting we have answered the question of the number of charisms proper to religious life, we must now reflect on their nature.

1. Vocational Gifts

A theological reflection on the nature of the charisms of religious life (the one that is common to all its forms, and the ones that are proper to each form) should be prefaced with the observation that we are dealing here with charisms that create a special type of Christian life in the Church.

Charisms are freely distributed by the Lord. The unconstrainable liberty of the Spirit is the first source of the variety of vocations in the Church, not the individual's decision. It is however, true, that since these gifts are intended to create a type of existence, the freedom of the human person is involved. In fact God ordained that we should forge our own lives through a dialogue with God that includes a call and an answer, the offer of a gift and its acceptance.

These gifts characterize a special vocation in the Church, make it possible, and give it visible form. They are not in the realm of the common Christian vocation, but in the realm of the various forms of discipleship. We may, in fact, add that the religious life is neither celibacy, nor anchoritism, nor community life as such. It is born from an all-embracing religious commitment: the commitment to live "exclusively" for the Lord. From this basic element emerge those charisms of religious life that make it possible. First of all comes celibacy, a charism that makes possible a type of life exclusively oriented toward the Lord and qualified only by its relationship with him. Then come the other charisms which determine the various forms of life dedicated to divine service.

2. Ecclesial Orientation

St. Paul's point of view, in explaining the variety of gifts of the Spirit which create different vocations among Christians is well known. The reason for this variety is that the Church, the community of believers, needs apostles, prophets, teachers, and administrators. We can develop his thought without falsifying it by saying that the Church needs celibates and married people, religious and secular people. It needs families, as well as communities whose only reason for being is the Gospel; Christians dedicated to prayer for the Church, and Christians consecrated to evangelization. It needs everyone in order to be able to reveal and realize its potentialities, and to accomplish all the services it has to render to humanity as an instrument of God's grace. From this point of view there is no privileged vocation. The Church needs them all.

In Chapter II we spoke of the ministerial orientation of religious life toward the Church, the visible society of Christ's disciples. Besides the apostolic ministry there are other ministries which the various forms of religious life carry out, all according to their particular gifts, on behalf of the ecclesial community. But in a deeper sense, religious life serves the Church by its very existence. From this point of view celibacy, poverty, and the other charisms that complete the principal one and differentiate the various forms of religious life have their own particular function: they cause religious life to become a visible sign of the presence of the Kingdom, and a meaningful expression of the universal call to follow Christ. This is a profoundly ecclesial fact.

The Church, God's people in their eschatological phase, is the result of God's grace penetrating it from within and giving it life. In Christ the Church is also the visible sacrament of salvific grace, revealing salvation not only as it is offered, but also as it is accepted by the human race. Here grace is already present in history, working effectively through the Word of God and the sacraments. K. Rahner rightly observed that religious life has a particular part in this. Through the charisms of religious life the Church shows that its eschatological faith is directed towards a goal transcending this world. Thanks to religious life, the Church appears visibly as a community animated by God's grace in which grace triumphs.[53] As Vatican II teaches, "This state manifests in a special way the transcendence of the kingdom of God and its requirements over all earthly things, bringing home to all men the immeasurable greatness of the power of Christ in his sovereignty and the infinite might of the Holy Spirit which works so marvelously in the Church."[54]

Thus one understands why, according to the same Council, religious life belongs to the life of the Church and to its holiness.[55] It belongs to the

Church in its pneumatic and charismatic dimension, as a community pervaded by the gifts of the Spirit.

3. Personal Orientation

Although the existence of various vocations in the Church is explained, first of all, by the needs of the community of believers, the choice of one or another state of life corresponds to a personal perception of the best way of achieving one's full human and Christian development. Note that the two aspects are inseparable. Humanly speaking one does not serve the community and grow in personal maturity separately. As one grows, one becomes useful to others, and as one becomes open to others, one grows. On the theological level, the way of serving the Church and the way of attaining perfection fully coincide. The question of vocation takes two forms: in what way does God want me to serve the Church, and in what way does he want me to reach my Christian maturity? It is a matter of finding out which is the best way for me to serve God in the Church and to attain the fullness of love. In theory all ways are open to the individual as equal possibilities. Each state has its own graces. The choice will depend on finding one's own personal calling, shown by one's psychological inclinations and the natural and supernatural gifts received.

4. The Charisms of Religious Life and Sanctity

This will suffice for the subjective side of the question which, in the final analysis, is the one that counts most. A hypothetically more direct approach might prove to be disastrous to some individuals. But having said this, it becomes necessary to look at the objective side of the question. Do the charisms of religious life have a special relationship to Christian perfection? We have already seen that they do, in the sense that religious life is a sign of the triumph of God's grace, of the sanctity that animates and pervades the Church. At this point, however, we are considering the question from a subjective-individual point of view.

Is there a relationship between religious life and the attainment of perfection? Evidently there is, since every form of Christian life is a means of attaining sanctity. It is also evident that religious life must have its own distinctive relationship to the attainment of perfection, since every form of Christian life has such a relationship inasmuch as each tends to embody charity in its own particular way and benefits from its own particular graces. A spouse who is inspired by intense faith is a most efficacious help for one's personal growth: charity is thus aided by the intimacy and closeness of conjugal love. All those who are married have the special grace of the sacrament of matrimony, a grace absent among celibates.

The distinctive bond between religious life and the perfection of charity originates from the very element which constitutes its special character: the fact that religious life is a form of Christian existence defined by its relationship with God and constructed exclusively on this basis. It presents an obvious unification of one's existence in God which, objectively, makes it easier to love God with an undivided heart, and one's neighbor as oneself, as the common vocation of all Christ's disciples requires.

Vatican II repeated this often, echoing an idea of St. Thomas. The idea, however, is very ancient. Tertullian, in commenting on Lk. 17:27-28 ("in the days of Noah people were eating and drinking, marrying wives and husbands. . . . In Lot's day people were eating and drinking, buying and selling. . . ."), said that marriage, and activities directed toward gain, can be an impediment to spiritual life.[56] St. Augustine wrote that one is not freed from sin by virginity, but that one promises one's Liberator something which one could, without sin, not have consecrated to him.[57] The theme that freedom is favored by the charisms of religious life is repeated often in conciliar documents.[58] Some of the texts do not offer any explanation.[59] In the paragraph of *Perfectae Caritatis* dealing with chastity, however, there is a reference to I Co. 7:32-35 which gives us an indication of the orientation of conciliar doctrine. This is shown clearly in a passage from *Lumen Gentium:* "the religious state of life (bestows) greater freedom from the cares of earthly existence."[60] In dispensing with these earthly concerns, the charisms of religious life free the Christian from "hindrances that could hold him back from loving God ardently and worshipping him perfectly."[61]

It is important not to misunderstand the Council's doctrine by giving it a Neo-Platonic or a more generally Hellenistic interpretation through which the service of the Lord becomes possible only by leaving the world and its cares behind. Every Christian is called to fervent charity and to the perfection of divine service. Other Council texts present marriage, raising children, and temporal activities as tasks which Christians assume in obedience to a divine call. Every mode of life has its graces and its particular difficulties. What the Council is affirming here is that religious life's special help on the road to holiness consists in this unification of existence in God, and that through this unification it is easier to attain charity. St. Thomas wrote that the ''counsels'' are not directed toward removing the obstacles which are contrary to charity, but toward those which hinder its actualization.[62]

Behind all this is the idea that in certain cases earthly cares may become obstacles in the practice of love. There is no opposition between the love of God and the love of one's family, between the love of God and the love of humanity to be served through one's profession. By loving people in God, one grows in the love of God. But in practice, since these occupations have a value and meaning of their own outside the realm of faith and divine love, attention to family and professional obligations may cause one to lose sight of their religious significance, thus preventing these duties from becoming effective means for the actualization of charity and consequently of growth toward perfection. Objectively speaking, the unification of one's existence in God through celibacy facilitates the undivided love to which we are all called. This is the measured and realistic teaching of the Council.

One should note that we are speaking of the unification of existence in God, that is, of an objective orientation of one's entire life toward the Lord, and of a life that is exclusively defined by one's relationship with him; we are not speaking of the elimination of reasons for concern. This would apply only to contemplative religious, especially to anchorites who abstract from all exterior activities. Religious who are consecrated to the various ministries of the apostolate or of charity are often busy with many things whose immediate end is not God but neighbor, such as teaching, hospitals, and administration. There is, nevertheless, a basic difference between religious dedicated to the apostolic life and secular Christians. The relationship of religious with their neighbor results *solely* from their relationship with God. It never has a meaning and value in itself, as the conjugal or parental relationship does, nor is it ever as clear-cut. The celibate's love of neighbor becomes a universal love, not bound to particular persons. In the apostolic life, religious change their location and their ministries, but the fundamental orientation of their lives does not change.

5. Charisms, the Church, and the Holy Spirit

The fact that the characteristic traits of religious life can be identified with vocational charisms (as we have seen, this is the only New Testament category that corresponds to them) permits us to see another important and essential aspect of the relationship of religious life to the Church. Religious life "belongs undeniably to the Church's life and holiness."[63] To put it more precisely, it belongs to the charismatic dimension which is basic to the Church. Vatican II spoke of this in *Lumen Gentium*.[64]

Charisms, which, in the broad sense of the term, include not only extraordinary gifts but also permanent vocational gifts, are the fruit of the Spirit's presence and action in the Church. Through them the Risen Lord continues to build up and vivify his Church. The charisms make it possible to realize one's being Church and to serve the community in highly diverse ways.

The Holy Spirit is at the source of all charisms, and hence of religious life.[65] We saw this in the first chapter. It is methodologically incorrect to narrow the relationship of religious life with Christ to the Lord's earthly existence. Religious life was born in the post-resurrection Church as a gift of the Risen Christ, bestowed by him through his Spirit. This is why the pneumatic aspect of religious life is as essential to it as the Christological aspect.

This relationship with the Holy Spirit explains why the charisms of prophecy, and of the spiritual understanding of history destined to renew God's people and bring them face to face with new problems, should have been granted so generously to the Founders.

6. Charisms, and the Charism of Institutes

Being obliged to include all the forms of religious life within one general scheme, we have had to limit ourselves to its common traits (celibacy-poverty, community or anchoritism). But doing so involves the danger that these charisms may lose their actuality. Common charisms are really indivisible parts of the one vocational charism which includes more varied and richer aspects. In the case of Institutes professing a "specialized" form of religious life centered on a specific ministry (intercession, apostolate, works of mercy), the specific gift is often the first one of which the Founders become aware and, around this, the common charisms attain their real significance. Celibacy-poverty and community are connected with a vocation to orient one's life toward prayer, toward evangelizing, or toward the care of the poor or of the sick. This explains the variety of forms in religious life.

Excursus: The Category of Evangelical Counsels

At the beginning of Chapter IV we explained why we prefer the term *charism* to the usual term *evangelical counsel,* which has been regularly used in reference to the distinguishing traits of religious life. In the first place, *charism* is a biblical concept, used by St. Paul to explain the different vocations in the Church. In the second place the idea of *evangelical counsel* raises numerous exegetical and theological problems. In the third place, *evangelical counsel* is systematically connected by St. Thomas Aquinas with the interpretation of religious life as a state of perfection, another problematical concept. It will, at any rate, be useful to summarize here the history of the usage of the term *evangelical counsel,* and to take a look at the problems involved.

1. In the New Testament

Since one speaks of evangelical counsels, one would expect to find the term in the Gospels. Yet in the entire New Testament the term *gnome* (counsel) appears only once, in I Co. 7:25, in regard to virginity, where St. Paul distinguishes between "directives from the Lord" and his own personal counsel. There is no question of a counsel given by the Lord and transmitted by the Apostle, but of a recommendation made by St. Paul. An examination of texts by the Fathers concerning virginity, denying that it is a precept, shows us that the category of counsel was basically inspired by this text of St. Paul, to which Ambrose and Jerome add Mt. 19:21, insisting on the "if you wish to be perfect."[1]

We have said that St. Paul does not speak of a counsel given by the Lord but of his own personal recommendation. The greater portion of the Fathers, as we shall see, were aware of this. As for Mt. 19:21, the excursus after Chapter I has already shown that there is nothing in the passage supporting the idea of a higher counsel. It will be enough at present to remember that according to modern exegesis, particularly after S. Légasse's analysis,[2] the words "if you wish to be perfect" do not refer to a higher degree of Christian life that is only counseled, since in Mt. 19:17 we have: "If you wish to enter into life, keep the commandments." In both cases it is a matter of respect for the individual's decision. The Kingdom is not imposed; it is offered. This explains why the term *counsel* is absent from almost all biblical dictionaries and encyclopedias.[3]

2. Precepts and Counsels

The use of the category of counsel presupposes differentiating between what has been commanded (the Decalogue), and what has not been—that is, what goes beyond the commandments. This differentiation is very ancient. We find it in two texts of the Shepherd of Hermas. A sort of initial hint is even found in the *Didache,* with the affirmation: "If thou canst bear the whole yoke of the Lord, thou shalt be perfect; but if thou canst not, do what thou canst."[4] The context shows that we are still in the midst of the discussion whether Christians converted from paganism were bound to observe the Torah, a problem to which the author gives a solution showing a Jewish tendency: the Christian (even though a Gentile) who observes the entire Torah is perfect. But if he is unable to observe all of it, let him do what one is able to do. The Sheperd of Hermas speaks of precepts and of that which goes beyond the precepts, in two different contexts. In *Mand* IV, 4.2, he says that if the widower remains alone he will receive additional glory, but that he will not sin if he remarries.[5] In *Sim,* V 2.1 and 3.9, he affirms that one is pleasing to God if one keeps the commandments, but that if one does something good beyond what has been commanded, one's glory will be greater.[6]

All later tradition will differentiate between things that are commanded and things that are counseled, as in the two passages of the Shepherd of Hermas where he speaks of what is obligatory and what goes beyond: a) in defining the place of virginity in Christian ethics, adding to it at times the renouncement of possessions (these are the counsels, in the technical sense given to the word by the theology of religious life); b) in exhorting Christians not to limit themselves to the minimum required by the commandments, while at the same time not taking away their peace of mind. The *consilium* is not binding in the same sense that the least of the commandments is binding. The concept of *counsel* is applied, by a certain tradition, to some of the Lord's sayings which are difficult to take literally, such as turning the other cheek, etc.

St. Thomas perceived the profound difference that exists between *consilium* in the former sense (theology of religious life) and the latter sense (moral theology). The former counsels are permanent traits of life, that is, constituent elements of a lifestyle, and are expressed publicly. Their aim is to extricate life from secular structures. Without the counsels, St. Thomas writes:[7] *"tota vita hominis implicaretur negotiis saecularibus"* (the whole of human life would be involved in secular concerns). The latter are acts of virtue (*consilia de melioribus actibus*) whose performance or omission does not alter the manner of one's life. The two types of counsels have only one thing in common: neither is obligatory.

3. Precepts and Evangelical Morality

Behind all this lies a question that is fundamental for an understanding of Christian life: the meaning and value of the Precepts (the Law) in evangelical ethics.

St. Paul's doctrine is well known. He insisted, especially in Romans and Galatians, that a morality based on a Law prescribing what must be done is not Christian. The Christian is no longer under the Law, whose highest expression is the Decalogue. In fact St. Paul is referring not only to ritual prescriptions, but also (and primarily) to the moral law (cf Rm. 7:5,7). The Christian is now subject to grace and to the Law of the Spirit. The law becomes interior and personal. It is the Spirit who suggests to each disciple of Christ what should be done to remain faithful to the grace received. Here we are not dealing with a morality reduced to a universal minimum but with a personal commitment. The Law is simply a pedagogue guiding one to Christ.

St. Paul's affirmations are not primarily to be placed in an ethical context, but in the deeper one from which Christianity, as a spirituality differing from Judaism, and not merely a current within Israel, was born. From whence does our justification come? Does it come from Jesus, his person and his works, or from the observance of the Law? The Apostolic Church reiterated that salvation is given by Jesus. Jesus, not the written Law, has become our Mediator. This affirmation (and it is St. Paul who speaks) has an immediate effect on practical Christian living: we are not primarily justified through the observance of the Law, but through faith in Jesus. The written Law of the Decalogue, the pedagogue and introduction to Christ, is replaced by the Law of the Spirit of Christ living within our hearts. To fulfill the minimum prescribed is far from being the characteristic criterion of Christian existence.[8]

The same problem concerning the relationship of the disciple and the Law is presented in the Sermon on the Mount in St. Matthew's Gospel. The theology in this Judaeo-Christian Gospel differs from that of St. Paul. Jesus did not come to abolish the Law, but to complete it (*plerosai:* Mt. 5:17). But here too, in this different context, the accent is placed on presenting Jesus and his ethico-spiritual message (already seen in Lk. 6:20-49) as going beyond a minimal ethics. Here one speaks of an abundance of justice (Mt. 5:20), in comparison with that of the Scribes and Pharisees, of a justice which goes beyond a mere literal interpretation of the Law. The logia, "You have learnt . . . but I say. . ." tend in the same direction. Among the "You have learnt" that need to be surmounted is the purely minimal interpretation of the Decalogue: do not kill, do not commit adultery, do not break your oath, etc. Against this background of going beyond the Law, even though not abolishing it (which has suggested the concept of a new Exodus and a new Moses), the ideal figure of the disciple, as described in the Beatitudes, is placed. The rabbinical differentiation between the *sadiq* (the just man) who keeps the Law, and the *hasid* (the pious man) who devotes himself to good works, has been superseded. Everything becomes a part of justice, because the new interpretation of the Law goes far beyond a literal minimum.[9]

We discover in the Gospels another way of posing the problem of the relationship of Jesus' disciples with the Law. The problem does not actually concern the ritual precepts of the Torah, but Torah ethics. Hellenistic Jews had already reduced the Torah to the Decalogue, classifying its ritual precepts as "human precepts." Rabbinical schools debated the question concerning which of the commandments was the first and essential one, the source of all the others. The question may appear to be academic, but the whole spirit of biblical ethics depends on the answer given to it.

The Gospels contain two traditions on this theme. The first is found only in the Synoptics, and deals with the twofold commandment of charity as a summary of the Law: Mk. 12:28-34; Mt. 22:35-40; Lk, 10:25-28. In answering the question of a Scribe, Jesus quotes the beginning of the *Shema* (Dt. 6:4-5), but makes an addition which is unusual for his surroundings: "and your neighbor as yourself" (Lv. 19:18). In Luke the answer is given by the Scribe himself, who is then praised for it by Jesus. The second tradition is found in the Synoptics, John, and Paul: love of neighbor sums up the Law: Mt. 7:12; Mk. 10:17-19; Mt. 19:16-19 (adding "love your neighbor as yourself"); Lk. 18:18-20; Jn. 12:34-35; Ga. 5:14.

Putting aside the question of the relation between love of neighbor and love of God, we are at present interested in emphasizing that the Law is summarized by love.

If, taking into account the different contexts, this is the Law of the disciple (the Spirit, the Sermon on the Mount, the precepts of love), there obviously are no "counsels" that go beyond the Law. This was clear to St. Thomas when he considered the counsels in relation to the negative precepts of the Decalogue and to the two precepts of love. While the counsels go beyond not stealing, not killing, or not committing adultery, they cannot go beyond love, on which no limit is placed.[10] In other words, there are certain acts of virtue, or traits of specific Christian vocations, that go beyond a merely literal and minimal reading of the Decalogue. But this minimal interpretation is the one that Matthew insists is not Christian! (And one should note that, with the Gospel of Matthew, we have a Judaeo-Christian approach to the problem.) If the Law consists in loving God with all our heart and our neighbor as ourself, the Law is all-inclusive. If the Beatitudes represent the new interpretation of the Law, it is difficult to imagine that one can go any further. If therefore one wants to use the category of *consilium,* one must conclude that the entire Gospel is actually a *consilium.* This, in fact, is the thought of St. Ambrose, the theologian of the *consilia.*

4. The "Counsels" in Religious Life

Let us now turn our attention to the "counsels" in the context of the theology of religious life. We have seen that the category of *consilium* was practically the only one used from the thirteenth century on in referring to the specific elements of religious life.

The question arose in regard to celibacy and virginity. The Shepherd of Hermas had already said that a widower who remarries does not sin, though he would attain added glory if he did not remarry.[11] Origen came closer to the text of I Co. 7:25 when, in his comment on the Letter to the Romans, he affirmed that Christians do things that go beyond duty, and gave the example of virginity: "Virginity is not embraced through duty, it is not required by a commandment, but it is proposed (*offertur*) as something that goes beyond the commandments.'"[12] St. John Chrysostom, commenting on the logion concerning eunuchs, repeated the same idea:

"Inasmuch as it would have been burdensome to impose virginity with force of Law, he aroused their desire for it. . . . He persuaded them to choose this type of life. . . . He mentioned the eunuchs in order to encourage them. . . . "[13] And again, in his fourth letter to Olympia: "Virginity is such a great thing, and requires such an effort that Christ . . . did not see fit to impose it, nor to raise it to the level of law. . . . He did not make virginity a precept . . . but left the choice up to his followers."[14] St. Jerome shares the same concern: "If Christ prefers virgins, it is because they give, of their own free will, that which had not been required of them."[15] Augustine says: "whoever does not obey a precept is guilty and must undergo punishment. But there is no sin in remarrying; if there were, it would have been forbidden by a precept. No precept exists with respect to virgins."[16]

Whoever is fairly well acquainted with the theology of virginity and marriage during the first five centuries will know why the Fathers felt impelled to repeat so insistently that virginity was not obligatory. They wanted to safeguard the legitimacy of marriage against the numerous and recurring encratite movements, of gnostic or Manichean origin, which were condemning marriage. Their entire culture, with its strongly spiritualistic orientation, tended to minimize the corporeal dimension. Thus the Fathers had to insist that celibacy is not imposed by the Lord, echoing St. Paul's teaching. But, though stating that virginity is not the object of a precept, the Fathers did not ordinarily assign it to any other category. Chrysostom described it with a series of verbs (*arouse the desire, persuade, encourage*) which suggest a particular calling and a gift.[17] Origen had said that virginity is proposed (*offertur*), evidently by the Lord.[18] Jerome[19] and Augustine[20] spoke of a counsel given by the Apostle. In one passage, however, Jerome tends to refer the counsel to Christ: "He says: 'if you wish to be perfect . . .' The great things are always left to the choice of his hearers. For this reason the Apostle does not impose virginity . . . he does not make an obligation of it; so that the will may obtain its reward."[21]

St. Ambrose, on the other hand, systematically used the category of *consilium* in explaining the importance of virginity as well as poverty, attributing it to the Lord, not to Paul. He does so in a long passage of his *De viduis*, in which he quotes both I Co. 7:25 and Mt. 19:21. With St. Ambrose, therefore, celibacy and poverty are not the objects of a precept, but of a counsel that comes from the Lord. It is necessary, however, to note the reason the Saint gives to explain why celibacy and poverty are objects of a counsel: "A precept is given to servants; one gives a counsel, rather, to friends. Where there is a precept, law dominates; where there is a counsel, grace rules."

The counsel, therefore, defines the standard of life proper to Christians, while the Law is proper to the Old Testament. We can conclude that, for Ambrose, the entire Gospel is a counsel of the Lord. Ambrose is eager to show that the Gospel message respects human freedom, treating us no longer as servants, but as friends. The Law was given in order to save nature (hence its minimal character). Grace, instead, draws toward what is good (hence its characteristic thrust toward the highest). For this reason also, celibacy (as well as poverty) are "not imposed, but proposed."[22] Just as Origen, without using the term *counsel,* had said,[23] and as Chrysostom had repeated.[24]

If subsequent theology had preserved the same meaning St. Ambrose gave to the term *consilium,* there would be no danger of misunderstanding in using it. The *consilium* does not exalt one type of Christian life above another. It indicates that Christian life as such is an existence beyond the Law and ruled by the grace of Christ. Thus it explains how vocations such as virginity and the renouncement of possessions may arise in the New Testament, even though they are not the object of precepts. Celibacy and poverty are therefore placed by St. Ambrose in the context of the Sermon on the Mount. They are offered by the Lord (we may consider them a gift and a calling) and are accepted and chosen by his disciples. There is still the need to explain why the *consilium* is given by Christ only to a few of his disciples, introducing the concept of a vocation reserved for a minority.

5. The Precepts of the Lord

The category of *counsel,* even when extended to cover the very essence of the New Testament, was not the only way of referring to what would later become the typical trait of religious life. Rather, in each of the two ways in which it was understood by separate traditions (single acts of virtue transcending the precepts, or traits of life), it is foreign to monasticism.

All the words of the Lord were "precepts," in early monasticism, from the desert Fathers, to St. Benedict, through Cassian and the *Regula Magistri*. It is a "precept" of the Lord to turn the other cheek (this is one of the texts in which the other tradition believes it has found a counsel of the Lord, in the sense of an act of virtue).[25] Humility is the first commandment of the Lord because he said, first of all, blessed are the poor in spirit;[26] even the Beatitudes have become commandments of Christ. It is the Lord's precept to correct one's brother first in secret,[27] and also not to wear sandals.[28]

St. Basil constantly spoke of the traits of his community, including celibacy and poverty, as *praecepta Domini*[29] or *Evangelii dogmata*.[30] It is known that St. Basil liked to define the rule of life he proposed as a faithful observance of the Gospel. Sulpicius Severus also spoke of evangelical precepts when he referred to the renunciation of one's goods.[31] St. Benedict wrote that the subject of the Abbot's teaching should be a life founded not on the counsels but on the precepts of the Lord.[32] St. Jerome was influenced by this monastic tradition when he spoke of those who receive the order to sell everything (*iubentur omni vendere*),[33] as was St. Augustine when he defined celibacy, fasting, and poverty as *praecepta evangelica*.[34]

In monastic tradition all the words of the Lord are *praecepta*, whether they recommend acts of superior virtue like turning the other cheek, or the renouncement of property, or practical ones such as not wearing sandals. One should remember that the Bible was the only rule of life, properly so called, that the monks had. They felt inwardly obliged to observe its pronouncements.

Two dangers were inherent in this way of interpreting the Lord's words: first, that of a great severity based on a literal interpretation; second, that of being unable to explain the situation of Christians who marry and keep their property: can one rightly say that they are not observing all the precepts of the Lord? This problem was solved by Gregory the Great, a monk who had become a bishop, when, in speaking of poverty through renunciation, he sees in it not a general precept, but one addressed by the Lord to a few: *perfectioribus imperatur*.[35] In this way it was possible to keep the category of *praeceptum Domini* (or *evangelicum*) without endangering the status of the secular Christian.[36] This solution was well accepted. We find it at the beginning of the eleventh century at the Council of Aachen.[37] Jonas of Orleans repeats it in *De Institutione laicali*.[38] Here, also, it is a matter of *praecepta specialia*, precepts reserved to certain people.

6. Conclusion

It will be useful to formulate the main conclusions resulting from our historical research:

1) The custom of designating the characteristic traits of religious life as *consilia* became general only from the thirteenth century on. It is foreign to monastic tradition.

2) The reference to virginity, and occasionally reference to the renouncement of possessions, in order to deny that they belong to the category of precepts, is due to the need of defending the legitimacy of marriage and secular life against all messalians, encratites, and in general, all dualistic movements. The category of *consilium Domini* or *evangelicum* was adopted in this context. The need to defend the legitimacy of marriage ceased many centuries ago.

3) St. Ambrose held that the Christian vocation, as such, is a *consilium*. Arguing from grace, and from the Christian's freedom, he explained how the vocation to virginity and the renouncement of material goods could orginate in the Church. St. Thomas Aquinas is basically faithful to this approach when he presents the *consilia* as means toward the attainment of the perfect charity to which the two main commandments call us, placing the *consilia,* at the same time, above the negative commandments. The problem arises when theologians go so far as to identify the observance of the commandments with the general Christian vocation, and limit the counsels to religious life, making it a state of perfection. This does not correspond to New Testament doctrine.

V

Celibacy for the Sake of the Kingdom

Celibacy is without doubt the most decisive characteristic of religious life. Vatican II affirms that celibacy is preeminent (*eminet*) among the manifold counsels proposed by the Lord in the Gospel.[1] In fact the conciliar documents always give it first place.[2] We note that it is the determining factor in creating the type of Christian existence called religious life, not primarily because it has to do with one of humanity's strongest instincts, sexual life and procreation, but because in a deeper sense it has to do with our being-in-relation which constitutes personhood.

In saying this we must, however, keep in mind two facts. First, the expressions of the following of Christ and the ways of witnessing to the Kingdom are not limited to marriage for the laity and celibacy for those who have made a canonical profession of religious life. Toward the end of Chapter I we noted that there is a gradation of forms: the married layperson; the single layperson, the celibate who, although not a religious in the canonical sense, decides to remain single for the sake of the Kingdom; those who unite marriage with a special witness in a lifestyle characterized by poverty and some sort of sharing of goods; and finally, religious in a canonical sense. We are here speaking of celibacy embraced willingly for religious motives. Considering it in this sense, we affirm that celibacy is the first and essential characteristic of what is traditionally known as religious life. We can say that the commitment to celibacy for evangelical reasons is so decisive in forming this type of life that all such commitments made for religious reasons, even outside the canonical state of religious, actually create religious life in a theological and spiritual sense.

At this point, however, a second fact emerges: monasticism apparently did not give any theoretical importance to the profession of celibacy. Descriptions of the basic traits of primitive monasticism mention it only now and then. When the monks began to make public commitments, the promise of celibacy was not included. It appears only in priestly (canonical) communities in the late Middle Ages. We shall later see that this objection is only apparent, since religious have always been celibates; in fact their life and spirituality are fundamentally shaped by celibacy.

I. Celibacy in the Bible and in History

1. The Terminology

Before entering into a discussion of our theme, it will be well to examine the question of terminology. The oldest ecclesiastical texts that speak of celibacy and celibates use the terms *agneia* and *agnos,* literally *chastity* and *chaste.*[3] Thus began a usage that becomes very common: in the language of the Fathers the terms *agnos* and *castus* often refer to those who refrain completely from the conjugal relationship.[4] Theological considerations, however, brought the Fathers to speak of a *castitas coelibum* and a *castitas nuptiarum.*[5] Thus chastity became a general virtue. In his *Summa,* St. Thomas Aquinas speaks of *castitas* in this ordinary sense,[6] and defines *virginitas* as the chastity belonging to those (women and men) who, through fidelity to a decision made for religious reasons, have never voluntarily experienced sexual pleasure.[7] In speaking of the *consilium* professed by religious, he systematically calls it *perpetua continentia,*[8] identifying it with the chastity proper to celibates.[9] Religious legislation generally speaks of "chastity,"[10] interpreting it however, in its comments, as *castitas perfecta* to distinguish it from conjugal chastity. Vatican II speaks of the counsel of *continentia perfecta* in virginity or in celibacy[11] but, referring to religious, it also speaks of *castitas Deo dicata* (chastity consecrated to God), of *castitas propter regnum caelorum* (chastity for the sake of the kingdom of heaven,[12] and of a profession of chastity).[13] On the other hand the Council systematically uses the term ''celibacy'' when it speaks of the state of priests in the Latin Church, defining it as *perfecta et perpetua propter Regnum caelorum continentia* (perfect and perpetual continence for the sake of the Kingdom of heaven).[14]

Vatican II, therefore, has put aside the term *perfect chastity,* and has systematically avoided speaking of ''chastity'' by itself, because in both cases there is a tendency to project a negative idea of marriage. For this reason Vatican II feels obliged to add qualifications that circumscribe the form of chastity professed by religious. For the same reason, however, St. Thomas preferred to speak of ''perfect'' (total) continence. If the Council did not as a rule follow him, it is because this expression places the accent on the physical, genital aspect, whereas the term *chastity* has a broader meaning: it is the virtue which regulates the sexual instinct, subordinating it to a life of faith and consequently excluding any sin. One is chaste insofar as one is free from sin in this matter, not insofar as one abstains from sex. The specific gift of religious life is not essentially a moral quality (a virtue), but a state of life which we designate by the term *celibacy.* What primarily constitutes religious life is this vocation to remain single, renouncing marriage. We are aware, however, that a vow of celibacy could be understood simply as a commitment not to marry, and this would not constitute a new claim for abstention from genital activities beyond ordinary Christian morality. Traditionally, at least from the thirteenth century on, the commitment also implied a promise of a total continence. For this reason, the *Normae secundum quas* of the beginning of the century thus defined the object of the vow: ''One is obliged to observe celibacy and besides, by a new title, that is by virtue of the same vow, to abstain from any act contrary to chastity.''[15] Having taken everything into consideration, the term *celibacy* seems preferable to the others.

2. Celibacy in the Bible[16]

A. In the Old Testament

While, in the Old Testament, virginity in women prior to marriage was praised (Dt. 22:14–29, cf. 2 Sm. 13:20), the idea of virginity or celibacy as a state of life is foreign to Israel's mentality and spirituality. It is significant that the Hebrew language does not have a word to express the idea of celibacy.[17]

A fruitful marriage was the ideal of every Israelite (Ps 30:1-2, 128:1-3), and therefore a woman's childlessness was considered shameful (Gn. 30:1-2; 1 S. 1:5-18; Is. 4:1). The daughter of Jephthah, who was to be sacrificed in fulfillment of her father's vow, wished to go with her friends to weep because she had to die a virgin, not because she had to die in her youth (Jg. 11:34-40).

Throughout the entire Old Testament there are only two cases of renouncing marriage. According to Jr. 16:1-4, God ordered Jeremiah not to marry, and to remain without progeny. The prophet's celibacy was to be a sign of the calamities (death through epidemics, hunger, and war) which he was about to send his people. Thus, in this case, celibacy is associated with death, in opposition to life.

Judith, who had become a widow and was apparently childless, refused several offers of marriage (Jdt. 16:22-24). In this case the renouncement of marriage seems to have been due to her fidelity in love, a fidelity that was stronger than the desire to have descendants. The book of Judith (end of the second century B.C.) strengthens a conclusion we can draw from various facts and tendencies: during the last two centuries before Christ there seem to be scattered rifts in this mentality opposed to celibacy.

B. In Judaism

According to the teachers in Israel, every person is obliged to marry. God's commandment in Gn. 1:28, repeated in his covenant with Noah (Gn. 9:7), applies to all human beings.[18] Since these teachers connect the fruitfulness of the human couple with the creative action of God, whoever does not contribute to the propagation and multiplication (of the human race) is blamed by the Scriptures for having diminished the image (the divine image in him or herself); thus taught Rabbi Jacob I, expressing the common opinion.[19] The rabbis repeat various sayings against celibacy: "He who does not contribute to propagation is like a man who sheds blood";[20] "The man who is without a woman is not a man."[21] A traditional saying gives the celibate first place among the seven types of men whom heaven itself has excommunicated.[22]

Obviously the rabbis were expected to be the first to obey the divine precept. However, some narratives and sayings show that it was entirely permissible for a rabbi to separate himself from his wife, for a time and with her consent, in order to dedicate himself entirely to the study of the

Torah. There is only one example of a rabbi who refrained from marriage, that of Shimon ben Ahaz. Since the other rabbis reproached him for his decision, he excused himself by saying: "My soul is entirely taken up by the Torah, and I have no time for marriage; let the world be preserved by others."[23] In Nb. 12:1,8, Miriam and Aaron complain because Moses had no intercourse with his wife, and was thus failing in his duty. God himself, however, justified Moses' conduct by revealing that he had required continence of him so that he might accomplish his mission.[24] At least in some extraordinary cases, and in relation to a special mission, God granted exemption from the law of procreation.[25]

C. In the New Testament

In Jesus' time the situation changes. The Essenes,[26] a sect characterized by a belief in the impending final intervention of God, and therefore convinced that they were living in the final days, seem, according to the information handed down by Pliny[27] and Josephus,[28] to have practiced celibacy. The *Manual of Discipline* at Qumran seems to foresee a community without women, but the *Rule of the Congregation* speaks of women and children, and lays down some rules for sexual behavior;[29] Josephus is acquainted with some married Essenes.[30] The Essene movement probably embraced both celibates and married people. And John the Baptist, a prophet who was likewise convinced that the eschatological judgment was imminent, seems to have been a celibate.

As for Jesus,[31] the Gospels do not explicitly state that he was either married or a celibate. It is significant, however, that, while his mother and his "brothers" are specifically mentioned during his public life (Mk. 3:20–21, 3:31–35, 6:3), there is never any reference to a family of his own. His spirituality and rule of life are those of a person without ties, consecrated to preaching the Kingdom (Mt. 8:18–19; Lk. 9:57–58); his family is composed of all those who do the will of the Father (Mk. 3:34–35). One should also note that in his case we are dealing with a strong eschatological orientation (Mk. 1:14–15). To suppose, therefore, as some have done, that since Jesus was a faithful observer of the Torah he must have been married, is to ignore a whole series of indications given in the New Testament and to forget the context in which he lived and worked. On the other hand to imagine, as more often happens, that his celibacy was the inevitable consequence of his being the Son of God, is to go beyond the idea of the

Incarnation which the New Testament gives us: a man like us in all things except sin (Rm. 8:3; Ga. 4:4; Ph. 2:7; Heb. 2:17; Heb. 4:15). The celibacy of Jesus was the result of his own choice, motivated by his exclusive dedication to his mission. Thus his celibacy becomes significant for those of his disciples who recognize themselves in the same personal vocation.

In Chapter I, in examining the discipleship texts, we saw that although Jesus was a celibate, and had required from his disciples a profound orientation of faith and love untrammeled by family ties, he showed great freedom of spirit in regard to their state of life. Peter, an eminent figure among the first disciples, was certainly married, and the same was probably true of most of those who followed Jesus. Among the sayings of Jesus recorded by the Synoptics, only one sentence can be referred to voluntary celibacy embraced for the sake of the Kingdom (Mt. 19:12). Paul says that he had not received any instructions from the Lord in regard to virginity, either for men or for women (I Co. 7:25), but that he himself had decided to remain single (I Co. 7:7), thus creating an exception to the rule that had generally been followed by the Apostles, among whom he specifically mentions Peter and the "brothers of the Lord" (I Co. 9:5).

3. Examination of Certain New Testament Texts

Turning our attention from history as it can be reconstructed through the texts, to the very idea of celibacy which the New Testament[32] proposes to us, we should study particularly two passages: Mt. 19:2-12 and I Co. 7. But first we should rapidly glance at a series of minor texts which are often quoted in connection with celibacy though they do not have a direct connection with the theme.

A logion originating from Q requires the disciples' hatred for father and mother, and for son and daughter (Mt. 10:37). Luke is more explicit, adding wife, brothers, and sisters (Lk. 14:26). This is obviously an explanatory addition; the original saying intends to speak of family ties, not only those of parents and children, leaving out the wife. Another saying recorded by Mark (Mk. 10:29) asks for the renunciation of one's "house," brothers, sisters, father, children, and land. To this Matthew (Mt. 19:29) adds "mother," while Luke (18:29) adds "wife" immediately after "house." Here, also, we are faced with a clarification, because the renouncement of one's "house" in the original text would seem to refer to one's wife also. Whatever Luke intended in making this addition, we will not stop to consider these texts because, as we believe we have shown in Chapter I, they do not require a renunciation that influences one's lifestyle. Otherwise, on reading these sayings, one would have to conclude that either Jesus or the Church had imposed celibacy as a condition for discipleship, and this is a totally false conclusion.

Another saying, belonging to the tradition represented by Mark (Mk. 12:25; cf. Mt. 22:30 and Lk. 20:34–35) compares the condition of those who, on rising from the dead, will not marry with that of the angels. Obviously this saying refers to the resurrection in order to reaffirm its reality, but at the same time to deny that it will be a repetition of our present state: "When they rise from the dead, men and women do not marry; no, they are like the angels in heaven." So say Matthew and Mark. Luke (20:34–35) gives us a somewhat different version, underscoring the contrast between the present world and the future one of the resurrection: "The children of this world take wives and husbands, but those who are judged worthy of a place in the other world and in the resurrection from the dead, do not marry because they can no longer die, for they are the same as the angels, and being children of the resurrection they are sons and daughters of God."

We are facing here a clear distinction between the two aeons in apocalyptic thought: marriage belongs to the present aeon which is ruled over by death, but has no place in the structure of the other aeon which begins with the resurrection. The text, even in Luke's version, does not directly consider the possibility of a celibacy that would anticipate the eschatological situation. It cannot, therefore, be taken as a justification for the vocation to celibacy in the Church on earth. It is true, though, that it can suggest one of the meanings of celibacy that is undertaken in obedience to a vocation which finds its justification elsewhere: celibacy would then appear as an anticipation of the eschatological condition. We will return to this theme later on.

Finally, the text in Rv. 14:4 ("the ones who have kept their virginity, and not been defiled with women; they follow the Lamb") is generally interpreted in the biblical sense of prostitution and adultery as synonyms of idolatry. It is a reference to those who have not submitted to the worship of the Beast.

4. Eunuchs for the Sake of the Kingdom[33]

A. The Pericope

Thus we come to the logion recorded exclusively by Matthew (Mt. 19:12) on the three types of eunuchs: "those who are such by nature, those who are made so by men, and those who have made themselves so for the sake of the Kingdom of Heaven." This saying is found in the context of the controversy between Jesus and the Pharisees on the subject of divorce. In Mark's version (10:1-12) it is merely the question of an aspect of Christ's doctrine. While he was teaching the crowds, some Pharisees asked him whether a man could lawfully divorce his wife. Jesus questioned them on the instructions given them by Moses, and they answered that Moses permitted them to give a writ of divorce. In the second part of the conversation, in an increasingly polemical tone, Jesus says that Moses had given them that precept because of the hardness of their hearts; he then refers to the original condition of man and woman in Gn. 2:24 (the scriptural argument), and concludes that it is not lawful for human beings to divide what God has united. At this point the public discussion finishes in Mark. But on returning home, in answer to a further unspecified question from his disciples, Jesus explains that a man or woman who is divorced and remarries commits adultery. The statement is absolute, and thus the narrative ends.

In Matthew's version some new elements appear, a few of which are very important. In the first place the Pharisees approach Jesus "to test him"; the polemical atmosphere is present from the beginning. In the second place the story is constructed in three phases, each consisting of a question-objection and an answer of Jesus. The polemical tone increases. In the first phase the testing Pharisees ask whether it is lawful for a man to divorce his wife "on any pretext whatever." The question put in this way seems to be in the context of a rabbinical discussion, and seems to admit the legality of divorce in some cases. Jesus answers from the outset by citing the indissoluble unity of a couple according to Genesis. In the second phase the Pharisees counterattack by quoting the Law of Moses. Jesus answers by giving the reason based on the hardness of their hearts, recalls again the original rule, and issues the condemnation of a second marriage of divorced people as adultery; this, in Mark's version, was expounded privately to his disciples.

In Matthew, however, a new clause is inserted, whose interpretation has consumed rivers of ink: "I am not speaking of fornication." (Does this mean "except" or "even"?) Some have thought that "fornication" referred to an illegitimate union, in which case there would be no real exception. Others maintain that Jesus accepted here the possibility of divorce in case of adultery; but this would weaken his affirmation of the original unity, and would be equivalent to showing that divorce is permissible in some cases. Others favor the translation: "even in the case of adultery," thus excluding all possibility of divorce, even in this extreme case. Modern exegesis has almost completely abandoned Dupont's theory, according to which this clause would permit separation without remarriage in case of adultery. In the third phase the disciples (not privately here) object: "If that is the way things are . . . it is not advisable to marry." To this Jesus replies with his famous logion on the three kinds of eunuchs, preceded and followed by two equivalent sentences: "It is not everyone who can accept what I have said, but only those to whom it is granted (by God). There are eunuchs born that way, . . . and there are eunuchs made so by men, and there are eunuchs who have made themselves that way for the sake of the kingdom of heaven. Let anyone accept this who can."

B. The Original Meaning of the Saying

The logion on the three types of eunuchs, which is omitted in Mark's parallel narrative was, to all appearances, added by Matthew rather than suppressed by the second Evangelist. J. Blinzer[34] claims that it was an already-existing saying which Matthew incorporated into the discussion on matrimony. The historical background for the saying should be found in the controversy between Jesus and the Pharisees concerning, in this case, the Lord's celibacy. Earlier we referred to some rabbinical sayings against celibacy which went so far as to state that the celibate was rejected by heaven itself. Having been called a glutton, a drunkard, and the friend of tax collectors because of his ministry among public sinners, Jesus was probably mocked as a "eunuch" because of his celibacy. The epithet was extremely offensive among Jews, even more than among Greeks. The Greeks, in fact, were familiar with many cases of ritual castration, while among the Israelites mutilation rendered not only men, but also animals, unfit for worship (Lv. 22:24). Jesus would hardly have used the offensive term "eunuch" in a context of positive praise unless it had been hurled at him in the midst of a controversy. In answer to this insult, Jesus would have pronounced his famous saying on the three kinds of eunuchs, those who are born so, those who are rendered so by others, and finally those who, like himself, choose to be so for the sake of the Kingdom.[35] In its original context, therefore, this saying would be a reaffirmation of the legitimacy of the celibacy which Jesus had chosen for himself, and an explanation of its religious motive.

C. The Meaning of the Saying in the Pericope

Having very probably been inserted by Matthew into the controversy over divorce, what meaning would this saying on eunuchs have in its actual context?

Traditionally, from St. Justin up to several exegetes of our own times, Jesus would be taking up his disciples' statement (to be translated as: "it is better not to marry") giving it a new and deeper meaning which reveals another possibility: to remain single for the sake of the Kingdom. The passage would proceed this way: "His disciples said to him: 'If this is the situation for men (indissolubility) it is better not to marry.' He answered: 'It is so, even though not everyone understands this word (which you are saying). Because there are eunuchs. . . .' ''

This interpretation has now been abandoned by a certain number of critics, because through it the pericope loses the unity of its structure. A new theme, that of celibacy is suddenly introduced, and one imagines that Jesus is playing upon the negative reaction of his disciples, accepting it, but with a different meaning.

In his *Mariage et divorce dans l'Evangile,*[36] J. Dupont offers a different interpretation which has been accepted by some exegetes and, above all, by theologians of religious life, after Q. Quesnel's re-examination of the whole question in 1968.[37] This interpretation was followed, even before Quesnel, by T. Fleming,[38] and after him, by W. Harrington and J. M. Van Cangh, and has been set forth favorably by Ortensio da Spinetioli.[39] Among theologians of religious life it has been adopted by J. M. F. Tillard and L. Gutiérrez Vega.[40]

According to this interpretation the "eunuchs for the sake of the Kingdom" would be those who, having been separated from their spouse, do not remarry, in obedience to God's word on the indissolubility of marriage. The possibility of accepting this Word for oneself depends entirely on grace. In support of this interpretation various reasons are adduced. First of all, it respects the tripartite structure and the ascending rhythm of the whole passage, in which each objection encounters a still more vigorous stand on the part of Jesus. Secondly, a saying in favor of celibacy would seem more typical of Luke (who does not record it). In fact Luke always includes the renouncement of a wife in the discipleship sayings (Lk. 14:26, 18:29). He stresses the contrast between the two aeons by affirming that marriage belongs to one, and not to the other (Lk. 20:34); he compares the Kingdom to an ordinary banquet (Lk. 14:15) and includes, among the excuses for not attending it, the fact of just having been married (Lk. 14:20).

But a saying on celibacy is more surprising in the Judaeo-Christian context of Matthew, who never explicitly lists the renouncement of a wife in his discipleship texts (Mt. 19:29; 10:37), who does not list the fact of getting married among the excuses for not accepting the invitation (Mt. 22:2–14), and who compares the Kingdom specifically to a wedding feast (*gamos:* Mt. 22:2).

Yet there is one main difficulty—apparently an insurmountable one—against this interpretation of the eunuchs as being separated spouses who cannot remarry: modern exegesis almost unanimously rejects the idea that the clause ''I am not speaking of fornication'' foresees separation without the possibility of remarriage. For the eunuchs to be separated spouses who do not remarry one must accept that interpretation of the clause.

There is, however, a third interpretation, according to which the saying concerning eunuchs refers indirectly to celibacy. That is, that the example of celibates would be adduced by Matthew as a more difficult situation than that of married people who cannot dissolve their marriage. It would not be that Jesus was appropriating, though with a different meaning, the negative reaction of his disciples to his words. Rather, he would be reaffirming what he had said on the indissolubility of marriage, and would be offering as an example the more difficult case of celibates, in order to show that it is possible.

The meaning of this last part of the pericope would be as follows: ''Not everyone can understand this word (my word concerning indissolubility), but only those to whom it is granted by God. Look about you; just as there are eunuchs from birth, and eunuchs made so by men, so there are eunuchs who make themselves so for the sake of the Kingdom of Heaven. Whoever can accept this, let him accept it.'' Thus Matthew would retain the provocative and offensive saying on the eunuchs in its original sense, and use it as a persuasive reason, or at least as an example. The polemical tone of the whole pericope retains all of its growing crescendo, and the saying keeps its original meaning. If this is true, we can note a similarity in construction between the pericope on the calling of the rich man and this one on indissolubility, which precedes it. In Mt. 19:16-27, following the affirmation of Jesus, "It is hard for a rich man to enter the kingdom of heaven," there is the disciples' discouraged reaction, "Who can be saved, then?" To which Jesus replies: "For God everything is possible." After this there is the encouraging example of those who have left everything to follow Jesus (Mt. 19:27). In Mt. 19:3-12, after the statement on indissolubility, came the negative reaction of the disciples: "It is not advisable to marry." In this case also, Jesus answers that acceptance of the Word on indissolubility is a grace from God (to those "to whom it is granted") and this is followed by the example of celibates to demonstrate this possibility concretely and forcefully.

All things considered, it seems to us that this third interpretation is to be preferred.

5. Celibacy and Virginity in I Co. 7

There is a long treatise in First Corinthians on celibacy, and on the significance of celibacy and marriage with respect to each other. In the second part of this letter, starting with Chapter 7,[41] the Apostle answers various questions posed to him by the Christians at Corinth. Judging from the context it would seem that in that community there were two tendencies in sexual matters, one permissive, the other of an ascetico-spiritual type, favoring continence. It is quite possible that the two tendencies were two manifestations of the same gnostic (or pre-gnostic) mindset in Corinth. We know that gnosis expressed its indifference toward the body either by permissiveness or by ascetical renunciation. St. Paul's teaching in this text is not, therefore, a simple doctrinal affirmation, but a concrete answer to an actual situation. Since we cannot take time here to analyze the whole chapter, we will consider only those statements which more clearly show St. Paul's doctrine on celibacy, leaving the rest to the commentators.

I Co. 7:1 seems to repeat a question posed by the Corinthians: "Is it a good thing for a man not to touch a woman?" Note the emphasis on the physical aspect of sexual continence. Paul, a celibate for the sake of the

Gospel, but aware of the different ideological background of the Corinthians, answers yes, "but since sex is always a danger, let each man have his own wife and each woman her own husband." This is obviously a general rule, not a law for everyone, since the celibate Paul continues by praising celibacy. In fact, after laying down some rules on married life which are inspired by a healthy realism (I Co. 7:3–7), Paul tells widows and celibates that "it is a good thing for them to stay as they are." This affirmation appears to contradict Gn. 2:18: "It is not good that man should be alone." Evidently we have here a re-examination of the human condition in the light of paschal mystery. In the new community created by the Risen Lord it is indeed possible and good for men and women to remain unmarried, since they are not alone (I Co. 7:8–9).

I Co. 7:7. Paul shows his (personal) preference for celibacy: "I should like (*thelō* expresses a desire, not a decision like *boulomai*) everyone to be like me, but everybody has his own particular gift (*charisma*) from God, one with a gift for one thing and another with a gift for another." The will of the Lord, who alone distributes his charisms, is above Paul's individual preferences. It is therefore obvious in these texts that Paul considers marriage and celibacy as fruits of the various charisms God bestows on the various categories of Christians for the common good. One does not marry or choose celibacy according to one's own will, but in obedience to a vocational gift.

I Co. 7:25–40. Hitherto Paul has not explained why it is desirable to remain single, or why he prefers celibacy. He does so in this section, adducing both an eschatological and a Christological reason.

V. 25: First of all, to avoid equivocation, he stresses that he has not received any directions (*epitagé*) from the Lord; he himself is giving advice, "as one who, by the Lord's mercy, has stayed faithful." It is therefore a matter of Paul's personal opinion, based on his own experience.

Vv. 26–31: The eschatological reason. Paul explains why one should stay as one is (without changing one's state of life): "in the present times of stress" (*anagke:* the great final crisis), in order to escape the imminent "tribulations" (*thlipsin*) of the last times (cf. Mk. 13:19; Mt. 24:21–29), because "time is growing short." *Anagke* is a technical term in apocalyptics, as is *thlipsis*. From Paul's examples—"if you are tied to a wife, do not look for freedom; if you are free of a wife, then do not look for one''—it is clear he is speaking of not changing one's state in life, not merely of remaining single, because in view of the end-time everything becomes relative. Putting it this way, the eschatological argument in favor of celibacy is weakened. But it is also true that, because if it is the end, celibates are more fortunate. They will be spared the tribulations of the flesh during the last days. One should keep in mind that the division of families and the sufferings of relatives during the great final crisis is a frequent theme in apocalyptics.

We know that Paul, as well as all of the primitive Church, believed the Lord's *parousia* was close at hand. In his earlier writings he reflects the opinion that the Lord would return before his death (I Th. 4:15–18; 5:23; cf. 1 Th. 1:9–10; 4:13; 5:11; 2 Th. 1:4–10). When he was writing his first letter to the Corinthians, the idea of the imminent *parousia* was still very much alive (1 Co. 15:51–52), even though the death of some Christians before the Return had already been experienced. Later he seems to be reconciled to the idea of his approaching death (Phm. 1:23).

Given this situation, one might raise the objection that, if Paul's doctrine on celibacy is connected with the idea of an imminent end, it cannot be accepted as a permanent message, valid for successive generations. This conclusion would be false for two reasons: first, because Paul gives a Christological (and ecclesiological) motive that remains always valid; second, because his affirmation regarding the relative importance, in an eschatological sense, of all earthly things including one's state in life or social situation, remains valid apart from the proximity of the End.

According to Paul, after the resurrection Christians are living in the *eschaton;* it is the resurrection of Jesus that has brought about a new existence in which all earthly values have become relative. Not even celibacy, as a concrete lifestyle, has a decisive importance, although Paul prefers it: if you are married, do not try to free yourself (v. 27). The idea of freedom in regard to everything that is not Christ and faith in him, which is so dear to St. Paul, is also revealed in his basic attitude of indifference (notwithstanding his personal preferences) concerning a state in life. It is evident though that the eschatological character of Christian existence, inaugurated by Christ's resurrection, renders celibacy both possible and praiseworthy.

1 Co. 7:32-34. In these verses St. Paul, by an antithetical parallelism, compares the existential situations of celibates and those who are married: first from the man's and then from the woman's point of view. "An unmarried man can *devote himself* to the Lord; but a married man has to *bother about* the world's affairs, and *devote himself* to pleasing his wife." It is clear that the Apostle is speaking to Christians about two types of Christian existence; the whole discourse (cf. v.7) shows this. As the context shows, the term *merimna* ("devotes himself" or "to bother about") points toward the characteristic occupation of a certain type of life, and not to a purely incidental occupation. It does not specify what "the Lord's affairs" to which the celibate dedicates himself may be; but to us, on the basis of Paul's own experience, it seems to mean the Church, and more specifically in this case, the preaching of the Gospel. The term "to please" (*areskein*) has a strong meaning in St. Paul: it means a manner of life directed toward the will of (the risen) Christ (1 Th. 4:1) or, in the case of the neighbor, toward his welfare; it is opposed to pleasing oneself, selfishly seeking one's own welfare or one's own satisfaction (Rm. 15:1-3). Thus the celibate lives for love of the Risen Christ.

The problems begin when we come to Paul's description of the married situation: married people (Christians, we must not forget) are busy "with the world's affairs"; that is, they are dedicated to secular pursuits and to the love of their spouses. In view of the parallelism, one would have expected to find: busy "with the affairs of his wife...." Here "the world" (not "this world" which in St. Paul has always a negative sense) has a positive meaning; and yet, by contrasting it with "the Lord's affairs," the Apostle intends to point out its transitory and earthly character. It is probably for this reason that he writes "the world's" affairs, and not "his wife's" affairs. Marriage belongs to this aeon. To devote oneself to pleasing one's spouse means a life dedicated to that particular love.

As we already said, this gives rise to some difficulties. It is clear that the affairs of the Risen Christ are understood by St. Paul in the strict sense of ecclesial ministry, of preaching the Gospel. In a broader, but equally correct sense, marriage is one of "the Lord's affairs," and a service to the Church. It became such, above all, when the Church became aware that it was not only called to announce and prepare for the *parousia* (thought to be imminent), but also to perpetuate throughout history the announcement of the Good News. Obviously the Apostle did not intend to say that married

Christians' lives are dedicated *only* to love of their spouses, and not to the love of the Lord. If that were so, the Christian would not be free either to marry or remain single, as the whole passage keeps repeating. What St. Paul affirms is that conjugal love is a distinctive trait of this type of Christian life, while celibates live *only* for the things of the Lord and for his love. This "living only for. . ." is the distinctive trait of their lives. Note that, in translating the idea into feminine terms, St. Paul no longer speaks of "pleasing the Lord," but of "being holy in body and spirit." It is the question of womanly devotion to the Lord, according to the social role of women at his time.

A second difficulty is encountered when we read the final statement of verse 33: "he is torn two ways." Obviously, if he is torn two ways, it is because of this dedication to worldly matters and to pleasing his spouse. There is a division between two forces, one impelling toward pleasing the Lord, and the other pulling back toward conjugal love and worldly pursuits. St. Paul well knows which is the first commandment: "to love God with one's whole heart." All must love God with their whole heart, that is, with a heart that is undivided. For Israel, however, the love of God includes every other legitimate love of his creatures, and first of all, of one's family. There are two types of love that belong on different levels. Obviously the Apostle is not saying that conjugal love causes a division of the heart in a theological or religious sense. He is simply noting a fact: a spouse, or anyone occupied in earthly pursuits, often experiences a tension. If Paul had meant to speak of a division of heart in the theological sense, marriage would no longer be lawful; and for St. Paul it is.

6. Virginity in the Hellenistic Church

The first references to virginity or male continence outside of the New Testament already show a certain change in perspecitve.[42] The earliest such reference is in Clement of Rome's *Epistula Prima ad Corinthios:* "He who is continent must not put on airs."[43] Chaste (*agnos*), originally "sacred," is taken here in the most ordinary sense of "not defiled," "virgin." St. Ignatius Martyr follows Clement of Rome closely in writing his letter to Polycarp: "If anyone can live in chastity for the honor of the Lord's flesh, let him do so without ever boasting."[44] Both texts refer to physical continence, even though it is embraced for religious motives. The accent is already on the physical. Both texts also reveal a fear that ascetic continence could lead to pride and, in Ignatius's text, to rebellion against the bishop. We are already in an encratite environment which placed great value on asceticism, and especially on sexual continence. This group of ascetics might constitute a danger to the unity of the Church, which was held together by a clergy who were usually married.

In Clement of Alexandria we find another warning, which already hints at the struggle against gnostic dualism: "One has left the way of salvation if one renounces marriage through hatred of the Creator and creation."[45] However, he also stresses the physical aspect: "It is beautiful to free oneself from concupiscence for the sake of the kingdom of heaven,"[46] but continence is a virtue only if embraced for the love of God.[47]

The number of those who embraced virginal continence in the Church of the Fathers became ever greater. Thus, beginning with the third century, a rich literature on virginity developed: Tertullian and Cyprian in Africa, the *Epistulae ad virgines* of the Pseudo-Clement of Syria, the *Symposium* of Methodius of Olympus in Asia Minor and, in Alexandria, the lost treatises on continence (*enkrateia*) by Clement and by the heretic Julius Cassian.[48] During the fourth and fifth centuries the tradition was enriched and amplified by Athanasius, Basil of Caesarea, Basil of Ancyra, Gregory of Nyssa, Chrysostom, Ambrose, Augustine, Jerome, etc.

It is not easy to summarize the development of Patristic thought on virginity in a few lines.[49] The following elements, however, seem to be the most common: 1) female virginity predominates; 2) virgins, together with widows, have a public position in the Church, exercise certain ministries, and so their virginity is given significance in the community and in the Church—some texts comparing virginity to martyrdom, inasmuch as it is a public witness;[50] 3) the theme of nuptial consecration to Christ is developed (the virgin reserves both spirit and body for the Lord); 4) although set in the context of faith and love, the integrity of the body is stressed, following the Greek and Roman tradition.

Tertullian and other African writers began to speak of *virgines sanctae*,[51] consecrated to God by the very fact of their physical integrity; and *velatio* or *benedictio virginum* became their "*consecratio*," a term that prevailed.[52] One realizes that, within certain tendencies, the fact of physical integrity had gained the ascendancy, since Tertullian refers to all unmarried women, even those who do not intend to remain virgins, as *sponsae Christi*.[53] We are confronted here with the Greek and

Roman concept of the adolescent or the virgin having a special relationship with divinity, a concept also found in other cultures.[54] Among Judaeo-Hellenists, Philo liked to repeat that God unites himself only with virgins,[55] although he was transferring the concept to an ethical and spiritual level.

7. Angelic Chastity and Adam's Virginity

A proof of the orientation celibacy had taken in Hellenistic Christian surroundings, where domination over one's body and physical integrity had acquired a value they do not have in the New Testament, is to be found in the theological traditions on virginal chastity as bringing about a resemblance to the angels, and representing the original human condition.

Monasticism is often called ''the angelic life'' because, by constant prayer, the monks imitate the angels who are always in the presence of God.[56] However the monks wanted to imitate the angels by constraining their bodies,[57] and above all by sexual continence.[58] John Cassian writes that there is no virtue that can make carnal man equal to angelic spirits.[59] In Serapion's text we are dealing with an anticipation of the eschatological condition; thus celibacy is placed within the biblical perspective of the history of salvation. In the other texts it is a question of rising into the superior sphere of spirits, following an ontological mentality which is typical of Neo-Platonism and of gnosticism. It is evident that, in this context, the orientation here stressed is not so much one of love as of dominating one's passions.

We must come to the same conclusion when, in examining Patristic treatises on virginity, we are led to consider virginity as a return to the condition of the first man and woman, and marriage as a consequence of our fall. In fact, these treatises say, Adam and Eve were virgins in Paradise, and had relations with each other only after they sinned. This affirmation, hinted at in the second century Acts of Andrew,[60] is repeated by Gregory of Nyssa,[61] by John Chrysostom,[62] and by Jerome.[63]

Thus arose the disputed question of how human beings would have reproduced themselves if they had not sinned, a question to which there are various answers, according to St. Augustine,[64] and which Gregory of Nyssa resolves in a rather curious way: if human beings had not sinned, they would have multiplied like the angels through their minds. He could not, however, ignore the fact that God created them male and female in

Paradise. To this he answered that God did so because he already foresaw that human beings would sin, and would consequently have to reproduce themselves like animals.[65] Now this statement is extremely important. We know, in fact, that in all primitive and ancient cultures the original situation of our kind was meant to express the true nature of humanity. The Fathers interpreted Paradise in this sense: paradise shows the real essence of humanity. In this context, to affirm that Adam and Eve were virgins in Paradise, and to affirm that there would have been no sexual relations had there been no sin, is tantamount to excluding sexuality and marriage from the true nature of humanity. Real humanity as God intended it is attained only in virginity, and sexual relations are an expression of the historical decadence of the human race.

This places us in the midst of a spiritualistic anthropology; in fact these texts compare the first human beings to angels. Since all spiritual life tends toward a return to the true human nature as it existed in Paradise,[66] virginity appears to be the logical means of attaining this end. Gregory goes so far as to say, "Inasmuch as marriage was the last step in the departure from the life of Paradise, renouncement of marriage is the first step that must be taken by anyone who sets out towards Christ."[67] This is no longer the evangelical and Pauline viewpoint of celibacy embraced as service, but the viewpoint of a non-biblical anthropology in which renouncement of sexuality is seen as a means for reestablishing the true human reality. This explains why marriage was considered a divine condescension toward the weak.

II. Theological Reflection

We now have at hand the data on celibacy which have been provided by the Word of God in the New Testament and by its interpretation in the Church's history. It is time to reflect on these data.

1. Celibacy, Not Simple Continence

The first conclusion which one derives from a study of the New Testament, especially when one compares it with the practice of the Hellenistic world, is that no text of the New Testament presents continence, abstention from sexual relations, as something that has a meaning and value in itself. In the New Testament, even in those segments of it closest to Hellenism, one does not find that opposition between spirit and flesh, between spiritual progress and physical fulfillment, which is typical of Greek thought and which practically all Hellenistic spiritual movements so insistently emphasized.

Chastity, the subjection of the body and its instincts to the Word of God, is certainly an evangelical virtue. Forbidden, therefore, are adultery, even of desire within the heart (Mt. 5:28), incest (1 Co. 5), relationships with prostitutes (1 Co. 6:12-20), fornication (1 Co. 6:18; 2 Co. 12:21; Ga. 5:19; Ep. 5:3). It is possible to sin in sexual love, just as it is possible to sin in any other aspects of human life. St. Paul points out, however, that all other sins are committed outside the body, while impurity is a sin against the body itself, the temple of the Holy Spirit. In all this we are within the confines of an abuse of sexual activity; nowhere in the New Testament is normal sexual activity opposed to life in the Spirit. The anthropology of Genesis 1 and 2 continues to guide the morals and spirituality of the New Testament.

We have seen, however, that little by little the Hellenistic opposition of spirit to matter, of soul to body, conditioned the preaching of the Fathers to such an extent that they identified the original state of Adam and Eve (man and woman according to God's will, before they sinned) with virginity, male or female. In certain texts continence (not celibacy) became an efficacious means for spiritual progress, while marriage was destined to be reduced from the category of a divine vocation to the state of those who are unable to practice continence.

2. Celibacy and Marriage: Two Charisms

In order to correct this tendency it is necessary to turn back to the statements of St. Paul in First Corinthians: celibacy and marriage are the result of two of the Lord's charisms. This is the only Pauline text in which the category of charism is connected not with a ministerial activity, or an ecclesiastical office, but with a type of Christian existence. There is, however, no reason to give the idea of charism in this passage a different interpretation from that of 1 Co. 12 and Rm. 12. Charisms are the different gifts granted by the Lord to various members of the Church for the common upbuilding of the people of God. While it is true that some gifts can consist in temporary manifestations of the Spirit, it is also true that the Apostle tends to speak of the permanent ones, those which are linked with a vocation within the Church. After having listed the charisms in 1 Co. 12:8–10, Paul affirms that "God *has given* the first place to apostles, the second to prophets, the third to teachers. . . ." We are therefore in an entirely vocational context. In Ep. 4:11–12, charisms are associated with various ecclesiastical offices.

Thus one is called by God either to marriage or to celibacy; these are two different ways of contributing to the building up of the Body of Christ. The reason for the vocation either to marriage or celibacy is basically to be found, therefore, in the respective orientation of each toward the common good of the Church, and not directly in the perfection of the individual. It is obvious, however, that one grows in Christ by obedience to one's vocation. Marriage taken up in obedience to Christ is, for some, an efficacious means for growing in the Spirit; for others celibacy is the best means.

3. The Christological-Ecclesial Motive

We have seen how, in 1 Co. 7:32–35, St. Paul drew a parallel between married persons and celibates. The first item which drew our attention was his use of the same verb both for those who marry and those who remain single; only the objects change. These are verbs that express relationship and orientation. Celibates devote themselves to the Lord's affairs and are intent on pleasing him; married persons devote themselves to secular affairs and are intent on pleasing their spouses. What characterizes celibacy or virginity is, therefore, a relationship and an orientation toward God and his affairs, just as what characterizes marriage is a relationship and an orientation toward the spouse and secular affairs. Celibacy is not, consequently, to be defined as an absence of relationship or orientation; it is a direction given to one's life, a dedication of one's person, just as marriage is. The radical difference between celibacy for the sake of the Kingdom and the situation of the ordinary bachelor consists in this: what gives meaning to celibacy is not the fact of being single, but the fact of being dedicated, of being in a different type of relationship. One should also note that never, in this Pauline treatise, does abstention from sexual relations appear as something valid in itself. In fact, abstention from sexual relations is not even expressly mentioned in this Pauline description of celibacy (I Co. 7:32–35).

What are the existential orientations of celibacy according to the Apostle? He refers explicitly to two: the objective one, of a characteristic occupation, toward the Church; and the subjective one, of an orientation of the heart, toward the Risen Christ. It is this double orientation, therefore, that gives celibacy its value and meaning as a type of Christian existence. One should note that this motive has nothing to do with the hypothetical nearness or remoteness of the *parousia*.

In order to express the subjective relationship with the risen Christ, Paul affirms that the celibate lives intent on "pleasing the Lord." We have already seen that "to please" (*areskein*) usually has a strong meaning in St. Paul. "To please God" expresses the basic orientation of biblical spirituality; here we are dealing with a search for the God who comes to meet us in the Risen Jesus. One should remember that the Christological motive is already present in the logion on the reward of renunciation which follows the narrative of the call of the rich man. Although, in Lk. 18:29, the reference is to those who leave their family "for the sake of the Kingdom of God," in Mk. 10:29 it is to those who renounce it "for my sake and for the sake of the Gospel," and in Mt. 19:29, "for the sake of my name." It is obvious, however, that while the saying (inserted by the Synoptics in the context of the narrative of a vocation to discipleship proposed to all) refers to problems which family ties can raise for whoever intends to remain faithful to Christ and his Gospel, St. Paul is referring instead to a lifestyle deliberately chosen in order to be able to concentrate on "pleasing the Lord." Thus, parallel with the conjugal relationship of love "to please one's spouse," the Christological motive is inserted into the dynamism of an existence growing in and for devotion to Christ. We are dealing, therefore, with something more than imitating the devotion of the celibate Jesus for his Father. This is not a New Testament concept; here the Lord is not the object of imitation, but the object of the relationship itself. But the religious experience for which the celibate, according to St. Paul, wants to live is a meeting with God in Christ. Writings on virginity, especially from the fourth century on, insisted a great deal on this motive.

Celibacy is also characterized by an objective orientation, by dedication to the Lord's affairs. We can see, to some extent, what St. Paul meant by this expression when we consider his own experience. In this same letter he repeats that he would have the right to be accompanied by a Christian woman (a wife,), just as all the other Apostles, brothers of the Lord, and Cephas were (1 Co. 9:5). Why did he not do so? He gives no explanation, but he suggests that it is because of his apostolic commitment to the Church, carried out in a radical way through his itinerant preaching of the Gospel (cf. 1 Co. 9:15–16), and his solicitude for all the churches (2 Co. 11:28).

4. A Choice between Values

This consideration of the value and meaning of a Christian celibacy, born from a choice to live entirely for the Lord and his concerns, has a clear confirmation in descriptions of the phenomenon of celibacy in general, such as the one by E. Schillebeeckx. Celibacy is not, in fact, an exclusively Christian phenomenon. There is also the religious celibacy of the Buddhist monks, as well as celibacy chosen because of devotion to secular values within all cultures. There are those who choose to remain single because they feel called to fight for the liberation of their people by revolution or guerrilla warefare. There are those who choose celibacy in order to take care of one or more dear ones. There are those who make the same choice for the sake of science or art. These secular values can, in certain cases, invite an exclusive dedication to them.

In these cases the choice of celibacy involves two premises. On the one hand, there is a positive estimate of marriage commitments: marriage requires mutual dedication and devotion, and the conjugal and family relationship would suffer if it were sacrificed or even limited for the sake of a profession that tends to entirely absorb one of the partners. On the other hand, the choice of celibacy implies that certain values are so highly prized as to arouse the need for a total or predominant dedication. One feels the need of giving one's life to the cultivation of these values, and thus discovers a personal vocation.[68]

The same premises apply to celibacy embraced for religious motives, whether in Buddhism, Christianity, or Hinduism. A religious value is perceived on the horizon of one's life, and begins to require a dedication exclusive of all other forms of dedication which might condition the person and the person's lifestyle. The man or woman then lives entirely to search for that value. Religion, which can intensely animate the life of a married individual, here becomes an element characterizing a lifestyle.

At this point, however, we are assailed by a doubt. Are we not, perhaps, toying with a concept of God and of his relation with creation which is typically Hellenistic, not biblical? Hellenistic spiritual movements speak of God or of the world; of God or of the human race. The world, time, and humanity must be left behind if one desires to dedicate oneself to seeking God. This is clearly not the point of view of the Bible, in which the wholehearted love of God does not exclude the love of creation (on another level). We have repeated often enough that it is possible to love God with all one's heart within a conjugal and family relationship that requires, on a different level, the orientation of one's entire person toward the loved ones. It is not, therefore, a matter of objective necessity, but of a subjective fact. In Christianity, as in other religions, some individuals may feel that they are called to cultivate exclusively religious values.

Thus we find that there is a root common to all forms of monasticism, in all faiths. Religious experience is a fundamental fact, and hence tends to pervade all sectors of life. Within those religions which favor a personal relationship with God, religious experience creates monastic life, fostering the vocation of men and women who decide to live their relationship with God exclusively, and who create a lifestyle in which religion appears as a visible and characteristic trait. Does this require a dualistic separation between God and the world? Not necessarily. In Christianity religious experience does not consist of a relationship with God which excludes his works, but of a relationship which embraces God together with his sons and daughters. In Christianity one renounces marriage and embraces celibacy in order to establish a religious relationship with God and the human race. One should remember that in the Pauline description of the celibate's state it is not only a matter of living for the love of the Lord, but of busying oneself with his concerns. The ecclesial ministry is an integrating motive in choosing celibacy. This is fully true also in regard to the ministry of intercession for the Church and for humanity.

Returning now to specifically Christian terms, the *sequela Christi*, which is the general condition for all Christian existence, may become a particular way of life through celibacy. One desires to live one's relationship of faith and love with Christ and in the service of the Church, excluding every other relationship capable of giving a fundamental meaning and orientation to life. Is this permissible? Should one not perhaps practice discipleship in the context of everyday life? Certainly this is what one should normally do, but it is not required. It is possible for a disciple to feel called to relive the life of exclusive dedication to the Father and his work which characterized Jesus of Nazareth, eunuch for the sake of the Kingdom. We give ourselves to God who comes to meet us in Jesus, and by choosing celibacy we make this common dedication the distinctive trait of our life. It is not necessary to repeat that in giving ourselves to the God of Jesus we are giving ourselves to his work, the salvation of the entire human race.

5. Celibacy and Love

Marriage and celibacy, since they are forms of Christian life, can only be understood by following both of them back to the common and essential elements of all Christian living. In answering a question put to him by the Pharisees, the Lord said that all of the Law and the Prophets—Revelation itself—can be summarized in the double precept of loving God with one's whole heart and whole soul and whole mind, and loving one's neighbor as oneself. Thus every disciple is aware of the fundamental rule of living according to God's Word: all must love God with their whole heart, with a love that does not allow any other love to condition or limit it. To love God "with an undivided heart" is, therefore, the vocation of every Christian. In rendering the biblical concept of the love of God more explicit, Jesus specifically linked it with the love of neighbor. From St. John's lofty point of view, the love of God for us becomes "perfect," that is, it unfolds all its potentialities, through our love for our neighbor.

By recalling the character of totality of divine love, and translating it into the common vocation to love God with an undivided heart, we are not only faithful to the biblical Word, but also to the directives of the ecclesiastical Magisterium as expressed by Vatican II. The Council, in fact, reconfirmed the common vocation to sanctity, and defined it primarily in terms of the two commandments of love.[69] It then affirmed that the gift of virginity or celibacy is granted to some in order that they may "devote themselves to God more easily and with an undivided heart."[70] With these last words, the Council document introduced a significant change from the preparatory text, which said that the "undivided heart" and the "consecration to God alone" belonged to celibacy: "Chastity consecrated to God . . . is a sign by which a person is totally dedicated to God."[71] In the definitive text, celibacy is a means by which one can attain that undivided heart and that consecration to God alone which form our common vocation. Unfortunately some versions of the Council documents do not take into account this shade of meaning, and express the thought of the preparatory text which the Council did not accept.

When we analyzed the sayings on discipleship and studied the call narratives, we found the same principle regarding the totality with which we must love. In order to be disciples one must hate one's family; that is, on the deep level where fidelity to Christ is found, no other love can penetrate, not even the most sacred. We have now seen that these sayings refer to all the disciples of the Risen Lord. To love God with an undivided heart and to place no limits to one's fidelity to Jesus are fundamental norms for all disciples, no matter what their particular calling may be. The law of the undivided heart applies to everyone.

Those married Christians who, after hearing certain sermons on celibacy, respond that their spouses are not an impediment to their love and total attachment to Christ are totally right. They live their fidelity to Christ in the context of a personal relationship of conjugal love, and this characterizes them. In the other's love they must find a support for their love of God and their adherence to Christ. What characterizes celibates for the sake of the Kingdom is not their undivided heart on the level of their theological relationship with God, but the attainment of unity in their lifestyle by eliminating the very telling interpersonal relationship of married Christians. Celibates are defined only by their search for the love of Christ, even in their lifestyle. On the other hand it is likewise true that the love of neighbor can never be absent from the heart of celibates for the sake of the Kingdom. They renounce only conjugal love. Thus love becomes universal, and as such, is the source of manifold ministries. In renouncing a family of one's own, one becomes dedicated to the education and care of the families of others.

Celibacy tends to further unify Christian life by orienting existence directly and exclusively toward the God who comes to meet us in Christ. St. Paul spoke of the divisions that are often present in the married Christian's life. To what sort of divisions was he referring? It seems to us that the question is not primarily psychological: the distractions of married persons compared with the peace of contemplatives. The very experience of the Apostle shows how much tension can fill the life even of a celibate for the Kingdom: the deviations of the Christians in Corinth, the disagreements and contentions among Judaeo-Christians, etc. Would he have encountered more tensions if he had married and remained with his family? Nor should one say that these great difficulties were caused solely by the service he was rendering to Christ, because similar difficulties are encountered by married Christians: concern for the children, and incidental personal and relational tensions and crises are inherent in the service of God and the Church which married people embrace in obedience to their divine calling. These are their means of ascetical purification, and the difficulties by which they can manifest their love.

Division arises primarily on the ethical plane, that is, in an orientation toward certain values. In some cases family love can be a temptation against fidelity to Christ. We are warned of this by certain sayings of Jesus which, although they were spoken in an eschatological context, have a broader meaning to which the discipleship sayings refer. Often the family relationship tends to become exclusive: life is directed toward the family without any reference to God. One should note, however, that this does not necessarily happen. One's own life in the Spirit can be supported efficaciously by a spouse whose faith is intense. Those who embrace celibacy also renounce this conjugal support.

6. A Sign of Transcendent Grace

In the past, frequent reference has been made to the eschatological meaning of celibacy, as founded on the logion: "for when they rise from the dead, men and women do not marry; no, they are like the angels in heaven" (Mk. 12:25; Mt. 22:30), and especially on the stronger formulation of Luke with its distinction between the two aeons: the present, dominated by death, in which there is marriage; and the future one, in which neither death nor marriage any longer exist.

As we have already said, even in the stronger Lukan formulation the logion does not affirm that celibates possess in advance the condition proper to the resurrection; it says nothing at all of celibates. The original version merely states that after the resurrection there will be no marriage. The Lukan version notes that marriage belongs to this world, and that it will not exist in the next. Actually the relationship between celibacy and the eschatological condition has often been interpreted naively, by imagining that in the glory of the Father we will all be celibates. In this connection one must remember that it is impossible to form an idea of our condition after the resurrection beyond the simple data of faith. We can, however, exclude the existence of either marriage or celibacy as such after the resurrection, since they are both states of life belonging to the Church on earth and are inseparably connected with it. The resurrection, in fact, brings about a different manner of existence, and consequently a different type of communion with God and with our neighbor. Celibacy is an exclusive orientation toward God carried into the sphere of one's lifestyle, and involves the renunciation of a value (marriage); in the resurrection a type of existence which includes renunciation of a value is inconceivable, because the resurrection implies complete fulfillment.

As Schillebeeckx has noted correctly, grace, not celibacy, anticipates life in the Kingdom, and God's grace is granted to celibates and married people alike.[72]

Celibacy is the prophetic announcement of the Kingdom, insofar as it expresses and embodies present grace. It is clear that in this sense there is a difference between marriage and celibacy.

Marriage and celibacy are two types of human existence (marriage is not imposed on the human person by the natural law) and two manners of living Christ's grace. They are two dimensions of the same reality, not two separate realities. Since they are types of human existence, marriage and celibacy must be two ways of progressing toward one's own fulfillment and of contributing to the upbuilding of human society. We have already seen that religiously-motivated celibacy allows earthly tasks as well. Since they are types of Christian existence, marriage and celibacy are two ways of living in Christ's grace. Both, consequently are means for growing in grace and signs of the faith which caused them to be undertaken. Grace is a gift that, at one and the same time, becomes incarnate in our humanity and transcends it.

In marriage we have a state of life in which two Christians live their relationship in Christ and in the Church. Marriage, undertaken in faith, is the concrete existential situation in and through which two Christians offer themselves to grace. It represents an incarnation of the Gospel in a particular lifestyle, but also represents the transcendence of grace over every human value, including the family relationship. The discipleship sayings regarding family life tell us it is necessary to love and to not love ("to hate") at the same time: to love with a love that nourishes life, but at the same time to be open to the superior demands of grace; to love God with all one's heart; to leave all in order to follow Christ. In marriage and secular life, too, grace preserves all its transcendence. One becomes justified as a human being, within a human manner of life, but not through a human agency. It is not conjugal love, nor work, that justifies, but the grace of God—or, from a subjective point of view, yielding oneself and one's life to the power of transcendent grace.

What to us seems typical of celibacy is that through its commitment to life exclusively for the Lord and his concerns, and its renouncement of the marriage relationship, the movement of all Christian existence toward the Kingdom becomes visible. Marriage is renounced for the sake of the Lord and his Church, and thus the transcendent value of the Kingdom is expressed. Ordinary discipleship is institutionalized, and becomes a specific lifestyle. Hence there is a difference between marriage and celibacy as forms of Christian life, since the choice of celibacy entails the renouncement of one's family, and therefore expresses the value of grace above all human structures. It expresses this by a specific lifestyle.

In marriage, on the other hand, we have not only a natural situation possessing its own value independent of faith in Christ, but a type of Christian life as well, which consists precisely in taking a human value as the orientation for one's existence. In marriage we have a sacramental structure in which an entirely human reality becomes a sign of grace and a means for meeting God. The sacramental reality is, of itself, ambiguous, by the very fact that it is a sign. Bread may be bread, or it may be the Body of Christ; wine may be the Blood of Christ, or it may be ordinary wine. In sacramental celebrations it is the action of the Church and the Word of God proclaimed by the Church which gives the significance to the sacramental matter. In the sacrament of matrimony it is faith, the acceptance of the Word, that converts human love into a sign and a means of encountering God.

In celibacy the sacramental structure is not present, because the choice of living only for the Lord and his concerns entails the renunciation of the family relationship. Objectively, then, celibacy as a way of life becomes a visible expression of grace which transcends the world. The celibate proclaims that one is saved not by conjugal love, nor by parenthood, but by grace. Clearly we may not overemphasize this difference by tying the visibility of the sign of grace with the sole fact of being single. Subjectively, in fact, the transcendence of grace becomes visible only when the religious motive for the choice is expressed in some way. Celibacy (being single) can also be an entirely human type of existence, dependent on natural motives.[73]

We believe, however, that the theme of celibacy as a sign of the transcendence of grace should be explored more deeply. How and why can celibacy become a sign of the Kingdom? Is it perhaps because of a human decision to direct one's life exclusively toward Christ and his service? Absolutely not. Grace alone can manifest its own transcendence. The Kingdom is made visible in celibacy because, in a certain sense, it is already present there; because Christ takes the heart of a disciple and dedicates it exclusively to himself and his concerns. Indeed, prior to being a human decision, celibacy is a charism, a gift of God which determines the place of certain people within the Church; it is therefore a vocation. It is Christ who calls to this form of discipleship, and gives the grace to follow him in this manner. The human decision is a recognition and acceptance of this grace. The profession of celibacy in the Church externalizes both the sovereign power of grace and the presence of the Kingdom which is already among us.[74]

VI

The Religious Profession of Christian Poverty

At this point in our reflection (between the consideration of two constituent charisms of religious life in its most usual form: celibacy and community) certain facts oblige us to speak of poverty.

In the first place, the renouncement of property and a life of poverty were the most characteristic expressions of religious life in its earliest form, among the anchorites. Second, within the cenobitical tradition, importance was always given to the individual's divestment as a preparatory step to acceptance into the community. Third, from the thirteenth century on, religious have always made a vow of poverty, and this has been considered an essential element of their religious life.

Moreover, in the discipleship sayings, and especially in the call narratives which are the constant source of inspiration for religious life, there was emphasis not only on abandoning family ties, but also on renouncing economic goods. It is therefore evident that the disciple's poverty, which discipleship texts seek to affirm, must be exemplified in a lifestyle constructed entirely around the following of Christ. The eschatological value of religious life is thus confirmed.

But in speaking of poverty at this point, between the chapter on celibacy and the chapter on community, we risk being misunderstood as intending to place celibacy and poverty on the same level, as two different charisms belonging to religious life. It does seem evident to us that poverty is a gift of the Spirit; we believe this will appear clearly when we speak of poverty in the New Testament. But we do not see it as a charism in the technical sense of the word, that is, as a special gift characterizing a special vocation, as does the gift of celibacy. Celibacy (we are not speaking merely of chastity but of *celibacy*) constitutes a different type of existence, while poverty belongs to the common Christian vocation and is practiced in different degrees. Some married Christians, some seculars, may feel called to an actual renunciation of possessions which is equal or superior to that which many religious embrace; yet they do not cease to be seculars, unless one considers the juridical act of renouncement as the crucial issue. But that we refuse to do, because it would overstress a factor which has little or no importance in revelation. In religious life there is a type of poverty consisting in personal divestment and the sharing of goods; this is typical of cenobitic life, but does not exist in hermitic life. It is not an element common to all religious life.

That is why we suggested in the preceding chapter that Christian poverty simply completes voluntary celibacy. We must also add that celibacy will be evangelical (oriented exclusively toward the Lord and his interests), and not mere bachelorhood, insofar as it is animated by evangelical poverty.

For these reasons we will now consider the poverty practiced by religious. But to avoid confusion we call this chapter "The Religious Profession of Christian Poverty." This time we will reverse the order of our discussion and speak first of poverty in the history of religious life. After that we will proceed to study poverty in the Bible, and will end with some theological conclusions.

I. The Poverty of Religious Throughout History

1. Poverty and the Monastic Vocation

In early Christian monasticism, poverty had a very important role. While other traits are mentioned or omitted in descriptions of monastic life written by the Fathers or by early monks, poverty is practically never overlooked, and is often the first to be mentioned. As evidence that it was a decisive factor in characterizing monasticism are the stories which recount how some Christians felt called to embrace it. We are referring, first of all, to the *Vita Antonii,* one of the most authoritative early monastic documents. In Chapter I, in speaking of the biblical inspiration for religious life, we quoted the initial account of how the famous hermit discovered his vocation. We said that this narrative should not be considered as the simple chronicle of a single event, but as a biography in the Hellenistic sense, that is, a description of an exemplary type of life, consequently as a rule for the many hermits who were living in the desert during that period. According to the *Vita Antonii,* the renunciation of one's possessions and their distribution among the poor constituted the first step for anyone who wanted to become a monk.[1] This idea was common among the first monks. We find in an anonymous apophthegm transmitted in the Coislin manuscript 283: "If you fulfill the Lord's commandment: 'Go sell all that you possess and give it to the poor.'"[2] In the sayings of the desert Fathers and Mothers, renunciation of one's goods and their distribution to the poor are closely connected in describing the first step toward monastic life. The very act by which certain Christians broke their ties with the world was, at the same time, an expression of communion with the poor. There are even various anecdotes about a secular Christian who had not made the radical act of renunciation, but nevertheless reached the same degree of perfection as some holy monks by giving to the poor everything left over from his simple and pious life.[3]

Thus ascetical renunciation and communion with the poor were two aspects of the same evangelical commitment. As we shall see later, the different Hellenistic movements of spirituality imposed varying degrees of renouncement of riches and material preoccupations on those who wanted to reach perfection, and interpreted the demand in different ways. Christian nuns and monks tied this renouncement to love for the needy. Obviously their linking of renunciation and charity had its source in the "Lord's commandment" to the rich man in Matthew 19:21. For this reason the linking of renunciation and charity reappears each time there is a radical return to the Gospel: in the Rule of St. Francis,[4] for example, Matthew 19:21 is the first of the fundamental Gospel texts to be quoted; the same is true in the Constitutions of the Society of Jesus.[5] The reason for distributing all the property one has abandoned to the poor at the point of breaking all ties with the world was indicated by St. Basil: everything owned by those who consecrate themselve to God belongs to God, and must therefore be given to the poor.[6] Here, on the basis of certain gospel texts (cf. Mt. 25:40), the poor appear as proxies of Christ.

Cenobites remained faithful to the tradition of the anchorites, retaining the renunciation of possessions as the starting point of their religious life.[7] But instead of giving their possessions to the poor, many of the first cenobites renounced them in favor of the community they intended to join. One should note that this had been the practice in the Essene community of Qumran. According to Cassian this practice was soon abandoned: because it was often an occasion for pride, and because those who returned to secular life demanded that their property be returned to them, causing many annoyances. Later the *Rule of the Master* and the *Regula Monasteriorum* of St. Benedict again gave the postulant the choice of distributing his possessions to the poor, or of donating them to the monastery by a legally sanctioned irrevocable renunciation.[8] St. Francis of Assisi, in obedience to Mt. 19:21, returned to the primitive practice by permitting his brothers to receive from new candidates only that for which they had a pressing need on the same basis as other poor people.[9] The poor are likewise the beneficiaries of the assets of those who seek admission to the Society of Jesus. But St. Ignatius of Loyola, in his great sensitivity to differing situations, foresaw the possibility of making exceptions in favor of the candidate's needy relatives, after due consultation with persons commendable for their life and doctrine.[10]

In later centuries the renunciation of possessions became an independent fact, necessary for the profession of the vow of poverty and for the profession of community of goods. The original relationship between renunciation and Christian solidarity with the poor has been lost. Obviously Canon Law, upon which it is customary to base the initial act of renunciation, could not include any reference to the recipients of the property, because of the multiplicity of individual circumstances. The theology of religious life, however, should have retained a reference to the poor as the ideal beneficiaries of the goods of Christians who dedicate themselves to divine service.

2. The Anchorites' Poverty

It was not enough for the anchorites to renounce their possessions when they embraced the monastic life; they had also to live like poor people. The practice of poverty among the first Christian hermits was, in fact, very strict. A number of the apophthegms exalt the life of extreme privation which some of the anchorites led.[11]

An essential element of their poverty was their work to support themselves.[12] Some cultivated a small garden, sufficient to care for the needs of their extremely simple life; others offered their services for hire to landowners for harvesting and mowing.[13] Many made baskets and clay vases which they sold now and then at the nearest market.[14] Since these hermits were not members of a community, they administered their own earnings. The important thing was that they should truly be poor. In order to remain so, they distributed among the indigent everything left after they had provided for their own immediate needs. They were strictly forbidden to save for their old age, or for sickness; God would provide. Thus a close connection existed between the obligation to work and solidarity with the needy. In a paragraph evidently seeking to summarize the basic traits of Anthony's rule of life, Athanasius writes: "He worked with his own hands, for he had heard that it is written that the person who refuses to work should not be fed (cf. 2 Th. 3:10). He used part of his earnings to obtain bread for himself; the rest he spent on the poor."[15] And Abbot Poemen's answer to one who asked him for advice was, "Work as long as you can, so that you may give alms."[16]

The desert Fathers were very cognizant of the negative side of poverty, for they mentioned it among the sufferings pertaining to their mode of life. But they embraced it as an effective means of growing in the fear of the Lord.[17] or reaching the Kingdom of heaven.[18] Thus their poverty was the expression of a life dedicated to the search for God, and they made the eschatological dimension of poverty visible. One should remember, however, that for Origen, Gregory Nazianzus, and Evagrius, the Kingdom of heaven actually begins in this life, in a sort of beatitude that culminates in the mystical experience.[19] In fact, some of the Fathers' sayings link poverty with peace of mind,[20] with prayer,[21] and with swift spiritual progress.[22] According to Evagrius's ascetical system, poverty is a radical means of liberation from the spirit of greed, one of the eight spirits which keep the soul in chains and obstruct its progress toward perfection.[23]

3. Divestment in Cenobitism

After the initial renouncement, the practice of poverty followed a different course in different religious communities. Pachomius and his disciples gradually discovered that it was important for community life, as well as for its theological significance, to have property in common.[24] Significantly the only reason St. Basil offers to explain why the sisters or brothers must not keep anything for themselves is that the Lord gave even his life for his friends.[25] Christian brotherhood, lived in a prototypal manner by the Apostolic Church in Jerusalem, had to express itself, among other means, through the sharing of material goods. This concept reaches its height with St. Augustine. For him what we now call religious life was, above all, a privileged expression of Christian communion. One should remember that the Doctor of Hippo was deeply opposed to private property and considered it to be the cause of every vice and social sin.[26] In this view the initial renunciation and subsequent poverty of the individual are conditions for a life of full communion.

The relationship of religious with material goods thus became rooted in the central Christian principle of mutual love; but this same fact brought about a profound change in their attitude toward these goods. The one thing that mattered, for them, was the individual's renouncement of goods before acceptance into the community, rigorously adhered to afterwards. From this point of view the anchorite's situation was stricter than that of the cenobite. Anchorites, as the hermit Poemen noted, did not possess even a drinking glass.[27] For the cenobite on the other hand, future security was assured by the institution, and thereby a typical characteristic of hermitical poverty was lost: their total insecurity for tomorrow and their complete reliance on the fatherly love of God.

Manual labor was retained.[28] The *Rule of the Master* orders that any priest who refused to work should be dismissed.[29] Since they were members of a community, the monks and nuns were not working only to provide for their individual needs; they were contributing toward the more numerous needs of the group. From the beginning they practiced a stringent organization of work, and worked the entire time their schedule prescribed. Since the work was financially productive, the cenobites soon began to accumulate wealth. Some communities became centers for agricultural production and marketing. They began to need servants; some even owned boats for transporting their wares to the city. But since it was not possible to calculate the immediate needs of large communities, and since their members produced much more than they gave to the poor, the connection between manual work and communion with the indigent was lost. In order to obviate these drawbacks, St. Basil wanted his community reduced to few members who should work only to provide for their needs, dividing the rest of their time between prayer and study of the Scriptures and of Origen. On the doctrinal level a number of ideologies were forged in an effort to legitimize the increasing resources of communities. Some writers spoke of poverty in the sense of "detachment of the heart."[30] But was not this what the Fathers required even of seculars? Others drew a distinction between individual and common ownership.[31] We shall later see that this was a subterfuge.

4. The Mendicants' Poverty

The mendicant orders introduced a profound change in the interpretation of religious poverty, a change which cannot be properly understood unless it is considered in the social context in which mendicant orders were born. Deep social changes had brought about the rise of the middle class, of the merchants, and of the first bankers. Money became a source of power in a new sense—a criterion for social discrimination—and private property received a new, narrow meaning. As a consequence of the economic changes many artisans were reduced to misery. Reaction was expressed by numerous movements which made real poverty the criterion of Christian authenticity. Christ's missionary discourse (Mt. 10 and Lk. 10), understood in terms of itinerant preaching and poverty, became a common source of inspiration. St. Dominic of Guzman obtained permission from a papal legate to adopt it as the rule for his preachers. St. Francis of Assisi discovered in it the summary of his aspirations toward authentic Christianity.

The mendicants' poverty began with an actual renunciation of goods and their distribution among the poor. From the middle of the preceding century, the custom of professing the three vows of chastity, obedience, and community of goods had become prevalent. St. Francis, perhaps at the suggestion of the Holy See, incorporated these three vows into the Rule, but he changed the vow of sharing goods into a vow of poverty. *Sine proprio* (without property) became the commitment not only of the individual but of the group as well. In the beginning the Friars Minor could work for other people, except in the administration of their goods; they could have their little workshops for their own support, or they could beg for alms together with the other needy people. The Mendicants continued sharing with the poor what they had received or earned for their own support, but the important thing for them was to embrace the condition of the poor. St. Francis, in his first Rule, says: "They should be glad to live among social outcasts, among the poor and helpless, the sick and the lepers, and those who beg by the wayside. They should not be ashamed to beg for alms. . . ."[32]

Thus religious poverty came to be understood as solidarity with the poor. Some modern congregations understand it in the same way."

5. Apostolic Poverty

We have seen that in the Order of Preachers, the first Institute founded for apostolic purposes, ministry and poverty were closely associated. When the Institutes for regular clergy appeared in the sixteenth century, poverty had already been the object of a special vow for three centuries, and was one of the "substantial" elements of religious life. Theological and canonical tradition had concentrated on it. Clerical Institutes accepted the various traditional tendencies, but referred them primarily to the individual's perfection and the protection of the spirit of the Institutes. Poverty in clerical institutes was expressed by renouncing benefices and dignities, and often by refusing to accept stipends for ministries. Among later congregations of missionaries, in particular, poverty often took the form of special attention to the spiritual needs of the underprivileged (peasants, the uninstructed, etc.). Some Institutes, like the Society of Jesus, were supposed to live on voluntary donations, and to be ready to ask for alms.[33]

The lay communities founded for ministries of Christian education and charity discovered a new expression for the poverty they professed in working to elevate the human and Christian level of the poor, or by caring for the neediest. Many communities were, in fact, founded exclusively or primarily to care for the poor. Some continued to work without any financial gain. In other cases, however, the ministries of education and charity proved to be profitable.

II. Poverty in the Bible

From the very beginning of monasticism, religious have constantly referred to the narrative of the call of the rich man, especially as recounted by

Matthew. They have also referred to other texts on the disciples' vocations and on Christian radicalism as sources of inspiration for their theology and practice of poverty.[34] We must therefore begin our reflection by comparing the theology of poverty with the biblical idea of poverty, particularly with Christ's practice of it.

1. In the Old Testament

The theme of poverty in the Old Testament is seen from different, at times opposite, points of view. We may say, however, that poverty always appears as a misfortune. In the Wisdom Books it is often shown as an evil brought on by one's sins (Pr. 6:6–11; 21:17; 23:21; Si. 18:32). The prophets have a completely different perspective. To understand them one must remember that they acted in the setting of a society without a middle class in the modern sense of the word—a society in which the wealth of a few contrasted with the poverty of an overwhelming majority, Justice was obviously in the hands of the rich, and was often turned to their own advantage. Therefore the terms *rich* and *oppressor* became synonymous.

The ancient Middle East thus developed a certain sensibility toward the rights of the poor, a sensibility manifested with special vigor by Israel's prophets. They often protest the arrogant impositions to which the poor are subjected: (Am. 2:6–8; Is. 3:13–15; Jr. 7:3–6; Mi. 2:1–2, 9–10). The poor are protected by God, the just Judge (Jr. 12:13; Is. 29:19), exactly as, in all of the ancient Middle East, the king was expected to protect the helpless. Following this line of thought, Deuteronomy, with its tendency to return to the sources, recalls the social equality of nomadic Israel, stressing that the land of Canaan had been promised to all the people, and that there must be no want among the Israelites (Dt. 8:9, 15:4). A third line of thought appears in the psalms of supplication and of thanksgiving: the poor place their trust in God, begging that he free them from their oppressors. It is perhaps from these sources that a spirituality of poverty ('*anawim*) developed in Israel, in which poverty is synonymous with piety, humility, and trust in Yahweh (Ps. 9–10, 12, 13, 18, 22, 24, 25, 34, 69, 120; 1 S. 1:1–10; Jr. 17:14). Finally, in the post-exilic period, all of Israel appears under the guise of the poor (Is. 49:13, 51:21). One must interpret the prophet's mission of announcing the good news to the poor in the light of this fact (Is. 61:1).

2. The Messiah of the Poor in the New Testament

In the New Testament, too, poverty appears with varying, and we might even say with distinct, meanings. On the one hand a saying recorded by Mark (14:7), Matthew (26:11) and John (12:8), but omitted by Luke, seems to show that Jesus considered the social condition of poverty an inevitable fact and a permanent situation: "you will always have the poor with you." We are aware that this was the common mentality of ancient peoples, for whom the poverty of the masses represented an inescapable natural law. But the typically evangelical note regarding economic poverty—the one found all through the New Testament—is the affirmation of the eminent dignity of the poor, who become images and proxies of Christ (Mt. 25:34-40).

In the Lukan infancy narratives (cf. the *Magnificat*) and in all of Matthew, one finds the rich Old Testament tradition of the spirituality of the poor. The Messiah appears as the Messiah of the poor (Mt. 11:5; cf. Lk. 4:18-19, 7:22). He himself is poor (*ani;* Mt. 21:5; cf. Zc. 9:9), and meek and humble of heart (Mt. 11:28-30). It is in this context that Matthew's version of the Beatitudes is introduced; divine blessings are bestowed on the poor in spirit, on the meek, etc. (Mt. 5:3-10). It is evidently in the light of a spiritual quality of poverty that one must interpret the sayings on the proper attitude toward material goods and the repeated warnings on the dangers inherent in wealth. The disciple's heart must be set on the search for the Kingdom and not, like the pagan's, on material preoccupations, because it is impossible at the same time to serve God and to be enslaved by riches (Mt. 6:19-23). The evangelical spirit requires faith in the providence of the Father (Mt. 6:25-34).

Luke, on this part, seems to stress poverty and wealth in their social reality. He alone records Jesus' first sermon in the synagogue of Nazareth, and describes him as one anointed in order that he may announce the Good News to the poor. Since he quotes Is. 61:1, this reference might be understood in the sense of the spirituality of the poor (cf. Mt. 11:5; Lk. 7:22). The Lukan Beatitudes attribute the Messianic blessings to the poor as a socio-economic class, and are followed by maledictions directed toward the rich (Lk. 6:20-26). It is clear, however, that in Luke, too, it is not material poverty as such which constitutes a blessing: that, on the contrary, is felt to be a misfortune. The blessedness of the poor does not consist in their destitution, nor in the promise of compensation in the other world (cf.

the Marxist criticism of religious belief in heaven as opium). Their blessedness depends, rather, on the fact that, in the person of Christ, God has put himself on their side. The poor and the afflicted are the objects of God's preferential love. God is very strongly with them. We are therefore within the tradition of the prophets of Israel, but with two new elements: on the one hand, Christ is fulfilling their predictions (Lk. 4:21); on the other hand, the disciples' solidarity with the needy, which has such a central place in the New Testament, is a consequence of God's love for the poor, the revelation of which culminates in Christ.

3. Poverty in the Life and Ministry of Jesus

So much for the explicit Gospel message on poverty and wealth. A careful reading of the texts permits us, however, to glimpse the place that poverty, as a social reality, had in the life and ministry of Christ. Jesus belonged to the great number of those who lived by their work (Mk. 6:3; Mt. 13:55). He enlisted his closest disciples from the ranks of lowly artisans and fishermen who did, however, possess their homes and their boats (Mt. 4:18-22, 8:14-15). Yet, Levi, Lazarus and some of the women who belonged to the group were well-to-do (cf. Mt. 9:9-13; Jn. 12:5; Lk. 8:1-3).

Most of the hearers of Jesus in Galilee must have belonged to that category of *'am ha-ares* (humble ones) whom the establishment in Jerusalem despised. But he showed particular kindness to all those who were considered public sinners: publicans and prostitutes, many of whom were well-to-do, like Zacchaeus (cf. Mt. 9:10-11, 11:19; Lk. 15:1-2). Thus one might say that rather than poverty as such, it was the fact of being discriminated against and excluded which drew the attention of Jesus.

Jesus accepted all the discomforts resulting from an itinerant apostolic life (Jn. 4:6-7), and he foresaw the same trials being met with by those who wished to follow him. In dedicating himself to the announcement of the Kingdom, Jesus left behind all material security and entrusted himself to the providence of the Father. The same spirit is evident in the rules he drew up for missionaries (Mt. 6:8-11; Mt. 10:5-14; Lk. 9:1-5). Thus total unselfishness, and the privations caused by their way of life, characterized the first Christian missionaries. This was particularly visible in St. Paul (1 Co. 4:11-12; 2 Co. 11:9-27; Ph. 4:11-14).

We must recall here what we have already discussed at length in Chapter 1. From the call narratives and the sayings on discipleship we cannot draw the conclusion that Jesus asked anyone to give up his or her possessions, either juridically or with a *de facto* cession in favor of others. The only passage which may point in that direction, Mt. 19:21 ("go, sell all you own and give..."), if taken literally, must refer to an exceptional test. Yet, more probably, it intends to express the same requirement as the other texts on discipleship: a call to transcend everything for the Kingdom of God, and a warning on the possible extreme situation in which fidelity to the Gospel may involve the loss of one's family and possessions.[35]

4. Poverty and the Disciples' Spirituality

Both the Old and the New Testament (the *Magnificat*) have presented poverty as the attitude of those who put all their trust in God. God is the refuge of the poor. From this point of view, poverty expresses faith. It places the believer in a sphere where prayer arises spontaneously. In the New Testament, Christ on the cross, entrusting himself to the Father even in his abandonment and solitude, shows us what depths the trust of the poor who rely on God must reach. In the New Testament, poverty is related to the search for the Kingdom. Those who seek God above all else are certain never to be disappointed.

St. Paul in 2 Co. 8:9, exhorting the Corinthians to be generous toward the poor in Jerusalem, offers as a motive the example of Christ who "was rich, but he became poor for your sake, to make you rich out of his poverty." A similar idea is suggested in the Christological hymn in Ph. 2:6–11, which speaks of the kenosis of Christ: "He did not cling to his equality with God, but emptied himself... and became as men are... even to accepting death, death on a cross." Here we have a radical interpretation of the poverty of Christ, and hence that of his disciples, as total detachment and generous dedication of self in obedience to the salvific will of the Father and for the redemption of his brothers and sisters. In this interpretation, which seizes the inner meaning of the poverty of Christ, poverty is shown to be a delicate expression of love. The disciples who give themselves to God and neighbor are poor. Poverty, in this sense, is in opposition to the narrow love of self, to egoism.

A typical trait of evangelical poverty is solidarity with the needy. St.

Paul places this solidarity in close connection with the ''poverty'' of Jesus. Just as the Lord became poor to come to meet us in our misery, so his disciples must come out of themselves generously in order to share in their neighbors' sufferings. It is through the disciples' love that the blessings of divine love descend on the poor.

III. Poverty, Between the Bible and Hellenism

In view of what we could find in Sacred Scriptures, it is clear that ''poverty of spirit'' is a special trait of Christ's disciples. It is a virtue springing from a life animated by the expectation of the Kingdom of God, vivified by a transcending love for God and trust in his Providence, and moved by generosity toward one's brothers and sisters. It is, therefore, a spiritual readiness to sacrifice wealth, comfort, and power when there is a question of fidelity to Christ or of love for God and neighbor. This availability is stressed in certain gospel texts having to do with the supreme importance of Christ, and is proposed in a practical way in call narratives. Poverty is more than actual renouncement of possessions; it is never described in the Gospels as a means of ascetic progress.

But if these ideas of actual poverty, and of its value as a means of attaining spiritual perfection were not biblical, how is it that from the time of the Fathers they should have penetrated so deeply into Christian spirituality as to give form to the life and spirit of the first Christian anchorites? Evidently we are dealing with a Hellenistic reading of Mt. 19:21: ''If you wish to be perfect, go and sell. . . .''

The category ''perfect'' in Matthew refers to an existential situation, but one which brings with it a deep inner transformation: they are perfect who adhere to Christ and accept his radical interpretation of the saving will of God. For the Greeks perfection consisted instead in a subjective state of goodness acquired through a long series of exercises (*askesis*). It was in this sense that Origen understood the saying in Matthew; hence he formulated the problem: how is it possible that one should become perfect merely by selling one's goods and giving the proceeds to the poor, when the perfect are only those who possess all virtues and no longer perform any action under the impulse of evil? Would those who, up to then, had allowed themselves to be dominated by anger suddenly stop being wrathful? And how could they, by that one act, free themselves from anxiety, and prove themselves superior to all the evils that might overtake them? Origen found this solution: one does not become perfect through the act of renunciation itself (this, one should note, is precisely Matthew's thought), but whoever does this act in obedience to Jesus will obtain a powerful aid in reaching perfection.[36]

This was an obvious exegesis for a Hellenistic Christian, also because a close connection between voluntary poverty and the search for wisdom or virtue existed in Greek tradition. Anaxagoras renounced his possessions in order to dedicate himself to the contemplation of nature.[37] Democritus divided his property and kept the lesser part for himself so that he could travel in search of philosophy;[38] from then on he lived in actual poverty.[39] Socrates lived a simple and austere life in order to be closer to the Deity.[40] He counseled others not to be concerned with their material interests but with the manner of reaching perfection in goodness and wisdom.[41]

Renouncement of wealth and comfort became more radical, and even ostentatious, among the Cynics. Crates sold his possessions and distributed the proceeds among his fellow citizens[42] or, according to another tradition, threw them into the sea.[43] From then on, humiliation and poverty became his domain.[44] Among the Stoics, Zeno considered that the loss of his possessions allowed him to dedicate himself more freely (*expeditius*) to philosophy.[45]

During the Hellenistic period, among the Neo-Pythagoreans and the Neo-Platonists, voluntary poverty took on religious connotations. As soon as he was of age, Apollonius of Tyana renounced his goods, gave part of them to his brother in hopes of gaining his good will and thus saving him from his vices, and distributed the rest among his needier relatives.[46] He prayed that the gods would grant that he have few things, and that he might need nothing.[47] Porphyrius praises the poverty of Plotinus and of his disciples, dwelling especially on the renouncement (*apostasis*) of his privileges as an imperial officer, and his refusal to live in his own house.[48] Conversely, Porphyrius stresses that another disciple, Serapion of Alexandria, was unable to renounce the base things of wealth and finance.[49] Plotinus carefully watched over the administration of the property of adolescents entrusted to him by their families until they had decided whether they would dedicate themselves to philosophy.[50] Marinus points out the poverty of Proclus.[51]

One may note certain facts in this rich Greek tradition on the poverty of philosophers. First, in the question of renouncing their possessions, they do it at the beginning of their journey, as a preliminary action which proves that they intend to give themselves to the search for wisdom or perfection, precisely as was done in early Christian monasticism. This initial renunciation (*apostasis,* in Porphyrius as also among the Christians) is mentioned in the life of Anaxagoras and that of Democritus,[52] in that of Apollonius of Tyana,[53] and in the life of Plotinus, where Porphyrius speaks of the disciples of the great Neo-Platonist. Second, Philostratus speaks of the "naked philosophers" (*gymnoi*) in Egypt, placing them on a level with the Magi in Babylonia and the Brahmins in India;[55] thus, at the beginning of the third century A.D., there was a philosophical sect in Egypt practicing a radical form of renunciation. Finally, it is well to remember what a profound impression the poverty of pagan philosophers made on the Christians. Origen explains Jesus' poverty by referring to Socrates and to the voluntary poverty of certain Greek philosophers, among whom he specifically mentions Democritus, Crates, and Diogenes.[56] Jerome recalls these men in a good number of texts.[57] According to Jerome, Crates believed that he could not be virtuous and rich at the same time.[58] It is very significant, then, that on the basis of these precise examples, Jerome felt obliged to conclude that renunciation of one's possessions is not, in itself, a specifically Christian act; it is also necessary to "follow Jesus" by imitating him.[59] It is this which distinguishes the apostles and believers.[60] However Jerome also held the opinion that radical renunciation of one's goods is an efficacious means for attaining perfection, and a requirement for following Christ. The relationship between voluntary poverty and perfection was obvious to Origen and Jerome, since it had already been perceived by pagan philosophers.

At first one has the impression that there is an actual convergence between the texts that speak of the voluntary poverty of the pagan philosophers and the Synoptic account of what Jesus asked of his disciples. Does there not seem to have been, in both traditions, the requirement of an initial renouncement before dedication either to philosophy or discipleship? Is it not true that, according to a certain tradition, Crates *sold his property and distributed the proceeds* among his fellow citizens?[61] And that Apollonius of Tyana distributed his goods among his needier relatives?[62] But these coincidences cannot hide the profound spiritual difference between Jesus and the Greek philosophers. Jesus was much more flexible in the use of material goods than were many of the Greek philosophers; he did not embrace poverty as such, but he did accept all the consequences resulting from his total dedication to announcing the Kingdom. For him the important thing was the spirit: to orient one's life toward certain values, to fix one's heart on certain realities. In the Gospel we do not find two of the attitudes that stand out in Greek philosophical tradition: first, scorn for the "baseness of money and finance"[63] (what the Gospels stress is the danger riches can present to our fidelity to the Gospel, thus placing us in the realm of Christian faith and love); second, the idea of renunciation as a liberation from many preoccupations, making it easier (*expeditius:* Seneca) to dedicate oneself to contemplation (either philosophical or religious), which is not a strictly biblical concept. One should note that this is the meaning St. Thomas gives to poverty: "Poverty is praiseworthy because, by freeing us from material concerns, it allows us to dedicate ourselves more freely to divine things."[64] We are not saying that this is not true in a life dedicated to prayer and silence, nor that it is contrary to Scriptures; we are only saying that this idea does not appear in the New Testament, and should not be taken as the basis for a theology of religious life.

Should we then conclude that total renunciation, extreme poverty freely embraced, cannot have a profound Christian meaning? Certainly not. What we must affirm with Jerome is that, by itself, it is not an evangelical reality. Actual and voluntary poverty becomes Christian only if it is bound together with the following of Christ, that is, with a specifically Christian reality. But here we must ask ourselves what the Christian realities are that can require the willing adoption of actual poverty.

IV. The Gospel Meaning of Poverty

1. The Kingdom Belongs to the Poor

Unquestionably poverty is one of the characteristic elements of the vocation of Christ's disciples according to the New Testament. Of course certain theological tendencies on poverty are typical of the individual evangelist, (e.g., Luke). Some elements are the result of post-resurrection reflections (2 Co. 8:9) and of socio-economic conditions among the great majority of the members of the primitive Church (1 Co. 1:26). Still, after a thorough analysis of the texts, one remains convinced that the theme poverty-wealth did have an important place in Christ's preaching. When formulating his mission in the words of Isaiah (61:1), he said that he was called to bring the Good News to the poor (Lk. 4:18), he called the poor blessed (Lk. 6:20), and he exhorted them to lift their hearts above daily worries (Mt. 6:25-34), warning them aginst the dangers of riches (Mt. 6:24, 19:23-26).

It therefore becomes necessary to investigate the basic meaning of poverty as taught and practiced by Jesus. His warnings against the dangers inherent in riches point in one direction only: toward the Kingdom of God. The Kingdom is already being offered, and it is precisely in this eschatological context that goods of this world become an obstacle and a danger. The Synoptic tradition attributes a hard saying to Jesus: "How hard it is for those who have riches to enter the Kingdom of God! . . . It is easier for a camel to pass through the eye of a needle. . . ." (Mk. 10:23-25, Mt. 19:23-24, Lk. 18:24-25)—a hard and also startling saying for his disciples, who may still have held the belief, found in Israel's Wisdom tradition, that wealth was a sign of God's favor (Pr. 3:33-35). Instead, the rich man who asks what he should do to enter into life, beyond keeping the commandments, is asked to become poor in order to gain the Kingdom. The same idea dominates the other call narratives. Matthew points in the same direction, though with individual nuances, in his first beatitude: the Kingdom belongs to the poor in spirit (Mt. 5:3). Since the Kingdom is offered through Jesus, one must make the radical decision to be converted from everything that was important in the old order of things. God's grace transcends all the values and standards that inspire the citizens of this world.

One should note that the motivation Jesus gave for voluntary poverty is exactly the same one he gave for celibacy in his famous saying on eunuchs: the Kingdom. For the sake of the Kingdom family ties are seen in a new light; all are invited to place the Kingdom ahead of their family, and some choose to remain single. Because of the Kingdom, possessions in this world become an obstacle; so all are called to place the Kingdom ahead of their own goods. Note that the question here is nothing less than that of transcending the primeval human vocation as expressed in the twofold command of the Creator in Genesis: "multiply . . . be masters. . . ." (Gn. 1:28).

But while Jesus mentions only occasionally the difficulties that can be caused by one's own family, he insists energetically and in absolute terms on the serious dangers entailed by wealth. It never occurred to him to say: "How hard it is for a married man or woman to enter the Kingdom" but he did say that it is hard for the rich to enter. Husband and wife can enter the Kingdom together, aided by their mutual love and fidelity to the Gospel, while the rich must, in one way or another, leave their wealth behind. We believe this can be explained by the essential difference between an interpersonal relationship (which aids growth by tending toward sharing and liberty), and the relationship with things, which begins as a humanizing factor (we need things in order to exist), but which soon becomes a cause of alienation. One ends by seeking power, security, and ownership; one closes one's heart to others and becomes selfish. In order to justify one's conduct, ideologies are devised, and one becomes deaf to the Gospel Word.

Jesus often refers to the obstacle of material goods. They cause countless worries (Mk. 4:19; cf. Mt. 6:21, 25-34), and they arouse the desire to possess even more (Lk. 12-15). It is therefore impossible to serve God and money at the same time; that is, one cannot be both a servant of God and a slave of riches (Mt. 6:24). However, detachment from money is a difficult thing. This is another reason why it is impossible to enter the Kingdom unassisted. It is made possible only through God's liberating grace (Mt. 19:26).

In all this we are within the context of a practical orientation of life toward certain values. We are not specifically in the ethical realm, of a choice between objective good and evil. Riches are not condemned as evil in themselves. They are dangerous because they inevitably tend to enslave, thus making one incapable of listening to the Word and, consequently, unfit for the Kingdom. But neither does a situation of material poverty allow one to enter the Kingdom automatically. The Kingdom of God is not a socio-economic entity. Through a voluntary renunciation of riches, variously performed according to the inspiration of the Spirit, it is possible for a life to be oriented toward the Kingdom which is offered as a grace in Christ, in order to submit oneself to the single standard of the Gospel. In a Christian sense, disciples are poor because the love of God and neighbor has taken such a hold on their hearts that they can no longer orient their lives toward any other good. Thus Matthew speaks of the "poor in spirit." On the one hand there is the Kingdom of God, and on the other there is comfort, security, and power; these are the two alternatives between which Christ's disciples must choose.

Here we encounter a difference between the poverty of Greek philosophers and evangelical poverty. There is one point of convergence between them: both imply the renouncement of economic goods for the love of a higher good. But the basic motivation, and consequently the spirit of the two is very different. Renunciation in Hellenism is based on the objective value of earthly goods: they are low things, and should be despised because they bind the soul to the material sphere. Or else it is a question of affirming one's superiority as a self-sufficient being, similar to the gods, as in Socrates and the Cynics. A horizontal division is drawn; one rises from a lower to a higher sphere of being. Hence comes the well-known insensitivity of impecunious philosophers to the misery of the needy.

In contrast to this attitude, the Gospels continue the biblical theme of human beings as beings in need. We are created from the earth—we are not souls fallen from heaven—and we need things in order to exist. Thus poverty willingly embraced becomes an acknowledgment of one's poverty in the sight of God, and at the same time is connected with one's solidarity with those who live in want. But Jesus reminds us that, in order to live, our greatest need is for the Word and the grace of God ("Not by bread alone. . ." Lk. 4:4). With a vertical cut which marks two stages in the history of salvation, Jesus affirms that the search for comfort and power can be a tragic obstacle to the Kingdom which is offered. What Jesus asks of us is that we should "seek first the Kingdom of God and his justice," that we should fix our hearts on the Kingdom of God.

2. Poverty and Discipleship

The close relationship between voluntary poverty and discipleship has been suggested above. As Peter said after the failure of the rich man, the disciples had abandoned everything to follow Jesus (Mt. 19:27). On his part, Luke summarizes the discipleship texts which he had received from tradition in the following words: "None of you can be my disciple unless he gives up all his possessions" (Lk. 14:33).

One must choose the Kingdom or riches; to follow Jesus or to have possessions. This is because following Jesus means to direct one's life, as he did, toward the Kingdom which he announces and which is offered through him. Just as he, being consecrated to his Father's affairs (Lk. 2:49), left his own family in order to form a community united by the will of God (Mk. 3:31–35) and just as he embraced an uprooted manner of life (Mt. 8:20, Lk. 9:58), so also must his disciples.

If the concept of poverty as an imitation of Christ is not explicit in the Gospels, the idea of sharing his destiny and his manner of life, uprooted because it is dedicated to preaching the Kingdom, is explicit. As we saw above, St. Paul links poverty to Christ's kenosis, a theme we will return to shortly. For now it will suffice to observe how the theme of poverty in the following of Christ becomes imitation and mystical identification with him. From St. Jerome's time the tradition of religious life spoke of poverty as a *sequi Jesus nudum et pauperem*. Certainly the monks, acting under certain influences and reacting to the particular situation of a Church which had become powerful, actually went beyond their model. The hermit who was praised because, when he died, he owned only a knife for his work,[65] or the cenobite who was punished because he let slip the expression, "my tunic,"[66] certainly were poorer than Christ in a material sense; or perhaps they were giving greater importance to the material fact of not possessing anything than Christ himself attributed to it. The cultural context was different. But the fact remains that they were acting in this way because they wanted to follow Christ in his poverty, and because they intended to live exclusively dedicated to the search for the Kingdom of God.

3. Poverty of Spirit and Actual Poverty

Thus the really important factor in the disciples' poverty as in that of Jesus is to have one's heart intent on the Kingdom, to place one's treasure in heaven (Mt. 6:19–21), to spend one's life in an effort to attain the Kingdom and its justice (Mt. 6:33). The expression "poor in spirit" should also be understood in this way, even though in Matthew it has wider implications.

Should we then say that what matters is the inner detachment of the heart? If that were so there would be the danger of falling back into that bourgeois ideology of poverty of spirit as an attitude of inner detachment, which has made so many rich people happy. In regard to that, K. Rahner points out that although Christian ethics is fundamentally an ethics of the conscience and the spirit, it must be carried out in concrete ways in the context of concrete reality.[67]

We, on our part, conclude that poverty of spirit must, of necessity, be real poverty. One should note that we are speaking of Christian poverty in general. Its forms and concrete expressions vary according to individual vocations, even within religious life. It remains true, however, that in one form or another poverty must be practiced in every Christian life. There is a requirement for simplicity on the one hand, and for solidarity with the poor on the other, that is common to every Christian vocation. The orientation of existence toward the Kingdom of God brings with it certain choices and, consequently, certain renunciations in one's manner of understanding the possession of earthly goods, of using personal power, and of enjoying life.

4. Poverty and the Kenosis of Christ

The necessity of incarnating poverty of spirit in life's concrete facts and choices is confirmed by the connection St. Paul establishes between renouncement of part of one's goods in favor of the needy and the kenosis of Christ, his becoming poor for our sake (2 Co. 8:9). We believe that J. Tillard has made a significant contribution to the theology of poverty by recalling, in this context, the law of compassion that dominates the history of salvation. God comes to meet us in our actual situation of misery and alienation in order to give us back our freedom and dignity. This movement of salvific presence culminates in Christ, through whom God descends to our level. Jesus is the witness of the Father's love, that is, of the Kingdom, because he has participated in the utter poverty of sinful humanity (Ph. 2:6-11).

If the Christian's poverty is to be a participation in the kenosis of Jesus, it must follow the pattern of the Incarnation expressed in the concept of kenosis. One takes upon oneself, in one way or another, the poverty of those in need. This is an integral part of evangelical poverty, which is a poverty of incarnation. Giving aid now and then, renouncing some pleasure in order to be able to increase giving, more effective politico-social action, renouncing a privileged position or the search for one's own advantage (in certain vocations of secular Christians as well) in order to live among the poor, the profession of religious poverty are all different expressions of one's assuming the condition of the needy. To act in this way is to manifest the presence of the Kingdom, of God's love which saves us and before which we are all equally needy brothers and sisters. The Kingdom unites what social sin has divided.[68]

Herein lies a second fundamental difference between the Stoic, Cynic, or Neo-Platonic type of poverty, and evangelical poverty. The renouncement of goods in Hellenism is, in itself, a liberating factor, and the goods may therefore be tossed into the sea, or given to rich relatives or friends. The gospel invitation to renounce wealth, the vocation to poverty, is connected with distributing wealth among the poor (Mt. 19:21). We have seen how Paul, in 2 Co. 8:9, points to Christ's poverty as the motive for solidarity with the poor. In Acts, renouncement of property is strictly connected with ecclesial communion (Ac. 2:44–45, 4:32–35). While in Matthew and Mark the renouncement of goods and their distribution among the poor are simply associated in the same logion, without making communion with the poor the nucleus of poverty, in Luke almsgiving and sharing with the needy are given a strongly ecclesial significance. This is the way to make the Kingdom visible in the ecclesial community. Renouncement of one's own property is a preparation for communion with the redeemed.[69] Thus while one renounces one's goods for the sake of the Kingdom, the Kingdom itself appears basically in the *agape,* in solidarity.

5. The Religious Profession of Poverty

Thus far we have discussed the various aspects of evangelical poverty, a basic requirement of the common Christian vocation. It is certainly an arduous vocation but the New Testament does not therefore limit it to an elite. We have spoken incidentally of the various forms by which evangelical poverty can be expressed. When we speak of "various forms," we are not referring only to the basic difference between the type of poverty of Christians called to live in the world and that of Christian religious, but also to the different forms of poverty within the secular and religious vocations. We have noted that in ancient times some secular Christians were thought to resemble monks because they gave to the poor the part of their earnings not required for the strict necessities of their simple life. In our day there are married couples who go to the Third World, and some militant Christians who renounce good positions in order to share the condition of the poor and contribute to their liberation. Among religious there is also a great variety of institutionalized forms of poverty. There is the more evident poverty of sharing in the Institutes founded either to serve the needy, or simply to incarnate the Gospel among the most unfortunate. And there is the poverty of the Institutes that administer funds in order to maintain their ministries.

It is the characteristic of religious life to be the visible expression of the presence of God's Kingdom in this world by concretizing the radical requirements of the following of Christ in a lifestyle freely chosen and publicly professed. This is done basically through the profession of celibacy for the sake of the Kingdom, which dedicates the individual's person and life totally to the Lord and his concerns. The public profession of Christian poverty continues this tendency to express and institutionalize certain fundamental demands of discipleship. It requires that the form of poverty embraced should be both visible and significant. The two dimensions of Christian poverty, namely the recognition of our own basic misery as sinners before God, and a descent together with Christ into the depth of human suffering in which so many brothers and sisters are submerged, must appear in this public profession of poverty.

Traditionally, from the time of the first hermits until now, this public profession of poverty has been accomplished by requiring that all religious divest themselves of their goods as an initial act of their religious life. It should be noted that the monasticism of both the anchorites and the cenobites, as well as the later forms of life dedicated to the divine service, have this divestment in common. In fact in monasticism the initial act of divestment was the significant expression of dedication to God.

Divestment is, therefore, the form of poverty required of religious. They renounce their property in order to create a type of Christian existence which reveals their total dedication to God and his service; in other words they desire to live in such a way as to be *possessed* by God's Word and his grace. According to Mt. 6:26, the possession of riches, with the resulting security and power, has the fatal tendency to end in enslavement, that is, in becoming property. The radical renunciation of religious is, objectively, an act of faith in God's Providence (one should remember that, for anchorites, saving for the future was one of the most serious sins against poverty), and of love for God and the neighbor in him, because they commit themselves to live only for God and for others.

In fact, divestment does not consist in renouncing only what one has at the moment, but also what one might possess in the future. This, in the final analysis, is simply the expression of a refusal to live for oneself (and for that projection of oneself which is one's family); a refusal to work for one's own social advancement and for one's own gain. Thus, while poverty carries on the tendency to go out of self in order to be entirely dedicated to the Lord and his affairs which is characteristic of celibacy, celibacy renders the practice of a radical form of poverty easier. The universalization of love, which is characteristic of celibacy, appears also in divestment. Ancient monastic tradition linked the act of renunciation with the distribution of property among the poor. Thereafter, all the rest of their lives, anchorites practiced divestment by turning their income over to the poor, keeping for themselves only what was strictly necessary for their immediate future.

Within today's new cultural and economic milieu, religious life must certainly retain communion with the needy as an essential part of that poverty of kenosis which is a fruit of compassion and of one's own evangelical spirituality.[70] It is not enough to assume a sort of abstract condition of poverty without any concrete reference to those who endure actual poverty. But the orientation toward sharing, which is innate in the profession of poverty, goes beyond solidarity with the indigent. Even for the hermit, to live exclusively for the Kingdom means to live for the Church. When poverty is professed by a community, it also means to work for others. Divestment implies a refusal to draw wealth, power, and prestige from one's work. This is very important in our times, especially for societies composed predominantly of a middle class, whose main source of security, and often of power too, is constituted by a higher level of education rather than by inherited wealth. Here we are dealing with an unalienable asset, often acquired with the help of one's religious community. The only way one can renounce this is to turn it to the advantage of others, of the brothers and sisters who form one's evangelical community, of the Church, of those who are deprived of these advantages.

6. Poverty in Communities

The great majority of religious profess poverty, together with the sharing of goods. Individual divestment is required for life in common. In analyzing the evangelical concept of poverty we have seen that it includes a movement toward solidarity. St. Luke makes this quite explicit in speaking of almsgiving and divestment as factors that permit the Church to emerge as a communion of hearts in which there are no class distinctions. Thus no opposition exists between poverty and sharing of goods, at least not on the ideological level. In practice the result is different. It has often been observed that the sharing of material goods actually limits real poverty. Membership in a community usually provides security for the future and, in many cases, a higher standard of living and level of education than would have been attained in the world. Father Régamey wrote: "It has too often happened, and still happens in prosperous communities, that the vow of poverty causes the reality of poverty to disappear."[71]

To counter this objection, which even fervent Christians frequently oppose to the statement that religious practice poverty, two types of answers are given.

The first answer says that it is the community which possesses the goods (sometimes very substantial ones), whereas the individual members are poor. This is a very old answer, already suggested by John Cassian.[72] It is old, but mistaken, as the history of religious life shows. If poverty is what the term signifies, then how can religious be called poor when they share in notable goods (luxurious buildings, country estates for vacations) merely because these are not legally theirs but belong to the community of which they are members? K. Rahner, in his study on the theology of poverty, reiterates that members of a rich community cannot be, or call themselves, poor.[73]

The second answer insists that religious cannot use the goods provided by the community without their superior's consent. But it is clear that dependence on the community, a consequence of the sharing of goods, is not sufficient in itself to make one poor. No human authority exists that can dispense from the common Christian vocation to poverty, nor transform into a visible profession of poverty something which is not poverty.[74]

One must remember that giving witness to the Kingdom of God and its transcendence is the task not only of the individual, but also of the Christian community. Thus the profession of poverty also applies to religious communities as such. Insofar as the community is poor, its members are poor. The sharing of goods is not in itself a specifically Christian circumstance; it becomes such only when it is animated by that spirit of poverty backed by facts, which is an inescapable trait of Christian existence. This requires simplicity and austerity of life for one thing, and openness on the part of the community toward the needy in various ways that are possible in different times and places, such as ceding part of their income to them, laboring for them, founding works for their benefit, and courageously defending the rights of the poor.

Forms of simplicity and austerity of life vary according to the times and the social environment. This historical variation depends on the economic evolution of society. But not everything is relative in regard to poverty: freedom from enslavement to well-being and protest against the fate imposed on the lowly are essential elements of poverty. Christians who are citizens of rich nations must not forget the great poverty that surrounds them within and beyond their borders.

As for the problem of owning or not owning of economic goods, on the part of religious communities, there is no single solution. On this level the forms of poverty vary according to the specific vocations. Communities which intend to incarnate the Gospel among the outcasts by sharing their actual condition, practice a form of poverty which differs from that of communities founded for the apostolate or for the benefit of the poor. In these cases the possession of material resources is necessary. The important thing, as we see it, is that these assets be effectively dedicated to their purpose (evangelization, education, and works of mercy), and that religious, individually and collectively, be mere administrators of these goods.

VII

Community Created by the Gospel

Within a few decades ancient monasticism underwent a Copernican revolution. It had been born under the sign of solitude, and this was the basic and typical expression of the monks' dedication to God's Kingdom. Their solitude was so basic that they were called monks (solitary ones) or, in the typical primitive form of monasticism, anchorites (those who go away). Solitude undertaken as a radical form of celibacy permitted them to be exclusively dedicated to the search for God's Kingdom through prayer and asceticism. This, at least in the exemplary models proposed by certain biographies (of St. Paul, of Anthony during many years of his life, of Mary the Singer, and others), meant renouncing the enrichment coming from a dialogue and confrontation with others and, in practice (although not as a consequence of their theology), the liturgical and sacramental mediation of the ecclesial community as well.[1]

Little by little the monks rediscovered the value of encounter-in-community. After seven years of training under a famous hermit, Pachomius found that he was unable to tolerate even a slight contradiction.[2] The monks also rediscovered the value of dialogue, not only as a means for training new candidates, but for adult monks, too. Thus it was common for them to go on pilgrimage in search of an enlightened monk, to ask him for a word of guidance: *"Dic mihi verbum"* (Speak the word to me).[3] They also began to see the value of blind obedience as a mortification of the spirit surpassing even solitude. Through all these approaches, complete or almost complete solitude was mitigated and gave way to various forms of more-or-less institutionalized relationships, succeeded after a few decades by the first monastic communities. From then on, community life became the most common form of religious life, and the only one recognized in the West up to our own day. The projected new Code of Canon Law, which is still being prepared, again recognizes the existence of a hermitic vocation, not necessarily bound to membership in any group.

Women religious, from the very beginning of monasticism, seem generally to have preferred community life, most likely because a woman living alone might be prey to numerous depredations. Nevertheless, there were female hermits (such as Mary the Singer), though at least one of them had to dress as a man for protection. In the third-century Church, groups of virgins lived together and, as the phenomenon of monasticism spread throughout the Church, women embraced it by augmenting these communities of virgins and giving them a new spirit. The founding of male *cenobia* (communities) gave new impetus to women's community life. Across the river from the Pachomian colony, the sister of Pachomius led a community of nuns. In the case of the Basilian group, it was Basil's sister Macrina, their mother Emilia, and some friends who first began the women's community. Later Basil, his brother Gregory, and some friends established their community across the river from the women.

I. Celibacy, Anchoritism, and Community

The few facts we have put together show that religious life, after its common profession of celibacy and poverty, branches out in two directions. On the one hand is born a type of religious life in which celibacy is further determined and radicalized by anchoritism. On the other hand a type of life takes shape in which the profession of celibacy results in the formation of a community created by a common search for the divine will.

We have noted that in the second type of religious life, cenobitism, the profession of celibacy has the goal of shaping a community founded on the Gospel. In fact, in the practice of this form of religious life (the usual form), celibacy and community are not two separate realities but two vocational gifts, two charisms which complete each other. First of all, celibacy (the fundamental charism of religious life) makes it possible to form a community founded solely on the Gospel, whose only bond is the search for and fulfillment of the salvific will of God. Celibacy eliminates all the ties upon which the primary human community, the family, is founded, and thrusts those who profess it toward the great community of the Church. As we have seen, it is for this reason that the hermitic vocation is also a type of existence open toward the great community of disciples, the Church. With religious-life-in-community, celibacy leads to the creation of a community whose sole reason for existence is to be Church. Thus the great community of believers is incarnated in a small group of disciples who live together the mystery of the Church.

In fact, as we have seen, celibacy does not destroy human sociality, and even less suppresses the vocation to communion in Christ which is essential to Christian life, since it is an evangelical reality. It merely excludes the more intimate and immediate way of expressing sociality and of living Christian communion: marriage. The vocation to religious community, therefore, and the gift of the Spirit which impels one to enter it, completes the charism of celibacy for the Kingdom, and reveals the potential for communion implicit in celibacy's exclusive self-dedication to the Lord and his affairs.

Yet solitude remains a possibility. Celibacy does not necessarily result in the formation of a community, since the individual is not bound by specific ways of expressing and fostering communion. The person transcends all the structures it has created in order to fulfill itself. Basically one is a person in God's presence, in dialogue with him. Neither family nor religious community is absolutely necessary for human or Christian fulfillment. Thus there are some Christians who are called to celibacy for the sake of the Kingdom, and also to solitude, in ways that greatly vary. In the hermitic solitude of lives dedicated to intercession before God for the human race and for the Church, the dialectic structure pertaining to personhood is developed on the interior level of faith and prayer. God becomes the only Other, and one lives by one's relationship with him. What must not be lacking, however, is the consciousness of one's communion with the Church in whose mystery one is immersed, and the expression of this union through the participation in sacramental worship. The sort of total anchoritism suggested by the lives of the great hermits is not acceptable, as St. Basil rightly perceived. Celibacy and solitude, in the form of a single life, can also exist in the midst of the secular city, often in conjunction with an apostolic vocation. Communion is then expressed in the setting of a local church, by sharing in its worship and its life.

II. The Origin of Community Life

We do not know how the first monastic communities began to appear. John Cassian transmits to us two different versions of a legend according to which the first monastic communities were the uninterrupted continutation of the first Christians' rule of life.[4] They would, therefore, have preceded hermitic life. But numerous data and indications seem to point in the opposite direction: anchoritism was the first form of monasticism, and cenobitism developed from it. The development probably came about in different ways: from small groups formed by a master and his disciples, from larger colonies presided over by a group of elders or a charismatic old monk, etc.

We have a concrete and easily discernible example in the type of community which is now the one best known to us among those existing in Egypt during the fourth century: the group of brotherhoods subject to a common Father, known as the Pachomian Congregation. These brotherhoods founded by St. Pachomius illustrate the process by which monasticism accomplished that Copernican revolution from solitude to community, of which we spoke earlier.[5]

While Pachomius was still a pagan, his first impression of Christianity was that of a religion whose members did all the good they could to their needy neighbors for the love of the God of heaven. He did not yet know the name of Jesus, but the echo of Christ's commandment of mutual love had reached him. Thus he made a vow to the God of heaven that, if he were freed from military service, he would consecrate his life to the service of others.[6] Having attained his liberty, he was baptized, but was carried away by the ascetic current then prevalent in the Church and went to seek his own salvation under the guidance of the anchorite Palemon. Seven years later his former concept of Christian life as communion re-emerged, and in the midst of a vocational crisis he remembered his vow to serve his neighbor.[7] It seems that he then decided to consecrate his efforts toward helping some other monks. With the aid of his brother John he built a series of habitations for them, including some space in common. An argument he had with John over the size of a wall humiliated him deeply, because he realized that after seven years of solitude he was still incapable of bearing a contradictory opinion.[8] He was discovering the value of relationship with others, and of encounter as a means of mutual purification. At first his disciples did not profess sharing of goods, but only contributed to the common expenses.[9]

Pachomius had, however, made a fortunate mistake: he had provided a common space for his monks who, up to that time, had been used to living apart from each other. This forced them to deal with one another, and little by little they discovered, as Pachomius had done, the central importance of fraternal communion as it had been expressed by the apostolic Church in Jerusalem. They soon discovered the necessity for a minimum of disciplinary order to formalize their being together. One might say that the first religious community was the by-product of town-planning.

The original group avoided using monastic terminology. They were not monks, because they were not hermits; they called each other "brother." They settled in an abandoned village in which some secular people soon came to live also. Pachomius and his brothers celebrated the Eucharist together with secular people on Saturday evenings, while keeping the Sunday celebration for the brothers alone.[10] But as the brothers became more numerous, they separated themselves from the seculars, surrounding themselves with a wall, and when the community was at prayer they did not allow anyone to enter the church without the permission of the *Apa* (Father)—not even priests or anchorites who might be passing by.[11] They established other local communities which were all subject to the direction of the Founder, and later to that of the *Apa*. Thus a centralized organization was founded. Each village (as they continued to call their dwelling-places) was formed of several hundred brothers under the guidance of a Father. Pachomius' sister founded the first community of "sisters" on the other side of the river, facing the congregation's mother-house.

The Pachomian community presented a strange combination of diverse elements. Brotherhood was the fundamental structure of their life: they considered themselves as brothers, and their spirituality was centered on communion. The greater part of the faults listed in their Code are faults against charity. On the other hand, they had been founded by Pachomius, and considered him to be their Father and Master. Since hundreds of brothers began to be gathered in the same village, following the Egyptian tendency toward large organizations, their mutual relationships became less close, and a strict disciplinary order was imposed. The brothers were distributed in various "houses" according to their specialized work, under the direction of a head; and the entire village was under the authority of an *Apa* and an administrative Vicar. Their code of life had a rigidly disciplinary and penal character.[12]

III. Community Throughout History

At this point it would be impossible to trace, in a few paragraphs, the historical development of religious communities beginning from this first rather well-known community. It seems easier to group, under their various types, the various kinds of communities which gradually appeared in the Church.

1. Community as an Aspect of an Evangelical Life

The first type of community is born in the setting of a vocation to live the total Gospel with particular fidelity. The important thing here is not primarily community, but dedication of self to the divine service by the public profession of a life according to the Gospel. Obviously we are speaking of a particular type of life characterized by celibacy, but what counts here is the totality of the Gospel that is professed. Fraternal relationships, communion, form a considerable part of evangelical spirituality. Consequently, those who feel they are called to such a life create a community. To us it seems that this is the genesis of community in St. Basil, in St. Francis of Assisi, in the Little Brothers and Sisters of Jesus, and generally in all movements for renewal of fidelity to the Gospel. There are, however, some differences between them. Let us look more closely at the Basilian group and the Franciscan group.

A. The Basilian Group of Brothers and Sisters

Basil, together with a group of young friends who had been converted to asceticism by the example of Eustachius of Sebaste, formed his own "brotherhood" in a rural area near a river. It was a group of former students.[13] They were actually following the example of Basil's sister, Macrina, who, along with her mother and some friends, had established an evangelical sorority on a family property. In his *Asketikon* Basil explains the origin of the group. They wanted to live according to the Gospel, without compromising with the world.[14] But the Gospel is basically summarized in the twofold precept of charity.[15] It is very difficult, if not impossible, to follow the Gospel in the midst of the world, among those who scorn the Lord's precepts. It is therefore necessary to separate oneself.[16] On the other hand the hermitic life was unacceptable to the Greek spirit of Basil, Macrina, and their friends, for both human and Christian reasons. For God has created us as social beings, not as wild and solitary creatures, and He has raised our sociality to the level of communion in the Church.[17] The conclusion is obvious: it is necessary to create a community separate from the world, bringing together those who have the same purpose of evangelical fervor.

We note here the influence of the ascetic and monastic idea that one must not hope to be able to live the Gospel fully in the midst of the world, but we also note an affirmation of the Christian principle of communion. Community, for Basil, is the natural consequence of the unity of the Christian vocation and of ecclesial unity. The evangelical community is, therefore, an expression of being Church.[18] Through it one shares in the charisms of the others (communion of charisms), one gives a concrete expression to charity, and each one preaches the Gospel to the other, helping each other to advance.[19] It becomes possible to practice more virtues and to keep more of the precepts, because whatever an individual member does on the part of the community is done by all the others vicariously.[20] The image of the apostolic community of Jerusalem often shows through Basil's words.

As to its concrete form, Basil and his friends created a horizontal community, often referred to as a brotherhood in the *Asketikon,* presided over not by a Father but by a president (*proestes*). Obedience was mainly mutual obedience among brothers, though gradually the need was felt to strengthen the authority of the president and, in harmony with monastic tradition, to require that all open their consciences to him.

After Basil was appointed Bishop of Caesarea, he rediscovered the reality of the Church in the midst of the secular city, and he summoned his brothers to serve the travelers, the poor, and the sick outside the walls of the city. The number of members was to be reduced, and all of them were to live by their own work, but to work only to the extent necessary for self-support; the remaining time was to be dedicated to the study of Scriptures and of Origen. In this way it was easier to preserve simplicity and poverty and to maintain deep community relationships.[21]

B. The Franciscan Brotherhood

More than eight centuries later, Francis of Assisi and a group of young companions began the same experience again.[22] They, too, proposed to live a life faithful to the Gospel, intending to be a leaven which would renew the whole Church. Francis too, as well as Dominic and the various movements of *Pauperes Christi* before them, discovered his vocation in the missionary discourse (Lk. 10): itinerant preaching, not being bound to anything or any place, poverty, insecurity, etc.[23] The self-supporting monastery was succeeded by rootlessness and mobility. A group holding property in common in imitation of the apostolic community in Jerusalem (which is no longer mentioned) is succeeded by a group of itinerant disciples. It is the Gospel in all its completeness and depth which has the primacy, rather than the community; indeed Francis and his followers react against the traditional monastic and canonical community. He prefers to call his group a brotherhood, never a community. The group is formed essentially by fraternal relationships which are extremely personal.[24] The friars are united by a common vocation to live according to the Gospel, by the example and charismatic authority of Brother Francis, and by the Rule in which the project of Franciscan life is expressed. This new type of brotherhood requires new structures. The friars are united among themselves around their minister, and at intervals they come together for general or provincial chapters called to facilitate mutual encounter and the sharing of government.

Little by little this movement of itinerant friars, which had surprised Europe at its inception,[25] became more stable. The friars founded convents (groups, assemblies) in the cities or close to them, and built churches.

2. Community as a School of Divine Service

We could have spoken of the Benedictine monastery as a community born from the Gospel. This community, too, was formed in response to a desire to live according to the precepts of the Lord. But the Benedictine monastery has special characteristics which distinguish it from other religious communities.[26]

In order to understand the basic orientation of the monastery described in St. Benedict's Rule, one should remember two of its initial affirmations: the intention to organize, through the Rule, a school of divine service,[27] and the definition of cenobitism which St. Benedict takes from the *Rule of the Master:* those monks are cenobites who serve together under a Rule and an Abbot.[28] The definition is surprising, especially when one compares it with the concept of the Basilian group of brothers and sisters, or the Augustinian community. One is a member of the same monastery because one is subject to the same Rule and the same Abbot. The monks are, of course, united because they are animated by the same purpose, and are dedicated to the same divine service. They are part of the same militia[29] and form an *acies* (an army);[30] but being subject to the same Rule and the same Abbot constitutes the main element of the monastic community. This vertical structure forms the central axis of Benedictine monasticism. First there is the Abbot or Abbess, a man or woman who represents Christ, then the monastery is formed around that person.[31]

In fact the second chapter of the Rule (the first normative one) deals with the abbot, and the third with his council. What characterizes the abbot, above all, is *docere:* he teaches the commandments of the Lord.[32] Thus we have a primarily didactic concept of the community, and one which reveals its origin in the groups of disciple-monks who surrounded their charismatic elders in the desert. The group has now become an established community, and the authority of the Father-Teacher has become institutionalized. One should note however that in the *Rule of the Master,* from which this concept of the monastery reached Benedict, the monastery has only this vertical structure; but the Benedictine Rule completes and balances it. The six chapters of the Rule preceding the last one, which are Benedict's own addition, deal with the relationships between the brothers; here there are some echoes of Augustinian texts. Hence the common attention to the Word of God from which the Benedictine monastery is born creates a communion in charity.

3. Community as the Basic Structure of an Evangelical Life

In the history of religious life we find another type, or rather another concept of community, whose incomparable master is St. Augustine.[33]

What we now call religious life is defined by him primarily as communion with one another, a union of hearts directed together toward God, a communion caused by the grace of the Resurrection and expressed in a special way by the sharing of goods. It thus aims to reproduce the original community which took shape after Pentecost.[34] Augustine states specifically in his *Praeceptum* that this is the central element of life dedicated to the divine service: *"Primum propter quod estis congregati, ut unanimes habitetis in domo, sit vobis anima una et cor unum in Deum. Et non dictatis aliquid proprium, sed sint vobis omni communia"*[35] ("You have come together first of all to live as one family in unity of spirit, in order to be one soul and one heart in God. Do not, therefore, claim anything as your own, but have everything in common"). The idea is clear: the unity from which community is born is not merely something added to a religious life consecrated as the individual's gift to God, nor is it, as in the Basilian and Franciscan tradition, merely an important aspect of the evangelical life. For Augustine, communion with one another is the very center of religious life, and community is its fundamental structure.

Life-in-community according to the Doctor of Hippo consists essentially in two things: first *caritas* (charity), a reality which is not merely emotional or psychological, but theological and ontological: the grace of unity which flows from the Trinity, unifying a group in their progress toward God;[36] second, the sharing of goods, beginning on the spiritual level, and ending in the community of material goods.[37] Actually Augustine founded various types of communities: first a lay community, for either men or for women, then a community of priests and laymen, and finally a community of the bishop with his priests. In spite of the presence of the bishop, a horizontal dimension prevails, and dialogue (the classic method of Bible study) is very important in the group's life, counter-balanced by the peace and silence which belong to those who spend their life listening to the Word.[38]

4. The Missionary Community

All religious communities are born from a common vocation within the Church, but the majority of those founded since the Mercedarian and Dominican Orders have been intended to carry out a common external mission toward the rest of the Church. The Constitutions of the Order of

Preachers are explicit: "This Order has been founded to preach the Gospel. . . ."[39] These communities do not originate from a desire to live the Gospel together, nor primarily to foster Christian communion or to learn to serve God better, but in order to render apostolic service. Indeed, often the first element to appear in the genesis of these religious families is their apostolate. This can be observed in the history of the Dominicans, the Jesuits,[40] the Daughters of Charity, the Redemptorists, the Sisters of Mercy, and the Claretians.[41]

Ministry is therefore a central element in the spirit and life of these communities. It shapes their spirituality, directs their training, inspires their administration, and conditions their actual lifestyle. They are communities gathered together for the sake of a mission. Does this mean that in these groups community is strictly functional, a means to facilitate work done in common? No, it does not. No Christian community can be purely functional. Once the community has been founded (for apostolic motives) it becomes the means by which a group of Christ's disciples express and nourish their communion, their being Church. Their coming together, their schedules, will be very flexible and will depend on their ministries. But they are called to live in an evangelical community, and their apostolic vocation and the mission they have in common are also an important part of their being-in-communion.

IV. The Human Community Created by Religion

While preparing to reflect on this theme, we are immediately faced with two terms: *community* and *religious*. Beginning with the first term, every community presents two aspects: first, it is a group of people united among themselves by various types of subjective bonds, which may greatly vary; second, it is a group having objective relationships based on the sharing of well-defined goods. Psychology studies primarily the subjective relationships; sociology the objective aspects. Putting both points of view together, we say that a community is "a group of persons united by sharing in the same goods." Both aspects are essential. A community is constituted by persons who relate one to the other, but that does not suffice. The interweaving of relationships becomes community only when it is founded on a sharing of given objective goods, and finds its expression therein. A simple friendly relationship with a distant person, even though intense, does not create community.

We are dealing here with the ''religious'' community. On the objective level this means that the goods which are shared and which create this kind of community are those of religion, that is, the relationship with God. On the subjective level this implies that the fundamental relationship is a religious one: it is the effect of a relationship with God, which provides the means of expressing and intensifying it. Communities created by religion are thus not restricted to the bounds of Christianity. Buddhism produced monastic religious communities centuries before Christianity. Judaism had the Essene community of Qumran. Obviously there are profound differences between the various communities created by the Buddhistic, Jewish, and Christian religions—differences arising from the distinct ways of conceiving and practicing religion.

The fact that these religious communities are born from the sharing of a fundamental good, the relationship with God, becomes the primary source of inspiration for community living and the supreme standard to which everything in community life is referred. Religious experience is a radical experience, reaching the person's innermost core and tending to influence all aspects of the individual's life. Consequently the relationship with others is reflected in one's personal relationship with God, and conversely. One is united with others on the profound level of one's own conscience. Whether this is true in practice, whether one's relationship with others is really religious, depends on the authenticity and intensity of one's relationship with God. Belonging to a religious community does not, of itself, guarantee that the members, and that the relations between members, will be truly religious. The relationships created may be merely formal ones. We will return to this theme later.

It is implicit in this entire reflection that the religious community is a human one, composed of human beings. One should note that, throughout history, the religious community never originates in societies or faiths whose religion consists only in a series of rites to be conducted at set times and places. Those concepts of religion which relegate it to a limited sector of life require only priests. Religious communities, groups born from religion and for religion, arise only where religion is seen as something reaching the very roots of being human, and consequently as something tending to animate all aspects of human living. It is only in this view of religion that it becomes possible for all life to revolve around religious experience. But this also requires that the communities created for religious purposes should actually make it easier for their members to attain their complete human fulfillment. The human being is a social, gregarious being who grows within a community and finds expression through social relationships. Joining a religious community means choosing to express oneself, as a human being, in this kind of community.

The religious community, therefore, has two dimensions which are distinguishable only in theory: a specifically religious dimension, and a strictly human one. St. Basil was the first to take note of this twofold dimension of religious community: that of promoting the relationship with God, and that of completing the human fulfillment of its members. In the first edition of his *Asketikon* he presented community in the light of scriptural arguments on Christian communion. In the second edition, guided by his lengthy experience of community life, he also speaks of the sociality of the human person. The community is therefore called to facilitate the attainment of these two aspects of the person's vocation.[42]

V. Community and Vocation

When we turn to specifically Christian religious community, we find a characteristic common to all communities created by religion: that the community exists because God called it together. Going beyond the ancient concept of a ''chosen people'' (a people who already exist but are chosen by Yahweh), Deuteronomy speaks of the people as *Qahal,* an assembly called together by God (Dt. 31:30). The idea of Church comes from this, although in a deeper sense. We are Church because we are drawn together by the Word and listen to it. The preaching of and the listening to the Word in faith is the root of the Church. The initiative is from God, who speaks to us through his Son.

As is well known, this Word is not to be understood in a purely Greek, noetic sense, but as the creating and redeeming Word of God. From this point of view, the Word and grace are one and the same thing. This was shown clearly in the Apostolic Church. After having been dispersed by the scandal of the Cross, the group of the disciples was brought together again by the Risen One and thus became the Church. The one heart and one soul of the apostolic Church was a fruit of the Resurrection. It was the risen Christ who sent the Spirit and bestowed faith. It was he who, according to Ac. 2:47, brought new members into the community. The grace of the Risen One unites all of us in ecclesial communion.

What happened in the apostolic Church happens in every community gathered together in Christ's name. This is true of the Christian married community as well as of the community of celibates for the sake of the Kingdom. Confining ourselves to the latter, the origin of every religious family is traced to the vocation its founder or foundress received, which characterizes the sons or daughters of each family.[43] In other words, the community is created by a charism received by the Foundress or Founder and his or her companions.[44] The same may be said of every existing community. One becomes incorporated in it because one recognizes a certain correspondence between its mission within the Church and one's own personal calling. Here, also, it is the Risen Lord who brings new members to the community.

The fact that the religious community is born from a common vocation of its members suggests two concepts which are fruitful for the theology of community. First, persons are united by a common mission in the Church. They are called to build up the Church through a common lifestyle and common ministries; they are called to actualize the Church in an identical way. One should recall St. Paul's doctrine on charisms: there are various concrete ways of being in the Church and of being Church. The fact that all these persons have been called to the same mission in the Church, and consequently to actualize their being Church in the same manner, constitutes a strong bond of religious communion.

The second concept is that communities are created to foster the development of persons through the fulfillment of their vocations. Here we come to the Church's teaching on the relationship between person and society: the human person ''is and . . . ought to be the beginning, the subject and object of every social organization.''[45] This statement is based on the transcendent value of the human person. It is likewise valid when applied to a religious community, and even when applied to the entire Church: *sacramenta propter homines*. As an institution the religious community is a simple social and temporal (earthly) structure, created to help the human person reach fulfillment.[46]

Note, however, that we are speaking here of the community as an institution, that is, of its laws, administrative organization, financing, etc., and not of community as a group of people. Although the person is above the institution, one cannot affirm that one individual is above the others, nor that the others are subordinate to the individual. People are for each other, since being in communion is an essential part of being a person. To place the institution above the person, deifying it, gives rise to a totalitarian point of view. To place one's self-interest above communion is to show an incapacity to take part in the dynamics of an adult community. One is an adult when one gives oneself to others. Self-enrichment and self-dedication go together.[47]

VI. The Evangelical Dimension

1. Community and the Word of God

In order to reflect on the religious community as a particular kind of Christian community, we must return to the starting point which we noted earlier: since it is a Christian community, it has been created by the Word of God. The members have come together because, under the light and impulse of the Spirit, they have discovered their common mission in the Church and have discerned therein their divine calling to form a particular Christian community. Through the revealed Word, as found in the Bible and preached in the community, the Spirit has inspired in them (often in an extraordinary way, in the case of the Founders) the *memoria Jesu:* the rememberance of Jesus the celibate prophet, leading an uprooted life, consecrated to the work of his Father, who left his own relatives in order to form a new family together with those who listen to the Word and seek to do the will of the Father. The preaching of and listening to the Word is therefore the founding moment of community. The Christian community constantly returns to the Word in order to find in it the strength and light for living. Thus, the reading of the Bible and the examination of one's own situation in its light is not merely an act of devotion but an essential moment for community life.

We must now repeat what we said in speaking of vocation: the ''Word'' must be understood not in a merely noetic, Greek sense, but in the Biblical sense of *Dabar*, a dynamic reality, the creative and redemptive Word of God. To state that community is founded on the Word is to affirm that it is the fruit of grace. One does not form a Christian community merely because one wants to, or because of a convergence of affections or ideas, but through the action and grace of God. A humble petition for the grace of communion is necessary for community life.

Beginning with the Pachomians of the fourth century, and on through the Canons Regular of the twelfth, religious have often repeated that their life together was an effort to return to the origins of Christianity when, immediately after Pentecost, the Church in Jerusalem was of one heart and one spirit. Thus the religious were imitating the example of the apostolic Church as described by Luke in the first chapters of Acts.[48] These passages constantly refer to the paschal event (Ac. 1:22; 2:24; 3:15; 4:2,10; 4:33; 5:3; etc.).[49] In describing Christian origins Luke thus presents communion and community as fruits of the Resurrection. An intimate connection exists, therefore, between the Resurrection and community. Through the gifts of the Spirit the Risen Christ reestablishes human solidarity which sin had destroyed, and gives the human race a new and superior bond: the Spirit which infuses *agape* into our hearts.

This idea, which pervades all the initial narratives of Acts, is explicitly taught by Paul. In 1 Co. 12:12–27 and Rm. 12:4–5, the local Christian community is Christ's body, because it depends on the Risen One and lives in him. In Paul's Captivity Letters the universal Church is identified with the risen body of Christ (Col. 1:14; Ep. 1:22), a symbol in Paul of the sanctifying activity of the Lord. The Church is a *pleroma*, the zone in which the salvific power of the Risen One expands and is exerted (Ep. 1:23).[50]

2. Religious Community, Church, Community of Disciples

In taking as their model and rule the summaries of Acts which describe the community in Jerusalem, Pachomius, Basil, and Benedict tended to offer the religious community as a local incarnation of the Church. To what extent is this so? Many communities are strictly lay groups, without ministers. Others include priests and deacons but lack the episcopacy, in which the Church finds its ultimate configuration.

In order to answer the above question one must remember that Christ's Church exists where the Word of God is preached and accepted in faith and where the Eucharist is celebrated. The Church which comes into being through preaching culminates in the Lord's Supper. We have here the two essential elements of the Church: *fides et fidei sacramenta,* as the Fathers stated and St. Thomas repeated.[51] A religious community is simply a group of disciples listening to the Word and gathered around Christ's table. All religious communities are actually Church, although only germinally so since, on the levels both of the Word and the sacraments, they lack an essential element, the very one which transforms a group of Christians into an individual local Church: the episcopacy. The bishop is the preacher of the Gospel and the first minister of the Eucharist, of which he is president or which is celebrated in communion with him. Therefore the religious community is, in a deep sense, Church, but not a Church; it is part of the life of the rest of the local Church in union with the bishop.

The religious community, however, has its own special way of being Church. It is not a preexistent human reality like the family, or, in a different way, like the parish, which faith has taken over and elevated. Its only reason to exist is, precisely, to be Church, because in the religious community the human reality is brought about by faith. People come together in order to develop a type of Christian life, and interpersonal relations are born within this evangelical context. Like the family, the religious community brings being Church to the point of shared life; but unlike the family, it exists only to be Church. Its being so results from concretizing discipleship into a lifestyle by renouncing the formation of a family of one's own and by the search for one's own development within the power structures of secular society. The members of these communities want only to be disciples; they intend only to form a group of disciples. Among the charisms of religious life celibacy, rendered complete by the profession of evangelical poverty, is not only a vocational gift of individuals but a fundamental trait of life in common; while obedience, listening together to the Word and together fulfilling the divine will, is the very root of community life.

3. *Agape*

In Acts, Luke describes the apostolic community as being "united, heart and soul." It is possible that we are dealing here with a single reality, translated both through a Semitic concept (heart) and a Greek concept (soul). In fact Luke seems to refer, in his summaries, to two Greek proverbs affirming that friends have one soul, and that "among friends everything is in common."[52] One should note, however, that all through the New Testament the heart is the seat of the Holy Spirit and of his gifts. One could, therefore, see in these words a description of community as a meeting of souls (psychological) and of hearts (pneumatic). In this way we should again find the two dimensions of community.

It is clear, however, that Christian community as such is created by the communion of hearts, that is, by charity.

The charity which creates ontological communion before psychological communion is the love of God, the love with which God loves his creatures (Rm. 5:5). Love of one another, St. John repeats, is nothing other than the love of God which permeates us and through us reaches our neighbor (Jn. 15:1-4). For this reason God's love for us becomes perfect, achieving and fulfilling its total potential when, under its impulse, we love our neighbor (1 Jn. 4:12). But God's love has characteristics which distinguish it from human love. First of all God's love is a creative love. Human love is directed toward (and presupposes) a goodness which already exists. Divine love always creates this goodness, because, before God has loved, nothing exists.[53] Thus divine love is a force that radiates goodness. Jesus invites us to imitate precisely the generous love of the heavenly Father, who bestows his gifts on the good and the bad. Herein charity differs from friendship, for charity discovers even in evil an occasion for extending itself. The second trait of divine love, manifested in the history of salvation and particularly in Jesus, is that of being a redemptive love. Jesus insistently entered into communion with outcasts, and pointed to the remission of their sins as a sign that the Kingdom has come (Lk. 5:27-32; Lk. 7:36-50; Lk. 15:1-32; Lk. 19:1-10; Jn. 4:1-43). Christian *agape* follows this same line: God wants to redeem us through the love of our brothers and sisters. This is the source of the concept of Christian community as mutual evangelization and redemption.

The third characteristic of Christian love, that in which its newness consists, is that Christ is its source and its model. Christian love expresses itself by giving one's life for the other (Jn. 15:12-13; 1 Jn. 3:16, 4:9-11; Ep. 5:1-2). To give one's life, according to John and Paul, does not mean only to die, but to live each day, for others. In community life one proposes to die each day to oneself so that our sisters and brothers may live in God. This type of death is already a resurrection.

Obviously we are not speaking sociologically, of day-to-day occurrences in religious communities or in any other kind of Christian community. We are speaking of what the community is called to be according to the Word of God. Daily reality is actually torn and weakened by sin. For this reason a Christian community cannot exist without a continuous movement of conversion by which one renounces sin, which disrupts, and adheres to Christ, receiving from him guidance for life in communion.

4. Communion

Created by listening to the Word, the community develops as a concrete realization of communion in faith, hope, and charity, which reaches the point of the community's living together.[54] This communion is celebrated sacramentally in the Eucharist, at which point community attains a sacramental level and becomes, more properly, Christ's Church. The religious become one body of Christ in the one bread-body of Christ. It has been noted that, in St. Paul, the concept of Church-body is closely related to worship and especially to the Lord's Supper.[55] Thus there is an intimate connection between Christ's presence and the joint presence of the members of the community. Christ becomes present among the disciples who are gathered together in his name and are, therefore, already in communion. Thus, in celebrating the Eucharist, they celebrate their own communion. But at the same time, Christ's presence in the celebration and the sacrament of the bread and wine unites the disciples among themselves with a sacramental bond. The Eucharist actuates and builds up community. It has a close relationship with the rest of community life.

Communion is also expressed in the sharing of goods. Discovered gradually by the first Pachomian group, the communion of goods, as a requirement for religious living and in the light of the summaries of Acts, has become a typical trait of religious life in common. In Acts, the renouncement of personal property and the sharing of goods with everyone is a tangible manifestation of that ecclesial communion which begins in the Spirit. Religious communities carry their being Church to its ultimate consequences by establishing among those who are united in the Lord the community of goods which is characteristic of families.

St. Basil understood the community of goods in its fullest sense when he defined community as a participation in each other's charisms.[56] Unfortunately, in the ecclesiastical legislation on the common life developed in the eleventh-century clerical reform, the community of goods had of necessity to be given a strictly economic meaning, even though this meaning was always seen in relation to the communion of hearts. In reality life in common consists in a sharing of goods which far transcends economics. Being united in one faith, one Lord, and one baptism as Christians, sharing a common mission in the Church as members of a given family, and called to live together as members of the same local community, religious place all their personal gifts, both spiritual and natural, at the service of the same mission, to their common advantage.

The sharing of material goods and the relative divestment on the part of individuals presents new aspects in our day. In the past, property, either inherited or obtained through one's own work, was the source of personal security and social power. In our present society, characterized by a large middle class, the source of earnings and security for the vast majority of citizens depends on the level of their professional education. The level of one's education is something one cannot leave behind; it is an asset that inheres in the very person. Thus the divestment required by community of goods must consist not only in refusing to draw personal advantage from one's professional training, but in using one's talents in the service of the Church and of one's own community. In many cases this corresponds to a duty of basic justice, because often it is thanks to the effort of the community that one has been able to attain such an academic level.

To avoid equivocation one must keep in mind that community of goods is not sufficient, in itself, to make a group a Christian community. Ideal communities, seeking a return to the Golden Age through a community of property, arose even within Hellenism: among the Pythagoreans, the disciples of Epicurus, and the Neo-Platonists. Christianity has nothing in common with an aristocratic elite which detaches itself from the present in order to form a perfect republic or a perfect group of friends. The community of goods is valid only as an expression of charity, and charity cannot be confined to the boundaries of one's own clan. A Christian community which is not open to the rest of the Church and of humanity is not feasible. On the other hand, Christian poverty is not only an individual vocation, but also the vocation of every group of disciples, and it is professed in a special and public manner by groups intending to be communities of Jesus' disciples. For both these reasons the religious community must remain open toward the poor outside it and, in a more general way, to the suffering and the needs of others, expressing solidarity with them as far as possible with material assistance.

In a society like ours, which makes an idol of private property and drives all, even the poor, to useless consumerism by creating artificial needs, communities of Christ's poor must adopt a prophetic stance of protest and denunciation, eliminating private property among themselves for the sake of a higher brotherhood, defending the rights of the poor, and refusing, by means of their simplicity of life, to allow themselves to be dominated by consumerism.

VII. The Human Dimension

Created by God's Word, animated by the Spirit's gift of love, and accomplished sacramentally in the Eucharist, the religious community is still a human group, a "collection of individuals who have relations to one another that make them interdependent to some significant degree."[57] Groups arise in response to various kinds of common interests biological or social; among those based on social interests there are economic, cultural, and religious groups. Some groups tend toward the satisfaction of the needs of their own members (inner-directed); others tend toward activities and goals outside the group. The two tendencies, however, are often connected.

Every social group follows certain laws: a) to a greater or lesser degree the group exercises an influence on its members; b) the members organize a more or less definite structure in regard to hierarchy and social roles; c) the members create a system of values, customs, and rules.

Putting aside any further discussion of human groups, we fix our attention on the characteristics which distinguish religious communities. We have already seen that there are different types of religious communities.[58] Some, for instance, are directed toward facilitating communion between their members (inner-directed), while others are founded in order to carry on an exterior activity (outer-directed). But they all have certain elements in common: a) the group is founded on religion; b) it involves living together, which means it is created by the human person as a direct projection of self, to express itself and grow through a system of face-to-face relationships; c) it is made up of persons of the same sex; d) generally (except in the case of monastic communities) the local community belongs to a larger body: to the Order or Congregation, and to a Province, and consequently its members often change houses and companions.

As we have already seen, the fact that the community is founded on religious motives is very important because it has a deep influence on the interior life of individual members. But it also has sociological consequences. The community is founded on a religious interpretation of the world and life. The doctrine which expresses this vision and formulates the characteristic values of the group has a fundamental importance for the life of the community and for membership in it.

The fact that the religious community requires living together also exercises a strong influence on the nature of the group. In fact it means that: a) the life of the group is interwoven with face-to-face relationships; b) it embraces not just certain aspects of its members' lives but their entire life; c) the group is structured like a family-commune.

Let us pause to consider the quality of the relationships the religious community tends to create. Since this is a basic community which involves living together and which tends to embrace the entire life of its members, the relationships within the group tend to be interpersonal even though they are functional, that is, even though they correspond to roles created by the group. In fact "whenever people are in sustained association with one another, they enter highly personalized relationships which impose special claims and obligations upon them that are independent of their respective conventional roles.'"[59] The human person needs to be treated as such, and will develop normally in a system of interpersonal relations. Religious naturally expect to find such relationships within the community where they are to live. It is their main human group.

Clearly, in a community composed of adults of the same sex, the most harmonious interpersonal relation will be that of friendship. While community on the theological level is *caritas,* community on the psychological level is friendship. St. Thomas Aquinas often repeated that charity is a form of friendship, a generous, benevolent love in which one seeks the other's good.[60] Long before that St. Luke, in speaking of the *caritas* of the apostolic community of Jerusalem, seems to have echoed two Greek proverbs on friendship. But friendship is not an automatic phenomenon; it requires a certain spiritual attitude, beginning with respect for the other and continuing with solidarity, recognizing the other as a member of the group. It is nourished by mutual help, and actually becomes friendship when it culminates in concern over the welfare of one's neighbor.

The above considerations make it clear that religious community on the human level may not be taken for granted. It is a task which must be carried out by the members working together. It must be created by all.

The religious community has often been compared to the family, but this is a bit too facile. Both groups certainly have something in common. Both are basic groups, living together, in which the members' personalities are meant to expand; and both consist of interwoven interpersonal relations (that is, when both the family and the community are truly such). But there are two profound differences between the two. First, the community lacks that basic intersexual relationship which gives solidity to the family; the human basis for the religious community is consequently much more fragile, and the family is richer and psychologically more varied. Second, all the members of a community are adults and are therefore on the same level, while the position of family members is very different: from grandparents, to parents, to children. If it is true that the community needs a leader in charge of promoting community life, the father or mother image is not adequate to express this role.

VIII

Religious Obedience: Communion in the Will of God

In order to avoid wasting time, we should remember that the obedience we are about to examine is the obedience to which religious have committed themselves, from the sixth century on, at the very moment of their incorporation into a community. We are not discussing the obedience of citizens in fulfilling civil laws, nor the obedience to God's will as revealed by Christ and preached in the Gospel, which is the common vocation of all the disciples of Jesus, nor the acceptance of the authority of the Church's ministers by all Christians. Later, in the course of our reflections, we will have occasion to see whether there are points of contact among these various types of obedience, and what they may be. But at present we would like to make clear that we are discussing the obedience of religious, as such.

We will give the following temporary definition, open to later revision, and based on data provided by common experience: religious obedience is submission, freely chosen as a distinctive trait of a certain type of Christian existence, to a human authority which, as such, is not part of the ecclesiastical hierarchy although it has an ecclesiastical significance. Religious promise an obedience to which they are not obliged as Christians and as members of the Church. They promise it as an important part of their commitment to live according to a given Rule of life, and as an efficacious means to attain their goal. Vatican II defines obedience in the following terms: ''By their profession of obedience, religious offer the full dedication of their own wills as a sacrifice of themselves to God. . . . Moved by the Holy Spirit (they) subject themselves in faith to those who hold God's place, their superiors. Through them they are led to serve all their brothers (and sisters) in Christ. . . .''[1]

It is useless to seek a New Testament basis for this kind of obedience. Although the entire New Testament speaks of obedience to the salvific will of God as the starting point of all Christian life, and although some texts recommend submission to Church ministers, there is no saying, either of Jesus or of the apostolic Church, recommending that one should submit freely to a human authority as a special profession of evangelical life. Although Jesus was a celibate, thus illustrating in a concrete manner a possible lifestyle, there is no event in Christ's life nor is there any text in which freely chosen submission to a human authority appears as a possible form of Christian existence. We can cite only the obedience of Jesus to the Father, which inspires all forms of Christian obedience but which is not by itself sufficient to establish religious obedience. The transition from God to a human being as the immediate object of obedience remains to be explained.

An effort has been made to establish the *locus evangelicus* (evangelical source) of religious obedience as prefigured by the disciples, in the *sequi Christum*.[2] But since this is a matter of *oboeditio fidei,* of accepting the saving will of God manifested uniquely in Christ, we are back where we began: union with the divine will, which is a basic element of all Christian life. The transition to obedience to a human will, and certain other traits of religious obedience, still need to be justified. In this connection nobody will think of referring to the Christ child's submission to his parents, or to his respect towards civil or religious authority (as regards the latter, only in certain instances), because these examples have to do with the normal situation of a child or a citizen. Authoritative records of the history of religious life have quoted Luke 10:16: ''Anyone who listens to you listens to me, and anyone who despises you despises me.'' But this *logion* is addressed to the disciples who are being sent to preach, and it seems to us to refer to the entire Church as herald of the Gospel.[3] Jesus here begins to identify himself with his *pusillus grex* (''little flock''). However, St. Basil does not quote this text as an initial justification of obedience, but as an indication of the attitude of faith with which one should obey an authority which has its foundations elsewhere.[4] But the *Rule of the Master* quotes this text repeatedly[5] in order to justify the theory that in the Church there exists, by divine institution, a hierarchy of abbots alongside the hierarchy of bishops—strictly an ideology, in support of an authority which was in a state of crisis.[6] And the Master's application of Lk. 10:16 had a following.[7]

So we will first have to trace the birth of obedience within ancient monasticism, followed by its successive development in later forms of religious life. Then we shall return to the New Testament to investigate the theme of general Christian obedience and to reflect on the particular conditions which explain its transformation into the special obedience of religious.

I. The History of Religious Obedience

1. Solitude vs. Obedience: Primitive Monasticism

The first fact that emerges in this history is that religious life began without obedience. Solitude was the basic structure of anchoritism. The first religious were called "monks" because they spent their lives alone, or "anchorites" because they lived far from everyone. Their *fuga* was not only from secular persons, but also from the other monks. In some cases, which are offered as models in their biographies, their solitude was absolute for long periods of time. Anthony first shut himself up in a cemetery and then, for 20 years, was walled up in a ruined fortress.[8] Another anchorite remained completely alone for 30 years,[9] and two others for 40 years, without ever meeting anyone.[10] According to St. Jerome, Paul lived almost his whole life in complete solitude,[11] and Mary the Singer never saw a human face during 18 years.[12] Aside from the historicity of these facts (generally there is no reason to doubt it), one should remember that the lives of these monks and anchorites are "biographies" in the Hellenistic sense: models being proposed, descriptions of a *way of life*. By applying to all the *Lives* what Gregory Nazianzus said of the work of Athanasius, we may call them monastic Rules presented in the form of stories.[13]

This solitude—interpreted by them as a radical form of celibacy, which permitted them to live an angelic life, constantly in the presence of God—excluded all human contact. In order to seek God's will the hermit had only the Bible. In this setting one cannot see how they could have given any importance to obedience. Obedience could scarcely have found any place in the lives of the exemplary hermits we mentioned above. Nor does obedience seem to have been considered a fundamental trait of monasticism even by monks whose solitude had been somewhat tempered, and who periodically met with each other. Obedience is simply absent from lists of characteristic traits of primitive monasticism.

In discussing the special charism of religious life we gathered an anthology of these traits, which one might reread. Where monastic renunciation is spoken of, renunciation of family and goods is pointed out but there is no mention of renouncing one's own will. Cassian, swayed by the classical tendency toward the triad, and wishing to add a third renunciation, spoke of the renouncement of "all things visible" after discussing that of family and goods.[14] We know of only one instance, in ancient times, in which the renouncement of all things (poverty) and of all persons and relatives (celibacy-solitude) is accompanied by the renouncement of one's will through obedience: that is in the case of St. John Climacus, in the seventh century.[15]

Yet the practice of obedience had an early beginning in the desert. At a certain point, when the Church had already recognized monasticism and it was becoming institutionalized as a lifestyle, there arose, in Egypt, the requirement that whoever wanted to become a monk or nun should spend some years under the spiritual guidance of an experienced father or mother before going into solitude.[16]

In his *Vita Antonii* Athanasius makes this quite clear, by repeating that Anthony went first to learn spirituality from an ascetic, and by praising him for wanting to learn from all the elders.[17] Later, those who wanted to be recognized by legitimate monks or nuns had to receive the habit from another monk or nun[18] who had first to instruct them in spiritual ways and to give them pedagogical norms in order to insure them practicing what they had heard, and in order to test them. Candidates were expected to be docile. They were free to choose the spiritual advisor they wanted, but once they had made their choice they had to be open to instruction. This was docility (*docilitas, docibilitas*), the quality of being teachable.

At times one pedagogical instruction sufficed for an entire year,[19] but candidates who lived with their teachers remained longer under obedience to them. There were certain old men who used the novices as servants, and others rebuked them for this. Apa Poemen counseled the spiritual fathers to ''be as a model, and not as one giving orders.''[20] In fact some of the Fathers refused to give orders.[21] Isaac of the Cells protested: ''Am I the superior of a cenobium that I should give orders?''[22]

Many novices were praised for their obedience, which in some cases was heroic. This master-disciple relationship, however, was usually temporary, and the occasion for obedience eventually came to an end. The anecdote of Anthony and his disciple Paul the Simple shows this. Anthony was not too sure of Paul's endurance (he was along in years) so he imposed on him a rigorous discipline which he made even harder toward the end of the probation. Then one day, after having subjected him to a final severe test, he told Paul, ''Now you are a monk; go into solitude to be tempted by the devil.''[23] When the novitiate ended, obedience ended. He who could rule himself, according to his own conscience, was a monk.

Only a few instances have been recorded of a young monk deciding to remain under the obedience of an elder for many years in order to better practice mortification and acquire greater merits.[24] But this entails a different concept of obedience, which we will examine.

2. Obedience as Renunciation

It is significant that although obedience to a master or superior was not a distinctive trait of the anchorites' profession, they soon began to praise this virtue. Indeed, one already notes this in an apophthegm attributed to Anthony and in another attributed to Pambo (d. 374). According to the apophthegm in the Anthonian collection obedience (*hypotagē*—submission) and continence (*enkrateia*) tame wild beasts.[25]

This is a very significant statement because, in monastic tradition, the taming of wild beasts was a privilege of those who had returned to the state of perfection of Adam and Eve in Paradise. Similarly, the *Historia Monachorum in Aegypto* relates that Paul the Simple, Anthony's disciple, received, precisely because of his extreme obedience, the charism of expelling devils: another indication of great perfection.[26] Obedience, in the desert, was also praised by comparing it with other virtues. Joseph of Thebes considers submission to one's spiritual teacher, and the entire renunciation of one's own will, to be more meritorious than patience during illness; even more meritorious than purity of actions.[27] For Pambo, living under obedience is more meritorious than fasting, than total poverty, than intense charity, because these virtues are attained through one's own will, whereas by submitting one does the will of another.[28] Rufus says that in submitting to a spiritual father or mother one attains a higher reward in heaven than by retiring to a hermitage on one's own decision, by being patient, by practicing hospitality, or by never seeing anyone in one's solitude.[29]

The terminology used and the comparisons made are extremely significant. First of all "living in submission to a spiritual father" and "renouncing one's own will" are spoken of. What stands out in these apophthegms is obedience as renunciation of personal freedom. The Antonian apophthegm couples obedience with *enkrateia* (continence), an ascetic virtue which includes chastity, fasting and abstinence, and vigils. Obedience–submission would be the asceticism of the spirit, while *enkrateia* would be that of the body. Finally, the other sayings tend to compare submission to other virtues of renunciation and suffering: absolute poverty, fasting, patience (Joseph of Thebes, Pambo, Rufus). In two cases (Pambo and Rufus) it is placed above great charity and the virtue of hospitality, which is saying a great deal.

But one should note that, in the beginning, submission to the father was a typical trait of the novice, not of the monk. Anthony and his disciple Paul, to whom we have referred, knew this well since Anthony sent Paul, after a final test, into the desert. It is true, however, that the placing of submission above solitude led to the mitigation of anchoritism and to the creation of cenobitical life.

Thus we find ourselves facing a conception of obedience called *hypotagē* (submission) and not *hypakoe* (obedience[30] properly so-called)—a conception which sees obedience as the renunciation of one's own will and consequently as a form of spiritual asceticism. The first monks had given great importance to corporal asceticism (fasting, abstinence, vigils, hard manual labor, etc., and continence). Now they more and more taught a spiritual asceticism which culminated in the renunciation of their own wills. As we know, primitive monks and nuns, influenced by the spiritual tendencies of their times (Neo-Platonism, various forms of gnosticism), had placed renunciation at the core of Christian spirituality. Within the Hellenistic culture, whose thought created dualisms and dyads (God on one side and people on the other, God vs. the world, eternity vs. time, spirit vs. matter, soul vs. body), the mystics, whether Neo-Platonist, gnostic, or Christian, ascended toward God insofar as they left the world behind. In this light one can understand the anchorites' total solitude, even to the point of spending many years without any contact with the visible Church; and the affirmation that the weaker the body becomes, the stronger the soul;[31] and finally, the search for detachment from self through renunciation of one's own will.

It seems evident to us that this tendency of primitive monasticism (whose spirituality was so vividly Christian in other respects) does not correspond to the spirituality of Jesus and of the New Testament. In the New Testament renunciation, as such, is not a means of growth. The New Testament does not speak of mortification of one's will, but of union with the salvific will of the Father; not of *hypotagē* (submission) but of *hypakoe* (to be listening). Disciples will have to be ready for the hardest renunciations, even of their lives if necessary, but only when it is required of them. St. Jerome stated this, and Chrysostom and the Angelic Doctor, at different times, repeated it: what makes disciples of us is not leaving, but following. In thinking of renunciation it is significant to note that primitive monastic tradition reiterated that St. John the Baptist was the founder of their manner of life; and we know how carefully Jesus contrasted his own spirit and lifestyle with that of his forerunner.

It seems to us that Cassian is much closer to the original meaning of the novices' obedience when he states that the novices should first learn to overcome their own will (*suas vincere voluntates*),[32] or when he writes that the first sign of humility consists in mortifying all one's desires (*voluntates*, in the plural).[33] He explains this in his famous sermon for the imposition of the habit: the fear of the Lord must transfix the inclinations of our will to such an extent that they are no longer subject to concupiscence.[34] In other words, not only should the will not be subject to the weaknesses of the flesh, but neither should it be attached to the things of this world.[35]

The doctrine of obedience-submission as being *in itself* the renouncement of one's will reaches its peak in the *Rule of the Master,* where it assumes special connotations.

The Master shows himself extremely pessimistic with respect to the trust one can place in one's own judgment. In order to recommend submission to the superior *in omni oboedientia*, he affirms that the disciple ''must take nothing on himself by his own judgment; as Scripture says, 'There are ways which people think right, but whose end plunges into the depths of hell.' And David likewise says: 'They are corrupt and have become abominable in their desires.' ''[36]

Earlier, quoting the same biblical texts, he had written: "As to our will, we are forbidden to do it."[37] If by "our will" we are to understand the individual's will as opposed to the divine will, there would be nothing here to find fault with. Nor could there be anything to criticize if "our will" referred to an attachment to one's own will to the detriment of the requirements of community life. This seems to be St. Basil's concept of self-will, in his *Asketikon*.[38] But in the *Master* it is the will itself, personal freedom, which must be mortified. Often the reason he gives for some precept or prohibition is simply to prevent the will of the monk from asserting itself.[39] He writes on another occasion, "All who still have folly for their mother ought to be subject to the authority of a superior so that, guided on their way by the judgment of a teacher, they may learn to avoid the way of self-will."[40] Going further, the monks should submit to the orders of the abbot "so as not to do their own will."[41] Note that they are not to renounce their own wills in order to obey the abbot, but to obey in order to renounce.

There is no need to say that we cannot agree with this pessimistic attitude toward one's own judgment and will. It appears that the Master was greatly concerned about remedying a serious crisis in cenobitism. In order to defend stability he required a total renunciation of possessions, so that anyone who left would remain without anything.[42] In order to guarantee monastic discipline, the Master introduced into the solemn act of incorporation a promise of obedience which, up to his time, had been done privately as a simple expression of availability. It was for this same reason, we believe, that he inserted into his doctrine on obedience some radical expressions which alter its nature to some extent. It is highly significant that St. Benedict, although he followed the Master in these first chapters, excised all these pessimistic reasons for obedience and eliminated every hint of obedience for the sake of obedience.

3. Obedience as *caritas*

A. In the Pachomians

To discover the beginnings of a certain practice of obedience which will later be developed by a long tradition, it is necessary to refer to the earliest cenobitical organization of which we know, the Pachomian Congregation.

Seen from without, through the eyes of the early hermits, of Jerome, and also of Cassian, the Pachomians seemed different because of their practice of obedience. This was noted by the above-mentioned authors, and has been mentioned again by modern authors, some of them well known.

If one examines Pachomian sources, one notes that: 1) the Pachomians passed from semi-anchoritism to full community through their progressive discovery of the value of Christian communion; 2) the Pachomian group went through some crises which made them understand the value of order in a community, to protect its union in charity;[43] 3) the necessity for discipline and organization was greatly emphasized by the fact that some Pachomian "villages" included more than a thousand members; 4) nevertheless the Pachomians did not insist doctrinally on obedience, nor did they attribute to it a great religious value.[44]

If we examine the Coptic texts, the two times we find obedience mentioned (by Theodorus) it is presented as the fulfilling of practical orders for the welfare of the community.[45] It is significant that on both occasions Theodorus buttresses his arguments for obedience with a reference to the "free choice" of community life which each one has made. Similarly in the *Praecepta et Instituta* there is a rule that no one should do anything against the instructions of the head of the house.[46] Obedience is therefore still a matter of discipline and good order. There is only one text, the *First Catechetics,* attributed to Pachomius, in which there is a reference to the pedagogical obedience which characterizes disciples.[47]

The Pachomian community had shaped itself around the idea of fraternal communion. Experience made it clear that order was important. Thus disciplinary and penal rules were written which speak, above all, of fraternal charity and of community life. Insistence is placed on the necessity of obeying orders, adducing the free choice one has made as the reason for it. Obedience is considered above all on the disciplinary level, and appears as a reflection of fraternal *caritas*.

B. In St. Basil

Thus we have discovered the beginning of a tradition which sees obedience as a protection for fraternal communion and as a requirement for community life. Obedience is seen in reference to the orderliness of the community. This concept appears again, with even greater clarity, in the

Basilian groups of brothers or sisters. We say that it appears there with greater clarity because the Pachomian congregation had arisen around the prestige of a man who, after a long initiation, had received the charism of fatherhood, and who had always remained the Father and Master of all; thus a vertical structure was given to a community born from a progressive (horizontal) discovery of brotherhood. The Basilian group, in contrast, is a small group of young people who come together in order to follow an evangelical life. They have no Rule except the Gospel (Basil's *Asketikon* is a catechism), nor do they have a charismatic Father or Mother. The group of men is repeatedly called a "brotherhood,"[48] and its members are "the brothers."[49] In the first version of the *Asketikon* the members already have a president or head,[50] but the accent is placed on mutual obedience among equals.[51] In the second version of the *Asketikon,* made after Basil's death, certain experiences have caused the accent to be placed on the authority of the prefect,[52] who remains, however, always a brother in charge of order in the community—not a father. The obedience spoken of is one which springs from charity (mutual obedience) and from a disciplined orderliness. As the foundation for obedience Basil never cites the value of renouncing one's own will, but rather the value of solidarity among members and the desire to preserve peace.[53] Peace requires that the initiative should not be taken by everyone, but should be left to the one in charge.[54]

Thus in Basilian obedience the orderliness of the community predominates, at least quantitatively. But it would be wrong to reduce Basilian obedience to a purely practical and functional concept. The Basilian group is a brotherhood or sisterhood gathered around the Gospel in order to experience it together. The head is one who answers not only for the good order of the community, but also for its spirit: by his or her decisions he or she must share God's Good News with the brothers or sisters; in fact leaders must share their own soul by giving themselves to them in charity.[55] Obviously in the second *Asketikon* this role is understood. The head is still in charge of the *communis rerum cura* (care of community affairs),[56] but it is also established that, in harmony with monastic practice, the members of the group should communicate all the secrets of their hearts to the leader.[57]

It is in connection with this disciplinary and spiritual communion (the former protecting the latter) that St. Basil recalls the example of Christ obedient even unto death[58] and declares that his example is the measure of our obedience.[59]

C. In St. Augustine

St. Augustine (as also St. Jerome) had been deeply impressed by the obedience practiced in some of the monasteries he visited.[60] The splendid fact remains, however, that he did not found his successive communities for the purpose of practicing obedience (for him obedience is not a *consilium*) but in order fully to live the Christian communion of charity and of goods as described in the summaries of the Acts. The Augustinian *Praeceptum* is explicit: *"Primum propter quod estis congregati, ut unanimes habitetis in domo et sit vobis anima una et cor unum in Deum. Et non dicatis aliquid proprium. . . . Sic enim legitis in Actibus Apostolorum.* (First of all, because you are gathered together, you must live in accord in the house and be of one mind and one heart in God. And do not speak of anything as your own. . . . for this you read in the Acts of the Apostles)."[61] His famous Sermons 355 and 356 stress this abundantly in connection with the community of priests he established after his episcopal consecration. The center of their evangelical life is to be charity, the one heart by which primitive Christianity is relived. Everything is brought back to this source.

What role, then, do authority and obedience play in this communication of hearts that is to be intensely lived? Augustine answers this in his *Enarratio in Ps. 99:* "let them love each other; let the ships move toward port without colliding with each other; but if a strong wind arises, then let a *cauta gubernatio* (a prudent leadership) intervene."[62] Fraternal charity should suffice to keep peace in the community; but when difficulties arise, authority should intervene with prudence.

The last normative chapter (the seventh) of the *Praeceptum* speaks of authority and obedience: all are asked to obey the head as their father or mother, and especially the priest who has charge over them. It is the duty of the head to see that the Rule is observed, and consequently to correct negligences,[63] to live the Rule in an exemplary manner, to reprove the restless, to console the pusillanimous, to provide care for the sick, to be patient with everyone, but to inspire fear even though he or she should prefer to be loved.[64] Theirs is not a rule of power but a service of charity. The brothers or sisters should obey not as servants, *sub lege,* but as free people, *sub gratia.*[65]

Thus we are dealing with an obedience which is simply a reflection of charity. It has reference both to the observance of the *Praeceptum* (we already have a Rule) and to the order and peace of the group.[66]

D. In St. Francis of Assisi

Following the same plan, we come to the Franciscan idea of obedience. The Franciscan brotherhood was the fruit of St. Francis's own personal vocation to live the Gospel in its entirety in a deeply renovative spirit. A "brotherhood" is formed around this vocation, which is shared by others.[67] Members of the brotherhood are called *fratres minores* (the lesser brothers).[68] We do not intend to say that Francis and his companions gathered together primarily and purposely to live the mystery of *caritas* as Augustine had done. The Franciscans are rather in the line of Basil: the Gospel brought them together, but the Gospel creates brotherhood.

When Francis appeared on the scene there was already a long tradition of monastic life as well as a shorter one of canonical life. The monks had established a promise of obedience. Among the canons the practice of a triple commitment was developing: that of chastity, obedience, and the sharing of goods. The three counsels already appear in the Rule of 1221 and, using the canons' language, profession is referred to as "being admitted to obedience"[69] or "promising obedience."[70] One should note that none of this was created by Francis; he received it from canonical tradition.[71] There were dangers involved in the first Franciscans' lifestyle: dangers from their itinerancy, and more serious dangers they might encounter through contact with the movements of the *Pauperes Christi,* who were often on bad terms with the hierarchy. Thus the Order was bound in a special way to the Apostolic See by a promise of obedience.[72] There were also the admonitions of Honorius III against vagabond religious who avoided obedience,[73] and Francis insisted upon the brothers' complete obedience to their ministers and upon the necessity of being provided with an *oboedientia* whenever transferring from place to place.

What appears original in St. Francis is his interpretation of obedience in terms of genuine brotherhood. From this interpretation stem the Franciscan prohibitions against using the title of prior[74] and against exercising any dominative authority;[75] the recognized privilege of the brothers to report to the Chapter those ministers who do not live according to the Rule, after they have been warned privately three times and have not reformed themselves;[76] and, above all, the insistence of both Rules that the minister's office is really one of service,[77] and the recommendation that all the brothers should obey and serve each other because "such is the true and holy obedience of Our Lord Jesus Christ."[78]

As far as the object of Franciscan obedience is concerned it is obvious that, since it began in an itinerant setting, it was not focusing on domestic order. Franciscan obedience refers primarily to the evangelical Rule of life; through this it becomes a means of spiritual growth.[79] Secondly, Franciscan obedience has mission as its object.[80]

E. Conclusion

Thus a long and rich tradition on obedience exists in which, though in various forms, it appears as a reflection of fraternal charity. Obedience is often interpreted on the level of discipline and the orderliness of the community. Submission to a given order is required to protect charity and community living. It is a social matter which, however, takes on a religious aspect in this setting. Often the concept goes deeper: obedience is seen as the fruit of the communion of souls professing the same Gospel. The object of obedience is, then, the Rule and the spirit that animates it.

4. Obedience as *auditio fidei*

There is another concept of obedience, more monastic in character, keeping pace with the long and rich tradition whose development we have observed from Pachomius to Francis. In this concept obedience is defined first of all as an *auditio,* or *docilitas:* an attitude of openness of the monks or nuns toward God's Word as it comes to them through their spiritual advisor and, later, through their abbot or abbess.

This concept originated in the monasticism of the desert, in which the monastic candidates were supposed to choose for themselves an enlightened elder who would instruct them in the ways of the spirit. From this came the original idea of community as a merely transitory situation, as a preparation for the hermitical life of the perfect.

We know, however, that, besides certain monks who chose to remain permanently under the guidance of a Father out of love for obedience, there were colonies of anchorites or semi-anchoritical groups with a charismatic elder as head. In these groups one could remain alone or could, periodically, come in contact with someone else. In his catechesis, Pachomius seems to have proposed the two possibilities when he wrote: "If you cannot be self-sufficient, follow someone who strives according to the

Gospel and you will make progress with him. Either listen yourself, or submit to one who listens; either be strong yourself and you will be called Elijah, or obey one who is strong, and you will be called Elisha.'"[81] We do not want to dwell, at this point, on the submissive relationship (which sounds strange on the lips of the founder of the first cenobitical congregation). We want to draw attention, instead, to the distinction made between those who listen to God directly, through their own purified conscience, and those who instead subject themselves to another, who listens directly. We have here, for the first time, the explanation of a practice common in the desert: obedience is a listening to the divine Word, through the instrumentality of a spiritual advisor.

This concept of obedience finds its highest expression in the *Rule of the Master* and in the *Regula Monasteriorum* of St. Benedict. Having defined monasticism as serving together *sub regula vel abbate* (under the Rule and the abbot),[82] they both interpret the role of the abbot as pivotal in all monastic life. One should note that the abbot's prerogative is: *docere, instituere, iubere* (to teach, to decide, and to give orders).[83] He is, first of all, teacher or master. Though it is true that, in the next verse, the *iussio* (order) precedes the *doctrina* (instruction),[84] it is later explained that the abbot must lead (*praeesse*) his disciples with a twofold manner of teaching: with his actions even more than with his words.[85] He sets forth the Lord's commandments, and indicates what is forbidden.[86] It is also very significant that the disciples' obedience is not considered in relation to the orders of the abbot but to his teaching.[87] The next chapter of the Rule states that it is fitting for the disciples to obey their master.[88] The orders of the abbot have a pedagogical value.

In order to emphasize the obligation of obeying the abbot, the Master likes to quote Luke 10:16: *"Qui vos audit, me audit."* He does so seven times. In five cases he explains that these words were directed by Christ "to our teachers;"[89] in the remaining two he refers them "to the abbots.'"[90] The spiritual father and mother have been institutionalized. Now it is no longer their personal sanctity which inspires confidence and convinces others that they express the true doctrine of Christ. Now they personify Christ and have the authority to speak in his name precisely because they are the head of the monastery. We have already said that the *Rule of the Master* tried to defend the existence in the Church of two hierarchies deriving from Christ: that of the bishops and that of the abbots; but this is not what we are interested in. What we want to stress is that obedience is understood in terms of listening: that is, of faith. Cassian, who had sought to show that God uses the elders to reveal his will,[91] repeatedly described the monk's attitude in obedience as an attitude of faith: *fides et devotio*,[92] *fides et profunda cordis simplicitas*,[93] *fervore fidei*.[94]

Whom does one obey? The cenobite is *sub regula vel abbate* (under the Rule and the abbot or the abbess.) Benedict states that everyone (even the abbot) must follow *magistram Regulam*.[95] Basic obedience is owed to the Rule. But we must emphasize that the Rule seldom appears as the object of obedience;[96] reference is made rather to the observance of the Rule.[97] Obedience is ordinarily directed toward the abbot or the abbess.[98] The head of the monastery is, in fact, the interpreter of the Rule.

In view of this concept of obedience as the disciples' docility toward their master, some have asked whether it would not be right to conclude that obedience should be a temporary condition as it was in the desert, where this idea originated; far from being a permanent vocation, the monastery should be simply a preparation for hermitical life.

Nevertheless, both the Master and St. Benedict look upon the community as a permanent entity to which one is bound by a promise of stability. In fact the answer is that St. Benedict often eliminates the term *disciple,* substituting *monk.* Thus the relationship with the abbot becomes more that of a monastery than that of a novitiate. Secondly, Father De Vogüé has pointed out that the Master's treatise on obedience is composed of two clearly defined passages essentially preserved by St. Benedict; moving from Luke 10:16 and John 6:38, they offer two different concepts of obedience, one as a listening to the abbot through whom Christ speaks (*Qui vos audit, me audit*), and the other as an imitation of Christ (*Non veni facere voluntatem meam ...*), following him to the point of martyrdom. If the disciple's obligation of obedience might disappear, that of imitating Christ remains until death.[99]

We are not convinced that by placing the two biblical texts side by side the Master and St. Benedict wanted to give two complementary views of monastic obedience, and still less that they actually did justify the permanence of the situation of obedience. It is, however, certain that obedience, both for the Master and for St. Benedict, is always an attitude of listening, of believing, and consequently is the characteristic attitude of the disciple. It is obvious that the relationship of the individual with the head of the monastery changes with the passage of time. The relationship of the young novice is different from that of the adult.

The monk or nun always remains a listener. The Master and St. Benedict say that this is because Christ speaks through the abbot. We, perhaps, might say that the abbot or abbess is the interpreter and intermediary of spiritual tradition for the individual. The member of the monastery who listens personally to the Word contained in the Scriptures, and who is well versed in his Rule, still remains open to the teaching of tradition represented by the head of the monastery and in relation to it. The experienced teacher who interprets a long and rich tradition is not an invention of the Master, nor of Christian monasticism. This concept existed in the Buddhist Orient for thousands of years. Nevertheless, it is evident that the function of monastic teacher acquires special connotations in Orthodox and Catholic Christian tradition.

The idea of obedience as an efficacious formative tool inserts itself into this basic concept of obedience as listening to the Word of God in the Rule and through its interpreter, as a link in the long chain of Catholic tradition: not only does one receive sound doctrine by obeying, but one learns to subject one's desires to the divine will and acquires humility. The anchorites were already aware that by obedience one learns to subdue and restrain one's desires, as we have previously mentioned. Cassian merely gathers their teachings.[100] Cassian himself, however, represents obedience as constituting the first four signs of humility,[101] which the Master, and subsequently St. Benedict, converted into degrees of humility.[102] Furthermore, in Cassian obedience often appears linked with humility.[103] The Master shows that he is keenly aware of how much suffering is involved in this apprenticeship of humility through obedience by comparing it to martyrdom.[104]

5. Obedience and Mission

We still have to consider obedience in the setting of the apostolic mission or of the various charitable ministries which form an essential part of the religious life of many Institutes from the twelfth century on.

In considering the meaning of obedience in these Institutes one immediately becomes aware that one is not dealing with a new concept. Their doctrine and practice, even though with some significant differences, can easily be traced to the concept of obedience as *caritas,* which we have already studied. One of the leading representatives of this broader tradition is St. Francis of Assisi, one of the first who linked obedience to the apostolic mission. In studying St. Ignatius of Loyola, one of the greatest doctors of obedience, and at the same time one of the Founders who have linked it most insistently with the apostolic mission, one notes how he, too, goes back to obedience as charity. He states this quite concisely in his Constitutions, with words which dispense us from further research: "Since this union is produced in great part by the bond of obedience, this virtue should always be maintained in its vigor."[105] We are not saying that St. Ignatius and other founders did not also introduce other elements of tradition into their doctrines on obedience, for instance the ascetical aspects, thus formulating syntheses which have special characteristics. But these elements engraft themselves onto the basic concept of obedience as charity.[106]

The truly new element in all these Institutes is the linking of obedience with the apostolic mission, or more generally, with the ecclesial mission. The Franciscan Rule of 1221 already reserves to ministers the sending out of the friars to various places.[107] Both Rules require the minister's permission before preaching,[108] and the later one adds the requirement of obtaining the bishop's permission.[109] The Constitutions of the Society of Jesus state specifically that the fourth vow, of obedience to the Pope, was established with the intention of being always available to go wherever His Holiness should desire; thus all ministries are received either directly from the Pope or through the superiors of the Society.[110] One of the most important responsibilities of the Propositor General is precisely that of assigning missions.[111] This idea of the Superior as the one who assigns the mission is to be found in the Constitutions of almost all apostolic Institutes.[112]

Two consequences result from this concentration of obedience on the apostolic mission which is the central element of these Institutes. In the first place it puts obedience in relation to the Church's mission of evangelization, and consequently to the necessity of being in communion with the hierarchy. St. Anthony M. Claret affirmed this with special emphasis in his *Autobiography*.[113] In the second place it establishes a special bond of obedience to the Apostolic See. This special bond exists, even though with different characteristics, in the Rule of St. Francis[114] and in the *Forma Societatis Jesu*.[115] St. Vincent de Paul begins his chapter *De Oboedientia* by speaking of the obedience due to the Pope and bishops,[116] and St. Anthony M. Claret deduces the special obligation to obey the Pope and to be valid helpers of the bishops precisely from his Institute's mission.[117] Obedience here touches its ecclesial roots.

II. Summary: Theological Reflection, Efforts Towards a Solution

We come now to the final and decisive point of our research: a study of the meaning and value of the obedience of religious as such, keeping in mind the various data presented to us by history, since we are discussing a reality which emerged as a type of Christian life within the Church's history. We believe that the disregard of all or of a large portion of these data has often led in the past, and still leads in our day, to an unsatisfactory theology.

1. At the Source: Christ's Obedience to the Father

In order to renew the theology of religious obedience we must go back to the first principle for renewal formulated by Vatican II: the following of Christ as taught in the Gospel.[118] This is valid because the Christian religious sense begins with Christ, who is therefore the reference point for the ethics of his disciples. It is also valid because religious life, from the Church's beginnings, has been conceived as a particular *sequela Christi,* a special manner of following the Lord, inspired by the New Testament figure of the disciple,[119] historically succeeding the martyr's following of Christ in death.[120]

In the New Testament Christ's life is shown as being, above all, inspired by a filial union with the will of the Father. This is the object of the third petition of the Our Father in Matthew's version: "Your will be done, on earth as in heaven" (Mt. 6:10), the prayer which the evangelist has included in his fundamental Sermon on the Mount. This petition was repeated by Christ in Gethsemane, (Mt. 26:39). While Matthew refers to the will of the Father who is in heaven, John attributes it to "the one who sent me" (Jn. 4:34, 5:20, 6:38–39, 7:16–17). The will of God thus takes on a more precise meaning: it is the very origin of the mission Christ wants to fulfill. The fulfillment of the will of the Father who sent him is the constant attitude of Jesus (Jn. 8:29, 55).

Moreover, according to John, the fulfillment of the will of the Sender is the nourishment and the very reason for Jesus' life: "My food is to do the will of the one who sent me, and to complete his work" (Jn. 4:34).[121] The centrality of the role of Christ's obedience appears in two Pauline texts, but this time in contrast to Adam's disobedience: "As by one man's disobedience many were made sinners, so by one man's obedience many will be made righteous" (Rm. 5:19); "He did not cling to his equality with God, but emptied himself to assume the condition of a slave.... He was humbler yet, even to accepting death, death on the cross" (Ph. 2:6–8). We discover in these two texts a close relationship between obedience and salvation which we will encounter more explicitly in St. John.

While it is true that the Father shows all things to Jesus (Jn. 5:20), it is also true that, coming as he does from God, Jesus listens to his words (Jn. 8:47). An attitude of constant listening is a distinctive trait of his spirit. One has often imagined that the will of the Father was on all occasions clearly revealed to Christ's humanity; this would not be in accord with a sound Christology. Although he was enlightened in the depth of his psyche by the awareness of his sonship, as a true man he also took upon himself a human-spiritual history; he had to seek and to formulate. Christ's ministry begins and ends with two trials, both of which have as object his mission: the temptations in the desert, and the agony in Gethsemane. "Although he was son," says the letter to the Hebrews, "he learned to obey through suffering" (Heb. 5:8).[122] He never lacked (nor could he have lacked) that complete willingness which the same epistle attributes to him on his coming into the world: "You... wanted no sacrifice or oblation.... Then I said, just as I was commanded in the scroll of the book, 'God, here I am! I am coming to obey your will.'" (Heb. 10:5–7). The hymn in Philippians reminds us to what extent Christ carried his obedience to the Father: even to death on the cross (Ph. 2:8).

The connection between the "will" which Christ must fulfill, the Father as the "One who sends," and his "work" already shows us what the divine will is: that Christ should bring salvation to all humanity by means of his ministry which culminates in his death. He states this in his discourse on the Bread of Life and the controversy which followed it: "Now the will of him who sent me is that I should lose nothing.... That whoever sees the Son and believes in him shall have eternal life" (Jn. 6:39–40; cf. also Mt. 18:14). The will of God is the salvation of the human race, and this is the mission of Christ. It is not, therefore, a coercive or oppressive will.

The interpretation that Jesus gives to the Torah as being summarized in the two commandments of love, points absolutely in the same direction (Mt. 22:37–40). The entire will of God, therefore, is concentrated in love. A precept is a vocation.[123] If, then, we go back to the Old Testament we

note that the precepts of the decalogue (the ethical Torah) are simply a call
to develop one's humanity fully in justice, truthfulness, etc. Israel attributed the ritual precepts also to God, in the absence, we may say, of the
category of ecclesiastical precepts. Feeling obliged in conscience to observe certain taboos and customs, many of which had existed in other
cultures and prior to Moses, these were all attributed to God through his
prophet. It is known that the Hellenistic Jews considered these ritual precepts as human precepts.[124]

2. The Obedience of the Disciple

If the fundamental attitude of Jesus in relation to the Father who sent him
is filial obedience to his salvific will, even to death on the cross, it is easy
to understand how the same basic attitude must be found at the roots of his
disciples' lives. The preaching of Christ's obedience was also intended, no
doubt, to offer a prototype.

But there is no need for us to carry out this transposition ourselves. Jesus
did it himself in a logion which is common to the Synoptics: "Anyone who
does the will of God, that person is my brother and sister and mother"
(Mk. 3:35).[125] This means that the disciples are united to Jesus by this
communion of obedience to the divine will. Reference is later made, also,
to knowing the will of the Lord, of Christ (cf. Lk. 12:47)—that is, of
knowing the will of God as manifested in Christ. In fact, the disciples are
referred to as "those who obey him" (Heb. 5:9).

It is evident that through this transfer from Jesus to his disciples the
meaning of obedience changes in part. In Jesus it was a matter of accepting
the will of God who wants everyone to be saved, and of accepting his own
mission, the means of that salvation. As regards Christians, the New Testament speaks of submitting to the faith (Ac. 6:7), to the Word (2 Th. 3:14)
or more commonly, to the Gospel (Rm. 6:17, 10:10; 2 Th. 1:8; 2 Co.
10:15; 1 Pt. 1:22).[126] The salvific will of God, revealed in Jesus, reaches
the disciples through the preaching of the Gospel accepted in faith. It is not
a matter, therefore, of moral behavior but of a religious attitude: the obedience of faith.

This same central idea is to be found in the call narratives, which were
shaped more and more as models of the adherence to Christ to which
Christians are called in post-resurrection times. The Synoptics stress that

the initiative belongs to Christ who calls, and they point out the promptness of obedience: "And at once they . . ." (Mk. 1:18; Mt. 4:20–22). Matthew (19:27) and Luke (in all his call narratives) describe the disciples as those who have left all to obey their calling (Lk. 5:11,28). Thus attention is drawn to the ultimate requirements of obedience. The meaning of this obedience, which is proposed as an example to all Christians remains, however, always the same: that of obedience in faith to the Good News of salvation. This becomes even clearer if we accept, with K. Berger,[127] that the Synoptics' call narratives follow the model of the conversion of pagans to Judaism, as Hellenistic Jews conceived it, and which the latter saw as being prefigured by Abraham's vocation and his obedience to it (Gn. 12:1–12). It is therefore a matter of narratives of conversion to the Gospel whose subjects are not pagans only but even Jews themselves. Paul's conversion is also defined as "knowing God's will" in the very act of his hearing the Word of Christ (Ac. 22:14). St. Paul himself refers to the conversion of the Christians in Rome by contrasting their previous obedience to concupiscence with their present obedience "without reservation to the creed you were taught" (Rm. 6:17).

It is in this deep sense of obedience-faith, common to all, that the relationship obedience-following is to be understood; certainly not in the sense of a particular "counsel."[128]

It is clear that, in the New Testament, the will of God which we must obey is not limited to universal salvation attained by acceptance of the Gospel. God wills that we should *live* according to the Gospel of salvation which we have accepted: "What God wants is for you all to be holy" (1 Th. 4:3). "Be happy at all times; pray constantly; and for all things give thanks to God, because this is what God expects you to do in Christ Jesus" (1 Th. 5:16). In St. Paul, the Law to which Christians owe obedience is the Law of the Spirit which gives us life and makes us free (Rm. 8). Matthew, instead, expresses the requirements of conversion to the Gospel in the Sermon on the Mount, seeing them as a radical interpretation of the Law (Mt. 5–7); in the Synoptics these requirements are the precepts of love; and in St. John, the Lord's precept of fraternal love.

Particular missions also come from God and must be accepted in humble obedience within the context of our common obedience to the salvific will which follows us all through our life. Paul repeats that he is an apostle by the will of God (1 Co. 1:1; 2 Co. 1:1; Ep. 1:1; Col. 1:1; 2 Th. 1:1). Therefore Paul knows that, like Christ and in him, he has received the mission of preaching the Gospel for the salvation of others, and he seeks to fulfill that mission.

Obedience to human beings is placed, in the New Testament, on a definitely lower level. In one case only, that of the obedience of Philemon to Paul, is the term *hypakoe* used in reference to obedience to a man. Generally the term *hypotassein* (submission) is used, indicating the obedience due to social order and civil society (Rm. 13; 1 Pt. 2:13-18), of woman to man (1 Co. 14:34; Ep. 5:24; Col. 3:18; Tt. 2:5), of children to parents (Lk. 2:51), of servants to their masters (Tt. 2:9). Paul advises his Christians to be subject to those who exercise the sacred ministry and to all those who cooperate with them within the Church (1 Co. 16:16).

This, essentially, is the New Testament doctrine on obedience. In its light all Christian life appears as the consequence of obedience to the will of God manifested in Christ Jesus: a will of universal salvation. By accepting this Gospel, not once but continuously, we are saved. In obedience to the Gospel of salvation we will have to keep all sin far from ourselves. There is therefore, throughout life, a search for the divine will which is essential to every Christian life. It is not a matter of seeking for details of a written law. The Christian's Law is the Spirit.

It is evident that we are in the presence of a divine will and an obedience that are not in the least oppressive but are, instead, deeply liberating. What God wants is the life and fullness of the human being. By entering into communion with this salvific will humanity is fulfilled, in spite of, or through, the sacrifices which fidelity to the divine will may entail. The Resurrection is God's answer to his Son's obedience unto death (Ph. 2:8-9); when all seems to be lost, all has been gained. The mission which the Father first confided to Jesus and then, through him, to the Apostles, is collaboration with the Father in his plan of salvation: whoever obeys this mission will be saved. The mission is not limited to a few. We all have our own charism in the Church (Rm. 12:6, 1 Co. 12:4-11). In obeying this grace-mission we cooperate with the Church and attain our completeness in the one Body. There is, also, a mutual submission of Christians which is the result of charity and the body of peace in the Church: "Give way to one another in obedience to Christ" (Ep. 5:21); and, for the same reason, a submission to those who have the same ministry (1 Co. 16:16).

It will not be superfluous to repeat here what we said at the beginning of our study: that nowhere in the New Testament is there an ascetical concept of obedience, still less a doctrine of renouncement of one's own freedom as a value in itself. The renouncement of such a great good can be required only by fidelity to a greater good: the salvific will of God, a mission entrusted by God, the requirements of the Gospel, the peace of the community. It is to this fidelity that the texts of Christian radicalism refer. Nor, in the New Testament, is there a *consilium oboedientiae* that is, submission to a human being as a distinguishing trait of a type of Christian existence.

3. Obedience to One's Vocation

Since the beginning of monasticism, Christians have embraced religious life in obedience to a divine call. Religious life, in fact, is born from an act of obedience to God who is assigning a mission within the Church. Christians asked God: *"Quomodo salvus ero?*—Show me the way of salvation."[129]

They were thus seeking the way in which the salvific will of God would be accomplished in them. In the case of Arsenius and others, the answer came directly from their consciences. Much more often it came through listening to, or reading, the Gospel. We have said repeatedly that the biblical figure of the disciple who leaves all in order to obey the Lord's voice and follow him has been the great source of inspiration for religious life.[130]

Subsequently all religious life presented itself as a constant search for the divine will. In seeking to discover a Rule of life, the first monks and nuns had recourse to the Scriptures. The divine words became *praecepta Domini* and the Scriptures were initially the only Rule. Basil did not write a Rule, but rather a catechism for his evangelical group in which various queries about individual and community life are answered by biblical quotations.[131] But even after the first Rules had been composed, the Gospel is still spoken of as the only Rule.

In his *Prologue,* St. Benedict writes that the Scriptures arouse us from our sleep and urge us toward conversion,[132] and that, since the Lord has spoken, we have only to answer him daily with our actions.[133]

Among the anchorites the contact with the Holy Scriptures as a rule of life was direct. The Bible, either read or learned by heart, was their great companion in solitude. In the paradigmatic cases of the great hermits, all human mediation was absent from this effort to find the will of God. For many years neither Paul, nor Anthony, nor Hilarion, nor Mary the Singer, nor Benedict during his years of hermitical life, had any outside help. In fact, according to the common opinion, a monk or nun was the one who could discern the will of God and was strong enough to carry it out alone.

One should recall again what the catechesis attributed to Pachomius said: ''If you cannot be self-sufficient, follow someone who strives according to the Gospel, and you will make progress with him. Either listen yourself, or submit to one who listens. . . .''[134] A monk is one who knows how to listen to God within himself. When Anthony was dismissing Paul the Simple, after subjecting him to a series of severe trials and finding that he was able to control himself completely, he told him: ''By this time you are a monk; go into solitude to be tempted by the devil.''[135] Precisely from this arose the concept of pedagogical obedience (*docilitas*) as a transitional situation, and the other very common idea of community as an ascetical preparation for solitude.

Obedience to a doctrine or to a human will as intermediaries of the divine will was not an essential element of primitive monasticism; nowhere, in fact, is it listed as a trait in the numerous descriptions of early monastic life.

This does not conflict with the fact that mature monks also felt the need to consult Fathers especially endowed with doctrine and spiritual experience. Often, when the anchorites met each other, they would ask each other for a saying: *dic mihi verbum,*[136] or they would ask each other questions.[137] The *Apophthegmata* originated from these sayings and questions. The anchorites felt the need of discovering God's will together and, at a given moment, they began to stress the value of monastic tradition. In hermitical and semi-hermitical colonies these consultations, as well as the habit of gathering now and then in groups to listen to the most prestigious Fathers or to the head of the spiritual colony, became common practice. But these meetings depended on the free choice of the individual. Within the same colony there were often different rules of life governing the greater or lesser degree of solitude, or the meetings.

At this point we must ask: are obedience to the divine call and the continual search for the divine will elements of religious life exclusively? Certainly not. Obedience to one's vocation and constant searching are the basis and the animating principle of all forms of Christian existence. Every Christian is called to perfection, and all Christians should choose their lifestyle in obedience to their divine vocation. It is the Lord himself who distributes the charisms adapted for the Church's welfare, among which are celibacy and matrimony (1 Co. 7:7). We have left behind the times in which the idea of vocation was restricted to celibacy or virginity, because marriage was considered a divine concession to the weak.[138]

As Paul forcefully states, the Lord is the only one to distribute his charisms, his vocational gifts. There is, strictly speaking, no possibility of human mediation in this matter. There is no one in the Church who has the authority to impose a vocation. In order to recognize their divine calling Christians can and should make use of another's counsel. But there is no such thing as obedience to human authority in regard to choice of one's state in life; this choice takes place within a relationship of faith and love between the individual and God.

4. Cenobitical Obedience, a Mystery of Communion

A study of the Sacred Books shows that obedience to a human authority, as a characteristic, distinguishing trait of a form of Christian existence, is not found in the New Testament. When the Fathers began to outline a theology of the ''counsels,'' they did not associate obedience with celibacy and poverty; and the descriptions of monasticism which the first monks have left us do not include obedience as one of its typical traits. Hence the question: What is the origin of religious obedience?

We have already said that it would not be logical to trace it to the imitation of Christ's obedience to the Father, without further additions and clarifications, because in this case one would have to justify the passage from obeying the saving will of God to obeying a human being; and that is what we are discussing here. On this point we must keep in mind the caution expressed by Father Karl Rahner on the subject of the imitation of Christ. Aside from the fact that Jesus could not practice faith as we do, nor conversion from sin, neither could he, within his finite human nature and history, assume all experiences and situations. He was neither a religious subject to a superior, nor a member of the Church subject to a hierarchy.[139]

We have also said that one cannot justify religious obedience simply by quoting biblical texts which speak of common Christian and civil obedience (obedience to the Gospel, submission to authority). According to Father Jacquemont, to do so would be altogether *malhonnête* (dishonest).[140] Among other things, one should remember that religious authority (if one wants to discuss this) does not exist for religious until they have taken upon themselves the commitment of obedience. Thus we are back where we started: why does one make this commitment of obedience? To deduce it simply from the *sequela Christi* embraced by the disciples would be to pass from a relationship of faith, from acceptance of the Gospel or of Christ proposed by the Gospel as the prototype of all Christian existence, to a relationship involving submission to a human being. And this passage is the very thing that needs to be explained.

Can we say that, since religious life is a prophetic sign of the Kingdom, the commitment to obedience is made in order to emphasize the central importance of evangelical obedience?[141] This does not seem justifiable to us either. For evangelical obedience means obedience to the Gospel, communion with the salvific will of God as revealed in Christ; and this was splendidly illustrated in the lives of the first anchorites, in which obedience to a superior had no part.

It is unnecessary to repeat that the origin of religious obedience is not to be sought in a decision to renounce oneself, because self-renouncement in the New Testament is not a value as such; still less can renouncement of one's freedom be justified by itself.

A sure path toward finding the solution is offered by a simple historical fact: obedience began to appear with the growing need for fraternal communion among anchorites and semi-anchorites, and manifested itself fully in the first communities of religious. Over the course of history the obedience of religious appears as an important aspect of their "life-in-communion."

It is known that, within a few decades, religious life went through a Copernican revolution, passing from complete solitude to community life. While Pachomius was still a pagan he discovered Christianity as charity toward others. Later he was asked to place himself at the service of others and in doing so found how useful the relationship with others could be in discovering his own defects. Little by little the Pachomians began to turn to the apostolic community of Jerusalem as an inspiration and as a model for their community.[142] Following that, Basil rejected total solitude and required that those who wished to live according to the Gospel should form an evangelical group of brothers and sisters, imitating the Church of Jerusalem.[143] Finally Augustine placed the *cor unum et anima una* at the core of religious life.[144]

Among the reasons St. Basil gives in favor of community life are some that are very significant because they all point in one direction: that hermits are in danger of becoming self-satisfied because, having no one with whom to compare themselves, they are unable to discover their defects; that those who are hermits may each, perhaps, have received a gift from God, but that those who are members of a community share in the gifts of others; that many of the Lord's precepts cannot be fulfilled by one person alone, but can be carried out in communion with others. By this reasoning Basil basically meant that community is an excellent means for discovering the will of God. Following Basil's lead we can go further: one is in community because one is animated by the same *propositum* of pleasing God. Certainly a community is created, or one joins it, because one has discovered a common vocation. All of the community's life consists in this constant effort to find the divine will and to fulfill it.

Religious obedience consists, first of all, in this common search for the divine will as it pertains to the group and the individuals who comprise it. St. Augustine represented community not only as a grace of the Risen Lord, in whom one glimpses the unity and plurality of the Trinitarian mystery, but also as the *cor unum et anima una in Deum*. God is not only the origin of life in common, but also the purpose toward which the *cor unum* is directed. Religious community is oriented entirely toward the divine will manifested in the Word. It is at one and the same time a communion of wills and a common search for the divine will. Obedience-faith animates community living. For the individual, therefore, obedience means finding God's will in communion with others. Mediation has been a term applied to this process. We would prefer to speak first of communion. The common search for the salvific will of God is carried out by listening to and meditating on the Scriptures together; by dialogue in community and in local chapters, by means of relationships between individuals, and, as St. Basil rightly saw, by means of messages and gifts which other individuals bestow on us. This process also takes place on a provincial or universal plane in the respective Chapters.

Religious obedience is, therefore, *fides* and *caritas: fides* because it consists essentially in listening to the Gospel, and *caritas* because the listening is done in communion with others. We believe that we can hereby correctly summarize the two traditional conceptions of obedience: the one originating in desert monasticism and culminating in St. Benedict's teaching (referred to likewise by St. Thomas);[145] and the other, originating above all in the teaching of Basil, Augustine, Francis, etc. The element uniting the two traditions is the *communio,* communion in faith and love.

5. Religious Obedience as Faith and as Charity

However, in order to more clearly define the content and hence the very meaning of religious obedience, it will be useful to go back to the two aspects of the subject which have been brought out in the two distinct traditions we have studied.

We have already emphasized that obedience is basically an attitude of faith, of listening to the Word which announces the salvific will of God to us. This characterizes the religious community not only as a group-that-listens, but as a group-that-seeks. Since every community has its own mission within the Church, it should periodically question itself on its fidelity to this mission, as well as on the requirements of this mission in different times and different societies. The life of the Church and the signs of the times are, on different levels, indications through which God's will for the group is discovered. In this search the community must measure itself by the various means through which God speaks to it.

First of all, the community must obey the Gospel, the one norm upon which all Rules and Constitutions comment, and which they apply to particular vocations. Second the community must profess fidelity to its Rule and Constitutions, which express its own charism and spirit. Since the Rule and Constitutions are approved by the Church, fidelity to them is not only fidelity to the Spirit who raised up the Foundress or Founder, but also to the Spouse of Christ. Finally, there is the ecclesial life itself with its various tendencies and movements, the signs of the times, through which the community rediscovers the requirements of its own mission and periodically renews itself for that mission. All this should also be applied by individuals to themselves.

Having come to the level of the actual decisions with which we build our existence, we must seriously analyze the concept of obedience to God as an attitude of listening in faith, which we found in the New Testament, and whose application had not, as yet, raised any problems. When we treat of the acceptance of the salvific will of God, revealed in Jesus and carried out by him, the terms *listening* and *accepting* adequately express the attitude of the believer. It is a question of something (the salvific will of God) which takes place beyond us, in the transcendence of grace; we have only to accept the Word which proclaims this event and makes it present to us.

But when it is a matter of the particular events that form our lives, the Christian's role may no longer be defined merely in the passive terms of listening and accepting. The human person collaborates actively in formulating in concrete and specific terms what corresponds to the salvific will of God here and now. In fact, God wants our salvation with an utterly pure and simple act including all that is good.

To the extent to which we can conceive of God's way of acting, we must say that God wants our individual good within the all-embracing and self-diffusive Good which he is as he communicates himself to us. Human beings proceed in the opposite way: their knowledge begins from what is particular, and their will follows their knowledge. The human being must, therefore, compare available concrete possibilities with the salvific will of God, and discern what corresponds to that will in the present situation. In doing this the believer must be ready to listen to the Word (Scripture, preaching, the life of the Church, signs of the times) and must be docile to the impulses and enlightenment of the Spirit; but the believer must also actively cooperate with God in discerning what corresponds to divine love in concrete cases. This discernment results from listening, but also from active cooperation.

In the second place there is the aspect of charity, which was more greatly stressed by the Pachomians, by St. Basil, and by St. Augustine. While the Master and St. Benedict spoke primarily of obedience to doctrine, here it is obedience to decisions that is spoken of. One is therefore on the level of community discipline. This is the type of obedience that modern Constitutions propose. One might infer that this obedience is simply a matter of accepting that minimum of community discipline necessary for any group of persons living together. Some authors protest against this concept of obedience, and yet this is what several great Founders have spoken of. In the case of Institutes dedicated to external ministries, obedience involves these ministries: dedication to one ministry rather than to another, work in one location rather than another. Here obedience reaches more deeply into the individual's life than mere questions of the orderliness of the community.

But even in this functional concept of obedience there is, beyond the sociological question, a deeply religious one. Obedience is at the service of mutual charity. Communion requires not only orderliness but, as far as possible, harmony between wills (*concordia animarum*): we are fully in the context of the second commandment of love. The "oneness of heart" is attained by hearts that are unified by the grace of Pentecost. St. Augustine greatly insisted on this accord and on the peace it brings as a gift of the Spirit. Thus one understands how both St. Basil and St. Francis inculcated mutual obedience among the brethren, and how, in the first Basilian *Asketikon*, mutual obedience is stressed more than obedience to the head. It is clear that we have here gone beyond the limits of obedience in its strict sense, and find ourselves in the midst of the mystery of charity, in which obedience is rooted.

Besides this, there is cooperation with the Church's own mission: religious carry out their ministry as members of a community, and in its name. St. Basil had already noted this when he gave credit to all for the works of mercy practiced by individual members.[146] The ministry is confided by the community to the individual; it should therefore be chosen together with the community and with those who are responsible for it.

6. Obedience, Communion, and Authority

It may have seemed strange that, during all the preceding discussion on religious obedience, the term *authority* has appeared only once, and then only to deny that authority could be the origin of religious obedience as a distinctive trait of a type of Christian existence. It is clear that we are not speaking of obedience in *actu executionis,* which always presupposes a mandate-decision, but of obedience as a specific trait that animates a whole life, that is, of obedience as a "counsel." We said that from this point of view religious authority does not exist for individuals before they take upon themselves the commitment of obedience. Having ascertained this, it becomes necessary to show the reasons for making such a commitment.

We have not yet spoken of authority because, on the deep level of community obedience to the Gospel, where we had placed ourselves, that category did not yet have a determining value. Communion creates obedience, which is an important aspect of the ecclesial communion lived within a group of sisters or brothers. The bond of obedience thus appears as a commitment to live evangelical communion to its fullest extent, in a community that is born not of flesh and blood but of the Gospel.

An essential part of cenobitical religious obedience, on this level, is the common search for the divine will for the group and, within certain limits, for the individual. One should not say that obedience is involved only in the case of a pre-existing command. We are not, in fact, on the level of the obedience *due* to authority: a potential part of justice. We are rather speaking of evangelical obedience lived within a community, a virtue and a characteristic of a lifestyle. This already exists as an attitude, and on the level of seeking.

But obedience is also actualization. Having begun in a common search for the divine will, obedience culminates in a personal contribution to the fulfillment of this will. Thus we pass from obedience as seeking to obedience as actualization. In regard to the first phase of obedience we spoke of communion carried out as prayer, reflection, and dialogue; now, instead, we must speak of the mediation of authority, an abstract term with a sociological rather than a specifically religious origin, which refers to the duty and right a person or a group has to make decisions affecting others. The origin of the term is sociological, but we are speaking specifically of the religious community as a social group which needs decisions to give it cohesion and security. Since the sociological existence of religious communities is simply the expression of their communion in faith and charity, the mechanism by which their decisions are made has its roots in this religious foundation and is at its service.

We have spoken of the mediation of a human office between an individual in the religious attitude of seeking, and God's will. This mediation is certainly not automatic, as an idolatrous concept of authority might be (e.g., that of the Roman Emperor, the Führer, or the ruling party). Christianity, through its martyrs, has always vindicated the individual's right to be a conscientious objector. In moral theology the immediate rule of morality is one's own well-informed conscience. It is the person, not the institution, who is the created means of dialogue with God, able to listen to the Word and to accept or reject it. But the person is a social being who grows and finds meaning in life together with others. Religious who profess obedience are people who have felt called to gradually find the salvific will of God in a community founded on the common search for that will. God is listened to in communion. Tradition has followed two trends in speaking of this mediation of authority in human life. On the one hand monastic life, entirely oriented toward religious experience, felt the need to be open to the doctrine and experience of previous tradition, because religious experience surpasses the limits of concrete personal experience.

This happens in all forms of monasticism, Christian or non-Christian. Authority is, thus, a matter of spiritual direction. Our age, in a secular way and on a purely human level, has rediscovered this need, seeking help for self-realization from every kind of analysis and counseling.

The second trend, on the other hand, has its source in the concept of communion. Religious give themselves to a community, and the community gives itself to them at the time of their profession, so that they may live the Gospel together. Thus an ecclesial reality, the religious community, appears. In the Church we are evangelized by each other. The community, as such, has the duty to announce the salvific plan of God as revealed in the Gospel. In living together, one has the obligation as a community to establish in the light of the Gospel the direction which should be followed, and to make whatever decisions are best able to foster the development of the community and its ministry.

In making these decisions the community presents to its members, who seek guidance, a norm they must consider. It is communion which requires human mediation in formulating the direction to be followed. Thus the decision becomes an expression of God's will, not objectively or absolutely, but for the benefit of the persons involved, in the sense that this decision affects the religious communion of the individuals and the community life to which God has called them. In fact, by accepting that decision one reaffirms one's membership in the community; by rejecting it one wounds and weakens it to a greater or lesser degree. One's own judgment, though possibly more correct in theory, is to be sacrificed in favor of communion, unless there are serious objections of conscience. The important thing for a mature person is not to be always right, but to be able to live with other people's opinions.

It is clear that we are always speaking of a community decision. Religious authority is always a community reality. Its only roots are in communion. The source of religious authority, which differs from the rights and duties belonging to Church ministers, is community, an ecclesial fact. It is irrelevant for theology whether the decision is made collectively or by an individual authority. Individual authority, in fact, originates within the community and acts in its name as its instrument. The difference between collegial authority and personal authority is simply juridical. Canon Law recognizes both forms of authority (chapters and superiors) and the history of religious life shows the most varied forms of government, often influenced by civil models.

7. Obedience, a Sign and a Service

It is obvious that the small religious community must make its decisions within the context of the great ecclesial community. Not only by being attentive to the Church's life and needs, but also by listening to those who, through the apostolic succession, have received the ministry of pastoral government.[147]

Religious obedience in itself, in its various phases of seeking, listening, and acting, is a service rendered to the People of God, because it is a sign. The religious community, through its constant search for the divine will, offers itself humbly as an indication of what every Christian and every Christian community must achieve. Thus the communion of a group with the divine will enriches the entire Church, which is a communion of faith and love. By sharing in Christ's obedience one contributes to the salvation of the human race. As for the Institutes dedicated to apostolic and charitable works, obedience is closely associated with the numerous services they render the Church.

None of this is possible unless we die to ourselves. In order to obey the salvific will of God one relinquishes the possibility of disposing freely of oneself. While the renouncement of one's free will is not a value in itself, it is certainly a requirement of the supreme value of communion with God and our neighbor. It should be noted that this holds true both for those who make decisions and for those who carry them out. In the search for the divine will, those who are invested with authority must also renounce their own tastes and desires in order to seek the will of God. If all human authority is a form of service, religious authority is a ministry, and Christian ministry is a participation in the Lord's death: we give our lives for each other. The example of Christ, obedient unto death, enlightens us as to the extreme consequences that are possible in exercising the ministry of authority and of obedience. It was in this sense that St. Basil was the first to quote Ph. 2:8.[148]

IX

The Religious Vow

For centries the vow was one of the fundamental elements of religious life. Canonically, the public vow was a decisive factor in being able to speak of a "religious state." In fact the Church recognized as religious only the state of those who, as formulated in canon 487, "commit themselves to observe the counsels, by means of the vows of obedience, chastity, and poverty." In the past, up to the time of Leo XIII[1] and practically until the promulgation of the Code of Canon Law, only the state of those who pronounced the three solemn vows was recognized as religious life. The simple vow, originating as a private vow, later became the commitment proper to those Institutes which resembled religious without actually being such, until first Leo XIII, and then the Code, gave the simple vow its full rights of citizenship within religious life. The theological point of view had been established by St. Thomas Aquinas[2] and St. Bonaventure.[3]

The situation has continued to develop during our own times. First, Pius XII required the public profession of the counsels, but not the profession of vows, in order for a life to be fully dedicated to the divine service and so recognized by the Church.[4] Then Vatican II, speaking of religious life in a new, broader sense (including therein the life of the secular institutes), associated with the vows "other sacred bonds, similar in nature to the vows." Let us leave aside the question of the differences characteristic of secular Institutes, which certainly do not result merely from the fact that the vow is not a determining element for them. We are interested in religious life as a life fully dedicated to the divine service and recognized as such by the Church; that is, we are interested in the fundamental theological nature of religious life as "a life dedicated to the divine service," a formula which the Council applied to secular Institutes as well. The recent openness to wider possibilities with respect to constituent bonds seems to us to have significant consequences for understanding the role of the vow in a life given to God. As always, in order to throw light on the various aspects of the question, we will undertake some historical research.

I. The Vow Throughout History

1. Introduction: The Vow in General

The Old Testament makes abundant use of the category of vow, above all in the sense of offering some object, or person, or oneself (Nazirite vow) to God. See Lv. 27:28-29 for the vow of anathema; Lv. 27:1-25 for the offering of persons, animals, houses and fields; Lv. 22:18-27 for the offering of animals. Since the offerings were often conditioned by the attainment of a grace, vows came to mean promises, and the idea of obligation prevailed: Nb. 30:2-2-16. In the New Testament the category of vow as a ritual act of consecration or of promise has no importance. Certainly the Lord does not attack the idea of the vow-offering (*qorban*), but only the evil use it is put to by certain practices (Mk. 7:11). Later, in order to make himself acceptable to the Jews, Paul twice makes the Nazirite vow in connection with trips to Jerusalem (Ac. 18:18, 21:24-26), while others make the anathema vow of not tasting anything until they have killed Paul (Ac. 23:14). A difficult question on the existence of vows within Christianity arises, not so much from the not-entirely-positive context of the above passages (Christ's condemnation of a certain practice, Paul's concession to his Jewish environment, the perverse vow of Paul's enemies), but from the New Testament's complete silence in respect to vows. Might this be due only to the decadence in the Jewish practice of vows, as Father Séjourné suggests,[5] or might it rather be that the spirituality of Jesus has a different orientation? This is a question which we will have to face squarely when we make our theological reflection.

The Greek Fathers spoke of the vow (*euchè*) essentially in the Greek sense of an offering to God. This is the basic meaning of the term in Origen[6] and in Gregory of Nyssa.[7] Influenced by Nb. 30:2, Pr. 20:25, and Qo. 5:4, Origen had already spoken of the vow that is a promise.[8] The Latin Fathers, instead, are influenced by the typically Roman concept of *ius sacrum*. It is the question of having promised God to do something. Thus the idea of obligation predominates, and categories typical of Roman culture are used: *votum suscipitur* or *concipitur;* the one who makes it becomes *voti reus* or *compos,* under obligation to fulfill the debt incurred; *votum solvitur, redditur.*[9] The idea and terminology appear in Cyprian[10] and Augustine.[11] One might mention here that it was logical in the Roman environment to apply the precise category of *votum* to the *dicatio virginum* (the virgins' consecration).[12] In this context, St. Cyprian uses the term *vovere* as a synonym of *dicare*[13] without, however, giving it the technical meaning it had in Roman culture.[14] In St. Augustine the transposition is already evident: he speaks of virginity, of total continence, and of the continence of spouses as being the object of *votum;*[15] on one occasion he applies *votum* to monks as well.[16] The discussion, in all these texts, is centered on the sacred obligation resulting from making the vow.

In Hispanic surroundings the concept of *pactum* (pact) was applied to the *dedicatio virginum*. We find this for the first time in Canon 13 of the Council of Elvira: *"virgines quae se Deo dicaverunt, si pactum perdiderint virginitatis...."* ("Virgins who dedicate themselves to God, if they violate the pact of virginity....")[17] And again in the Rule of St. Leander: *"si pactum quod cum Christo pepigistis servaveris ..."* ("If you have served the pact you have made with Christ").[18] The pact was thus a contract with Christ.

2. Renouncement and the Habit in Monasticism

The vow does not play any part in the origins of monasticism; it simply does not exist. The first anchorites and cenobites were monks, living for the service of God without entering into any explicit commitment. The beginning of a monastic life was expressed by the renouncement of goods and the abandonment of the earthly city (anchoritism). They spoke of their renunciation as an initial and decisive moment: "from the moment when I renounced (all) and entered into the desert. . . ."[19] Other texts speak of the moment in which they began to live in solitude.[20] Even after the early creation of an initial period of testing under the guidance of an elder, no act to indicate the passage from this initial period to the monastic state was immediately established. After having put Paul the Simple to the test, Anthony recognized that he was already a monk because of his virtue, built him a cell three or four miles away, and ordered him to settle there in solitude.[21]

At a certain point the monks and nuns began to wear special garb, and the beginning of monastic life was marked by being clothed in the habit. Since monasticism had, by that time, become institutionalized, it was agreed that the habit should be given to the candidate by an elder in order to distinguish true monks or nuns from capricious and eccentric people who might imitate them. To prove the monastic professions of Pachomius or of Benedict, it is stated that they received the habit from a holy monk.[22] When the first coenobiums were established, the act of incorporation into the monastic community consisted in receiving the habit.[23] Later, when the act of incorporation following the period of probation was enriched by other elements, the investiture remained its crowning act.[24] To be clothed with the habit signified, for the monk, total renunciation[25] or the purpose of living a life according to God.[26] Consequently the exhortations will speak of the habit as a reminder of the commitment which has been made.[27]

The ancient custom of considering oneself dedicated to God through the act of being invested with a habit is recalled again toward the end of the eleventh century by St. Anselm of Canterbury, in a letter to a nun who had returned to the secular state with the excuse that she had not been consecrated by a bishop, and had not read the act of profession. Anselm gives weight to the commitment resulting from the *propositum* and the habit: "even though you were not consecrated by a bishop and did not read the act of profession in his presence, you have made your profession public by the single undeniable fact that you have worn the habit of your holy intention in public and in private, and in this way you have stated to everyone that you are consecrated to God no less clearly than if you had read your profession. Because, before it became customary to make this profession and consecration of the monastic purpose as we do now (*ista nunc usitata monachici propositi professio et sacratio*), many thousands of women and men professed this purpose through the habit alone."[28]

3. The Monastic *propositum*

In Anselm's text we have seen the habit and the *propositum monachicum* united. He thus summarized the point of view of ancient tradition. Indeed, leaving the city and being later clothed with the habit were merely visible expressions of an inner act of dedication to the divine service upon which monastic literature insisted: the *propositum* or decision. This term already appears in writings concerning virginity. Hippolytus stated that a virgin was constituted as such entirely by the *propositum* (*proairesis*), and not by an ordination.[29] St. Cyprian and St. Jerome also speak of the virgin's *propositum*.[30] The same concept reappears in the earliest monastic literature. The *Vita Antonii* often mentions the *pròthesis* (*propositum*, decision) as the decisive factor in the Saint's monastic life.[31] St. Basil speaks of the propositum (*skòpos, gnomê*) in the sense of a decision and choice of vocation.[32] The term is stressed in the same manner in the *Rule of the Master* where, however, a semantic evolution which had already appeared in Basil's text becomes stronger: the *sanctum propositum* is here identified with monastic life.[33] Thus the *propositum* in the literature on both virginity and monasticism is the decision by which individual believers give themselves to God. Since the first monks did not express this *propositum* with any special public act (except for the renouncement of their goods and the departure from the city), the primitive theology of monastic spirituality based itself on this interior act, and tended to credit it with special importance as a gift to God.

4. Incorporation into the Community

For those who were about to enter a coenobium, an act of introduction to the community was soon instituted as an initiation to monastic life. First of all the candidate had to be received (*suscipi, recipi*).[34] In the Pachomian community incorporation took place in a simple manner. Following a certain period of testing and instruction, the candidate laid aside his secular garments, was clothed in the monastic habit and, while the community was at prayer, was presented by the door-keeper to all the brothers (*adducat eum in conspectum omnium fratrum*), and was assigned a place.[35] No public commitment exists here: the postulant is accepted first by the superior, and this implies an expression, on the candidate's part, of the desire to serve God and be a good member of the community; but this obvious commitment is not made in any solemn way. The candidate begins to be recognized as a monk because he is clothed in the habit and has been introduced to the community. We may say that he becomes a monk because of his decision (*propositum*) to dedicate himself to the divine service, and that he becomes a member of the coenobium because it has accepted him.

Obviously the visible act of incorporation (by means of the habit) soon tends to become the social expression of the inner *propositum*. One notes this change in Cassian: the candidate is introduced to the assembled brothers (*in concilio fratrum productum in medium*), and in their presence the abbot takes the candidate's garments from him and clothes him with the monastic habit; after which the abbot preaches a sermon on the monastic calling and spirituality.[36] It should be noted, however, that in Cassian this first *receptio* with the vesting does not indicate a definite incorporation into the community. In fact, after this ceremony the candidate is entrusted to the monk who is in charge of pilgrims and guests, who instructs him and tries him for a year, after which time he is incorporated into the community (*admiscendus ex hoc congregationi fratrum*), by placing him in a group of *juniores*. The incorporation thus is gradual, and the various stages are not marked by any public commitment. In Cesarius of Arles' Rule, towards the beginning of the sixth century, virgins have already received their habit at the end of their novitiate.[37]

5. Beginning Monastic Life, a Commitment to God

It is natural that the nuns and monks should have practiced their *propositum* of serving God as an act of dedication to the divine service, even though they had hitherto made no public commitment (anchorites), or had only manifested their desire to adapt themselves to the discipline of the community (cenobites), without any formal commitment of a religious nature.

In a passage of the *Vita Antonii*, the beginning of monastic life is understood as a promise made to God, as pledging oneself to him; thus Anthony's faults are reckoned only "from the moment when he became a monk and made his promise to God."[38] Although no profession exists as yet, the beginning of monastic life understood as a commitment to God takes on such importance that it is considered almost like a second baptism. Cassian shows the same tendency to consider the *propositum* as a dedication of self to the divine service and a commitment. Even though incorporation into a monastic community did not yet include a public commitment, in his *Cenobitical Institutes* he encouraged the candidates to fidelity not only by threatening them with grievous punishment in the other world, but by reminding them of the passage in Qo. 5:4 (LXX): *"melius est non vovere quam vovere et non reddere"* ("it is better not to promise, than to promise and not fulfill"), an expression in which we find the term *vovere* connected with monastic commitments.[39]

In his *Conlatio IX* on prayer, the Abbot Isaac speaks of the various types of prayer, basing his discourse on the Greek term *euchè*. As we know, *euchè* in Greek means prayer in general, but also means *vow*. This caused a confusion of terminology which Cassian was unable to solve; he translates *oramus* where he should, perhaps, have said *vovemus: "Oramus cum renuntiantes huic mundo spondemus nos. . . . Oramus, cum pollicemur. . . . Oramus, cum promittimus. . . ."* But this confusion does not concern us here. The important thing is to note that, for him also, becoming a monk represented a commitment and a promise:

> We pray (*oramus* = *vovemus*) when, in renouncing this world we commit ourselves (*spondemus*) to live as though dead to the world's manner of existence, and to serve the Lord with all the intensity of our hearts. We pray when we promise to despise worldly honors and material goods, and to unite ourselves to the Lord with complete contrition of heart and poverty of spirit. We pray when we promise to observe perpetually a most pure chastity of body and a most firm patience, or when we commit ourselves (*vovemus*) to extract from our hearts the very roots of anger and sadness which cause death. Now, if we are later overcome by sloth and, returning to our former vices, we neglect all things, we will be guilty (*rei*) of our prayers and of our vows, and we will be told: "it is better not to promise, than to promise and not fulfill."[40]

It is clear from this passage that renunciation of the world and the profession of monastic life had come to be interpreted more and more as a commitment made with God. To us it seems that this appears quite forcibly in Cassian, in connection with the text of Qo. 5:4 and perhaps of St. Athanasius.

6. The First Promises to the Community

In the meantime, however, a promise and commitment to the community had been inserted into the period of probation. We already know from the

Praecepta Pachomii that during the few days of postulancy the candidate was warned of the great sacrifices entailed in the monastic vocation in order to test his character.[41] This practice must have existed even earlier, among anchorites, because the *Historia Lausiaca* tells us that Anthony acted thus when his disciple Paul the Simple came to knock at his door;[42] and the *Lives of Pachomius* states that the anchorite Palemon dealt in the same way with Pachomius.[43] Obviously, in answer to the objections and difficulties presented to them, the candidates reaffirmed their decision. "I will do whatever you teach me to do," said Paul: and Pachomius answered, "I trust that with God's help and your prayers I will bear everything." Rather than a promise, this was proof of their good intentions.

Into this encounter with one who warns of the difficulties of monastic life, Sulpicius Severus introduces the concept of a promise of obedience: *"omnem oboedientiam polliceri"* ("to promise total obedience");[44] *cum prima ei lex oboedientiae poneretur ac perpetue pollicetur ad omnia vel extremam patientiam"* ("when the law of obedience is first proposed to him and is perpetually promised in everything, even extreme suffering").[45] An effort was made in the coenobiums to protect community life from all disturbing elements by requiring the postulant to promise obedience to the rule. In this one notes the tendency to pass from a proof of one's good intentions to a promise of subjecting oneself to community discipline. This step is strongly stressed in the *Rule of the Master:* during the days of postulancy not only will the gravest difficulties be expounded to the candidates, but they will also be told that they will never be free to do as they please;[46] the entire *Rule* will be read to them, and they "will promise to truly keep it."[47] After this the novitiate will begin.

In St. Benedict's Rule postulants do not make any specific promise, but simply give a good account of themselves.[48] During the novitiate, however, the Rule is read to them three times, and they are left free each time to decide whether they will be able to observe it.[49] Clearly the candidates will then promise to observe the Rule, even though the term *promittere* is only used on two occasions: immediately after entering the novitiate,[50] and after the last reading of the *Rule* at the end of the novitiate: *"promiserit se omnia custodire et cuncta sibi imperata servare"* ("when the candidates will promise to keep the Rule and fulfill every order").[51]

7. The Basilian *homologia*

Proof of good will and promises were made to the superior or in a private conversation; obviously this was not an example of profession. We must go back to St. Basil in order to see the origin of the act of profession. In his Epistle 199 St. Basil noted that, while virgins made a profession (*homologia*) of virginity,[52] "we are not aware that men make any profession, excepting those who join the order of monks, and these seem to embrace celibacy silently." Basil is not satisfied with this custom, which was universal up to his time.

> I believe however, that it is fitting that they also should do it at the beginning, that they should be questioned and that a clear and unequivocal profession (*homologian*) be received from them. Thus those who perhaps later will return to a life of sensuality and self-gratification may be punished if they commit sins against purity.[53]

This is precisely what Basil ordered for his communities. In his *Asceticum parvum* he dedicates one chapter to the inquiry which must be conducted regarding the candidate,[54] and the following chapter to the proper time for offering oneself to God and making one's profession of virginity. From his answer it is clear that, although he holds that it is well to begin training children and adolescents in asceticism early, the religious profession of virginity should be made by those who have dedicated themselves to the divine service in adulthood. The infringement of the *propositum* would be equivalent to a transgression before the Lord (*quo teste*) of the pact contracted by the confession (*homologia* equals profession), and would therefore be a sin against God.[55] The *Asceticum magnum* takes up all these points and adds others. Above all, an increased use of terminology in respect to the consecration is to be noted.[56] The *homologia* or profession is also spoken of more often.[57]

What does St. Basil mean by *homologia?* The term *homologein,* in classical Greek, means specifically "to show oneself in agreement with" and therefore "to confess that," "to promise to do," and "to commit oneself," while the noun *homologia* has the more precise meaning of an accord, pact and contract. In Patristic Greek the term soon takes on the sense of "confession": confession of faith in martyrdom and in baptism (in which case the renunciation of Satan is also included), but also a recounting of one's sins. Clement of Alexandria uses *homologia* for continence,[58] and St. Basil and the *Apostolic Constitutions* use it in reference to virginity. In these cases it appears to be equivalent to a public assertion of commitment.

This term, in the Greek of the Fathers, has a strongly ecclesial meaning. Except for the martyr's confession of faith before the pagans, the *homologia* is carried out before the Church: in baptism, in the liturgy, and in reconciliation. We believe this to be the meaning of *homologia* within the Basilian group as well: it is a declaration made to the community. It is true that Clement speaks of continence being the fruit of a *homologia* (commitment) to God (*pros Theòn*). But we must remember that in one passage St. Basil speaks of the mutual commitment the members make to live together.[59] On the other hand it seems that the Basilian *homologia* was made, like the baptismal one, in answer to questions asked by the superior, or perhaps by the prefects of the Churches.[60]

According to Pseudo-Dionysius the monastic profession was made in answer to questions asked by a priest.[61] This declaration of commitment by which one becomes associated with life of the community has, undoubtedly, an intensely religious meaning. According to the *Asceticum Parvum* those who fail in the *propositum* sin against God, before whom (*coram quo*) they have violated the pact of their confession: "*quo teste confessionis suae pactum transgressi sunt.*"[62] The Greek text of the *Asceticum magnum* is still more explicit: God is not only the witness of their transgression, but is likewise witness and recipient of their commitment; hence they would sin against God before whom and with whom (*eis on*) they deposited the confession of their pacts.[63] We may thus conclude that the *homologia* is required by and made to the community, but God is also involved both as the witness (and thus it becomes an oath), and as the final recipient (*eis on*).

We must add, however, that St. Basil never introduced the term *euchè* (vow) and that his doctrine, like that of monasticism properly so-called, is rooted in the concept of a firm purpose. *Homologia* has become a community and religious declaration of the *propositum* (the vocational decision). We must, however, add that even if St. Basil does not use the term *euchè,* his description of *homologia* as an oblation, dedication, and consecration is an exact rendering, in other terms, of what pagans and Christians meant by *euchè:* an offering to God, rather than a binding commitment in the Roman sense.

As we have seen, St. Basil sometimes uses the term "pact." In his

Asceticum parvum "*the pact of the homologia*" is spoken of,[64] and in his *Regulae fusius* the terms are inverted: "the confession of the pacts."[65] It seems to us that the term "pact" serves here merely to strengthen the meaning of *homologia,* without adding anything new. We could translate the expression: a binding *declaration* (*homologia*) of commitment (*synthekôn*). One should also remember that, as we have already seen, Hispanic writers (Council of Elvira and St. Leander) also spoke of a pact of virginity (*virginitatis pactum*). Through the two concepts, the profession of virginity became comparable in a certain sense to baptism. This line of thought was followed by those who, in speaking of the monastic profession as a second baptism, called it "*secundum foedus, professio secunda.*" Baptism too, with its profession of faith and its renouncement of Satan and sin, was understood as a commitment. The resemblance to the baptismal liturgy is more evident when one recalls that probably with St. Basil, and certainly with Pseudo-Dionysius, the *homologia* consisted in answering a set of questions.

What was the object of this commitment pact? The *propositum,* as we know, was to live the Gospel in the radical, ascetical manner in which monasticism understood it. But in regard to the public act, Basil speaks only of the *homologia* of virginity. There are those who ask whether, perhaps, the *homologia* did not include other commitments besides that of virginity. It seems to us that such commitments were not expressed at that time. During the initial probationary period the candidate evidently was questioned on all the commitments of the group, but in regard to the public act of incorporation into the community Basil speaks specifically only of virginity. We know from his Epistle 199 that he wanted to extend to the monks the liturgical ceremony of the *homologia* of virginity which virgins made in the presence of the Church. A passage in the *Asceticum magnum,* which is not in the *parvum,* describing this ceremony, confirms that this innovation was suggested by the virgins' act of commitment; adolescents were consecrated with a typically feminine terminology: virginity, holiness of the body as something consecrated to God, etc. Ministers of the Church were even called in as witnesses, so that through them the holiness of the body could be offered to God.[66] This is all terminology from the *consecratio virginum*. From this we must conclude that very probably the solemn public *homologia* was made only for virginity. We are no longer specifically in the monastic environment. In fact Basil, in the above-mentioned letter, presents this as an innovation.

8. Other Eastern Professions

Within Eastern monastic tradition, from some aspects of which St. Basil purposely detached himself, various types of public profession arose. The profession established by Shenoutè, who reformed Pachomian cenobitism in the fifth century, is very significant. With him incorporation into the community no longer consists simply in receiving the habit and being introduced to the group. The candidate, "in this holy place and before God," reads a formula in which he commits himself not to sully his body and to fulfill the commandments of the decalogue: "If I fail in my promise, I will see the Kingdom of God but I will not enter into it. God, in whose presence I am making this pact, will destroy my soul and my body in the gehenna of fire." Since Shenoutè was averse to making vows, this is possibly in reference to a pact with the community made under oath in the presence of God, a pact required in a period of decadence and necessary to protect the established reform. In any case the content of the pact was intended to keep the coenobiums free from the more gross and serious faults: lust, theft, false witness, etc.[67] Whatever the reason may be, it is significant that even among Pachomian cenobites the need was felt to express their commitments explicitly in the presence of the community.

Pseudo-Dionysius is both closer to St. Basil regarding the liturgical character given to religious profession, and more faithful to monastic tradition regarding the object of the commitment. In his *On the Ecclesiastical Hierarchy* the monk professes (*homologein*) that he renounces everything, not only in practice but also in his affections, and that he wants to live according to the rule of monastic life. We are therefore in the presence of a profession of renouncement and of dedication to the divine service in all its breadth. But this *homologia* is made in a liturgical ceremony, in answer to questions posed by a priest, just as in baptism. The liturgical character of the profession in Pseudo-Dionysius is notable, and its baptismal connotation is evident.[68]

9. Promises in the Latin Profession

In the West, the *Rule of the Master* and St. Benedict's *Regula Monasteriorum* document another step in the historical evolution of monastic commitments. We have seen that during meetings preceding admission to the novitiate (the Master) or during the novitiate (Benedict) the candidate had to promise to observe the rule. We find this same promise in Sulpicius Severus. The two rules of Aurelianus (for women and for men) dwelt on this same point: the candidates listened to the reading of the Rule *in salutatorio* ("in the ceremony of welcome") and, if they promised to fulfill it, they were admitted.[69] St. Isidore of Seville required first the renouncement of possessions and then a written promise of perseverance, like the one required from those who join a militia or army: *"nisi prius ibi scriptis suae professionis spoponderit permansurum."*[70] No special ceremony, however, is provided for. The *First Rule* of St. Fructuosus provides that, after a year of probation, the candidate should receive a blessing in church, and then be presented to the community;[71] his *Second Rule* orders that, after having put aside secular garments and being vested in the religious habit, the candidate should be inscribed in a pact with the group.[72]

Thus in the Hispanic setting during the second half of the sixth century and the first half of the seventh, there was a tendency to formalize the monastic commitment. According to Isidore this was done by means of a written promise of perseverance, though he later speaks of a promise which is either oral or written.[73] This, and the fact that he justifies this by referring to the practice followed for those who are enrolled in the military legions, seems to suggest that it is a new matter. Fructuosus, on the other hand, speaks of a pact signed by the members of the community. We are not in a position to establish the precise origin of this pact: did it derive from the *pactum virginitatis* of the Council of Elvira and from St. Leander in his Rule for virgins, or from the influence of Visigothic law? The formula which follows the *Regula communis* includes elements outlining the rights and obligations of the abbot and monks (the pact), but it also speaks of a *traditio animarum* to God and to the abbot.[74]

The Rule of the Master and St. Benedict's Rule, which were written between 500 and 560 and hence were earlier than the Hispanic Rules—more or less contemporary with those of Aurelianus—show that a definite step forward had been taken in Italian monastic circles. Besides the preliminary promises of stability and observance of the Rule,[75] the Master requires that stability should be assured[76] by distributing one's goods to the poor or by transferring them to the monastery.[77] Those who choose to distribute them to the poor will not be required to sign a document of stability;[78] but those who give them to the monastery must sign such a document, transferring their goods irrevocably.[79] Candidates who claim that they have no goods must find guarantors who will sign with them, and must also endorse a penal clause.[80]

All this is only preliminary to incorporation into the monastery. The end of the novitiate is marked by a simple ceremony, carried out in chapel at the end of Prime, in which the candidate tells the abbot that he has "something to propose, first to God and this holy oratory, then to you and the community: I wish to serve God in your monastery through the discipline of the Rule read to me." The abbot asks him whether he truly wants this, and he reaffirms his decision. After this the abbot warns him that the promise has not been made to him, "but to God and to this oratory and to this holy altar." The abbot calls on God and the community as witnesses on Judgment Day.[81] After this the new monk places the document of the transfer of his goods upon the altar.[82]

These texts from the *Rule of the Master* have a great importance for the history of the religious profession. It is the first time in the West that we find an explicit declaration, in the presence of the community, of the individual's monastic *propositum,* and the first time this declaration is used to formalize incorporation into the monastery.

In St. Basil we had already seen a profession or public commitment, limited however to virginity, following the manner used in the *consecratio virginum.* Here, instead, that *propositum,* which included, from the beginning, the monk's dedication to the service of God, is declared publicly in all its fullness: "I wish to serve God" with the addition—since it is a matter of cenobitical life—"in your monastery." The Master adds his own formula: "through the discipline of the Rule read to me."

One is acquainted with the Master's tendency to stress the necessity of observing the Rule and consequently of obeying the abbot. Was this a defensive stance taken during a period of crisis for monastic life? It seems so. The same defensive attitude is to be noted in the initial precautions taken to defend stability. However this may be, the observance of the rule associated with the fundamental *propositum* (to serve God in the monastery) is included in the public declaration: the Latin *professio.* In St. Basil we found the same defensive attitude on the part of the institution that requires guarantees. He wanted the monks to make a public declaration, like the virgins, so that they might be punished in case they were unfaithful to their commitments.[83] In reconstructing the history of the religious profession one must also keep in mind this sociological factor.

But it would be very nearsighted to seek to trace the origin of public commitments to this defensive attitude alone. The public commitment was born, on the ecclesial and community level, as a natural counterpart to the individual *propositum*. One is aware of this not only in St. Basil, where *homologia* is described as a dedication of oneself to God, but also in the Master. The novice takes the initiative by declaring that he has something *suggerere* (to propose humbly) "first to God and this holy oratory, then to you and the community." It is a religious commitment to the divine service; but the superior and the community are not merely witnesses of the commitment made to God, they are also its recipients. The commitment, therefore, is to God and to the community.

St. Benedict takes his cue from the Master. After the preliminary promises of fidelity to the Rule and of stability, he likewise prescribes a public act of commitment at the end of the novitiate in which the candidate

> promises, in the presence of all in the oratory, stability, conversion of his life, and obedience, before God and his saints, so that if he were later to act in a contrary manner, he knows that he will be condemned by the One he mocks. He shall make a written document (*petitio*) of this promise in the name of the saints whose relics are there, and of the abbot; he will sign it and place it on the altar.[84]

From that moment the candidates are members of the community,[85] and so they are immediately clothed in the habit.[86] If they have possessions, the Rule indicates that they should distribute them among the poor or cede them in a solemn way (legally) to the monastery.[87]

It is clear that, although St. Benedict starts out like the Master, he has introduced some new elements. First of all the ceremony no longer takes place almost suddenly, at the end of Prime, as in the Master: it appears to be an act by itself. Furthermore, the object of the profession is already threefold because, first, the promise of stability which is preliminary in the Master is here introduced into the *professio;* second, while the Master mentions the "discipline of the Rule" only in passing, obedience in St. Benedict's Rule becomes the explicit and direct object of a promise; finally a promise of conversion is spoken of. We believe this to be the new way of expressing the traditional *propositum*, which the Master indicated with the words "to serve God." In fact "to be converted" and "to serve God" are equivalent expressions, both of them characterizing monastic life. To this *propositum* St. Benedict adds the promise of stability and that of obedience (to the Rule and to the abbot or abbess). We are aware of the great importance the Rule had during the novitiate: it was read three times, and three times the novice was required to show his willingness to observe it. Thus we come from the context of a mere defense for a tottering institution to the understanding of obedience in a deeply theological and spiritual sense. It becomes the means by which the nuns and monks vow themselves to the divine service.

The promises are made *coram omnibus*[88] and *coram Deo et sanctis eius*.[89] The *petitio,* the document with the promises, is no longer an act of donating property, but seems to have become, in virtue of the promises, an act of donating oneself; it is done in the name of the saints whose relics are there, and of the superior. What does it mean to promise "in the presence" (*coram*) of everyone and "in the presence" (*coram*) of God and his saints? Might one possibly interpret the term *coram* differently in each case, either making God the recipient of the promise and the community simply the witness, or, on the other hand, making the community the recipient and God the witness? In the second interpretation we would have a promise made, under oath, to the community (with God as witness).

This hypothesis should not cause surprise, because up to now in our monastic history we have already treated of promises made to the community, except in the case of St. Basil. In the *Master* and in St. Benedict, moreover, the promises of stability and observance of the Rule, which are now being reintroduced into the *professio,* have already been made to the community. Could St. Benedict, then, merely have wanted to make the promise to the community more solemn by having it repeated before God and the saints of the oratory, giving it the force of an oath? One fact prevents us from accepting this hypothesis: in the Master the *suggestio* or the *propositum* to serve God is made, first to God and the oratory, then to the superior and the community. Neither of the two parties is simply a witness; each is the recipient of the *professio,* in the degree proper to each. For this reason we are surprised that, in commenting on the Rule of St. Benedict, the celebrated Father De Vogüé should have said: "in the *Rule of the Master* one promises to God and to the oratory," (*"chez le Maître on promet à Dieu et à l'oratoire"*), quoting as proof RM 89, 6.11 which, however, speaks also of the abbot and the community.[90]

Just as in the Master the two parties are related in the same manner to the *suggerere,* so in St. Benedict the terms *omnibus* and *Deo et sanctis eius* are bound to the *promittere* in the same manner: in both cases by the word *coram*. The promise is consequently made to God and the saints whose relics are on the altar and, on a different level, to the sisters or brothers. The two communities, the celestial and the monastic, are recipients of the profession. Thus the *promissio* is religious, binding with God, but it is also communitarian and ecclesial. However, St. Benedict never uses the term *votum* to express the religious character of the promises, and certainly one cannot apply to the Rule ahead of time all the canonical and theological definitions which originated later. The fact that St. Benedict does not use the term *votum* shows, once again, how much closer he is to earlier monastic tradition than to St. Augustine.

10. Toward the Vow

We cannot follow here, step by step, the theological evolution which ended by making of the monastic promises *vota* in the technical sense; and it is not necessary to do so. We have seen that St. Augustine used the category *votum* frequently; and even though at times, in commenting on the Greek term *euchè*, he interprets "vow" in the sense of a ritual offering,[91] he ordinarily takes it as it is from the Roman religion whose related terminology he uses in its entirety, applying it both to virgins and to the monks' dedication to the divine service.[92] His point of view, however, did not exert an immediate influence over the great monastic tradition; Cassian and St. Gregory the Great were only marginally affected, inasmuch as they sometimes used the category of vow in condemning the unfaithfulness of those who fail in their commitments.[93] The category was foreign to St. Benedict.

A few centuries later the idea of *vota* took hold. The aspect of a contractual obligation was then stressed more than that of an offering, and the *lectio professionis* was stressed as the source of the obligation.[94] Sometimes quoting St. Augustine, St. Bernard applied all the binding force of the *votum* to the profession.[95] The interpretation of profession using the category of *vow*, understood according to the Roman *ius sacrum*, was already common before St. Thomas. We will end our historical research at this point because we shall have occasion to return repeatedly to St. Thomas's thought in the reflection that follows.

II. Theological Reflection

Having traced the history of the religious vow in its fundamental lines, we now are prepared to reflect on its nature. What is the significance for religious of binding themselves with a vow, and what is the value of this act of commitment?

1. The Vow in the New Testament

The first problem to draw our attention, one raised by Luther and constantly repeated by Protestant theologians, has to do with the place of the vow in Christian life as shown in the New Testament.

The Gospels speak only once of the vow as a ritual offering to God, and that is to denounce a religious distortion: one may not offer God something which, according to the divine will, is due in justice to others (Mk. 7:11). Clearly this text is not concerned with the vow as such, but with a deviation in its use. The Gospels foresee the ritual offering of objects: "if you are bringing your offering . . ." (Mt. 5:23-24) without, however, specifying whether it is the question of an offering made to fulfill a previous commitment with God (a vow properly so-called). However, in examining the vow as shown in the New Testament, one encounters a serious problem: the almost complete silence of the New Testament concerning the practice of binding oneself with a vow in one's relations with God—a practice which was extremely common among the Jews of Jesus' time, as likewise among the Greeks and, especially, among the Romans. We speak of an *almost* complete silence in order to take into account the logion of Mk. 7:11 (which, however, refers to the vow only in passing), of the Nazirite vow taken by Paul on one occasion (Ac. 18:18), and of Paul's participation in a vow made by others—this time to calm the apprehensions of his fellow Jews (Ac. 21:33-34).

The New Testament's silence on the question of vows, which were so important at that time, has often been a source of embarrassment for Catholic theologians who have dealt with it, especially in their dialogue with Protestants. To say with Father Séjourné[96] that Jesus did not speak of it in order not to be misunderstood, in view of the abuses that vitiated its practice among the people, seems a mere expedient to us. It seems to us that Jesus was silent because, like the great prophets of Israel, he was opposed to an interpretation of religion exclusively or predominantly in terms of ritual offerings and rites. He enlarged and radicalized the religion of the prophets: "What I want is mercy and not sacrifice" (Mt. 9:13, 12:7; cf. Ho. 6:6). There would be no basis to deduce from this that Jesus was opposed to offerings made to God to obtain help, or in thanksgiving for his gifts. The theses of liberal Protestantism which reduced the religion of Jesus to a sentiment or to simple ethics have been set aside by later New-Testament criticism. Christ's attitude regarding the Law and worship was much more subtle than it was said to be almost a century ago. Jesus opposed an interpretation of religion in a purely or predominantly ritual key. For him religion consisted, first of all, in an existence lived under the sign of love. Thus ethics has the primacy over ritual, but the Gospels do not oppose ritual expressions of faith. Already in the Synoptics, what Jesus rejected was an interpretation of religion in which the multiplicity of rites and legalistic observances crushes the human being. Whenever there was opposition between the welfare of the human being and the observance of a ritual, Jesus decidedly took the side of the human being: "The sabbath was made for people, not people for the sabbath" (Mk. 2:27).[97]

What we have said so far provides only the general framework in which the religious vow can be re-examined in the light of the New Testament. It is only a framework, because the religious vow does not draw its inspiration from an offering of things: a fact which was accepted as obvious among Christ's followers though never expressly stated by him. His interest was focused in another direction: toward religion as a totality of life. The Christian baptismal commitment and its reconfirmations throughout life, especially in the decisive moments when one chooses a type of Christian life, are born precisely from this point of view.

The story of the commitment of religious life begins in the individual, with a call and a charism which come from God. This is evident in the Lives of the Fathers (Anthony or Hilarion, for instance), of Francis of Assisi, of Anthony Claret, of Antonia Paris, and is repeated in a less striking manner, but through an equally overwhelming experience, in each religious. The monastic candidate in the *Rule of the Master* declares that "first it is God's (will), so then (it is) also mine."[98] In answering the divine call Christians offer themselves to the creative and redemptive Word of God, without which there is no possibility of discipleship, in order to be transformed and refashioned. Every Christian commitment has its origin in grace and is an answer to it. For this reason every Christian commitment is an act of theological hope and a challenge to human weakness. Such is the baptismal confession, such is the pledge to form a family submissive to the Word of God, in marriage, and such is the commitment to live the form of discipleship characteristic of religious life. "I trust in God's help" was Pachomius's answer to Palemon.[99]

The *propositum* (commitment) is also an oblation of self. Religious confirm their baptismal offering but, at the same time, and responding to grace, make a special offering of themselves in order to live entirely in the presence of God in a relationship excluding all other types of specific and binding relationships on the level of a lifestyle. Origen already spoke of the choice of virginity as being a special dedication to God.[100] The constant reference to monastic life as divine service implies such a dedication. From this point of view the vocational decision (*propositum*) is already an offering, a vow in the same sense that the term *euchè* (an offering-vow) has for the Greek Fathers.

It is evident that Christians must give themselves in a commitment which is in answer to the Word of God. Jesus opened the way by his two experiences in the desert: the one that followed his baptism, and the one in the solitude of Gethsemane. Christ gave himself to his ministry and to his death in obedience to the Father who was calling him. The author of the Letter to the Hebrews summarized, theologically, this attitude of the Son upon entering into the world: "And this is what he said, on coming into the world: you who wanted no sacrifice or oblation, prepared a body for me. You took no pleasure in holocausts or sacrifices for sin; then I said, just as I was commanded in the scroll of the book, '"God, here I am! I am coming to obey your will'" (Heb. 10:5–7).

The religious commitment, the act of dedicating oneself to God, is an imitation of this obedience of Jesus to the Father. It is therefore an act of faith and of hope. Insofar as it is an offering, it is made *per Jesum Christum Dominum*. Insofar as it is a commitment to a form of Christian life, it is a dedication to him (discipleship) who has given himself for us. Origen had rightly seen in this the root of all gifts of self:

> To offer oneself to God . . . is more perfect and higher than all other vows. Whoever does this is an imitator of Christ . . . who gave himself. In fact, God so loved the world as to give his only begotten Son for the life of the world. What merit, then, can human beings have in offering themselves to God, when he has first given himself to them?[101]

The call narratives in the Synoptics show the disciples' attitude when they answer Jesus' call as an all-comprehensive and radical one. This decision-offering to Christ constitutes the very essence of discipleship seen from a human standpoint; it must, therefore, animate every Christian vocational decision. The religious commitment is a special form of such a decision. Religious simply commit themselves to live as disciples in a manner that brings *sequela* to the level of a lifestyle.

2. Religious Bonds or the Religious Bond

The history of religious life makes one fact clear: it is the dedication of one's own person and of one's own life to God in an exclusive relationship that creates religious life. Vatican II repeats that the basic act of religious life is *"Deo totaliter mancipari"* ("to give oneself wholly to God"),[102] *"totam vitam Dei famulatui mancipare"* ("to give one's whole life to the service of God").[103] St. Thomas Aquinas had repeated this often.[104] It was thus throughout history: primitive monasticism took upon itself an all-inclusive commitment, not specific ones. In the *Rule of the Master*, during the first half of the sixth century, the profession is still all-embracing: "I want to serve God," that is, I want to live only for him and in his presence, listening to his Word.[105] This constituted the object of the *propositum* which had characterized monasticism from the first, and which now, with the Master, was beginning to be expressed in a public act.

In St. Benedict's Rule there is something new: the central object of the promise is conversion. This is not the proper moment to pause and analyze the historical development of this concept of monasticism. But on the basis of the tradition preceding Benedict, from the desert to Basil, to Cassian, to the Master, it seems to us that, when they speak of the monastic *renuntiatio,* the commitment is the all-inclusive one of Christian life, and is in this sense a simple reconfirmation of the baptismal confession, and at the same time a commitment to live only for the Lord. It is not a question merely of moral conversion, but of the exclusive orientation of one's life. The two means of stability and obedience, that is, the two commitments related to the structure of cenobitical life, were added as objects of this one promise, this fundamental vow which repeats the traditional monastic *propositum.*[106]

We must then conclude that what really constitutes religious life in its general theological sense (applying to the secular Institutes as well,) is an offering of oneself to God, a commitment to live entirely for him. Religious are such because they give themselves to God in a relationship which establishes a form of Christian life. This can simply be called a commitment to religious life, a *vinculum (votum) religionis*. Again St. Thomas, in seeking to attribute a religious profession to the Apostles (in order to justify the vows) wrote: "the Apostles are understood to have vowed things pertaining to the state of perfection when they left all things and followed Christ"—that is, with a global and radical commitment.[107] The specific commitments of stability-obedience among the Benedictines, of chastity, communion of goods, and obedience in the twelfth-century communities of canons, of chastity, poverty, and obedience from St. Francis' time on, are either aspects of the one basic commitment, or practical means for its attainment.[108]

3. Manifesting the *propositum* to the Church

Inasmuch as it is the choice of a lifestyle, the decision to embrace religious life already has a social projection. By choosing a lifestyle, a person is choosing not only a means of self-fulfillment, but also a way of contributing to human society and a type of relationship with others. Distinct lifestyles have social significance. For this reason there is a strong tendency to impart to others the important decisions one makes with respect to the definitive arrangement of one's life, such as marriage, work, or entrance into religion. This manifestation is not only an expression of communion on the part of the person in question, but is also a recognition of the mutual solidarity of all concerned. We are all interested in the decisions of those who are close to us and, to a certain extent, we are all involved in them.

Proceeding from social life to the life of the Church, each choice of a Christian lifestyle has an essential relationship to the entire community of believers, because the various vocational gifts are not only means for individual self-fulfillment but also different ways of contributing to the common upbuilding of the Church. Especially so, in a manner all its own, is the choice of religious life, because it makes visible the requirements of our common vocation to discipleship.[109] Thus it is clear why the decision to give oneself entirely to the divine service was brought before the ecclesial community very early, either by investiture with a habit, among the anchorites, or by a ceremony of incorporation into the community, among the cenobites. Thus profession is a way of informing the Church of one's decision to dedicate oneself to Christ, and of having the Church share in it. On this level it is the ecclesial manifestation of the inner reality of a vocational decision. Inasmuch as this decision consists in listening to the Word and dedicating oneself to it, it is already in itself an ecclesial event.

In the instance of a profession of the member of a community, a communitarian manifestation of one's commitment, accompanied by vesting in a habit or by a promise, is entirely natural. Human groups (we are here returning to the sociological level) tend to make public the active and passive incorporation of a member. It is historically clear that the group's need to defend and provide for itself has influenced the creation of binding commitments. Basil desired that monks, too, should make a vow of celebacy, like the virgins, so that they might be called to account in case they were unfaithful to the monastic rule of life.[110] John Cassian used the category of vow to forestall any falling away from the monastic commitments.[111] In the *Rule of the Master* some of the cautionary provisions connected with professions show an effort to defend the monastic institution which was in crisis at that time.[112] But we have already said that it would be nearsighted for anyone to trace the origin of binding commitments, on a sociological and historical level, solely to the need to protect institutions. Profession originated as a natural social expression of the individual's inner decision.

4. Profession, a Bond with the Church

Profession is much more than the manifestation of what has already been decided in one's heart. Through their act of profession religious repeat, this time with an ecclesial act, their dedication to God and make their public gift to the Church, while the Church accepts and acknowledges their gift. Every gift of self to the Word of God calling to some form of Christian life is already an ecclesial reality, a fruit of faith, but it is also oriented toward the welfare of the Church. We said this earlier in speaking of charisms being oriented toward the Church. But in the public profession we have an act of dedication to the Church as a society. In fact the public profession is not only made to God (otherwise the inner *propositum* would be sufficient), but to God through the Church, following that sacramental structure which is typical of Christian spirituality. The Church is materially represented and embodied by this community of disciples with whom one desires to be united. The rite of profession in the Master's Rule expresses this very well: "I have something to propose, first to God and this holy oratory, then to you (the abbot) and the community. . . ."[113] St. Benedict's Rule reaffirms this: "I promise in the presence of all . . . in the presence of God. . . ."[114] Neither God nor the community are mere witnesses to the offering that is being made, both of them are, although on a very different level, recipients of the gift.

Thus the offering of self acquires the character of a ritual offering (*euché* in the Greek sense); it is an act of ecclesial liturgy. It also takes on the value of a contract between the new members, who are giving themselves to the group, and the community, which accepts the new members and offers itself to them. From this one comes to understand better how the Church recognizes in itself the power to dissolve the bonds resulting from such an offering.

5. The Binding Character of the Commitment

Thus we come to the difficult question of the obligation deriving from the commitment. The obligation has been attacked on the basis of a perhaps-too-abstract concept of human freedom. For human beings construct their lives by choosing and committing themselves. There are few things as binding as the choice of a state in life or a profession. Among the numerous possible ways of self-realization for men or women, each person makes fundamental choices. Freedom consists precisely in this choice of the manner of self-realization. The decision is much more binding when it involves a religious choice: the choice of marriage and of a spouse, the choice of celibacy and of a community. These choices are made because of a conviction that one is responding to a call and to a gift from God. At this point the human person achieves a deep level of dialogue with God, wherein the manner of fulfilling oneself as a human being and a Christian is decided. *Quomodo salvus ero?* ("How can I be saved?") is the question that many monks, together with Apa Arsenius, asked themselves.[115] Even avoiding a narrow view of the relationship vocation-salvation in which the infinity of divine love appears constrained within the limitations of the human response, it is evident that the choice of a life devoted to the divine service and placed under the aegis of religion is extremely binding. The first hermits, even before the establishment of any act of profession, described the embracing of monastic life as a promise made to God.[116]

At this deep and intimate level of response to grace, the decision takes place between the human person and God, without any intervention on the part of the community. Only the person in question can hear the Word of God calling. The Church cannot, nor does it ever intend, to dispense a Christian from fidelity to grace. But the commitment to God was made publicly; it was made in a liturgical act witnessed by the Church, and it was made with the Church, too. It is from this public commitment that the Church dispenses. It does not do so gladly, or easily, because it is common knowledge that the choice of a state in life involves obligations, and a change in the orientation of one's life is always a source of suffering, and often very traumatic. The Church dispenses, however, for pastoral reasons, subordinating everything to human salvation: "The sabbath was made for people. . . ." One must not forget that in certain cases there may be a temporary vocation: some canonized saints left the community in which they were professed in order to found new ones. It is also possible, in some cases, for one to discover after some years that one is not called by God to the religious life: this explains temporary commitments. But it is also true that a commitment made in past years may, at a given moment, become a crushing fact rather than a liberating reality and a means of salvation, owing to the individual's changed spiritual and psychological condition. Without passing judgment on the fidelity or unfaithfulness of the person in question (a fact which is enacted within the individual's heart) the Church dispenses from the obligation contracted with itself and with God through it.

6. Vows?

So far we have spoken of the moment of commitment to religious life as an act of dedication of self to grace which is calling; a self-giving which begins with a vocational decision, the binding choice of a form of discipleship, and which culminates with a public act of ritual dedication made within the Church and through the Church. This public liturgical act is a vow (*euché*) inasmuch as it is an offering of oneself to God, this being the predominant meaning of the word among the Greek Fathers. St. Thomas

Aquinas, though using the category *votum* which was already common in his time, interprets it fundamentally in the same way: an offering of oneself and of all one's life to God.[117]

Up till now we have not used the term *vow,* for the reason that the vow is only one of the forms that public commitment may take. We have seen that the technical category of *vow* is foreign to the great monastic tradition: to the desert Fathers, to Pachomius, to the Master, and to Benedict. In our day one may belong to a community of evangelical life and one can be a religious in the theological sense of the term without making public vows. The important thing, even from the canonical point of view, is the public act of dedication to God in his Church. It is for this reason that Vatican II insists (as St. Thomas does) on the *dedication of self* as the basic fact of religious life on the part of the individual (its ultimate foundation is the grace that calls), and then refers to the forms this dedication can take as "vows or other sacred bonds." From what has been said earlier on the nature of this public dedication to God through the Church, one gathers that the public act is not only a canonical fact, but characterizes religious life theologically as an existence dedicated to God within the community of believers.

Certainly what counts in the final analysis is the decision to live exclusively for the Lord and his interests, a decision made in one's own heart and in God's presence, in answer to his call. Thus those who choose to remain celibate for the love of the Lord, even though they live in the world, without joining any institution, are already religious in a certain sense. But those are religious in a proper sense who bring their decision before the Church and make their commitment to it. Profession is the full manifestation of the ecclesial meaning of religious life. The public character of the commitment has its roots in the ecclesial meaning and value of a life dedicated to the divine service. The public commitment, and the bond which results from it, is not only a juridical fact but also a determining factor on the theological level.

This ecclesial value of the religious commitment is preserved either by the vow in its stricter sense, or by any other bond recognized by the Church. The fact that some people bind themselves to live according to the special charisms of religious life (celibacy-poverty, community-obedience) by means of vows, while others bind themselves to do the same thing by means of promises only, does not change the theological nature of a state dedicated publicly to the service of God in the Church. As we well know from history and from theology, the first constituent element of religious life on the theological level is not a commitment on certain definite points (celibacy, poverty, etc.), although these are important, but the total dedication of oneself to God made through the Church. This take place in every public commitment.

One might object to this equating of all commitments, reasoning that religious make public vows of celibacy, poverty, and obedience which members of secular Institutes do not make, and that, therefore, the dedication which religious make of themselves to God through the Church (the same as that which the others make) takes on, in the case of religious, a votive character. In other words, since religious vows are simply the concrete expression of total dedication of self, this dedication assumes through them a votive nature, differing not only canonically, but also theologically from the dedication made by members of other institutes of evangelical life. But to us it seems that the theological essence of the religious vow, from a Christian standpoint, is preserved in all total dedications of self made through the Church. Therefore every dedication of self through an ecclesial act is, in a Christian sense, a votive act, whether or not one has made vows in the canonical sense on specific important points.

One must be careful not to attribute a fundamental importance to a fact (the *votum*) which is, in a strict sense, technical, which is ignored by the New Testament, which is foreign to a large part of ecclesiastical tradition, which was introduced into theological thought under the influence of the Roman *religio* (in early times by Augustine alone), and which was obviously modified and brought back to a Christian inspiration by theological reflection (Thomas Aquinas) and by ecclesiastical practice. Recall that the Roman *votum*, simply by its formulation, introduces the object of the vow, whether it be a person or a thing, into the divine sphere, the precincts of the *sacrum*. The *votum* is something automatic (it presupposes an almost magical concept of religion) and one does not evade its force except by fulfilling the vow. St. Thomas was forced to have recourse to this Roman concept of the *votum sacrum* in a given context, in order to explain why, according to a canonical source which he considered definitive, not even the Pope could dispense from the solemn vow of continence.[118] We shall speak of this in the subsequent excursus.

The fact that the Church has recognized its power to grant a dispensation, even from a public vow, shows that to apply the concept of the Roman *religio* to the religious commitment is erroneous. In fact St.

Thomas himself usually tends away from this concept, by defining the religious vow as a personal dedication through which one offers all one's subsequent life to God under the form of a commitment (*obligatio*). The religious vow consists in the person's dedication to God through the Church and, consequently, in the public commitment to live as a dedicated person: "You wanted no sacrifice or oblation (objectifying vows) . . . Here I am! I am coming to obey your will." The Christian vow has a personal and dynamic quality which the Roman *votum* does not have. We conclude therefore that if the Christian vow is theologically a dedication to God through the Church, and a commitment to God through the Church, the same is also true of the dedication of self made by those who do not pronounce vows in the canonical sense. Theologically, what counts is that the commitment be made with God through the Church, so that it will have a public character. The dedication that members of Institutes of evangelical life make of themselves is also a public ecclesial act and constitutes a state of life in the Church.

Excursus: The Consecrated Life

1. Starting Point: Vatican II

In speaking of the total dedication of self to God which constitutes the religious profession, Vatican II has repeatedly used the terms *consecrari* and *consecratio*. The most important texts are to be found in number 44 of *Lumen Gentium*, and in number 5 of *Perfectae Caritatis*, which treat the nature and fundamental elements of religious life. To these passages one must add number 45 of *Lumen Gentium* which speaks of the relations with the Church and its hierarchy. In the first text, the Council affirms that the religious

> as a baptized Christian . . . is (already) dead to sin and dedicated to God; but he desires to derive still more abundant fruit from the grace of his baptism. For this purpose he makes profession in the Church of the evangelical counsels . . . in order to consecrate himself in a more thoroughgoing way to the service of God. The bonds by which he pledges himself to the practice of the counsels show forth the unbreakable bond of union that exists between Christ and his bride, the

Church. The more stable and firm these bonds are, then, the more perfect will the Christian's religious consecration be.[1]

The same doctrine, with slight variations, is found in *Perfectae Caritatis:* "They have dedicated their whole lives to his service. This constitutes a special consecration and is a fuller expression of it."[2] In number 45 of *Lumen Gentium* the *consecratio* is placed in relationship to the liturgical act in which profession is made: "Besides giving legal sanction to the religious form of life and thus raising it to the dignity of a canonical state, the Church sets it forth liturgically also as a state of consecration to God."[3]

The Council refers to the "consecrated life" also in: a) the introduction to *Perfectae Caritatis,* saying that it is such "by the profession of the counsels";[4] b) in number 46 of *Lumen Gentium,* to remind us that the consecration does not alienate religious from the rest of humanity; c) in number 11 of *Perfectae Caritatis,* to apply it also to the secular institutes; d) in number 17 of the same decree, to present the habit as a sign of consecration; e) in the decree *Ad Gentes,* echoing the doctrine of *Lumen Gentium* and *Perfectae Caritatis:* "Through the deeper consecration made to God in the Church, [religious life] clearly shows and signifies the intimate nature of the Christian vocation."[5]

Before continuing, it will be well to point out three facts: 1) The Council rejected the recommendation of three of the Council Fathers to give the title *De Consecratis* to chapter VI of *Lumen Gentium;* this would have made the idea of consecration the center of the Conciliar doctrine on religious life.[6] 2) The chairman noted that in composing the text, the commission had refrained from providing definitions in a strict sense.[7] 3) The Council speaks of "a certain special consecration" (*peculiarem quandam*), thus suggesting that the term *consecratio* can be employed in various ways and only in a certain way does it suit the profession of the counsels.

Having stated this in advance, we note that the Conciliar texts on the consecration of those who profess the "counsels" raise some questions which are closely connected and of some importance: 1) In what sense can the profession of the "counsels" be called a consecration to God? 2) What are the relationships between this special consecration and the baptismal consecration to which the Council refers in the two fundamental texts of *Lumen Gentium* 44, and *Perfectae Caritatis* 5? 3) What relationship exists between being consecrated, and the liturgical action spoken of in *Lumen Gentium* 45?

Since Vatican II wanted to summarize traditional doctrine without entering into controversies, we believe it will first be very helpful to glance rapidly at the development of doctrine on this point, in order to solve the problems which have arisen.

2. The Consecration of Virgins

At the beginning of the third century Hippolytus wrote in his *Traditio Apostolica:* ''There shall be no laying on of hands in the case of a virgin, because it has been her own decision (*propositum, proairesis*) to make herself a virgin.'' With these words he drew a distinction between the ministers who became such through the laying on of hands, and the virgins who were such because they gave themselves to God through a commitment.[8] Hippolytus uses the concept of *propositum* which will later become decisive in the history of primitive monasticism.

Soon, however, Tertullian began to use the expression *virgines sanctae,*[9] an expression which is found again in the extant version of the *Epistulae Clementis ad Virgines.*[10] The expression becomes common in the fourth century. At this time, too, appear the first references to a liturgical act of commitment for virgins, and a blessing on the part of Church ministers. While St. Ambrose prefers to call this act the *velatio virginis,* the African Church favors the designation *consecratio,*[11] which was also used by St. Jerome toward the end of the fourth century,[12] by Leo I a half-century later,[13] and in the *Gelasian Sacramentary.*[14] The ceremony, however, is also called *velatio* and *benedictio.*[15]

In our opinion, two ideas are involved in this concept of consecrated virginity: 1) virginity becomes consecrated when the virgin's *propositum* has been offered to God in a liturgical act reserved to the bishop; 2) virginity, or bodily integrity, tends in itself to be what makes a woman sacred. The first idea corresponds to historically proved data, and causes no problem. But the second also seems certain to us. In fact Tertullian, who was the first to call virgins *sanctae* according to the Roman ritual sense, even before a ceremony of consecration appears to have existed, gives the name of *sponsae Christi* to all unmarried Christian women, although they may not have decided to remain virgins.[16] Certainly the decision of those who want to remain virgins is inspired by the love of Christ: all the literature of the third and fourth centuries proves this abundantly. But physical integrity is a decisive factor of sacredness. As we know, the idea was very much alive in Roman culture, and was a part of other ancient civilizations as well. Physical integrity as such created a special relationship with the Divinity.[17] This explains why a liturgical ceremony, the *velatio* or *consecratio*, was created early for women, while for monks and ascetics profession began to appear very slowly, and was at first mainly a commitment to the community.

3. Consecration and Monasticism

The history of the term *consecratio* in monastic literature is very different. First of all we must note that this and related terms are practically not to be found in all the ancient Rules, including St. Benedict's *Regula Monasteriorum*, where profession begins to appear.[18] They do not even appear in the *Vita Antonii*, nor in the numerous Lives that followed it (of Hilarion, Paul, Martin, the Fathers of the Jura, etc.), nor in the Coptic or Greek *Corpus Pachomianum*. A reading of the other monastic sources shows us that the idea of consecration, in a specific sense, does not play an important role in primitive monastic tradition.

Having made this general statement, we must now be more precise. It would at first seem that there is an important exception in the *Interrogatio XV* of St. Basil's *Regulae fusius* where, in speaking of the "profession of virginity" made by the adolescents educated within the community when they reach a given age, there is the precise instruction: "Church authorities should be called as witnesses of this decision (*gnome, propositum*) so that, through them, the holiness (*hagiasmon*) of the body may be consecrated to God (*kathieroustai*) as a sacred thing (*anathema*), and that the event may be confirmed by their witness."[19] Here we would have the first case in which the profession of virginity by adolescent men is consecrated by ministers of the Church. One should note, however, that this entire paragraph is lacking in the Latin version which Rufinus made from the original Greek text; we may therefore conclude that St. Basil's original text did not provide for any liturgical rite, nor did it speak of the commitment as a consecration.[20] Thus we are dealing with a later development.

The term *consecrari* was also introduced in two Latin versions of monastic Greek texts. Thus, where Athanasius wrote in his *Vita Antonii:* "... after [Anthony] became a monk and offered himself to God (*epeggeílato to Theô*)," Evagrius's Latin version says: "*ex quo . . . sese consecravit,*"[21] while the first Latin version by an anonymous author says: *ex eo . . . promisit Deo.*"[22] Similarly the *Life of Pachomius,* translated by Dionysius Exiguus, states that Palemon consecrated Pachomius while giving him the monastic habit: *Habitu monachi consacravit.*[23] But if we consult the second Greek Life, which reproduces a Greek text very similar to one used by Dionysius, we find that Palemon simply gave the habit to Pachomius.[24] Finally, the term *sacred* is used once in the *Rule of the Master,* referring to the habit in a particular context: in the case of anyone who decides to return to the world, the order is given that his holy garments and the sacred habit should be taken from him, because the habit belongs to Christ.[25] One should note, however, that the same Rule attributes consecration exclusively to priests, in contrast to monks and lay people.[26]

But the scarcity of references to the concept of sacredness should not cause surprise in connection with a movement like monasticism, which had its origins among the laity and was founded on the personal decision to respond to an internally perceived vocation. As Hippolytus already clearly saw in the previously cited passage, the *propositum,* the decision in this matter, is the root of everything. Yet in treating of an existence entirely dedicated to the divine service, and consequently belonging in the sphere of the divine, it would be very strange if the concept of sacredness, as an objective quality of things and persons *set apart* and allotted to God (*quadòs̀, hèrem* in Hebrew; *hagios* in Greek; *sacer* in Latin), had not been applied. It is significant that the concept was introduced in two texts which have to do with the deplorable eventuality of a monk's return to the secular state. St. Basil used the term purposely in a text which is, this time, undoubtedly authentic since it is to be found in the Greek text of the *Regulae brevius* and in Rufinus's version of the *Asceticum Parvum:* "Sacredness (*hagiasmòs*) consists in being entirely dedicated to the all-holy God, and in busying oneself always, without ceasing, with the things that please Him. Because that which is mutilated cannot be placed among sacred gifts (*anathēmasin*), and it is an impious and dreadful thing to reduce to common and human use what was once dedicated (*anatethen*) to God."[27]

And the Master, without making such explicit use of the terminology of the sacred, restates the same idea in order to explain why one may not give back to a monk who returns to the world what he brought into the monastery when he made his profession: "*quia omni rei ingressae ad*

Deum in monasterio perseverantia opus est . . . ideo res Deo oblata revocari saeculo ab homine non debet'' ("because perseverance is required of everything that makes its way to God in the monastery . . . therefore something offered to God must not be recalled to the world of man").[28] Since the monk has free will, he cannot be detained against his will; but with material things it is otherwise. The meaning is clear: the monk also has offered himself to God and could not, rightly, return to the world; but others cannot stand in his way.

4. Pseudo-Dionysius and the Monastic *teleiosis*

The writings of Pseudo-Dionysius the Areopagite, a Christian Neo-Platonic writer of the late fifth century, show a process which had developed in the Eastern Church: the act of monastic profession had been introduced into a liturgical rite in which the minister's role tended to prevail over that of the monk being professed. We have seen that a text in Basil's *Regulae fusius*[29] called for the presence of Church authorities during the adolescents' "profession of virginity," in order that, through them, the holiness (*hagiasmon*) of the body should be consecrated (*kathierousthai*) to God as a sacred thing (*anathema*). Since this passage does not appear in Rufinus's Latin version, it may present a post-Basilian development.[30] As early as Pseudo-Dionysius the monastic profession is described as a consecration, with terminology that is explicitly liturgical and almost mysterial. He speaks of it in the fifth chapter of his *De Ecclesiastica Hierarchia,* devoted to a discussion of the various *ordines* dependent on the initiating action of the priests: that is, to the various types of Christians whom we now would call the laity. At the apex of these are the monks (who are also laymen), whose profession is termed *teleiosis* (*perfectio, consummatio*) by Dionysius. He uses this term in the sense of a consecration, and applies it both to Baptism and to Holy Orders; but he takes care to explain that the "prayer of consecration" recited over the monks is not of the hierarchical type reserved for sacred ordinations, but of lesser degree. Its object is to call down upon the monk the grace necessary for his high vocation. During the liturgical ceremony the one who is to be consecrated a monk remains standing behind the celebrant, who recites the invocation before the altar. The celebrant then questions the candidate on his commitments (act of profession), makes the sign of the Cross over him, and gives him the monastic habit.[31] Throughout this account the terminology of consecration is very explicit (*teleiosis, teloumenous, aphierōtikês, epiklēseos, ierourgikes*). But the meaning is very clear: consecration has to do with an invocation by which one asks God for the perfecting grace (*telestikên charin*) necessary in order to observe the monastic commitments.

5. The *consecratio* in St. Thomas Aquinas

Thus we come to St. Thomas, by whose thought the compilers of the Conciliar texts on religious life were more directly inspired.[32] In reading Aquinas's various passages on religious life it is clear that the terminology of consecration plays a minor role in Thomistic doctrine. The terms which St. Thomas most frequently uses, and to which he gives most importance, are those which express the subjective commitment of the religious and the bond which this commitment establishes with God: the religious *se obligat*,[33] *totam vitam obligavit*,[34] *obligatio fit cum quaedam solemnitate professionis et benedictionis*,[35] *Deo serviturum promisit*,[36] *totam vitam suam divino servitio deputet*,[37] *totam vitam Deo exhibere*,[38] *se totaliter mancipat divino servitio*,[39] *totaliter se debet praebere ad serviendum Deo*.[40] These are all key expressions of Thomistic doctrine on religious life, and they all express the act of commitment by which religious place their entire life at the service of God. In order to indicate this dedication words connected with offering follow, and often assume sacrificial connotations: *offert, oblatio, holocaustum*.[41]

The term *consecrari* appears incidentally in *Contra Impugnantes*: "*perfecta religio triplici voto consecratur*" ("religious life is consecrated by the three vows"),[42] and more pointedly in two other texts: in his *In Sent.*, IV, dist. 2, and in *Secunda Secundae*, q. 88. In his commentary on the *Fourth of the Sentences*, St. Thomas introduces the idea of consecration by a quotation from Pseudo-Dionysius, cited as an objection. In the ninth objection of article II, the text of Dionysius (*De Ecclesiastica Hierarchia*, VI) is cited as including, in the opinion of the person formulating the objection, the monastic *consummatio* or *consecratio* among the sacraments. In his answer St. Thomas notes that, on the contrary, the *consecratio* of monks, like that of kings, is not a sacramental act, but another kind of hierarchical act intending to implore the special aid of grace for those who commit themselves to grave responsibilities.[43]

Question 88 of *Secunda Secundae*, instead, has to do with whether the Church can grant a dispensation from the solemn vow of continence. St. Thomas is provided with the decretal *Cum ad Monasterium*, which states specifically that it is impossible even for the Roman Pontiff to dispense from such a vow. St. Thomas examines one after another various arguments sustaining the impossibility of this: the greatness of chastity, the perpetuity and universality of the vow, etc., arguments which he refutes for various reasons. There are those who say that the pope can grant a dispensation in certain cases, but for St. Thomas the text of the decretal is definitive. Thus he concludes that the reason for this impossibility is to be found in Leviticus (27:9–10, and 28):

> Whatsoever has once been sanctified to the Lord cannot be put into any other use. For no ecclesiastical prelate can make that which is sanctified to lose its consecration, not even though it be something inanimate, for instance a consecrated chalice to be not consecrated, so long as it remains entire. Much less, therefore, can a prelate make a man that is consecrated to God cease to be consecrated, so long as he lives. Now the solemnity of a vow consists in a kind of consecration or blessing (*in quandam consecratione seu benedictione*) of the person who takes the vow.[44]

He had already explained this in the seventh article of the same question: the solemnity of the religious vow consists in a blessing which is bestowed by a minister.[45]

The following facts emerge from our research on St. Thomas: 1) He decidedly puts the accent on religious life as such. Although he uses the category of *status* (state), his preference is for the dynamic concept of *vita* (life) which one begins by assuming certain obligations. Note, for example, how often the noun *vita* appears as the object of the verbs we listed above. From this it is clear that he prefers, to the more static and objective category of sacredness, the dynamic and subjective concepts of obligation, commitment, dedication, etc. 2) With St. Thomas the religious profession always appears as a subjective act: *vovet, offert, praebet, deputat, exhibet*, etc., to which, in a very limited number of texts, the minister's *benedictio* or *consecratio* is added. 3) The term *consecrari* is used once in reference to the triple vow,[46] and again, while explaining a passage of Pseudo-Dionysius, to the liturgical action of the presiding minister. 4) Finally, the concept of sacredness as an objective quality of a person or thing set aside for the Divinity was applied to religious by St. Thomas in order to explain why, according to a decretal, not even the pope could dispense from the solemn vow of continence. According to him the solemnity of the vow is due to that *consecratio seu benedictio* bestowed by the priest and spoken of by Pseudo-Dionysius.

The affirmations of St. Thomas in question 88 of *Secunda Secundae*, according to which the solemnity of the vow comes from this priestly *benedictio* or *consecratio*, soon aroused some serious objections among Thomists. Cajetan himself called attention to the fact that such a blessing played a very secondary role in the Dominican rite of profession, and Suárez added that it practically did not exist in the Society of Jesus; the same is true of many institutes which were founded later.[47]

Leaving aside, at this point, the question of the *solemnitas* of the vow, we must note that the same problem exists with respect to the consecrating character of profession. How can such a character result from something added to profession, such as the priest's invocation to obtain the grace of fidelity for the professed? And how can one explain that such an invocation either had no importance or was practically nonexistent in the Latin rites of profession before Vatican II? If one desires to attribute the idea of objective sacredness to the person of the religious, can this quality result from such an invocation?

Actually, in the two passages referred to—from his commentary on the *Fourth of the Sentences* and in the *Secunda Secundae*—St. Thomas was influenced by two sources that he considered definitive: Pseudo-Dionysius, whom he thought St. Paul's disciple, Dionysius the Divine; and the authority of the decretal which affirmed the absolute impossibility of granting a dispensation from the vow of chastity—an affirmation for which St. Thomas could find no reason except the concept of *sacredness* applied to religious. He well knew that a consecration, in the strict sense, can result only from an action of the ecclesiastical hierarchy, and he found the support he needed in the more liturgically inclined tradition of the East, emphasized by Dionysius. But both of these presuppositions have since been superseded. Dionysius is no longer a decisive authority, and the Church now recognizes in itself the power to dispense from public vows, whether solemn or not.

6. Theological Reflection

Having thus examined, in its main stages, the historical development of the concept of *consecratio* as applied to religious life, we must now try to answer the problems raised by Vatican II's statements on consecrated life.

A. Consecration, an Existential Orientation

Religious life is, first of all, a life in the sense both of an objective lifestyle (*genus vitae*, a type of existence), and of a person's development in time. One is a religious because, through an ecclesial commitment, one embraces a life characterized by celibacy, poverty and obedience; and then actually, in an existential sense, because one continues to profess this life. This life begins with the dedication religious make of their entire existence to God, committing themselves to live for him alone by following Christ. This can be called a consecration because it is a dedication of life to God alone. God thus becomes the only reason for a human existence. In this sense *consecration* signifies a direct and explicit orientation of an existence toward God. To indicate this one speaks, in fact, of a *vita per consiliorum professionem consecrata* (a life consecrated by the profession of the *counsels*).[48] Tradition however, and therein St. Thomas in particular, ordinarily preferred a terminology indicating the commitment of the subject: *deputat, exhibet*, etc.

Profession, brought back to this commitment of the subject which is its fundamental element, is therefore not a consecration in a ritual and narrow sense. The fact that it is not a sacrament shows that profession does not belong to that ontological type of consecration which is given by some sacraments. St. Thomas was already aware of this and for this reason spoke, on the ritual level, of "a certain spiritual blessing or consecration" (*aliqua spiritualis benedictio vel consecratio*) of the professed.[49] In this manner of speaking of the rite of profession we find in St. Thomas the same intentional openness of the term *consecratio* to a broader sense through the use of the adjectives *aliqua, quaedam*, which we had noted in *Perfectae Caritatis*.[50]

But St. Thomas also once wrote "*perfecta religio triplici voto consecratur*," words which we might translate as, "religious life is consecrated by the three vows."[51] The concept of the vows is thus introduced into the argument, a concept which is decisive in the Thomist theology of religious life.[52] Recently Father B. Häring has reconnected consecration with the vows: "consecrated . . . are all the religious whom the Church appoints to the divine service through the acceptance of their vows and the bestowal of her privileges. The objective consecration, essentially conferred by the Church, is rendered more intimate and perfect by a personal act of consecration (the vow), in a very special way by the vow of religion which the Church confirms as a choice and distinction oriented toward the glory of God."[53] These affirmations of Father Häring's offer the occasion for some remarks on the role of the vow, and on the relationship between the subject's personal act of consecration and the objective consecration conferred only by the Church.

As regards the vow, if the consecration were considered to depend on it there would be room for serious equivocation, since the consecratory vow could be understood in the almost-magic sense it held in the religion of pagan Rome. We have a right to ask ourselves whether that category, which is not represented in the New Testament, can rightly claim citizenship in the Christian religion; or whether it does not rather belong to another way of understanding relationships with the Divinity.

For the fact remains that for centuries monks did not pronounce any vows properly so-called, and that the idea of consecration is now also extended to the members of secular Institutes, who do not depend on vows for their identity. Thus, in discussing the fact of consecration, one must speak of commitment rather than vow. St. Thomas explains the necessity of the vow precisely by the *obligatio* of the commitment to God, by the necessity of offering one's whole life to God in one moment, because totality is characteristic of religious life and because one cannot offer all of life by an action (which is a development), but only by an *obligatio*, by a commitment.[54] The important thing is this binding of oneself, this *exhibere totam vitam*, this placing of one's whole life before God, which is accomplished by a commitment of one's entire existence.

As regards the relationships between the personal act and the consecration bestowed exclusively by the Church, Father Häring rightly notes that the consecration has strong ecclesial implications. Obviously *consecratio* is related etymologically to public worship: some thing or some person is publicly set aside from the profane sphere in order to dedicate it to divine worship. But even leaving aside these considerations, which raise some troublesome problems because of their non-Christian origins, it is a fact that in Christianity every gift to God is a gift to the Church.

Yet, in the paragraph cited, Father Häring distinguishes between the "objective consecration, essentially conferred by the Church," and the "personal act of consecration," that is, the subject's dedication through a public commitment. Actually, starting from a strictly ritual concept of consecration, Father Häring was obliged to give priority to the consecration bestowed by the Church, which "is rendered more intimate . . . by a personal act of consecration." The personal commitment would thus serve to complete and make more intimate the consecration carried out by the Church. One should note, however, that St. Thomas had already warned that the *cultus* to which religious are consecrated is to be understood not in a narrow sense of ritual-worship, but in the sense of *servitium Dei*, that is of lives entirely oriented toward union with God.

It is for this reason that the Christian's commitment (the "personal act of consecration") is more decisive than its acceptance by the Church through the hierarchy. The point of view should therefore be reversed: the personal act does not make the Church's action more intimate but, on the contrary, the Church's acceptance of the Christian's commitment makes the latter visibly and publicly ecclesial. The Church is already present in the very act of dedication made by the religious, since those who give themselves to God already belong to his Holy People and share in the common priesthood of the faithful.

One should remember that Vatican II presents religious life as an ecclesial reality in its very birth in the hearts of the faithful, as a gift of the Risen One and the work of the Spirit, even before its acceptance by the hierarchy.[55] The decision to dedicate oneself is already a reality of the pneumatic Church. Christians, however, through this public act of commitment, this ecclesial act, bring their decision before the community, complete it in its presence, and thus make it an act of dedication. The commitment thus becomes doubly ecclesial; the religious is consecrated publicly. Basically, however, the consecration consists in this commitment of one's life, made in the presence of the Church and accepted by it. Whether this is done by means of a vow properly so-called, or of some other approved bond, does not affect the reality of the consecration itself.

B. The *consecratio vel benedictio* in Profession

There is, therefore, a clear difference not only between the consecration of religious and sacramental consecrations (Baptism and Holy Orders), but also between the consecration of religious and ritual consecrations administered by the Church. In a strictly technical sense a consecration is a liturgical act carried out by a minister and, in certain cases, only by a bishop. In fact, in order for an object to be set aside for ritual use, the intervention of the minister of worship is necessary. Similarly, in the case of the consecration of a person set aside for divine worship (by Baptism and Holy Orders), this intervention is necessary. But the religious consecration is a lifetime commitment, and such a commitment can only be made by the free will of the individuals who feel Christ's call. No one else in the Church can make the commitment for them. The Church's role, which is essential for accepting the commitment and making it public, is secondary on the ritual level. It is right that the Church should be liturgically present in order to associate the self-offering of the religious to Christ's own offering[56] and to obtain the grace of perseverance for them (Pseudo-Dionysius, St. Thomas). This, however, is secondary (it comes later), and it is not this that renders profession a consecration. St. Thomas saw correctly that the ritual consecration involves a simple propitiatory blessing.

C. Consecration and Baptism

In the two principal texts we have quoted,[57] Vatican II stressed the relationships that exist between the consecration made through professing the religious life and baptismal consecration. We state that the consecration of religious, understood as a dedication of self and the living out of a commitment, is entirely based on the consecrating power of Baptism. As we have seen, the public act of dedication and commitment is not a sacramental consecration, nor is it a more-generally ritual one reserved to the ministry. All its power comes from Baptism, which makes Christians members of God's Holy People and assigns them to the divine service. Through this dedication the Christian, now a religious, has decided to live exclusively for the worship and service of God. Thus religious consecration expresses fully the fact that one belongs to God as a result of Baptism. Toward this end the religious renounces not only sin, but also all those things that might be obstacles in the path of total dedication to God. This is why, though profession is neither a sacramental nor a ritual act of consecration, religious bind themselves to God's service *novo et peculiari titulo* (by a new and special claim). They become, as ancient tradition expressed it, servants of God in the highest sense, specifically because of this commitment to express their baptismal consecration to God through a life of discipleship.

We know that ancient Patristic tradition spoke of profession as a "new" or "second" Baptism. The texts are numerous. This affirmation, already suggested in the *Vita Antonii,*[58] is found in St. Jerome,[59] in St. Peter Damian,[60] in St. Bernard,[61] and on up to St. Thomas.[62] At first, profession (in its broader sense) was compared to Baptism because it also obtains the remission of all previous sins (*Vita Antonii,* and St. Thomas). But the comparison was likewise based on the fact that profession represents a radical conversion. Following this line of thought we can say that religious life is merely a radical application of what has already been accomplished sacramentally in Baptism. Guerricus of Igny wrote: "That which has been done *specie* in the first Baptism, was done again *veritate* in profession":[63] *specie,* that is, in the sacramental sign; *veritate,* that is, in actual life. From this deeper perspective, one should speak of expressing the consequences of Baptism visibly rather than of a second Baptism.[64]

D. Consecration and *sequela*

The Council also establishes a close relationship between consecration and the profession of the "counsels." Going deeper, we might say that it is the *sequela Christi,* the adherence to Christ in his entire devotion to the Father, that consecrates a life. The three counsels of later tradition are nothing more than the specific traits embodying such a life, and the necessary means for attaining the complete freedom to live it. They orient all of life toward God. For this reason they are effective means for attaining the perfection of charity. The objective orientation thus achieves subjective communion.

E. Consecration and the Human World

Finally, the Council has reminded us that the consecration of religious does not alienate them from other people and their problems. This is a typically Christian concept of consecration. On the one hand, as religious they renounce some temporal possibilities and, from this point of view, separate themselves, step aside. But as Christians, those who consecrate themselves to God in the following of Christ, they give themselves to humanity. The Christian God is a saving God, and Christ is the Redeemer. Those who meet Christ meet humanity with its ills, its alienations, and its sufferings. This is true even of hermits and other contemplatives. To consecrate oneself to God in Christ is to be deeply immersed in the mystery of redemption.

Notes

NOTES TO CHAPTER I

1. *LG*, 44.
2. *PC*, 1.
3. *PC*, 2.
4. *PC*, 5.
5. *PC*, 8.
6. *PC*, 2a. Cf also *PC*, 1.
7. *PC*, 1; *LG*, 44.
8. *PC*, 5.
9. *PC*, 5 and 8.
10. *PC*, 2.
11. *Vita Antonii*, 2 (PG 26, 841). Eng. trans. by M. E. Keenan, in *ECB*, pp. 135-6.
12. *Enciclopedia Italiana Trecani*, s.v. "Biografia Letteratura Classica" F. Leo, *Die griechische-römische Biographie* (Leipzig, 1901). D. S. Stuart, *Epochs of Greek and Roman Biography*, in Sather Classical Lectures, 4 (1928).
13. S. Légasse, *L'appel du riche* (Paris: Beauchesne, 1966).
14. *Vita Hilarionis*, 3 (PL 23, 31). Eng. trans. by M. L. Ewald, in ECB, p. 247.
15. *Vie d'Hypatios*, 1; *Vie de Kyriakos*, 3, in A. J. Festugière, *Les Moines d'Orient* (MO), 2: 16-17; 3, 3: 40.
16. Palladius, *The Lausiac History*, 14. 4.
17. Théodore, 2 Catéchèse, in T. L. LeFort, *Oeuvres de Saint Pachôme et de ses disciples*, CSCO, 159, p. 38.
18. F. Halkin, *Sancti Pachomii Vitae Graecae*, 1. 24 (Brussels, 1932) p. 15: 2-4.
19. J. Cassian, *Instit. Coenob.*, 7. 27, *SC*, 109, p. 328.
20. *La Règle du Maître*, ed. A. de Vogüé, 87. 13-14, 39; 91. 44, in *SC*, 106, pp. 358, 362, 406. Eng. trans. *RM*, pp. 254, 255, 263.
21. Ibid., 91. 15-18, in *SC*, 106, p. 400. Eng. trans. *RM*, p. 268.
22. *Rule* of 1221, c 1, Eng. trans. *OS*, p. 31.
23. *Rule* of 1223, c 2, Eng. trans. *OS*, p. 32.
24. Cf. P. Vallium Sarnai, *Historia Albigensis*, n. 21, ed. Guébin (Lyon-Paris, 1926), p. 23.
25. T. de Celano, *Vita Prim.*, c. 9, n.

22, *Analecta Franciscana* (Quarrachi, 1941), p. 19.

26. Cf. A. Jiménez Oñate, *El Origen de la Compañía de Jesús* (Rome, 1966). A. Ravier, *Ignace de Loyola fonda la Compagnie de Jésus* (Paris: Desclée de Br., 1974), pp. 458–472.

27. St. Anthony M. Claret, *Autobiography*, 494 (Chicago: Claretian Publications, 1976), p. 157; (Madrid: BAC, 1959), p. 328.

28. *2 Catéchèse*, in Lefort, p. 38.

29. *Haer.*, 61 (*PG* 41, 1044).

30. *Hist. Eccles.*, 4. 23 (PG 67, 512).

31. *Ordo Monasterii*, rec. crit. D. De Bruyne, *Revue Benedictine* 42 (1930): 318–326.

32. *Rule* 3, in Holstenius, *Codex Regularum*, 1: 188–189.

33. Ed. Kaeppeli, *Arch. Fr. Praed.* 6 (Rome, 1936), p. 145: 21–22.

34. *Fontes Narrativi S. J.*, 2, (Rome, 1951), p. 310.

35. "To D. José Caixal," 5 September, 1849, *Epistolario Claretiano*, ed. J. M. Gil (Madrid, 1970), 1: 318.

36. *TDNT*, s.v. "akolouthein," 1: 210–216; s.v. "mathetēs," 4: 415–461. T. Aerts, "Suivre Jésus: Evolution d'un thème biblique dans les Evangiles Synoptiques," EThL, 42 (1966), 476–512. On the meaning of "akolouthein" in Matthew, cf. J. D. Kingsbury, "The Verb *akolouthein* (to follow) as an Index of Matthew's View of His Community," JBL 97 (1978): 56–73.

37. On the institution of the Twelve by Jesus himself, and its meaning, cf. B. Rigaux, "Die zwölf in Geschichte und Kerygma," in *Der historische Jesus und der kerygmatische Christus*, ed. H. Ristow and K. Mathias, 2 ed. (Berlin, 1961), pp. 468–486.

38. For a study of the relationship between the Twelve and the disciples, cf. E. Best, "The Role of the Disciples in Mark," NTS 23 (1976–77): 377–401.

39. M. Hengel, *Nachfolge und Charisma* (Berlin, 1968), pp. 68–70.

40. Ibid., pp. 94–96.

41. A. Schulz, *Nachfolgen und Nachahmen: Studien über das Verhältnis der neutestamentliche Jüngerschaft zur urchristlichen Vorbildethik* (Munich: Kösel, 1962).

42. Hengel, *Nachfolge*, pp. 46–63.

43. Cf. C. H. Dodd, "Jesus as Teacher and Prophet," in *Mysterium Christi: Christological Studies by British and German Theologians*, ed. G. K. A. Bell and A. Deissmann (London, 1930), pp. 53 ff. J. J. Vincent, "Did Jesus Teach His Disciples?" in *Studia Evangelica* 3 (Texte und Untersuchungen, 88), ed. K. Aland (Berlin, 1964), pp. 105–118.

44. Hengel, *Nachfolge*, pp. 20–27.

45. Ibid., pp. 83–84.

46. Ibid., p. 82.

47. P. Hoffmann, *Studien zur Theologie der Logienquelle* (Münster: Aschendorf, 1971), p. 262.

48. Cf. K. Stock, *Boten aus dem Mit-Ihm-Sein* (Rome: PIB, 1975).

49. R. Bultmann, *Die Geschichte der synoptischen Tradition*, 6th ed. (Göttingen, 1964), p. 173; H. D. Betz, *Nachfolge und Nachahmung Jesu Christ im Neuen Testament* (Tübingen, 1967), p. 27; H. Schürmann, *La tradizione dei detti di Gesú* (Brescia: Paideia, 1966, 1967), pp. 22–23.

50. A. Schlatter, *Der Evangelist Matthäus* (Stuttgart, 1933), pp. 350–351.

51. G. Theissen, "Wanderradikalismus, Literatursoziologische Aspekte des Überlieferung con Worten Jesu im Unchristentum," ZThK 70 (1973): 245–271.

52. G. Kretschmar, "Ein Beitrag zu Frage nach dem Ursprung

frühchristlicher Askese," ZThK 61 (1964); 27-67.

53. E. Käsemann, "Zum Thema der urchristlichen Apokalyptik," in *Exegetische Versche und Besinnungen,* 2: 78-80, 115. Cf. also H. R. Baltz, *Methodische Probleme der neutestamentlichen Christologie* (Neukirchen, 1967), pp. 167-174. Both quoted in P. Hoffman, *Logienquelle,* p. 236.

54. P. Hoffman, *Logienquelle,* pp. 236 ff.

55. H. D. Betz, *Nachfolge und Nachahmung,* pp. 33, 41.

56. Ibid., p. 32. Best, "Role of the Disciples in Mark."

57. The study of these differences goes beyond the limits of our research. One may read the paragraphs dedicated to this theme in Betz, *Nachfolge und Nachahmung,* pp. 31-43, together with the ample bibliography prepared by him. Cf. also Aerts, "Suivre Jésus," pp. 500-512. For Matthew, U. Lutz, "Die Jünger in Matthausevangelium," ZNTW (1971): 141-171. For Mark, Best, "Role of the Disciples in Mark."

58. G. Klein, "Die Berufung des Petrus," in *Rekonstruktion und Interpretation* (Munich: Kaiser, 1969), pp. 11-48.

59. F. Hahn, "Die Jüngerberufung Joh.1, 35-51," in *Neuen Testament und Kirche* ed. J. Gnilka (Freiburg, Herder), pp. 172-190.

60. P. Lamarche, "The Call to Conversion and Faith: The Vocation of Levi," in *Lumen Vitae* 25 (1970); 301-312.

61. K. Berger, *Die Gesetzesauslegung Jesu, 1: Markus und Parallelen* (Neukirchen, 1972), pp. 422-427.

62. J. Dupont, "Reconocer à tous ses biens," NRT 93 (1971): 561-582.

63. There is a danger inherent in starting out from a predetermined interpretation of religious life and reading the biblical texts in light of that interpretation.

64. D. Bonhoeffer, *The Cost of Discipleship,* 2nd ed. (New York: Macmillan, 1966).

65. *LG,* 40.

66. *LG,* 40, 41, 42.

67. *LG,* 42.

68. *LG,* 41.

69. *LG,* 41. Cf. I Co 12, Rom 12.

70. Bonhoeffer, *Discipleship,* pp. 38-39.

71. *Did.* 11. 8.

72. *Vita Antonii,* 2 (PG 26, 841). Eng trans. in *ECB,* pp. 135-136.

73. *Praeceptum* 1; *Sermo* 355, 1; *Sermo* 356, 1 (PL 32, 1377; 39, 1568-1569, 1574-1575).

74. Celano, *Vita Prima,* 9. 22.

75. *Autobiography,* nn. 113-120.

76. Basil, *Asceticum Parvum,* int. 3 (PL 103, 494-496); *Regulae fusius,* 7 (PG 31, 928-933).

77. *RB,* 4.

78. A. Harnack, *Monasticism, Its Ideals and History,* trans. E. E. Kellett and F. H. Marseille, 2nd. ed. (London: Williams and Norgate, 1913), pp. 35-36. Bonhoeffer, *Discipleship,* pp. 38-39.

79. *Exhort. ad Mart.,* 12, 14, and 37 (PG 11, 577-580, 581, and 613), quotes Mt. 16:24-27; Mt. 19:27; Lk. 14:26; Jn. 12:25.

80. Cf. *Vita Antonii,* 47 (PG 26, 912), *ECB,* p. 178. Jerome, *Ep.* 108, 31 (PL 22, 905). Augustine, *Sermo* 4, 34 (PL 38, 52). *Vie de Pachôme* S², in Lefort, p. 9: 1-17.

81. *Vie de Daniel,* 31 and 47, in Festugière, *MO,* 2: 132, 164.

82. A. Rischl, *Rechfertigung und Versöhnung,* 3 vols., 1870-1874, 1888.

83. J. Weiss, *Die Predigt Jesu vom Reiche Gottes,* 1892.

84. For a complete and accurate history of this discussion cf. N. Perrin, *The Kingdom of God in the Teaching of Jesus* (Philadelphia: Westminster Press, 1963).

85. R. Bultmann is the only great exegete who has insisted on the exclusively future character of the Kingdom, in the context of his existentialist interpretation of the Christian message. His disciples, however, reintroduced the tension between present and future.

86. Gregory Naz., *Or.*, 40, 45 (PG 36, 424). Evagrius, *Praktikós*, 2, *SC*, 171, p. 500. Eng. trans. (Spencer, Mass: Cistercian Publications, 1970), p. 15.

87. W. Rauschenbusch, *A Theology of the Social Gospel*, 1919.

88. *In Matth. Hom.*, 64 (PG 58, 609).

89. *In Matth.* 3. 20, *CSEL*, 77, 170–177.

90. 2-2, q. 184, a. 3, ad. 1.

91. *Asceticum Parvum*, int. 4 (PL 103, 496–497). *Regulae fus.*, int. 8 (PG 31, 933–941).

92. It is true that this raises the problem of the relationships between monasticism and secular life. We will discuss this later.

93. The limitations of Canon Law with respect to different forms of Christian life are necessary. Laws do not create forms of life, but recognize and regulate them. Only the Spirit creates. Hence it is understandable that law and theology always tend to be a century or more behind the action of the Holy Spirit. On the other hand, the Church cannot officially recognize, still less institutionalize, all vocations.

94. The difficulty of classifying not only Christian life but also religious life itself was seen during the years 1976–1977 in the difficulty several religious institutes experienced in trying to recognize themselve in the typology proposed by the new draft of Canon Law.

NOTES TO EXCURSUS,
CHAPTER I

1. R. Bultmann, *Die Geschichte der synoptischen Tradition*, 6th ed. (Göttingen, 1964), pp. 56–57.

2. K. Berger, *Die Gesetzesauslegung*, p. 402.

3. "Die Frage des Reichen nach dem ewigen Leben," EvTh 19 (1959): 97.

4. Berger, *Die Gesetzesauslegung*, pp. 362–365.

5. W. Harnisch, "Die Berufung des Reichen: Zur Analyse von Markus 1, 17-27," *Festschrift für Ernst Fuchs* (Tübingen: Mohr, 1973), pp. 161–176 (esp. 173 ff).

6. *L'appel du riche* (Paris: Beauchesne, 1965), pp. 50-57.

7. Harnisch, "Die Berufung," pp. 171–173.

8. Ibid., p. 174.

9. For further details cf. Légasse, *L'appel*, pp. 97–110.

10. *In Matth.*, 19 (PG 13, 1289–1301).

11. *De viduis*, 11. 71—12. 74 (PL 16, 255–257).

12. *Ep.* 66 *ad Pammachium*, 8 (PL 22, 643).

13. Légasse, *L'appel*, pp. 188 ff.

14. G. Barth, "Das Gesetzesverstandnis des Evangelisten Matthäus," in G. Bornkamm et al., *Überlieferung und Auslegung im*

Mathhäusevangelium (Neukirchen, 1968), pp. 88–93. Barth also refutes a two-stage morality: commandments for everyone and counsels for a few; but he sees the call to discipleship as a general affirmation which radicalizes the love of neighbor still more. The *quid novum* in his interpretation would be this fuller love which leads to the renunciation of goods in favor of the poor. If this were so, the climax of the anecdote would not be "follow me" (consequently Christ), but "sell and distribute."

NOTES TO CHAPTER II

1. Cf. B. D. Dupuy, "Theologie der kirchlicher Amter," in *Mysterium Salutis: Grundriss heiligeschichtlicher Dogmatik,* 4, part 2 (Einsiedeln: Benziger, 1973), pp. 511–513; with bibliography.

2. Clement Roman., *Ad Vor.,* 1. 38 (PG 1, 284). Ignatius Martyr, *Ad Polycarpum,* 5 (PG 5, 867).

3. *LG,* 43b, 44d.

4. *Vita Ant.,* 23 (PG 26, 876–877). *ECB,* p. 156.

5. *Vita Ant.,* 28 (PG 26, 885). *ECB,* pp. 161–162.

6. *Vita Ant.,* 49, 57, 58, 61, 64 (PG 26, 913; 921; 925; 932; 933). *ECB,* pp. 179, 186, 190, 191.

7. Isaac Cell., 8 (PG 65, 225); *SDF,* p. 86.

8. Poemen 182 (PG 65, 365). Cf. Felix (PG 65, 433); *SDF,* pp. 161–162; 202.

9. Ammonathas (PG 65, 136); *SDF,* p. 32.

10. *Vitae PP. Iurensium,* 68. 3; 70. 12; 96. 6; 147. 4, in *SC,* 142, pp. 314, 318, 342, 396, 418.

11. *Saeculi homines,* 172. 1, *SC,* p. 424.

12. PG 65, 168–169; *SDF,* p. 51.

13. Spyridon, 1–2 (PG 65, 517–520); *SDF,* pp. 191–192.

14. Epiphanius, 4 (PG 65, 164); *SDF,* p. 49.

15. Anthony, 24 (PG 65, 84); *SDF,* p. 5.

16. Or 6 (PG 65, 437–440); *SDF,* pp. 206–207.

17. *Conlat.,* 21. 14, in *SC,* 64, pp. 89–90. Cf. *Conlat.,* 6. 3, in *SC,* 42, pp. 221–223.

18. Syncletica, 2 (PG 65, 421g). *SDF,* p. 193.

19. *Vita e detti dei Padri del Deserto* (Assisi: Citta Nuova, 1975), 2: 198.

20. *Reg. Mag.,* 90. 69–70, in *SC,* 106, p. 390.

21. *Moral. in Job,* 26. 51 (PL 76, 380).

22. *RB,* 4.

23. Sinuthii Archimand., *Vita et Opera Omnia,* ed. H. Wiesmann, *CSCO,* 96, (Louvain, 1932), pp. 6–7.

24. *De Eccles. Hierar.,* 6. 2 (PG 3, 533).

25. *Regulae fusius (RF),* 8. 3 (PG 31, 940). *Reg. brev. Proem.* (PG 31, 1080).

26. *RF,* 26 (PG 31, 985). *Reg. fus. Proem.,* 4 (PG 31, 987).

27. *RF,* 6 (PG 31, 925).

28. *RF,* 6. 2 (PG 31, 928).

29. *RF,* 5 (PG 31, 920).

30. *RF,* 6 (PG 31, 925).

31. *RF,* 7 (PG 31, 928).

32. *RF,* 8. 3 (PG 31, 940).

33. J. Gribomont, "Le Renoncement au

monde dans l'idéal ascétique de saint Basile," *Irenikon* 31 (1958): 282-307, 460-475.

34. Ibid., pp. 303-307.

35. *Reg. fus. Proem.*, 3-4 (PG 31, 893-901).

36. *Parvum Asketikon Proem.* (PL 103, 487).

37. *Reg. fus. Proem.* (PG 31, 889 ff.).

38. Jerome, *Epis.*, 22 (PL 22, 405-406). Augustine, *De s. virginitate*, 18 (PL 40, 404).

39. Jerome, *Epis.*, 22. 15 (PL 22, 403).

40. *Adv. Iovinian.*, 1 (PL 23, 231).

41. *De virginitate*, 25, in *SC*, 125, p. 174.

42. *De virginitate*, 26, in *SC*, 125, pp. 174-176.

43. *De virginitate*, 16-17, in *SC*, pp. 146-154.

44. *Adv. Iovinian.* 1. 7 (PL 23, 230).

45. *De perpetua virginit.*, 21 (PL 23, 214).

46. *Ex actis Andreae*, 5, Lipsius Bonnet, 2, 1. 40.

47. Gregory of Nyssa, *De virginitate*, 12. 4, in *SC*, 119, p. 418. John Chrysostom, *De virginitate* 14. 3; 15. 1; 17. 5, in *SC*, 125, pp. 140, 144, 154. Jerome, *Epist.*, 22. 19 (PL 22, 406).

48. *In Hebr. hom.*, 7. 4 (PG 63, 68).

49. *Adv. oppugn. vitae monasticae*, 3. 14 (PG 47, 372).

50. *In Gen.*, 21. 6 (PG 53, 183).

51. *In I Thess.*, 5. 1 (PG 62, 423).

52. *In Matth.*, 7. 4 (PG 63, 67).

53. *In Matth.*, 7. 4 (PG 63, 67).

54. *In Gen. hom.*, 43. 1 (PG 54, 396).

55. Cf. J. M. Leroux, "Monachisme et Communauté chrétienne d'après saint J. Chrysostome," *Theologié de la Vie Monastique* (Aubier, 1951), pp. 143-190. "Saint Jean Chrysostome et la monachisme," in *Jean Chrysostome*

et Augustin, Actes du Colloque de Chantilly 1974, Théologie Historique 35 (Beauchesne, 1975), pp. 125-144.

56. *Moral. in Job*, 26. 51 (PL 76, 380).

57. Cf. ibid., 19. 13 (PL 76, 109).

58. Disparia merita: Ibid., 30. 6, n. 23 (PL 76, 536).

59. *Regula Pastoralis*, 3. 27 (PL 77, 101).

60. *De Institutione Laicali*, 1. 12 (PL 106, 145-146).

61. Ibid., 2. 16 (PL 106, 197-199).

62. Ibid., 3. 18 (PL 106, 271).

63. Ibid., (PL 106, 172).

64. Urban II, *Epistolae et Privilegia*, 58 (PL 151, 358): "From the beginning Holy Church has offered two types of life to her children: one sustains the frailty of the weak; the other perfects the blessed life of the strong. One remains in the low valleys of Segor, while the other ascends to the mountain peaks...." In regard to the Premonstratensians, cf. *Sacri et canonici Ordinis Praemonstratensium Annales*, Carolus Ludovicus Hugo, (Nancy, 1743) vol 2: Probationes tomi primi Monasteriologicae Praemonstratensis, col. 8-9.

65. *Comm. in Matth.*, 19 (PG 13, 1289-1301).

66. *Parvum Asketikon*, 4 (PL 103, 496-497). Cf. *Regulae fus.*, 8 (PG 31, 933-941).

67. *Regulae fusius*, 8 (PG 31, 936).

68. *Parvum Asketikon Proem.*, (PL 103, 487).

69. 2-2, q. 184, aa. 3-4.

70. 2-2, q. 184, a. 4.

71. 2-2, q. 184, a. 3.

72. *Adv. Iovin.*, 1. 8 (PL 23, 231).

73. 2-2, q. 183, aa. 2-3.

74. *Comm. in Rom.*, 7. 7 (PG 14, 1122).

75. Ps. Macarius, *De Oratione*, 11 (PG 34, 861).

76. 2-2, q. 184, a. 3.

77. *LG*, 40.

78. 2-2, q. 184, a. 3.

79. *LG*, 41.

80. 2-2, q. 183, a. 2c.

81. *LG*, 44c.

82. E. Schillebeeckx, *Celibacy* (New York: Sheed and Ward, 1968), pp. 82–85.

83. *LG*, 44a.

84. *LG*, 44c. Cf. LG, 46b: "a closer imitation."

85. *PC*, 1.

86. *LG*, 44a.

87. *LG*, 44c; PC, 1.

88. *LG*, 44c.

89. D. Wiederkehr, "Die kirche als Ort vielgestaltiger christlicher Existenz," in *Mysterium Salutis*, v. 4, pt. 2 (Einsiedeln: Benziger, 1973), p. 563.

90. Clem. Alex., *Strom.*, 3. 12 (PG 8, 1189B); 7. 12 (PG 9, 497–500).

91. *Adv. Iovin. Libri Duo*, (PL 23, 206–338).

92. *De Votis Monasticis*, 1, in D. Martin Luthers, *Werke, Kristliche Gesammausgabe*, 8 band (Weimar: H. Böhlau, 1889), p. 585. Cf. *Luther's Works, The Christian in Society*, trans.

J. Atkinson 1, (Philadelphia: Fortress Press, 1966), p. 264.

93. Sess. X, can. 10 de matrimonio (*Denziger-Schoenmetzer*, 1963, n. 1810): "Si quis dixerit statum coniugalem anteponendum esse statui virginitatis vel celibatus, et non esse melius ac beatius manere in virginitate aut celibatu, quam iungi matrimonio, A. S."

94. AAS (1954): 161–191.

95. *Optatam totius*, 10.

96. *LG*, 42.

97. *LG*, 42.

98. K. Rahner, "On the Evangelical Counsels," *Theological Investigations*, 8: 147–149.

99. 2-2, q. 152, a. 4.

100. *De s. virginitate*, 8 (PL 40, 400). *De Civit. Dei*, 1. 18 (PL 41, 31–32).

101. *LG*, 42.

102. Sacr. Conc., 98 and 101. The document reflects the usage of the Holy See, resulting from the desire to include religious and secular institutes in the same general category. In *Vatican Council II*, ed. A. Flannery, it is translated "religious" in both cases.

103. 2-2, q. 184, a. 4.

NOTES TO EXCURSUS, CHAPTER II

1. *Apoph. Patrum*, Pambo, 3 (PG 65, 369), *SDF*, p. 165.

2. *De Coenob. Instit.*, 4, *SC*, 109, pp. 118ff.

3. CF. R. Reitzenstein, *Historia Monachorum und Historia Lausiaca* (Göttingen, 1916), p. 104.

4. Cf. Mss. Coislin 126, n. 17 in *Vita e detti dei Padri del Deserto* (Assisi: Citta Nuova, 1975), pp. 224–225.

5. Anthony, 20; Cassian, 7; Macarius the Egypt., 2 (PG 65; 81, 245, 260). *SDF*, pp. 4, 98, 106.

6. *De Coenob. Instit.*, 2. 3.2; 4. 1; 4. 23; 4. 27; 5. 32.2; 7. 15, *SC*, 109, pp. 60, 122, 152, 160, 242, 310.

7. Ibid., 4. 34, *SC*, p. 172.

8. *Vita Martini*, 3. 5, *SC*, 133, p. 258. *Vitae PP. Iuren.*, 14. 3, *SC*, 142, p. 276.

9. *Vita Martini, loc. cit.*

10. Ibid., 25. 4, *SC*, 133, p. 310.

11. Ibid., ep. 2. 7, *SC*, 133, p. 238.

12. *RM*, 3. 94; 86. 7; 86. 21; 87. 20, etc.

13. *RB*, 7. 8.

14. *RB*, 64. 17.

15. Cf. comment of De Vogüé, in *SC*, 186, p. 1202.

16. *Vitae PP. Iuren.*, 165. 8, *SC*, p. 416.

17. *RM*, 3. 94.

18. *Vita Martini*, 1. 3, *SC*, p. 250.

19. *RM* thp 23.

20. *De Coenob. Instit.*, 4. 28, *SC*, p. 162.

21. Ibid., 7. 26, *SC*, p. 328.

22. Ibid., 4. 36.1, *SC*, p. 176.

23. Ibid., 4. 14, *SC*, p. 138.

24. Arsenius, 12; Agathon, 1; Andrew; Longinus, 1; Pistos; Tithoes, 2 (PG 65; 89, 108-109, 136, 256, 375, 428. *SDF*, pp. 9, 17, 32, 103-104, 166-167, 198.

25. *Parvum Asketikon*, 4 (PL 103, 496). *Reg. fus.*, 8 (PG 31, 936).

26. *Conlat.*, 3. 6, *SC*, 42, pp. 145-146.

27. *De Coenob. Instit.*, 4. 39.1, *SC*, 109, p. 180.

28. Ibid., 7. 26, *SC*, p. 328.

29. 2-2, q. 186, a. 2 ad. 3.

30. Alonius, 1 (PG 65, 133). *SDF*, p.

31. Apphy (PG 65, 133). *SDF*, pp. 30-31.

32. Theodora, 8. *Mss. Coislin.*

33. John the Dwarf, 10 (PG 65, 208). *SDF*, p. 74. *Reg. Mag.* 50. 20; 50. 42.

34. Pistos (PG 65, 373). *SDF*, pp. 166-167.

35. *Vita Antonii*, 14 (PG 26, 865). *ECB*, pp. 148-149.

36. *RB*, 4. 21.

37. *Vita Martini*, 25.4, *SC*, 133, p. 318.

38. *Conlat.*, 11. 6.2, *SC*, 54, p. 105.

39. *Conlat.*, 21. 14.2, *SC*, 64, p. 89.

40. *Conlat.*, 1. 5, *SC*, 42, p. 83.

41. *Conlat.*, 24. 2.4, *SC*, 64, p. 173.

42. Cf. R. Bultot, *Christianisme et valeurs humaines*, I: *La Doctrine du mépris du monde en Occident de s. Ambroise à Innocent III, 4,* (Nauwelaerst, 1963, 1964). M. de Certeau et al., Le mépris du monde (Paris: Cerf, 1965). F. Lazzari, "Saint Pierre Damien et le *contemptus mundi*," RAM 40 (1964): 185-196.

43. T. M. Gannon and G. W. Traub, *The Desert and the City* (Toronto: Macmillan, 1969).

44. Carion, 2 (PG 65, 249). *SDF*, pp. 100-101.

45. Milesios, 2 (PG 65, 297). *SDF*, pp. 124-125.

46. Arsenius, 40 (PG 65, 105). *SDF*, pp. 15-16.

47. *Vitae PP. Iuren.*, 68. 13-14, *SC*, 142, p. 314.

48. Arsenius, 13 (PG 65, 92). Cf. Arsenius, 1-2 (PG 65, 88). *SDF*, pp. 8 and 9.

49. "Cella-mundi turbines": *Vitae PP. Iuren.*, 2. 12, *SC*, 142, p. 238.

50. Agathon, 1 (PG 65, 108-109). *SDF*, p. 17.

51. *Asketikon Parvum*, 2 (PL 103, 494). Cf. *Reg. fus.*, 5 (PG 31, 920-924).

52. *Reg. fus.*, 6 (PG 31, 925A-B).

53. *Asket. Parv.*, 1-2 (PL 103, 488-494). *Reg. fus.*, 1-3 (PG 31, 905-917).

54. *Reg. fus.*, 6 (PG 31, 925A-B).

55. *Reg. fus.*, 32: PG 31, 993-997).

56. Cf. J. M. Lozano, "La Comunità Pacomiana dalla comunione alla instituzione," *Claretianum* 15 (1975): 237-267.

57. *Reg. Mag.*, 95. 17-19, *SC*, 106, p. 446. *RM*, p. 284.

58. *RB*, 66. 6–7.

59. *Reg. Mag.*, 95. 22–23, *SC*, 106, pp. 446–448. *RM*, p. 284.

60. *RB*, 66. 7.

61. *Reg. Mag.*, 95. 17–21, *SC*, 106, p. 446. *RM*, p. 284.

62. *RB*, 67. 4–5.

63. It is quite significant that some of the earliest sources for the Franciscan Movement repeat that the brothers' monastery or convent is the whole world. In *Sacrum commercium* (1127) when Lady Poverty asks to see their convent, the brothers show her "the entire world" and tell her, "This, O Lady, is our cloister" (6, n. 63 in *Omnibus of Sources*, p. 1593). Jacques de Vitry in his *Historia Orientalis* (1219–1221) affirms that the new Order lives in the "vastness of an open cloister" (ch. 32, cited by K. Esser).

64. 2-2, q. 187, a. 1.

65. 2-2, q. 187, a. 2.

66. 2-2, q. 187, a. 4–5.

67. 2-2, q. 188, a. 3.

NOTES TO CHAPTER III

1. G. Kittel, s.v. "akolouthein," *TDNT*, 1: 210–216.

2. *Vita Antonii*, 65 (PG 26, 936). *ECB*, p. 192.

3. *Vita e detti dei Padri dei Deserto* (Città Nuova, 1975) 1: 241.

4. *Hom. 6 ad monachos* (PL 50, 448).

5. *Conlat.*, 3. 3, *SC*, 42, p. 141.

6. *Vita Antonii*, 18 (PG 26, 936). *ECB*, p. 192. Gregory the Great, *Dialogues* 2, 5, and 31. Eng. trans. in *The Fathers of the Church*, 15: 67, 99.

7. J. Cassian, *Conlat.*, 3. 5, *SC*, 42, p. 143.

8. *RB*, Prol. 45.

9. *Vita Antonii*, 85 (PG 26, 964); *ECB*, p. 209. *Apoph. Patrum*, Longinus, 3 (PG 65, 257): *SDF*, p. 104. Jerome, *Vita Hilarionis*, 8. 2 and 3. 1; *ECB*, pp. 250, 271. J. Cassian, *De Coenob. Instit.*, 1. 2.2; 2. 2.2, *SC*, 109, pp. 40, 60.

10. 2-2, q. 81, a. 2; a. 3, ad. 2.

11. 2-2, q. 186, a. 1.

12. 1-2, q. 108, a. 4; 2-2, q. 88, a. 11; q. 186, a. 1, ad. 1; a. 5, ad. 1; q. 188, a. 2, ad. 2.

13. *De perf. vitae spir.*, C 11; 2-2, q. 186, a. 1, ad. 2; a. 6, ad. 2.

14. 2-2, q. 186, a. 2.

15. 2-2, q. 186, a. 1, ad. 3.

16. *LG*, 44.

17. *PC*, 5.

18. *LG*, 44.

19. *PC*, 5.

20. 2-2, q. 184, a. 3.

21. 2-2, q. 184, a. 2.

22. 2-2, q. 184, a. 2c.

23. Just because the concept is Greek does not make it false.

24. Later, when we discuss celibacy, we will return to the question of the legitimacy of this expression through actual renouncement, in the light of God's word.

25. H. Küng, *On Being a Christian*, 1. 3 (New York: Doubleday, 1976), pp. 195–200.

26. It should be clear, however, that

this is equally true of secular life. It is not permissible to assign to matrimony or to secular life the exclusive right to embody the service of God, as some tend to do. This is equivalent to basing oneself entirely on Genesis, ignoring what has been added by Christ's example and by his eschatological hope. It represents, in fact, a typically Old Testament perspective.

27. 2-2, q. 81, a. 2; a. 3, ad. 2.

28. 2-2, q. 186, a. 1.

29. 1, q. 8, a. 7, ad. 1.

30. E. Schillebeeckx, *Celibacy,* pp. 91-92.

31. J. Weiss, *Die Predigt Jesu vom Reiche Gottes,* 1892, 2nd ed. 1900. *Die Idee des Reiches Gottes in der Theologie.* A. Schweitzer, *Das Messianäts und Leidensgeheimnis, Eine Skizze des Lebens Jesu,* 1901. *Von Reimarus zu Wrede,* 1906.

32. J. Jeremias, s.v. "Pais Theou," *TDNT,* 5: 654-717. M. A. Gervais, s. v. "Servant of the Lord," *New Catholic Encyclopedia,* 13: 126-130.

33. Cf. H. Braun, *Jesus der Mann aus Nazareth und seine Zeit* (Stuttgart: Kreuz, 1969), pp. 161-166.

34. *Apoph. Patrum,* Arsenius, 1-2 (PG 65, 88). *SDF,* p. 8.

35. Arsenius, 13 (PG 65, 92). *SDF,* p. 9.

36. St. Teresa of Avila, *Way of Perfection,* 1. 3; *Life,* 32; *Relation,* 3, *Complete Works,* trans. E. Allison Peers (New York: Sheed and Ward, 1944), 2: 3-10; 1: 217, 317.

37. Thomas Merton, *Faith and Violence* (Notre Dame: Univ. of N.D. Press, 1968), pp. 106-110, 121-129.

38. *PC,* 1; *LG,* 43.

39. *LG,* 44b; *PC,* 2b-d.

40. *LG,* 43.

41. *PC,* 1.

42. *LG,* 73; *Dignitatis humanae,* 4; *Apostolicum actuositatem,* 19.

43. *Les Vies Coptes de saint Pachóme,* Ed. T. Lefort (Louvain, 1943), pp. 99, 220-223.

44. *RB,* 64. 3-6.

45. Arsenius, 1; Hieras, 1 (PG 65, 88 and 232). *SDF,* pp. 8, 89. *Vie de Pachôme* Bo n.115, p. 190. 16-17. *Oeuvres de saint Pachôme,* p. 28. 26. Cyril de Scythopolis, *Vie de Jean l'Hesychaste,* 20, in *MO,* 3. 3, pp. 17, 28-29.

46. Gregory Naz., *Carmen de se ipso,* (PG 37, 1029f.).

47. Augustine, *Sermo,* 255. 5-6 (PL 38, 1186-1189).

48. *De Civ. Dei,* 19. 19 (PL 41, 647).

49. S. Thomas, 2-2, q. 184, a. 3; S. Bonaventure, *Apologia Pauperum,* 3. 3 (Quaracchi, 1898), 8: 245.

50. *LG,* 44.

51. F. Hahn, *Mission in the New Testament* (Naperville, Ill: A. R. Allenson, 1965.) A. Chavasse et al., *Eglise et Apostolat* (Paris: Tournai, 1954). C. Journet, *L'Eglise du Verbe Incarné,* 2, 2nd ed. (Paris, 1962), pp. 1223-1252.

52. *Ad Gentes,* 2.

53. Augustine, *In Johan.,* 58 (PL 35, 1793).

54. 2-2, q. 132, a. 1, ad. 1.

55. Vie de Pachôme S³ and S¹, *Les Vies Coptes,* pp. 60. 21—62. 16 and 1. 5-11.

56. 2-2, q. 188, a. 2, ad. 1.

57. *Contra impugn.,* c. 1.

58. *Quodlib.,* 3, a. 17, ad. 6.

59. 2-2, q. 186, a. 1, ad. 2.

60. It is well to be aware than monastic tradition has also interpreted divine service in a broader sense, going beyond the limits of liturgy and prayer, even though these remained the preeminent expression of that service. In primitive monasticism one became a

servant of God not only because one set constant prayer as a goal, but also because one sought to fulfill the gospel Word by ascetic combat. At that time, too, one was a servant of God, of Christ, by having been consecrated to him through radical renunciation. St. Benedict retained this broad concept of divine service. The new element in St. Thomas consists in his inclusion of

apostolic and charitable activities in the service of God toward which religious life is directed.

61. 2-2, q. 188, a. 2. The above translation, as well as the previous one, is taken from the translation of the *Summa* by the fathers of the English Dominican province. (First complete American ed., 3 vols., New York: Benziger, 1947.)

NOTES TO CHAPTER IV

1. E. Bettencourt, s.v. "charism," *Sacramentum Mundi* (New York: Herder, 1968), pp. 283–284. A. Bittlinger, *Gifts and Graces* (Grand Rapids: 1976); *Gifts and Ministries* (Grand Rapids, 1973). H. Conzelman, s.v. "charism," *TDNT* 9: 402–406. B. N. Wambecq, "Le mot charism," NRTh 97 (1975): 345–355.

2. Ambrose, *De Viduis*, 11. 71—12. 74 (PL 16: 255–257).

3. Origen, *Comm. in Rom.*, 9. 14 (PG 14, 1275).

4. Note the inadequacy of the motive: it would be burdensome to impose virginity!

5. J. Chrysostom, *In Matth. Hom.*, 62. 3–4 (PG 58: 599–600).

6. *LG*, 43, 44, 45, 46, 47; *PC*, 1, 2, 5, 6, 10, 11.

7. *LG*, 39.

8. *LG*, 42.

9. *LG*, 39.

10. *PC*, 1.

11. *PC*, 8.

12. *LG*, 42; *PC*, 12.

13. *LG*, 43.

14. *LG*, 12.

15. *LG*, 43.

16. *Lg*, 43.

17. *LG*, 44.

18. 2-2, q. 186, aa. 3–5.

19. 2-2, q. 186. a. 6.

20. *Orat. 6 de pace*, n. 11 (PG 35, 724).

21. PG 65, 136. *SDF*, p. 32.

22. PG 65, 336. *SDF*, p. 147.

23. PG 65, 185. *SDF*, p. 61 (translates "poverty, obedience, and fasting").

24. PG 65, 216. *SDF*, p. 79.

25. PG 65, 180. *SDF*, p. 58.

26. *Praecepta*, 49 (PL 23, 73).

27. *Reg. fus.*, 8 (PG 31, 936).

28. *Tract. ad Eulogium*, 2 (PG 79, 1096).

29. *Conlat.*, 3. 6, *SC*, 42, pp. 145–146.

30. *Scala Paradisi*, 3 (PG 88, 668).

31. John Chrysostom, *In Primam ad Cor.*, 9. 2 (PG 61, 77).

32. Ambrose, *De Viduis*, 11. 71—12. 74 (PL 16, 255–257).

33. Augustine, *Contra Celsum*, 5. 9 (PL 40, 225).

34. *Enarr. in Ps. 103*, 16 (PL 37, 1371). CSEL, 40. 1513–1514.

35. Bernard, *Sermo 27 de div.*, 3 (PL 183, 613).

36. Int. 7 (PL 103, 498).

37. *Epist.*, 199. 18 (PG 32, 720B).

38. *Reg. Mag.*, 89. 8–16, *SC*, 106, pp. 372–375. *RM*, pp. 258–259.

39. *Reg. Mag.*, 89. 1–2, *SC*, 106, pp. 370–372. *RM*, p. 258.

40. *RB*, 58. 17–20, *SC*, 182, p. 630.

41. *Sermo 30 in festo S. Augustini* (PL 198, 1790).

42. PG 88, 657.

43. Odo, abbas S. Genoveffae, *Epis.*, 1: "In professione igitur nostra quam fecimus, tria, sicut bene nostris, promisimus: castitatem, communionem, obedientiam" (PL 196, 1399).

44. *Reg. Ordinis SS. Trinitatis*, in L. Holstenius, *Codex Regularum* (Augsburg, 1759), 3: 3.

45. *Regula* 1221, c. 1.

46. Innocent IV, in J. H. Sbaralea, *Bullarium Franciscanum*, 2: 474.

47. 2-2, q. 186, aa. 3–7.

48. J. Chrysostom, *In I Cor.*, 9. 2 (PG 61, 77). Ambrose, *De Viduis*, 11. 71—12. 74 (PL 16, 255–257).

49. Augustine, *Contra Celsum*, 5. 9 (PL 40, 225). *Ennar. in Ps. 103*, 3. 16 (PL 37, 1371). *CSEL*, 40, 1513.

50. Bernard, *Sermo 27 de div.*, (PL 183, 613).

51. K. Rahner, "The Theology of Poverty," *Theological Investigations*, trans. D. Burke (London-New York, 1971), 8: 182–183.

52. 2-2, q. 186, a. 2, ad. 3. He added, however, a vague reference to the religious vows, probably to include obedience also among the "counsels."

53. K. Rahner, "On the Evangelical Counsels," *Theol. Invest.* 8: 163–165.

54. *LG*, 44.

55. Loc. cit.

56. *Ux.*, 1. 5.4 (PL 1, 1395).

57. *De s. virginit.*, 14–15 (PL 40, 402–403).

58. *LG*, 44a (twice), 46b; *PC*, 1b, 12a; *PO*, 16b.

59. *LG*, 46b; *PC*, 1b, 12a.

60. *LG*, 44c.

61. *LG*, 44a.

62. 2-2, q. 184, a. 3.

63. *LG*, 44.

64. *LG*, 12. Cf. H. Küng, "The Charismatic Structure of the Church," *Concilium*, 4: The Church and Ecumenism (New York: Paulist Press, 1965), pp. 41–61.

65. L. Artigas, *El Espíritu Santo y la Vida Religiosa* (Salamanca: Secret. Trinitario, 1975).

NOTES TO EXCURSUS TO CHAPTER IV

1. Ambrose, *De Viduis*, 11. 71—12. 74 (PL 16, 255-257). Jerome, *Ep. 66 ad Pamm.*, 8 (PL 22, 643).

2. S. Légasse, *L'appel du riche* (Beauchesne, 1966).

3. S. v. "counsel" (evangelical) in the following dictionaries: J. Bauer, *Diccionario de Teología Biblica* (Barcelona: Herder, 1967). J. Bonsirven, *Vocabulaire biblique* (Paris: Lethieleux, 1958). *Catholic Biblical Encyclopedia* (New York: Wagner,

1949). *Dictionnaire de la Bible* (Supplément) (Paris, 1934). *Dictionnaire encyclopédique de la Bible* (Paris: Turnhout, 1960). X. L. Dufour, *Dictionary of Biblical Theology*, 2nd ed. (New York: Seabury, 1977). H. Fries, *Encyclopédie de la foi* (Paris: Cerf, 1965). J. L. Mackenzie, *Dictionary of the Bible* (Milwaukee, 1965). F. Spadafora, *Dizionario Biblico* (Rome: Studium, 1957). J. J. Von Allmen, *Vocabulaire biblique*, 4th ed. (Lausanne, 1969). Cf. M. Sauvage, *Les Fondements évangeliques de la vie religieuse*, Lasallianum, 16 (1973): 34.

4. *Did.*, 6. 2-3. Translation by Charles Bigg, *The Doctrine of the Twelve Apostles* (New York, 1922).

5. *Mand.*, 4. 4.2.

6. *Sim.*, 5. 2.1.

7. 2-2, q. 186, a. 2, ad. 3.

8. Cf. S. Lyonnet, "Christian Freedom and the Law of the Spirit According to St. Paul," in De la Potterie and Lyonnet, *The Christian Lives by the Spirit*, trans. J. Morris (Staten Island: Alba House, 1970) 5: 145-174. B. Häring, *The Law of Christ* (Westminster, Md.: Newman Press, 1961) I: 252-263.

9. J. Dupont, *Les Béatitudes* (Paris: Gabala, 1969, 1973) esp. 3: 245 ff. W. D. Davies, *The Setting of the Sermon on the Mount* (Cambridge: Cambridge Univ. Press, 1966). P. Hoffman, V. Eid., *Jesus von Nazareth und eine christliche Moral* (Herder, 1975). F. Andrusso et al., *Rivelazione e Morale* (Brescia: Paideia, 1973).

10. 2-2, q. 184, a. 3.

11. *Mand.*, 4. 4.2.

12. Origen, *In Rom.*, 10. 14 (PG 14, 1275).

13. J. Chrysostom, *In Matth. Hom.*, 62. 3 (PG 58, 599).

14. J. Chrysostom, *Epis. 4 ad Olymp.*, 7 (PG 52, 563).

15. Jerome, *Adv. Iovin.*, 1. 3(PL 23; 213, 227-228).

16. Augustine, *De s. virginit.*, 14. 14 (PL 40, 402-403).

17. J. Chrysostom, *In Matth. Hom.*, 62 (PG 58, 600).

18. Origen, *In Rom.*, 10. 14 (PG 14, 1275).

19. Jerome, *Epist. 66 ad Pamm.*, 8 (PL 22, 643).

20. Augustine, *De s. virginit.*, 14. 14 (PL 40, 402-403).

21. Jerome, *Epis. 66 ad Pamm.*, 8 (PL 22, 643).

22. Ambrose, *De viduis*, 11. 71—12. 74 (PL 16, 255-257).

23. *Comm. in Rom.*, 10. 14 (PG 14, 1275).

24. *In Matth.*, 62. 4 (PG 58, 599).

25. 4, *SC*, 133, p. 310. 156). *SDF*, p. 43. *RB*, 7. 42.

26. *Apoph. Patrum*, John of the Thebaid (PG 65, 233). *SDF*, p. 90.

27. *RB*, 23. 2.

28. J. Cassian, *De Coenob. Instit.*, 1. 7.9, *SC*, 109, p. 48.

29. *Reg. fusius*, 17. 2, 26 (PG 31, 964 and 987).

30. Ibid., Proem. (PG 31, 890).

31. Sulpicius Severus, *Vita Martini*, 25.4, *SC*, 133, p. 310.

32. *RB*, 2. 4.

33. *Epist.*, 146 (PL 22, 1192).

34. *Contra Faustum*, 5. 9 (PL 40, 224).

35. Gregory the Great, *Moralia in Job*, 26. 51 (PL 76, 380).

36. Whether this status was fully protected is an entirely different matter, to which we will return in chapter 8.

37. Cf. *Doc. Christ. Perf.* (Rome, 1931), pp. 69-70.

38. *De Instit. Laic.*, 1. 20 (PL 106, 161).

NOTES TO CHAPTER V

1. *LG,* 42.

2. *LG,* 42, 43; *PC,* 1 (twice), 12.

3. Clement Rom., *Epist. 1 ad Cor.,* 1. 38 (PG 1, 284). Ignatius Mart., *Ad Polyc.,* 5 (PG 5, 867).

4. Cf. Liddell and Scott, *A Greek-English Lexicon* (Oxford: Clarendon Press, 1968). Gingrich and Arndt, *A Green-English Lexicon of the New Testament and Other Early Christian Literature* (trans. and ed. W. Bauer) (Chicago: Univ. of Chicago Press, 1957).

5. Augustine, *De bono coniug.,* 22 (PL 40, 392).

6. 2-2, q. 151.

7. 2-2, q. 152.

8. 2-2, 1. 186, a. 4.

9. 2-2, q. 186, a. 4, ad. 2.

10. Francis of Assisi, *Regula* 1221, c. 1; *Constitutiones S. J.,* 5 P c 3.3 and 6, c 4. 2 and 4. *Examen S.J.,* 1. 3; 1. 9; 1. 10. *Normae secundum quas S. Congregatio,* n. 99, pp. 129–131. Cf. CIC, canon 487.

11. *LG,* 42. Cf. *PC,* 12.

12. *PC,* 12.

13. *PC,* 1.

14. *PO,* 16, *Optatam totius,* 10.

15. *Normae secundum quas,* p. 129.

16. B. Proietti, "La scelta celibataria alla luce delle S. Scritturas," in *Il celibato per il Regno* (Milan: Ancora, 1977), pp. 7–75.

17. L. Koehler, *Der hebraische Mensch* (Tübingen, 1953), p. 76.

18. Strack-Billerbeck, *Kommentar zum Neuen Testament aus Talmund und Midrash* (Munich, 1922–1926) 2: 372–373. John Schneider, s. v. "eunuchos" in *TDNT,* 2: 765–768.

19. Jeb. 63b (Bar).

20. R. Eleazer, c. 90: Jeb 63b (Bar).

21. Ibid. c. 270: Jeb. 63a.

22. Pes 113b. T.C.G. Thornton in his short note, "Jewish Bachelors in the New Testament Times" (JThSt 23 [1972]: 444–445) has collected data which seem to indicate some Jews around the time of Jesus delayed the age of marriage.

23. T. Jeb. 8.4. Cf. Strack-Billerbeck, 1: 807.

24. S. v. "eunuchos," *TDNT,* 2: 767.

25. Cf. J. J. De Vault, "The Concept of Virginity in Judaism," *MarSt* 13 (1962): 23–40. G. Vajda, "Continence, mariage et vie mystique selon la doctrine du judaïsme," in *Mystique et continence, Etudes Carmelitaines* (Bruges, 1952), pp. 82–92.

26. A. Guillaumont, "A propos du célibat des Esséniens," in *Hommages à A. Dupont-Sommer* (Paris, 1971), pp. 395–404. A. Marx, "Les racines du célibat essénien," *RdQ* 7 (1969–1971): 323–342.

27. *Hist. Nat.,* 5. 17.4.

28. *Bell. Jud.,* 2. 8.2.

29. 1QSa, 1. 4–8.

30. *Bell. Jud.,* 2. 8.13.

31. M. Adinolfi, "Il celibato di Gesú," *BeO* (1971): 145–148. J. Galot, "The Celibacy of Jesus," *Emmanuel* 76 (1970): 151–159. J. Guillet, "La chasteté de Jésus-Christ," *Christus* 66 (1970): 163–176.

32. For an all-inclusive inquiry into the subject of celibacy in the New Testament, see the study of B. Proietti in *Il celibato per il Regno,* p. 7–75.

33. J. Blinzer, "Eisen eunuchoi. Zur Auslegung von Mt. 19, 12," *ZNTW* 48 (1957): 254–270. Blinzer, "'Zur Ehe unfähig. . . .' Auslegung von Mt. 19, 12," in *Aus der Welt und Umwelt des N. T. Gesammelte Aufsätze* (Stuttgart,

1969), pp. 20-40. J. Dupont, *"Mariage et divorce dans l'Evangile"* (Bruges, 1959), pp. 161-222. T. Fleming, "Christ and Divorce," *ThSt* 24 (1963): 106-120. W. Harrington, "The New Testament and Divorce," *Irish Theol. Quarterly,* 39 (1972): 178-182. M. Laconi, "L'invito evangelico alla verginatà: Mt. 19, 3-12," *PAF* 65 (1972): 72-87. F. Marin, "Mas sobre Mt. 19, 12," *SalTer* 61 (1973): 533-546. B. Rigaux, "Le Célibat et le radicalisme évangelique," *NRTh* 94 (1972): 157-170. G. Ruiz, "Eunucos por el Reino (Mt. 19, 12): Dos interpretaciones contradictorias?" *SalTer* 61 (1973): 83-92. G. Segalla, "Il testo piu antico sul celibato: Mt. 19, 12," *StPat* 17 (1970): 121-137. W. Thüsing, "Die Intention Jesu und der Zölibat," *Diak* 3 (1972): 363-377. D. W. Trautman, *The Eunuch Logion of Mt. 19:12: Historical and Exegetical Dimensions as Related to Celibacy,* (Rome, 1966).

34. "Eisin eunuchoi," *ZNTW* 48 (1957): 254-270.

35. Rabbinical tradition knew of two kinds of eunuchs: those made so by others, and those who were so by nature (Jeb. 8. 4-6; s.v., "eunuchos," *TDNT,* 2: 767). Jesus therefore has added a new category.

36. Bruges, 1959.

37. Q. Quesnel, "Made Themselves Eunuchs for the Kingdom of Heaven," *CBQ* 30 (1968): 335-358.

38. "Christ and Divorce," *ThSt* 24 (1963): 106-120.

39. J. M. Van Cangh, "Fondement évangelique de la vie religieuse," *NRTh* 95 (1973): 635-647.

40. J. M. R. Tillard, "Le fondement évangelique de la vie religieuse, *NRTh* 91 (1969): 929.

41. M. Adinolfi, "Il matrimonio nella libertà dell'etica escatologica di I Cor

7," *Anton* 51 (1976): 133-169. E. Alzas, "L'apôtre Paul et le célibat: étude exégétique sur 1 Cor. 7, 25-40," *RThPh,* 2 series 38 (1950): 226-232. J. K. Elliot, "Paul's Teaching on Marriage in 1 Corinthians: Some Problems Considered," *NTS* 19 (1972-73): 219-225. J. M. González Ruíz, "Un celibato apostólico? (1 Cor. 7, 25-38)," *XVII Semana Biblica Española* (Madrid, 1958): 275-291. L. Legrand, "Sao Paolo e il celibato," in J. Coppens (ed), *Sacerdozio e celibato: Studi storici e teologici* (Milan, 1975), pp. 427-450. X. Léon-Dufour, "Mariage et continence selon saint Paul," *A la rencontre de Dieu: Mémorial A. Gelin* (Le Puy, 1961), pp. 318-330. Léon-Dufour, "Mariage et virginité selon saint Paul," *Christus* 42 (1964): 179-194. P. H. Menoud, "Mariage et virginité selon Paul," *RThPh,* 3 series 1 (1951): 21-34. E. Neuhäusler, "Ruf Gottes und Stand des Christen: Bermerkingen zu i Ko. 7," *BZ* 3 (1959): 43-60. L. Swain, "Paul on Celibacy," *CleR* 51 (1966): 785-791. T. Williams, "The Forgotten Alternative in First Corinthians 7: A Case for Celibacy," *ChrTo* 17 (1973): 870-872. P. Zerafa, "Matrimonio, Verginità e Castità in s. Paolo," *RAMi* 12 (1967): 226-246.

42. P. T. Camelot, "Les traités de virginitate au IV siecle," *Etudes Carmélitaines* 32 (1952): 278ff. V. Grossi, La Verginità negli scritti dei Padri: La sintesi di s. Ambrogio," *Il celibato per il Regno* (Milan: Ancora, 1977), pp. 131-164. S. Frank, *Angelikos Bios* (Münster, 1964). J. M. Lozano, "Celibato e solitudine nel deserto," in *Il celibato per il Regno,* pp. 165-207. T. N. Zissis, *Techne parthenias: The Fathers' Arguments on Celibacy and Their Sources* (Bonn, 1973).

43. *Prima ad Cor.,* 1, 38 (PG 1, 284).

44. *Ad Polyc.,* 5 (PG 5, 867).

45. *Strom.*, 3. 10. 70.4.

46. *Strom.*, 3. 7. 59.4.

47. *Loc. cit.*; and *Strom.*, 3. 6. 51.1.

48. Justin, *I Apolog.*, 15 (PG 5, 349).

49. Cf. V. Grossi, "La Verginità negli scritti dei Padri....," pp. 131–164.

50. Athanasius, *De Incarn. Verbi*, 48 (PG 25, 181).

51. *De virg. vel.*, 2. 3. 5. *CSEL*, 2: 1211, 1212, 1224.

52. R. Metz, *La consécration des vierges dans l'église romaine* (Paris, 1954), p. 74, note.

53. *Ibid.*, p. 51.

54. M. Adriani, s. v. "Verginità," *Enciclopedia delle Religioni* (Firenze, Vallecchi), 6: 174–179.

55. *Cher.*, 49–50, 51–52.

56. Cf. *Vita Antonii*, 44 (PG 26, 908). *ECB*, p. 175. *Apoph. Patrum*, Amos 2, Bessarion 11, John the Dwarf 2, Cronius 5, Poemen 155 (PG 65; 125, 141, 204, 249, 360. *SDF*, pp. 26, 35, 73, 99, 159.

57. Palladius, *The Lausiac History*, 1.3; 2.3, pp. 16.4, 18.1.

58. Serapion, *Ep. ad. monachos*, 7 (PG 40, 932). J. Climacus, *Scala Paradisi*, 15, scholia (PG 40, 932). Isidorus, *Epist.*, 192 (PG 78, 1280).

59. *De Coenob. Instit.*, 6. 6, *SC*, 109, p. 270.

60. *Ex Actis Andreae*, 5, Lipsius Bonnet 2, 1.40.

61. *De virginitate*, 12. 4, *SC*, 119, p. 418.

62. *De virginitate*, 14.3; 15. 1; 17. 5, *SC*, 125, pp. 140, 144, 154.

63. *Epist.*, 22. 19 (PL 22, 406).

64. *De bono coniug.*, 2 (PL 40, 373–374).

65. *De hominis opif.*, 17 (PG 44, 188–192).

66. Cf. *Vita Antonii*, 20 (PG 26, 873B).

67. *De virginitate*, 12. 1, 6–7, *SC*, 119, p. 422.

68. E. Schillebeeckx, *Celibacy* (New York: Sheed and Ward, 1968) pp. 83, 94.

69. *LG*, 40.

70. *LG*, 42.

71. *Schema Constit. De Ecclesia: Textus prior non emendatus* (Vatican City, 1964).

72. Schillebeeckx, *Celibacy*, p. 104.

73. We are not taking into account the various non-religious, more-or-less subconscious motives which can condition the choice of celibacy. It would not be honest to speak of these only in connection with celibacy, since obviously every human choice, including marriage, is conditioned in some way by unclear factors. Ours is always a conditioned freedom. What counts is that the decision is consciously made for the sake of the Lord and his concerns.

74. Cf. K. Rahner, "On the Evangelical Counsels," *Theological Investigations* 8: 164–165. R. Balducelli, "The Decision for Celibacy," *ThSt* 36 (1975): 226–227.

NOTES TO CHAPTER VI

1. *Vita Antonii*, 2 (PG 26, 841). *ECB*, p. 135.

2. *Vita e detti dei Padri del Deserto*, 2: 230.

3. Anthony, 24, Eucharistos (PG 65; 84, 169). *SDF*, pp. 5, 51.

4. *Rule* 1221, ch. 1. *OS*, p. 31.

5. *Examen S. J.*, 4. 2.

6. *Asceticum parvum*, 5 and 31 (PL 103, 497 and 510-55). *Reg. fusius*, 9 (PG 31, 941).

7. Pachomius, *Praecepta*, 49 (PL 23, 70); Augustine, *Praeceptum*, 1 (PL 32, 1377-1378). J. Cassian, *De Coenob. Instit.*, 4. 4, *SC*, 109, pp. 124-126. *Reg. Mag.*, 87, *SC*, 106, pp. 354-366. *RB*, 58. 24-25, *SC*, 182, pp. 360-362.

8. *Reg. Mag.*, 87. 1-24, 35-37, RM, pp. 354-362. *RB*, 58. 24-25; pp. 630-632.

9. *Rule* 1221, ch. 2, *OS*, pp. 32-33.

10. *Examen S.J.*, 4. 2-3.

11. Megethios 1, Pambo 6 (PG 65, 300 and 369). *SDF*, pp. 126, 165.

12. J. Cassian, *De Coenob. Instit.*, 7. 17.1; 8. 18, *SC*, 109, pp. 316, 320.

13. John the Dwarf 6, Isaac of the Cells 7, Macarius Aegypt. 7, Pior 1, Serenus 2 (PG 65,205; 225; 265; 373; 417. *SDF*, pp. 74, 85-86, 108, 167, 191.

14. Agathon 16, Isidore Scet. 7, Pistamon (PG 65, 115; 221; 376). *SDF*, pp. 16, 85, 168.

15. *Vita Antonii*, 3 (PG 26, 844). *ECB*, pp. 136-137.

16. Poemen, 69 (PG 65, 337). *SDF*, p. 148. Cf. "Vie d'Euthyme," in Festugière, *MO*, 3. 1, pp. 65-66.

17. *Syncletica* 10, Poemen 181 (PG 65, 425; 365). *SDF*, pp. 195, 161.

18. Isidore 2-3, Hyperechios 6 (PG 65, 236; 420). *SDF*, p. 91. Evagrius Ponticus, *De octo spiritibus malitiae*, 8 (PG 79, 1153). Basil, *Reg. brev.*, 92 (PG 31, 1145).

19. Origen, *Lib. de oratione* (PG 11, 496). Gregory Naz., *Orat.*, 40 (PG 36, 424). Evagrius Ponticus, *Praktikon*, 3, *SC*, 171, p. 498.

20. Syncletica, 5 and 10 (PG 65, 421 and 425). *SDF*, pp. 194-195.

21. Nilus, 4 (PG 65, 305). *SDF*, p. 129.

22. Evagrius Ponticus, *De octo spiritibus malitiae*, 7 (PG 79, 1152).

23. *Praktikon*, 6. 9, 18, *SC*, 171, pp. 508, 512, 546. *De octo spiritibus malitiae*, 7-8 (PG 79, 1152-1153).

24. Horsiesius, *Règlements*, in Lefort, *Oeuvres de Saint Pachôme, CSCO*, 160, (Louvain, 1956), p. 96. 31-35. *Liber Horsiesii*, 50 in *Pachomiana Latina*, ed. A. Boon (Louvain, 1932), p. 142. 14-26. *Les Vies Coptes de Saint Pachôme*, S⁵ nn. 120-121, ed. Lefort, pp. 268. 19—269. 7.

25. *Asceticum parvum*, 29 (PL 103, 510). *Reg. brev.*, 85-86 (PG 31, 1144).

26. *Enarr. in Ps. 131*, 5 (PL 37, 1718-1719) in *CSEL*, 40, 1913 and 1914.

27. Poemen, 152 (PG 65, 360).

28. Horsiesius, Règlements, *Oeuvres de Saint Pachôme*, p. 87. 1-3.

29. *Reg. Mag.*, 83. 17, *SC*, 106, p. 344.

30. Gelasius, 5 (PG 65, 152). *SDF*, p. 41.

31. *De Coenob. Instit.*, 4. 14, *SC*, 109, p. 138.

32. *Rule* 1221, ch. 9. *OS*, p. 39.

33. *Constitutiones S.J.*, 6, ch. 2, n. 2.

34. S. v. "ptochos," *TDNT*, 6: 885-915. S. v. "pénes," *TDNT*, 6: 37-40. S. v. "ploutos," *TDNT*, 6: 319-332. A. Gelin, *Les pauvres de Yahvé*, (Paris: Cerf, 1953).

35. Cf. excursus on the call of the rich man at end of Chapter I.

36. *In Matth.*, 15. 16-17 (PG 13, 1300-1304).

37. Diogen. Laert., *Lives of the Eminent Philosophers*, 2. 3 (Chicago: Loeb Classical Library, 1958).

38. Ibid., 9. 35-36, p. 444.

39. Ibid., 9. 39, p. 448.

40. Xenophon, *Memorab.*, A 6. 1-10, ed. K. Hude (Stuttgart, 1959), p. 41.

41. Plato, *Apologia*, 26, in *Plato I* (Chicago: Loeb Classical Libr. 1960), p. 128.

42. Diog. Laert., *Lives*, 6. 87, p. 90.

43. *Loc. cit.*

44. Ibid., 6. 93, p. 96.

45. Seneca, *De tranquil. an. Dialogorum Libri*, 9–10 (Turin, Paravia, 1946), p. 30.

46. Philostratus, *Vita Apolonii*, 1. 13, in *Flavii Philostrati Opera*, ed. C. L. Kayser (Hildesheim, 1970) 1: 11–12.

47. Ibid., 1. 34, p. 35.

48. Porphyrius, *Vita Plotini*, 7. Cf. Plotinus, *Opera*, Loeb Classical Library, (Chicago: University of Chicago Press, 1966) 1: 24–28.

49. Ibid., p. 28. 47–50.

50. *Vita Plotini*, 9, in *Opera*, p. 30. 13–16.

51. *Vita Procli*, 4. See L. J. Rosán, *The Philosophy of Proclus* (New York, 1949), p. 15.

52. Diog. Lart., 2. 3 and 9. 35–36.

53. *Vita Apolonii*, 1. 13.

54. *Vita Plotini*, 9, in *Opera*, p. 30. 13–16.

55. Philostratus, *Vita Apolonii*, 1. 2, p. 2.

56. *Contra Cels.*, 2. 41 (PG 11, 861).

57. *In Matth.*, 3. 19 (PL 24, 138–139), *CSEL*, 77, 172. *Epist*. 58 *ad Paulinum* (PL 22, 580). *Epist*. 66 *ad Pammachium* (PL 22, 644). *Epist*. 71 *ad Lucinium* (PL 22, 670). *Adv. Iovin.*, 2. 9 (PL 23, 311–312).

58. *Ad Paulinum* (PL 22, 580).

59. *In Matth*. 3. 19 (PL 26, 137–139), *CSEL*, 77, 170–172.

60. *In Matth*. 3. 20 (PL 26, 144–145), *CSEL*, 40, 172.

61. Diog. Laert., 6. 87, *Lives*, p. 90.

62. Philostratus, *Vita Apolonii*, 1. 13.

63. Porphyrius, *Vita Plotini*, in *Opera*, p. 38. 47–50.

64. *Contra Gentiles*, 3. 133.

65. Megethios, 1 (PG 65, 300).

66. J. Cassian, *De Coenob, Instit.*, 4. 13, *SC*, 109, pp. 136–138.

67. K. Rahner, "The Theology of Poverty," *Theol. Invest.* 8: 187.

68. Ibid., p. 185.

69. S. Légasse, *L'appel du riche*, pp. 97–110.

70. Cf. J. Cassian, *De Coenob. Instit.*, 4. 4–5, *SC*, 109, p. 126: "ad humilitatem Christi descendens . . . ad Christi paupertatem et inopiam descendisse . . . "

71. S. v. "poverty," *New Catholic Encyclopedia*, 11: 650.

72. *De Coenob. Instit.*, 4. 14, *SC*, 109, p. 138.

73. K. Rahner, "The Theology of Poverty," pp. 172, 201.

74. Cf. *PC*, 13: "haud sufficit in usu bonorum Superioribus subici" ["It is by no means enough to be subject to superiors in the use of property"] (*Vatican Council II*, ed. A. Flannery, p. 618).

NOTES TO CHAPTER VII

1. According to Anthony's biography, he certainly did not enjoy these advantages during the entire time he was in the necropolis, or during the twenty years he spent walled up, or even toward the end of his life when he fled deep into the desert to a place rarely crossed by caravans (*Vita Antonii*, 8, 12, 14, 49–50: PG 26; 853, 861, 864, 916). Paul, too, renounced them since, according to Jerome, he spent his entire life in complete solitude (*Vita Pauli*, 6 : PL 23, 21–22). Also remember that St. Benedict once discovered it was Easter day only because a priest brought him some bread (Gregory the Great, *Dialogues*, 2. 1: PL 66, 130).

2. *Les Vies de Saint Pachôme* . . . , ed. Lefort (Louvain, 1943) S¹, pp. 1. 19—2. 3.

3. *Apoph. Patrum*, Poemen, 69; Sisoes, 35, 45; Sopatros; Serapion, 2 (PG 65, 404; 405; 413; 416. *SDF*, pp. 148, 184, 185, 189, 190.

4. J. Cassian, *De Coenob. Instit.*, 2. 5, *SC*, 109, pp. 64-68. *Conlat.*, 18. 5, *SC*, 64, pp. 14-16.

5. Cf. H. Bacht, "Pakhome der grosse Adler," *Geist und Leben* 22 (1949): 370-379. "L'importance de l'idéal monastique de saint Pachôme pour l'histoire du monachisme chrétien," *RAM* 26 (1950): 308-326. "Pachôme et ses disciples (IV siecle)," *Théologie de la Vie Monastique* (Aubier, 1961). J. M. Lozano, "La comunità pacomiana," *Claretianum* 15 (1975): 237-267. A. Levis, "Koinonia e Comunidade no monacato Pacomiano," *Claretianum* 15 (1975): 269-273. M. M. Van Molle, "Aux origines de la vie communautaire chrétienne, quelques équivoques déterminantes pour l'avenir," in *VS. Supplément* 88 (Feb. 1969): 101-121. "Vie commune et obéissance d'après les institutions premières de Pachôme et Basile," *VS. Suppl.* 93 (May 1970): 196-225. P. Tamburrino, "Koinonia, die Beziehung monasterium-Kirche im frühen pachomianischen Mönchtum," *Erbe und Auftrag* 43 (1967): 5-21.

6. *Les Vies Coptes de Saint Pachôme* . . . , Bo.p. 82. 23-26; S⁴ p. 293. 31—294. 2. Cf. J. M. Lozano, La comunità pacomiana, pp. 241-242.

7. *Les Vies Coptes*, S³ p. 60. 21—61. 15. Lozano, La comunità. . . . , pp. 243-244.

8. Ibid., S¹ pp. 1. 19—2. 3 and 2. 20—3. 5; S³ pp. 61. 20—62. 31.

9. Ibid., S³ p. 65. 25-31.

10. Ibid., S⁵ n. 25, pp. 236. 30—237. 9; Bo. n. 95. 23—96. 9.

11. Praecepta 51, *Pacomiana Latina*,

ed. A. Boon (Louvain, 1932), p. 27. 4-8.

12. This explains the strictly disciplinary and military idea one formed of the Pachomian community when it was known only through the various texts of the *Praecepta* in Jerome's Latin version.

13. J. Gribomont, "Saint Basile," *Théologie de la Vie Monastique* (Aubier, 1961), pp. 99-113. *Histoire du texte des Ascétiques de Saint Basile* (Louvain, 1952). D'Amand, *L'ascèse monastique de Saint Basile, Essai historique* (Maredsous, 1948).

14. Basil insistently refers to the manner of life he proposes as "the faithful observance of the Gospel," cf. *Regulae fusius*, Proem. 4; 8. 3; 26 (PG 31, 897; 940; 985). *Reg. brevius*, Proem. (PG 31, 1080). Cf. our fuller treatment in chapter 2.

15. *Reg. fusius*, Interr. 1-3 (PG 65, 905-917). Basil made significant progress on this point. In his *Moralia* he placed the idea of conversion (very correctly) as the foundation of his system, but immediately afterwards spoke of detachment as its natural consequence (*Moralia Regulae*, 1-3: PG 31, 700-705), before coming to the theme of the two precepts of love (*Moralia, Regulae* 3-5: PG 31, 705-709). In his *Asketikon Parvum* instead, he speaks of charity first (Interr. 1-2: PL 103, 488-494) and only later of retirement (Interr. 3: PL 103, 494-496).

16. *Asketikon Parvum*, Interr. 3 (PL 103, 494-496). *Reg. fusius*, Interr. 6 (PG 31, 925-928).

17. *Reg. fusius*, Interr. 3. 1 (PG 31, 917).

18. *Reg. fusius*, Interr. 8 (PG 31, 932).

19. *Reg. fusius*, Interr. 7. 1 (PG 31, 929).

20. Loc. cit.

21. Cf. J. M. Lozano, "La comunità

religiosa nel suo sviluppo storico," in *Vita Comunitaria* (Milan: Ancora, 1979), pp. 14-19.

22. Cf. F. DeBeer, "La genesi della fraternità francescana secondo alcune fonti primitive," *Studi Francescani* 65 (1968): 66-92. K. Esser, *Origins of the Franciscan Order* (Chicago: Franciscan Herald Press, 1970). A. Ghinato, *Una Regola in cammino* (Rome-Vicenza, 1973). D. Filod et al., *La naissance d'un charisme: une lecture de la première Regle de saint François* (Paris, 1973).

23. *Regula* 1221, 14. T. de Celano, 1. 29.

24. Regula 1223, 6.

25. Esser, *Origins*, pp. 60-66.

26. A. De Vogüé, *La Communauté et l'abbé dans la Règle de saint Benoit* (Desclee de Br., 1961). De Vogüé, "Le monastère, Eglise du Christ," *Studia Anselmiana* 42 (1957): 25-46. E. U. Heufelder, "San Benedetto di Norcia e la Chiesa," in *Sentire Ecclesiam* (Rome: Paoline, 1964) 1: 291-308. B. Steidle, *Die Regel St. Benedikts* (Beuron, 1952).

27. *RB*, Prol. 45.

28. *RB*, 1. 2.

29. *RB*, Prol. 3 and 40; 1. 2, etc.

30. *RB*, 1. 5.

31. De Vogüe, *La communauté et l'abbé*, p. 127.

32. *RB*, 2. 4. Cf. 14. 1.19-22.

33. A. Sage, *La Vie Religieuse selon St. Augustin* (Paris: La Vie Augustinienne, 1972). C. Lambot, "Le monachisme de Saint Augustin," in *Augustinus Magister*, 3 (Paris, 1955). pp. 64-69. A. Manrique, *Teología Augustiniana de la vida religiosa* (Salamanca, 1964). D. Sanchis, "Pauvreté monastique et charité fraternelle chez Saint Augustin: note sur le plan de la Regula," *Augustiniana* 8 (1958); 5-21. Sanchis, "Pauvreté

monastique et charité fraternelle chez saint Augustin: Le commentaire augustinien des Actes 4, 32-35," *Studia Monastica* 4 (1962); 7-33. C. Vaca, *La vida religiosa en San Augustín*, 4 vols. (Madrid, 1955-1964). L. Verheijen, *La Règle de Saint Augustin*, 2 vols. (Paris, 1962).

34. *Sermo* 355, n. 2 (PL 39, 1569). *Sermo* 356, n. 1 (PL 39, 1574).

35. *Praeceptum*, ch. 1. Verheijen, *La Règle...*, 1: 416.

36. *Epist.*, 238. 16 (PL 33, 1044). *Sermo* 103, n. 4 (PL 38, 614-615). *Tract. in Johan.*, 14. 9 (PL 35, 1508).

37. *Sermo* 356, n. 6 (PL 39, 1573).

38. Cf. J. M. Lozano, "La comunità religiosa nel suo sviluppo storico," in *Vita Comunitaria* (Milan: Ancora, 1979), pp. 27-36.

39. *Constitutiones Ordinis Praedicatorum*, Proem.

40. D. Bertrand, *Un Corps pour l'Esprit: Essai sur l'expérience communautaire selon les Constitutions de la Compagnie de Jésus*, Christus, 38 (Desclée de Br., 1974), J. De Guibert, *La spiritualité de la Compagnie de Jésus* (Rome, 1953). J. C. Futrell, *Making an Apostolic Community of Love: the Role of the Superior According to Saint Ignatius of Loyola* (St. Louis, 1970). J. Osuna, *Amigos en el Señor: estudio sobre la génesis de la comunidad en Compañía de Jésus* (Bogota, 1975).

41. J. M. Lozano, *Misión y espíritu del Claretiano en la Iglesia* (Rome, 1967). *The Claretians* (Chicago, 1980).

42. *Asketikon parvum*, 3 (PL 103, 494-496). *Reg. fusius*, 7 (PG 31, 928-933).

43. Cf. J. Nadal, *Commentarii de Instituto Societatis Iesu* (Rome, 1962), p. 799.

44. Paul VI, *Evangelica testificatio*, 11. Cf. J. M. Lozano, *El fundador y su familia religiosa* (Madrid, 1978).

45. *Gaudium et spes*, 25. Pius XII, "Radiomessagio natalizio del 24 dicembre 1942," *AAS* 35 (1943): 12. John XXIII, *Mater et magistra, AAS* 53 (1961): 453.

46. This also applies to communities founded for external ministries. They were born for a purpose outside the community, but accomplish this by incorporating individuals called to that mission and by fostering the development of their vocation and personality.

47. Cf. M. Driot, "Vie communautaire et vocation personelle," *VS. Suppl.* 93 (1970): 171–195.

48. Pier C. Bori, *Chiesa primitiva, l'immagine dell comunità delle origini nella storia della Chiesa antica* (Brescia: Paideia, 1974). J. M. Lozano, "De Vita Apostolica apud Patres et scriptores monasticos . . . apud canonicos regulares . . . apud Ordines Mendicantes," *CpR* 52 (1971): 97–120, 193–210, 300–313. On Basil, cf. D. Amand, 'L'ascèse monastique de Saint Basile (Maredsous, 1949), p. 129. On St. Benedict, cf. A. De Vogüé, "Le monastère Eglise du Christ," *Studia Anselmiana* (Rome, 1957), pp. 25–46.

49. On the origin and nature of the summaries in Acts, cf. L. Cerfaux, "La composition de la première partie du Libre des Actes." in *Recueil Lucien Cerfaux* (Gembloux, 1954) 2: 63–79. Cerfaux, "La première communauté chrétienne a Jerusalem," ibid, pp. 125–156. P. Benolt, "Remarques sur les sommaires des Actes," in *Exégèse et Théologie* (Paris, 1961) 2: 180–192. J. Dupont, "La comunità dei beni nei primi tempi della Chiesa," in *Studi sugli Atti degli Apostoli* (Rome: Paoline, 1971), pp. 861–889. K. Lake, "The Communism of Acts II and IV–VI and the Appointment of the Seven," in F. J. Foakes Jakson and K. Lake, *The Beginnings of Christianity*, 5 vols. (London, 1953) 1: 140–151. B. Reicke, *Glaube und Leben der Urgemeinde: Bemerkungen zur Apg 1–7* (Zurich, 1957).

50. L. Cerfaux, *Théologie de l'Eglise suivant saint Paul* (Paris: Cerf, 1965), esp. pp. 223–237, 271–283.

51. 3, q. 64, a. 2, ad. 3.

52. Cf. Aristotle, *Ethic. ad Nicomachum*, 8. 9; 9. 8, ed. J. Voilquin (Paris, 1961), pp. 378, 432. Cicero, *De Offic.*, 1. 16.15. Seneca, *De Benef.*, 7. 4.1. It is significant that the proverb on the "one heart" should have been attributed by Diogenes Laertius to Pythagoras, the founder of a community which sought to recreate the Golden Age (*Vita Pythagorae*, 8. 10).

53. Thomas, 1, q. 20, a. 2c; 1–2, q. 110, 1c and ad. 1; 3, q. 86, 2c.

54. D. Bonhoeffer, *Life Together* (New York: Harper and Row, 1954), pp. 18–21.

55. E. Schweitzer, *La comunità e il suo ordinamento nel Nuovo Testamento* (Turin: Gribaudi, 1971), p. 74.

56. *Reg. fusius*, 7. 2 (PG 31, 932).

57. D. Cartwright and A. Zander, *Group Dynamics: Research and Theory* (New York: Harper and Row, 1948), p. 46. M. G. Sherif, *Groups in Harmony and Tension* (New York: Harper and Row, 1953), pp. 150–151.

58. Cf. W. W. Meissner, *Group Dynamics in Religious Life* (South Bend: Univ. of Notre Dame Pr., 2nd ed., 1966).

59. Tamotsu Shibutani, *Society and Personality* (Englewood Cliffs: Prentice-Hall, 1961), p. 331.

60. 2-2, q. 23, a. 1.

NOTES TO CHAPTER VIII

1. *PC,* 14.

2. Thomas, 2-2, q. 186, a. 8, ad. 1.

3. Among the rules recorded in the missionary discourse and referring to Jesus' identification with others, there seem to be two categories. In the first (Mk. 9:3; Mt. 10:42), Jesus identifies himself with the "least ones": whatever is done to them is done to him. We are far from the idea of authority. But this saying was transformed in ecclesiastical tradition into one identifying Jesus with the humblest members of the Christian community (or perhaps with the community in its entirety as being composed of humble people) (cf. Mk. 9:41; Mt. 10:40,42—"because he is a disciple"). In the second category, probably formed within ecclesiastical tradition and inspired by a common rabbinical saying, Mt. 10:41 (cf. Strack-Billerbeck 4: 590), Jesus is identified with Christian prophets: in receiving a preacher of the Gospel, one receives Jesus. Mt. 10:40 was modified in this manner and inserted into the missionary discourse. Lk. 10:16 transforms receiving into listening, and Jn. 13:20 broadens it to include all disciples. Cf. R. Bultmann, *History of the Synoptic Tradition,* trans. J. Marsh, rev. ed. (New York: Harper and Row, 1963), pp. 142-143, 147-148.

4. Basil, *Reg. brevius,* Interr. 38 (PG 31, 1108).

5. *Reg. Mag.* 2. 6; 2. 68; 10. 51; 11. 11; 12. 6; 57. 16; 89. 20.

6. *Reg. Mag.* 1. 89-92; 11. 8-12; 14. 13-14. Cf. the explanation by De Vogüé, *La communauté et l'abbé dans la Règle de saint Benoît,* pp. 129-134. *La Règle du Maitre,* 1, *SC,* 105, pp. 110-116.

7. Cf., for example, St. Ignatius of Loyola, "A los Padres y Hermanos de Portugal, 1 febrero 1553," *Obras*

Completas (Madrid: BAC, 1952) p. 835.

8. *Vita Antonii* 8; 12-14 (PG 26, 853; 861-864). *ECB,* pp. 142-143, 146-149.

9. Cyril of Scythopolis, "Vie de saint Sabas," in Festugière, *Les Moines d'Orient* (Paris, 1962) 3/3, pp. 34-35.

10. Macarius Egyp., 2 (PG 65, 260). *SDF,* p. 128.

11. *Vita Pauli,* 6 (PL 23, 31). *ECB,* pp. 228-229.

12. Cf. Festugière *MO,* 1: 43-44.

13. Gregory Naz., *Orat.,* 21. 5 (PG 35, 1088).

14. *Conlat.,* 3. 6, *SC,* 42, pp. 145-146.

15. PG 88, 657.

16. Poemen, 65 (PG 65, 337). *SDF,* pp. 147-148.

17. *Vita Antonii,* 3-4 (PG 26, 844-845). *ECB,* pp. 138-139.

18. Epiphanius, 4 (PG 65, 164). *SDF,* p. 49. *Historia Monachorum in Aegypto,* 10. 9, ed. A. J. Festugière, (Brussels: Société des Bollandistes, 1961), p. 79. Cyril of Scythopolis, "Vie de Kyriakos, 4, in *Les Moines,* 3/3, p. 41. Gregory the Great, *Dialog.,* 2. 1 (PL 66, 128), trans., *The Fathers of the Church,* vol. 39, pp. 55-56.

19. Ares (PG 65, 131-133). *SDF,* pp. 29-30. There were some disciples who lived in solitude: Agathon, 20 (PG 65, 113-115). *SDF,* p. 20.

20. Poemen, 174 (PG 65, 364). *SDF,* pp. 160-161.

21. Sisoes, 29; 35; 45 (PG 65, 401; 404; 405). *SDF,* pp. 183, 184, 185.

22. Isaac Cell., 2 (PG 65, 224). *SDF,* p. 85.

23. *Lausiac History,* 22, p. 73. 7-8.

24. Heraclius; Pambo, 3 (PG 65, 185; 369). *SDF*, pp. 61-62, 165.

25. Antonius, 36 (PG 65, 88). *SDF*, p. 7.

26. Festugière, *Historia Monachorum*, 24. 1-10, pp. 131-133.

27. PG 65, 241. *SDF*, p. 165.

28. Pambo, 3 (PG 65, 369). *SDF*, p. 165.

29. Rufus, 2 (PG 65, 389-392). *SDF*, p. 177.

30. Anthony, Joseph of Thebes, and Rugo speak of *hypotage;* only Pambo speaks of *hypakoe.*

31. Theodotus I (under the name Theodore of Eleutheropolis) (PG 65, 197). *SDF*, p. 68.

32. *Instit.*, ;4. 8, *SC*, 109, p. 130.

33. *Instit.*, 4. 39.2, p. 188.

34. *Instit.*, 4. 34, pp. 172-174.

35. *Instit.*, 4. 35, p. 174. Cf. 4. 43, p. 184.

36. *Reg. Mag.*, 10. 45-48, SC, 105, p. 428. *RM*, p. 134.

37. *Reg. Mag.*, 10. 30-33. Cf. 7. 39-40. SC, 105, pp. 424, 390-392. *RM*, pp. 133, 122.

38. *Asketikon Parvum*, Int. 12, 81, 88, 176 (PL 103, 505; 521; 523-524; 546 (La). Interrogatio 12 measures the individual's will against the dictates of Scripture or, if this does not say anything, against what the Spirit suggests as well as what the neighbor's welfare requires. Here one's will is *nobis placere.* In interrogatio 81 it is a question of a personal whim as opposed to the good order of the community, while 88 speaks of those who, following their own will, are unable to fulfill their duties through excessive fasting. Interrogatio 176 has a statement that in an uncertain case one must act not on one's own, but according to the opinion or with the consensus of the others or of those in charge. In this case, too, it is a matter of good order in the community. We must thus conclude that, while the Master seems to depend on Basil in regard to the *voluntas propria*, he lacks the reference to mutual charity and to the common good which in Basil justifies the renunciation of *voluntas propria*, and his condemnation takes on an absolute and general character.

39. *Reg. Mag.*, 81. 15; 82. 19; 87. 18; 90. 5; 90. 48; 92. 10. *RM*, pp. 245, 247-248, 254, 260, 263.

40. Ibid., 1. 87. *RM*, pp. 110-111.

41. Ibid., 2. 35. *RM*, p. 113.

42. Ibid., 87. 14-24, 35, 43-48. *RM*, pp. 254, 255-256.

43. Cf. J. M. Lozano, "La comunità pacomiana della comunione all'instituzione," *Claretianum* 15 (1975): 237-267.

44. F. Ruppert, *Das Pakomianische Mönchtum und die Anfänge klosterlichen Gehorsam* Münsterschwarzach, 1971 (see esp. pp. 371 ff.).

45. 3 Catéchèse, *Oeuvres de saint Pachôme*, p. 45. 18—46. 3; p. 49. 18-32.

46. *Praecepta et Instituta*, n. 16, in ibid., p. 36. 4-5.

47. Pachomius, 1 Catéchèse, in ibid., p. 6. 17-22.

48. *Asketikon Parvum*, Int. 6 and 71. *Reg. fusius*, 10, 11, 14, 28, 29, 30, 35, 36, 49, 54.

49. *Asketikon Parvum*, Int. 31, 36, 39, 43, 70, 101, 107. *Reg. fusius*, 7, 15, 45, 46, etc.

50. Int. 15 (PL 103, 506-507). Int. 81 (PL 103, 521-522).

51. Int. 13, 46, 64-65 (PL 103, 505-506; 514; 517-518). Basil also dedicates one entire question to demonstrating that one must obey only what is in accord with the divine precepts in Scripture: Int. 13 (PL 103, 505-506).

52. *Reg. fusius,* 45–46 (PG 31, 1032–1036). *Reg. brevius,* 303 (PG 31, 1296–1297).

53. *Reg. brevius,* 125 (PG 31, 1168).

54. *Reg. brevius,* 303 (PG 31, 1297). On the duties of the superior, see *Asketikon Parvum,* cf. Int. 80 (PL 103, 521).

55. Int. 15 (PL 103, 506–507).

56. Int. 24 (PG 31, 984).

57. Int. 26 (PG 31, 986–987).

58. Int. 45 (PL 103, 517–518).

59. Int. 49 (PL 103, 518).

60. *De Morib. Eccl. Cath.,* 31. 67 (PL 32, 1338). Cf. Jerome, *Epist.,* 22. 35, *CSEL,* 54. 197.

61. *Praeceptum,* 2–3. Cf. Verheijen, *La Règle de saint Augustin* (Paris, 1967) 1: 417–418.

62. *Enarr.* in Ps. 99. 10 (PL 37, 1277).

63. *Praeceptum,* 7. 2, Verheijen, p. 435.

64. *Praeceptum,* 8. 3, Ibid., p. 436.

65. *Praeceptum,* 8. 1, Ibid., p. 437.

66. Cf. A. Zümkeller, "Der klosterliche Gehorsam beim hl. Augustinus," *Augustinus Magister* (1954), pp. 265–276. A. Manrique, *La vida monástica en San Agustín* (El Escorial, 1959), pp. 333–339.

67. J. M. Boccali, *Concordantiae verbales opusculorum S. Francisci et Stae. Clara assisiensium* (Assisi: S. Maria Angelorum, 1976), p. 437.

68. Ibid., pp. 433–438.

69. *Rule* 1221, ch. 2. Cf. *rule* 1223, 2. *OS,* pp. 32, 58.

70. *Rule* 1221, 2. Cf. *Rule* 1223, 2. *OS,* pp. 32, 59.

71. K. Esser, *Origins of the Franciscan Order,* trans. A. Daly and I. Lynch (Chicago: Franciscan Herald Press), pp. 60–62.

72. *Rule* 1221, prol.; *Rule* 1223, 1. *OS,* pp. 31, 57. *La Leggenda dei Tre Compagni* infers that this bond of

obedience originated from an initiative of the Curia. (*The Legend of the Three Companions,* pp. 51–52. *OS,* pp. 936–937). If this is true, it would have been a question of prudence by which the Holy See bound to itself a movement not yet completely formed, at a time when many groups of the *Pauperes Christi* were having trouble with the hierarchy.

73. Bull *Cum secundum consilium,* Sept. 22, 1220. Cf. *Rule* 1221, 2. *OS,* p. 32.

74. *Rule* 1221, 6. *OS,* p. 37.

75. *Rule* 1221, 1. 5. *OS,* pp. 31, 35.

76. *Rule* 1221, 5. *OS,* p. 35.

77. *Rule* 1221, 4; *OS,* p. 35. *Rule* 1223, 10; *OS,* p. 63; cf. *Admonitum* 4; *OS,* p. 80.

78. *Rule* 1221, 5. *OS,* p. 36.

79. *Rule* 1221, 2; *OS,* p. 32. *Rule* 1223, 2; *OS,* p. 58; cf. *Rule* 1223, 10; *OS,* p. 63.

80. *Rule* 1221, 4, 6 and *Rule* 1223, 10, 12. *OS,* pp. 34, 37, 63, 64.

81. Pachomius, 1 Catéchèse, in Lefort, *Oeuvres de saint Pachôme,* p. 6. 17–21.

82. *Reg. Mag.,* 1. 2. *RM,* p. 105. *RB,* 1. 2.

83. *Reg. Mag.,* 2. 4. *RM,* p. 111. *RB,* 2. 4.

84. *RB,* 2. 5. *Reg. Mag.* has *iussio, monitio, doctrina* (2. 5).

85. *Reg. Mag.,* 2. 11–12. *RM,* p. 112. *RB,* 2. 11–12.

86. *Reg. Mag.,* 2. 12–13. *RM,* p. 112. *RB,* 2. 12–13.

87. *Reg. Mag.,* 2. 6. *RM,* p. 111. *RB,* 2. 6.

88. *RB,* 3. 6.

89. *Reg. Mag.,* 2. 6; 6. 68; 10. 51; 12. 6; 57. 16. *RM,* pp. 111, 124, 134–135, 149, 224.

90. *Reg. Mag.,* 11. 11; 89. 20. *RM,* pp. 141, 259.

91. *Conlat.*, 2. 14–15.

92. *Instit.*, 4. 10; 4. 28.

93. *Instit.*, 4. 24.

94. *Instit.*, 4. 27.4.

95. *RB*, 3. 11.

96. *RB*, 62. 4; 63. 11.

97. *RB*, 3.7; 3. 11; 60. 2, 9; 64. 20; 65. 17.

98. *RB*, 5. 5; 5. 8; 5. 12; 5. 15. Cf. 3. 6; 4. 61; 71. 4.

99. De Vogüé, *La communauté et l'abbé*, pp. 266 ff.

100. *Instit.*, 4. 8, *SC*, 109, p. 130.

101. *Instit.*, 4. 39.2, *SC*, 109, p. 180.

102. *Reg. Mag.*, 10. 42 ff. *RB*, 7. 31–48. Cf. De Vogüé, *La communauté*, p. 262.

103. *Instit.*, 4. 24.1; 4. 29; 4. 43; 5. 10; 7. 9, *SC*, 109, pp. 154, 164, 184, 204, 302.

104. *Reg. Mag.*, 7. 57–66 (esp. 59): *velut in martyrio patienter*. Cf. *RB*, 5. 10–13, and De Vogüé, *La communauté*, pp. 266 ff.

105. *Constitutions S. J.*, 8, cap. 1, n. 3. Cf. ibid., nn. 4, 6, 7, 9. Cf. "Carta a los Padres y Hermanos de Portugal," n. 7, *Obras Completas*, p. 842.

106. Cf. John C. Futrell, *Making an Apostolic Community of Love* (St. Louis, 1970), pp. 157–159.

107. *Rule* 1221, 4. 1. Cf. 6. 1–2; 16. 3–4. *Rule* 1223, 10. 4–5; 12. 1–2.

108. *Rule* 1221, 17. 1–2; *Rule* 1223, 9. 2.

109. *Rule* 1223, 9. 1.

110. *Constitutions S. J.*, 7. 1.

111. *Constitutions S. J.*, 8. 16; 9. 3.9.

112. St. Vincent de Paul, *Regulae C. M.*, 11. 2–3, in *Constitutiones ac Regulae C. M.* (Paris, 1948), p. 134. St. Alphonsus Liguori, *Regole* I, cap. 1, n. 2, in *Constitutiones et Regulae C. SS. R.* (Rome, 1936), p. 12. St. Anthony M. Claret, *Constituciones C.*

M. F. 1857, cap. 3, n. 17, and *Constituciones C. M. F.* 1865, I, cap. 3, n. 8, in *Constituciones y textos sobre la Congregación de Misioneros*, ed. J. M. Lozano (Barcelona, 1972), pp. 177, 365.

113. St. Anthony M. Claret, *Autobiography*, nn. 192–198 (Chicago: Claretian Publications, 1976), pp. 72–74.

114. *Rule* 1221 and *Rule* 1223, beginning.

115. Paul III, 'Regimini militantis,'' *Institutum S. J.* (Florence, 1892), 1: 4. Cf. *Constitutions S. J.*, 7. 1.

116. *Regulae*, 5. 1, pp. 111–112.

117. *Constituciones C. M. F.*, 1865, I, cap. 1, n. 1, p. 359.

118. *PC*, 2a.

119. Cf. Athanasius, *Vita Antonii*, 2 (PG 26, 841); *ECB*, pp. 135–136. Jerome, *Vita Hilarionis*, 3 (PL 23, 31); *ECB*, p. 247. Lefort, *Oeuvres de saint Pachôme*, CSCO, 159, p. 38.

120. Origen, *Exhortatio ad Mart.*, 12, 14, 37–38 (PG 11, 577–581; 612–613) applies to martyrs the texts on the *sequela Christi* which will later be applied to monks. Cf. also *Reg. Mag.*, 7. 57–66. St. Thomas Aquinas, *De perfectione vitae spiritualis*, cap. 10, *Opuscula Theologica* (Turin: Marietti, 1954), 2: 124, n. 600. In regard to the martyr-monk relationship, cf. E. E. Malone, "The Martyr and the Monk," in *Antonius Magnus Eremita, Studia Anselmiana* 38 (1956): 204–228.

121. Cf. G. Schrenk, s.v. *thelema*, *TDNT*, 3: 52–62.

122. For the relationship between "consciousness of the divine Sonship" in Christ and its gradual evolution in regard to its objectification, cf. Rahner, "Dogmatic Reflections on the Knowledge and Self-Consciousness of Christ," *Theological Investigations* 5: 193–215.

123. Cf. St. Thomas on the precepts of charity as a vocation to fulfillment (2-2, q. 184, a. 3).

124. In this regard cf. K. Berger, *Die Gesetzesauslegung Jesu* (Neukirchen, 1972), 1: 474–477.

125. Cf. Mt. 12: 50.

126. Cf. s.v. *hypakouo* and *hypakoe, TDNT,* 1: 223–224.

127. K. Berger, *Die Gesetzesauslegung Jesu,* I: *Markus und Parallelen* (Neukirchen, 1972), pp. 422–427.

128. Cf. 2-2, q. 186, a. 8, ad. 1.

129. Arsenius, 1 (PG 65, 88). *SDF,* p. 8.

130. *Vita Antonii,* 2 (PG 26, 841); *ECB,* pp. 135–136. *Vita Hilarionis,* 3 (PL 23, 31); *ECB,* p. 247. T. de Celano, *First Life,* cf. *OS,* pp. 246–247. *Legend of the Three Companions,* ch. 8, *OS,* p. 915. St. Anthony M. Claret, *Autobiography,* nn. 113–120, pp. 48–50.

131. PL 103, 487–554.

132. *RB,* prol. 8.

133. *RB,* prol. 35.

134. 1 Catéchèse, *Oeuvres de saint Pachôme,* p. 6. 17–22.

135. *Lausiac History,* 22, p. 73.

136. Anthony 19, Arsenius 9, Ammona 1, Ammoe 4, Daniel 2, Euprepios 7, Elias 8 (PG 65, 81; 89; 120; 128; 153; 172; 185). *SDF,* pp. 4, 8, 22, 30, 43, 53, 61.

137. Anthony 3, Arsenius 4, Agathon 9, Ammonas 7, Achilles 6, Amoun Nitr 3, Alonios 4 (PG 65, 76; 89; 112; 121; 125; 128; 133). *SDF,* pp. 2, 8, 18, 23, 25–26, 27, 30.

138. J. Chrysostom, *De virg.,* 16–17, 25, 26, *SC,* 125, pp. 146–150, 174–176. Gregory the Great, *Reg. Past.,* 3. 27 (PL 77, 101): "non valet.... " Jonas of Orleans, *De Institutione laicali,* 3. 18 (PL 106, 272): the monk "valet" (is able), the secular "nequit" (is not able).

139. K. Rahner, "Christ as the Exemplar of Clerical Obedience," in *Obedience and the Church* (Washington: Corpus Books), pp. 1–2, 11.

140. P. Jacquemont, "Autorité et obéissance selon l'Ecriture," *VS Suppl.,* 1968, pp. 340–350. Cf. pp. 346–347.

141. Ibid., p. 346.

142. We have studied the development of a communitarian spirituality among the Pachomians in our essay, "La comunità pacomiana dall comunione all 'instituzione," *Claretianum* 15 (1975): 237–267.

143. *Asketikon Parvum,* Int. 3 and 19 (PL 103, 496 and 510). Cf. *Reg. fusius,* 7 (PG 31, 928–933); *Reg. brevius,* 85 (PG 31, 1144).

144. *Praeceptum,* 2–3, in Verheijen, *La Règle de saint Augustin,* 1: 417–418.

145. 2-2, q. 186, a. 5: *instruantur, exercitentur, discipuli.*

146. Int. 3 (PL 103, 494–496). Cf. *Reg. fusius,* 7. 1 (PG 31, 929).

147. L. Gutiérrez Vega, *Autoridad y obediencia en la vida religiosa* (Madrid: Inst. de la Vida Religiosa, 1974).

148. Int. 45 (PL 103, 517–518).

NOTES TO CHAPTER IX

1. Leo XIII, Const. Ap. *Conditae a Christo* (Dec. 8, 1900), in *Enchiridion de statibus perfectionis,* n. 241, Rome, 1949, 1: 241–247. Our remark refers only to official statements of the Holy See. Until the publication of *Conditae a Christo,* the policy followed by the Roman Congregation for Bishops and

Regulars was not precise. In some cases, the Vatican Congregation applied to religious congregations the canon law for Regulars; in other cases it excluded them. Yet we must note that as early as 1857 the noted canonist D. Bouix wrote that it was already an opinion at his time that the solemn nature of the vows does not belong to the essence of the religious state, and therefore those who only take simple vows are to be considered religious. This new opinion was based on the constitution *Ascendens* of Gregory XIII, which recognized as religious those religious who only take simple vows. Cf. D. Bouix, *Tractatus de Iure Regularum* (Paris, 1857) 1: 53.

2. 2-2, q, 186, aa. 6-7. *De perf. vit. spir*, c. 12, 15. *Contra Impugn.*, 1.

3. *Apol. paup.*, c. 3, n. 2. 11.

4. *Provida Mater* (February 2, 1947), in *AAS* 39 (1947); 120 ff.

5. S. v. *voeu*, *DTC*, 15: 3189.

6. *De Oratione*, 3 (PG 11, 425 B-C).

7. *De orat. domin.*, or. 2, c. 2 (PG 44, 1137-1138).

8. *De oratione*, 3 (PG 11, 425D-428).

9. A. M. Di Nola, s.v. "Romana, Religione," *Enciclopedia delle Religioni* (Firenze: Vallecchi), 5: 513-515.

10. PL 4, 752 and 471.

11. *Epist.* 127 *ad Armentarium* (PL 33, 487). *Enarr.* in Ps. 76, 16.

12. Cyprian, *Epist.* 62; *De habit. virg.*, 4 (PL 4, 378-379; 445-446).

13. *De habit. virg.*, 4 (PL 4, 445-446).

14. Cf. *Ep.* 62 (PL 4, 378).

15. *De s. virg.*, 29 and 30 (PL 40, 412). *Enarr.* in Ps. 76, 16 (PL 36, 997). *Sermo* 224. 3 (PL 38, 1094). *Sermo* 132. 3 (PL 38, 736). *De doctr. Christ.*, 21, n. 48 (PL 34, 113). *De bon. viduit.*, 9 and 11 (PL 40, 437-438).

16. *Enarr.* in Ps. 76, 16 (PL 36, 967).

17. PL 84, 303.

18. *Regula*, c. 21 (PL 72, 893).

19. *Lausiac History*, 10. 6; 13. 1; 35. 1; 44. 1.

20. Ibid., 10. 6; 23. 3; 38. 12; 47. 1.

21. Ibid., 22. 8-9.

22. *S. Pachomii Vitae Graecae*, ed. F. Halkin: *Vita prima*, 6; *Vita secunda*, 8 (Brussels, 1932), pp. 5, 174. St. Gregory the Great, *Dialog.*, 2. 1 (PL 66, 128C).

23. Pachomius, *Praecepta*, 49 (PL 23, 73). J. Cassian, *De Coenob. Instit.*, 4. 5, *SC*, 109, p. 126.

24. *RB*, 58. 26-27.

25. J. Cassian, *De Coenob. Instit.*, 4. 5-6. *RB*, 58. 26-28.

26. Basil, *Reg. fusius*, 22. 3 (PG 31, 980B).

27. *Oeuvres de saint Pachôme*, trans. Lefort, *CSCO*, 24 (Louvain, 1964), pp. 28. 7; 40. 2, 32; 67. 31.

28. Anselm of Canterbury, *Epist.*, 157 (PL 159, 191).

29. B. Botte, *La Tradition Apostolique de saint Hippolyte* (Münster, 1936), p. 32.

30. Cyprian, *De habit. virg.*, 18 (PL 4, 470). Jerome, *Epist.*, 22. 14-15 (PL 22, 403).

31. *Vita Antonii*, Proem. and 5 (PG 26, 837; 848). *ECB*, pp. 133-134, 138-139.

32. *Asketikon Parvum*, 7, 11, 31 (PL 103, 499; 503; 504; 510). *Reg. fusius*, 22. 2-3 (PG 31, 980).

33. *Reg. Mag.*, 1. 9, *SC*, 105, p. 330; 11. 10, *SC*, 106, p. 10; 58. 5, p. 274; 61. 19, p. 282; 90 tit., 90. 68, 80, 82, pp. 390, 393, 394.

34. Basil, *Asketikon Parvum*, 6-7 (PL 103, 498-499). J. Cassian, *De Coenob. Instit.*, 4. 3, 5, 7, *SC*, 109, pp. 124, 126. *Reg. Mag.*, 87. 1, *SC*, 106, p. 356. *RB*, 58. 14, 17.

35. Pachomius, *Praecepta*, 49 (PL 23, 73).

36. *De Coenob. Instit.*, 4. 5, *SC*, 109, pp. 126-128. Cf. an example in the same work, 4. 32-43, *SC*, 109, pp. 170-184.

37. Caesareus, *Ad virgines*, 3-4 (PL 67, 1107).

38. *Eppeggeilato to Theou, Vita Antonii*, 65 (PG 26, 936A). *ECB*, p. 192.

39. *De Coenob. Instit.*, 4. 33, *SC*, 109, p. 172.

40. *Conlat.*, 9. 12, *SC*, 54, pp. 50-51.

41. Cf. Pachomius, *Praecepta*, 49 (PL 23, 73).

42. *Lausiac History*, 22. 2-4.

43. *Les Vies Coptes de saint Pachôme*, trans. Lefort, Bo. 10 (Louvain, 1943), pp. 84-85. *Vitae Graecae*, ed. F. Halkin; *Vita prima*, 6; *Vita secunda*, 8, pp. 5, 173-174.

44. *Dial.*, 1. 18 (PL 20, 195).

45. *Dial.*, 1. 191.

46. *Reg. Mag.*, 90. 2-7, 62, *SC*, 106, pp. 378-380, 388.

47. *Factis implenda promittatur: Reg. Mag.*, 90, 64, *SC*, 106, p. 388.

48. *RB*, 58. 1-4.

49. *RB*, 58. 9, 12-13.

50. *Si promiserit de stabilitate sua perseverantia: RB*, 58. 9.

51. *RB*, 58. 14.

52. Basil, *Epist.* 199, n. 18 (PG 32, 720B).

53. *Epist.* 199, 19 (PG 32, 720).

54. Inter. 6 (PL 103 497-498).

55. Inter. 7 (PL 103, 498-499).

56. Cf. *Reg. fusius*, 9, 14, 15 (PG 31, 941B; 949C; 952A; 958C).

57. *Reg. fusius*, 14, 36 (PG 31, 949; 956B; 1008C). *Reg. brevius*, 2 (PG 31, 1081C).

58. *Strom.*, 3. 1 (PG 8, 1104).

59. *Kathomologesamenous allelois: Reg. fusius*, 36 (PG 31, 1008C).

60. Cf. *Asketikon Parvum*, 6 (PL 103, 498). *Epist.* 199, 18 (PG 32, 720): *siano interrogati*.

61. *De. Eccl. Hierar.*, 6. 2 (PG 3, 533).

62. *Asketikon Parvum*, 7 (PL 103, 499A).

63. *Ten homologian ton synthekon katetheto: Reg. fusius*, 14 (PG 31, 949C).

64. *Confessionis pactum:* PL 103, 499A.

65. PG 31, 949C.

66. *Reg. fusius*, 15. 4 (PG 31, 956B).

67. On Shenoute's attitude against the vows, cf. J. Leipold, *Shenoute von Atripe und die Entstehung des national Aegyptisches Christentums, Texte und Untersuchungen*, 25 (Leipzig, 1903-1904).

68. *De. Eccles. Hierar.*, 6. 2 (PG 3, 533).

69. *Reg. monachorum*, 1 (PL 68, 387). *Reg. ad virgines*, 1 (PL 68, 399).

70. *Reg. monachorum*, 4 (PL 103, 558).

71. *Percepta in ecclesia benedictione, fratrum societati donetur: Regula*, 1. 21 (PL 87, 1109).

72. *Regula*, 2. 18 (PL 87, 1125).

73. *Regula*, 2. 18 (PL 87, 1125). Cf. Leander, *Reg. virginum*, 21 (PL 72, 803).

74. PL 87, 1127-1130.

75. *Reg. Mag.*, 88. 1, *SC*, 106, pp. 370-372.

76. *Reg. Mag.*, 87. 12, *SC*, 106, p. 356.

77. *Reg. Mag.*, 87. 14-24, *SC*, 106, p. 358.

78. *Charta perseverantiae: Reg. Mag.*, 87. 28, *SC*, 106, p. 360.

79. *Reg. Mag.*, 87. 35, *SC*, 106, pp. 360-362.

80. *Reg. Mag.*, 87. 43-48, *SC*, 106, pp. 362-364.

81. *Reg. Mag.*, 89. 3-16, *SC*, 106, pp. 372-374.

82. *Reg. Mag.*, 89. 17, *SC*, 106, p. 374.

83. *Epist.* 199, 19 (PG 32, 270).

84. *RB*, 58. 17–20.

85. *RB*, 58. 23.

86. *RB*, 58. 26.

87. *RB*, 58. 24–25.

88. *RB*, 58. 17.

89. *RB*, 58. 18.

90. *La Règle de saint Benoît*, 2, *SC*, 182, p. 630, note 18.

91. *Epist.* 149, 16 (PL 33, 637).

92. *Enarr.* in Ps. 75, 16 (PL 35, 967–968).

93. Cf. Gregory the Great, *Epist. Lib.*, 1. 34 (PL 77, 488). On the contrary, *Lib.*, 1. 42 (PL 77, 4954 ff.).

94. Anselm of Canterbury, *Epist.*, 87 (PL 159, 123). St. Anselm himself, in a passage already quoted, states that vows were a recent practice in monasticism and it was considered sufficient to wear the habit as a sign of personal commitment (PL 159, 191).

95. *Liber de Praec. et Disp.*, 1. 2 (PL 182, 862). *Epist.*, 2. 6 (PL 182, 83).

96. S. v. *voeu*, *DTC*, 15: 3189.

97. The freedom Jesus shows toward ritual obligations, in the sense that he submits to them for the good of the person, must be taken as a source of inspiration in pastoral activity. An oppressive vow, which is so because of the changed psychological, economic, etc., condition of the person who took it, should be dispensed. The Sabbath is for the person, not the person for the Sabbath. This explains why the Church grants dispensation from vows.

98. *Reg. Mag.*, 89. 11.

99. *Les Vies Grecques*, *Vita prima*, 6, p. 5; *Vita secunda*, 8, p. 174.

100. *Contra Celsum*, 7. 48 (PG 11, 1492). *In Num. hom.*, 24 (PG 12, 761A).

101. *In Num. hom.*, 24 (PG 12, 760D–761A).

102. *LG*, 44.

103. *PC*, 5.

104. 2-2, q. 186, a. 1, ad. 2; a. 6, ad. 2.

105. *Reg. Mag.*, 89. 8, *SC*, 106, p. 372.

106. Cf. J. Leclercq, ''Autour de la Règle de saint Benoît,'' *Collect. Cister.*, 3 (1975), 200–203.

107. 2-2, q. 88, a. 4, ad. 3.

108. St. Thomas, 2-2, q. 186, a.2, ad. 3.

109. Cf. *LG*, 44c.

110. Basil, *Epist.* 199, 19 (PG 32, 720).

111. J. Cassian, *De Coenob. Instit.*, 4. 33, *SC*, 109, p. 172.

112. *Reg. Mag.*, 89. 1–2, 11–16, 17, *SC*, 106, pp. 370–372, 374.

113. *Reg. Mag.*, 89. 6, *SC*, 106, p. 372.

114. *RB*, 58. 18.

115. Arsenius 1-2, Biare, Euprepios 7, Macarius Aegypt., 23 and 25 (PG 65, 88; 272; 172; 272. *SDF*, pp. 8, 37, 53, 111–112.

116. Athanasius, *Vita Antonii*, 65 (PG 65, 936); *ECB*, p. 192. Pachomius, Catéchèse, in Lefort, *Oeuvres de saint Pachôme*, CSCO, 160, p. 24.

117. 2-2, q. 186, a. 6, ad. 2.

118. 2-2, q. 88, a. 11; q. 186, a. 8, ad. 3.

NOTES TO EXCURSUS, CHAPTER IX

1. *LG*, 44.

2. *PC*, 5.

3. *LG*, 45.

4. *PC*, 1.

5. *Ad Gentes*, 18.

6. Cf. *Modi a Patribus*, 5, ch. 6 (Typis Vaticanis, 1964), p. 3.

7. Ibid., 10, p. 5.

8. Cf. Botte, *La Tradition Apostolique de saint Hippolyte* (Münster, 1963), p. 32.

9. *De virg. vel.*, 2, 3, 15, *CSEL*, 2: 1211, 1212, 1224.

10. Clement Rom., *Epist.*, 1. 1 (PG 1, 380). Cf. 2. 9 (PG 1, 438).

11. R. Metz, *La consécration des vierges dans l'Eglise romaine* (Paris, 1954), p. 74 note.

12. Jerome, *Adv. Iov.*, 1. 13 (PL 23, 240).

13. PL 54, 1208.

14. *Liber Sacramentorum Romanae Ecclesiae*, ed. H. W. Wilson (Oxford: Clarendon Press, 1894), p. 156.

15. Metz, *La consécration*, pp. 97-99.

16. Metz, *La consécration*, p. 51. Koch, *Virgines Christi* (Leipzig, 1907), pp. 71-76.

17. S. v. "verginità," *Encicl. delle Relig.*, 6: 174-179.

18. Cf. E. Kasch, *Das Liturgische Vokabular fer frühen Lateinischen Mönchreglen* (Hildesheim, 1974).

19. *Reg. fusius*, 15. 4 (PG 31, 956B-C).

20. Cf. *Asketikon Parvum*, 7 (PL 103, 498-499).

21. PG 26, 935-936.

22. *Vita di Antonio*, ed. Bartelinck, (Mondadori), p. 126.

23. *Vita Pachomii*, 2. 8, *Vita Graecae*, p. 174. 9-10. Identical reading in *Vita Graecae*, 1. 6, p. 5. 4-5.

24. *Vita Graeca* 2. 8: Halkin, p. 174. 9-10. Identical reading in *Vita Graeca* 1.6, p. 5.4-5.

25. *Reg. Mag.*, 90. 85-87, *SC*, 106, p. 394.

26. *Reg. Mag.*, 77. 4, 83. 8, 94, *SC*, 106, pp. 316, 344.

27. Basil, *Reg. brevius*, 53 (PG 31, 1177). *Asketikon Parvum*, 147 (PL 103, 538).

28. *Reg. Mag.*, 90. 88, *SC*, 106, p. 396.

29. *Reg. fusius*, 15. 4 (PG 31, 956B-C).

30. Cf. *Asketikon Parvum*, 7 (PL 103, 498-499).

31. *De Eccles. Hierar.*, 6 (PG 3, 529-538).

32. Cf. Vatican II, *Schema Constitutionis De Ecclesia* (Typis Vaticanis, 1964), pp. 162-163, 166.

33. *Contra Impugnantes*, 1. 1, n. 7, *Opuscula Theologica*, (Marietti, 1954), p. 7.

34. *De perf. vit. spir*, 15, in ibid., p. 134.

35. 2-2, q. 184, a. 5.

36. *Contra Impugn.*, 1. 1, n. 10, *Opuscula*, p. 8.

37. 2-2, q. 186, a. 2, ad. 2.

38. 2-2, q. 186, a. 6.

39. 2-2, q. 186, a. 1.

40. 2-2, q. 188, a. 1, ad. 1.

41. *Contra Impugn.*, 1. 1, n. 9, *Opuscula*, p. 8; 2-2, q. 186, a. 1; q. 186, aa. 7, 8.

42. *Contra Impugn.*, 1. 1, n. 9, *Opuscula*, p. 8.

43. *In Sent.*, 4, d. 2, q. 1, a. 2, ad. 9.

44. 2-2, q. 88, a. 11c.

45. 2-2, q. 88, a. 7c and ad. 1.

46. *Triplici voto consecratur: Contra Impugn.*, 1. 1, n. 9.

47. Cf. A. Boni, "Note storico-giuridiche sul concetto di consecrazione nella professione religiosa," *Vita Consecrata* 8 (1972): 666-682.

48. *PC*, 1.

49. *Quaedam consecratio seu benedictio voventis*: 2-2, q. 88, aa. 7, 11.

50. *PC,* 5.

51. *Contra Impugn.,* 1. 1, n. 9, *Opuscula,* p. 8.

52. 2-2, q. 186, a. 6.

53. *La Legge di Cristo,* 2/2, c. 3, 1 (Brescia: Morcelliana, 1964), pp. 237-238.

54. Cf. 2-2, q. 186, a. 6c and ad. 2.

55. *LG,* 43, *PC,* 1.

56. *LG,* 45.

57. *LG,* 44, *PC,* 5.

58. *Vita Antonii,* 65 (PG 26, 936).

59. Jerome, *Epist.,* 39. 3.4, *CSEL,* 54, p. 299. *Epist.,* 130, 7.14, *ibid.,* p. 186.

60. PL 145, 300 and 377.

61. *De Praec.,* 17. 54 (PL 182, 889).

62. 2-2, q. 189, a. 3, ad. 3. For minor medieval writers, cf. J. Leclercq, *La Vie Parfaite* (Turnhout, 1948), pp. 133-141; also *Studia Anselmiana,* 31, pp. 124-140; H. De Lubac, *Exégèse Médiévale* (Paris: Aubier, 1959), 2: 576.

63. *Epist.,* 4. 7 (PL 185, 63).

64. On baptismal conversion and religious life, cf. Basil, *Asketikon Parvum,* 4 (PL 103, 196-197).

ABBREVIATIONS IN NOTES

The following abbreviations are used in the notes to this book. It is presumed the reader is familiar with certain standard abbreviations such as those for the Migne Patrology.

Constitutions S. J. = *The Constitutions of the Society of Jesus.* Trans. by G. Ganss. St. Louis: Institute for Jesuit Sources, 1975.

DTC = *Dictionnaire de Théologie Catholique.* Paris: Letouzey-et-Ané.

DESP = *Dizionario Enciclopedico degli Stati Perfezione.* Roma: Ed. Paoline.

DSpir = *Dictionnaire de Spiritualité.* Paris: Beauchesne.

ECB = *Early Christian Biographies.* R. Deferrari, ed. *The Fathers of the Church,* v. 15. Washington: Catholic University of America Press, 1952.

Lausiac History = Palladius, *The Lausiac History.* Trans. by C. Butler. Cambridge: 1891-1904.

OS = *St. Francis of Assisi, Omnibus of Sources.* Chicago: Franciscan Herald Press, 1975.

RB = The *Rule* of St. Benedict.

RM = *The Rule of the Master.* Trans. by L. Eberle. Kalamazoo: Cistercian Publications, 1977.

SDF = *The Sayings of the Desert Fathers: The Alphabetic Collection.* Trans. by B. Ward. Kalamazoo: Cistercian Publications, 1975.

Strack-Billerbeck = P. Billerbeck and H. L. Strack, *Kommentar zum Neuen Testament aus Talmud und Midrasch,* 4 vols. Munich: 1965 (supplements to their work were published Munich: 1956 and 1961).

TDNT = *Theological Dictionary of the New Testament*. G. Kittel, ed. Trans. by
      G. Bromiley. Grand Rapids: Wm. B. Eerdmans.

*Standard abbreviations are used for the documents of the Second Vatican
Council, especially the following:*
LG = Lumen Gentium
PC = Perfectae Caritatis
PO = Presbyterorum Ordinis
      Translations of these documents are taken from: *Vatican Council II: The
Conciliar and Post-Conciliar Documents*. A. Flannery, ed. Northport, N.Y.:
Costello Publishing Co., Inc., 1975.

Bibliography

1. Theology of Religious Life

Alonso Rodríguez, S. *La Vida Consagrada*. Madrid: Publicaciones Claretianas, 197-.

Artigas, L. *El Espíritu Santo y la Vida Religiosa*. Salamanca: Secr. Trinitario, 1975.

Asiain, M. A. *La Vida Religiosa en la Iglesia: Contribución à un Eclesiologia de la vida religiosa*. Salamanca: Secr. Trinitario, 1977.

Aubry, J. *Teología della Vita Religiosa*. Torino: Elle-Di-Ci, 1970.

Augé, M. "Notas para una Teología de la Vida Religiosa que emerge de los ritos de profesión religiosa y de consagración de vírgenes." *Misc. Lateranense* 1975: 458-470.

Balducci, E. "Teologia della Vita Religiosa." *Studi Francescani* 65 (1968): 9-18.

Bandera, A. *Siguiendo á Jesucristo: Teología de la Vida Religiosa*. Guadalajara, 1970.

Bayerlein, W. "Der Grundauftrag der Orden und anderer geistlichen Gemeinschaften aus Sicht eines Laien." *GuL* 50 (1977): 365-370.

Beltrán, J. M. *La vida religiosa y el Vaticano II: Orientación Bibliográfica, 1960-1968*. Madrid: Verda y Vida, 1969.

Beth-Gery, F. "Bibliographie sur la vie religieuse depuis le Concile." *Vocation*, janvier 1970: 133-136.

Beyer, J. *De vita per consilia evangelica consacrata*. Roma, 1969.

———. *La Vita Consacrata*. Roma, 1977.

Boff, L. *Testigos de Dios en el corazón del mundo*. Madrid: Instituto vida religiosa, 1977.

Boni, A. "La vita religiosa nel suo contenuto teologale." *Vita consa.* 7 (1971): 265-276.

Brinkman, M. "Toward a Theology of Women's Religious Life." *RRel* 30 (1971): 563–577.

Cabestrero, T. "La vida religiosa debe ser signo histórico de la Pascua de Jesus." *Vida rel* 37 (1974): 148–154.

Cambier, J. *Théologie de la vie religieuse aujourd'hui.* Bruxelles: CEP, 1971.

Castro, F. M. de. *La vida religiosa á la luz del Vaticano II.* Madrid: Studium, 1972.

Catazzo, E. *La vita religiosa nel magistero pontificio postconciliare.* Vicenza: ESCA, 1969.

Ciappi, L. *Vita religiosa e santità.* Milano: Ancora, 1970.

Clarke, T. E. *New Pentecost or New Passion: The Direction of Religious Life Today.* New York: Paulist Press, 1973.

Codina, V. *Teología de la vida religiosa.* Madrid: Razón y Fe, ²1969.

———. *Nueva formulación de la vida religiosa.* Bilbao: Mensajero, 1972.

Colorado, A. *La vida religiosa á la luz de la teología actual.* Salamanca, 1965.

Comblin, J. "Os fundamentos teologicos da Vida Religiosa." *REB* 29 (1970): 308–352.

———. "A vida religiosa e os sinais do reino de Deus." *Grande Sinal* 24 (1970): 200–208.

Connole, P. F. "Spirit and Life: The Holy Spirit in the Life of Religious." *Sursum Corda,* 33 (1971): 403–411.

Delalande, V. "La théologie de la vie religieuse: État des recherches." *Vocation,* janvier 1970: 93–100.

Tollanaere, M. De. Filosofische antropologie aan de basis de drie geloften: I De armoede; II De maagdelijkheid; III Gehoorzaamheid. *Tijdschr. voor Geest Leven* 30 (1974): 442–460, 505–529; 665–685.

Favale, A. "Orientamento bibliografico post-conciliare sulla vita religiosa." *Per una Presenza viva dei Religiosi nella Chiesa.* Torino: Elle-Di-Ci, 1970: 887–930.

Faricy, R. *Spirituality for Religious Life.* Paulist, 1976.

Fox, E. J. "The Raison d'être of Religious Life." *Supplement to Doctrine and Life* (1974): 3–9.

Gambari, E. *Manuale della vita religiosa alla luce del Vaticano II: Svolgimento e practica della vita religiosa.* Roma: Centro Mariano Monfortano, 1971.

———. *Consacrazione e missione. Dottrina e Diritto di vita religiosa.* Milano: Ancora, 1975.

Gelpi, D. L. *Discerning the Spirit: Foundations and Future of Religious Life.* New York: Sheed and Ward, 1970.

Genuyt, F. M. "Approche philosophique de la vie religieuse." *Lumière et vie* 19 (1970): 91–110.

Gonzalez, P. C. *El Misterio de la vida religiosa.* Bujedo: Centro Vocación Lasalle, 1970.

Gozzelino, G. *Una vita che si raccoglie su Dio.* Torino: Elle-Di-Ci, 1978.

Granero, J. M. "La sociedad moderna y la vida religiosa." *Manresa* 42 (1971): 243–251.

————. "Más sobre la vida religiosa" *Manresa* 43 (1971): 115–122.

Guerrero, J. M. *El religioso, signo de denuncia y reconciliación.* Bilbao: Desclée de Br., 1974.

Gutiérrez Vega, L. *Teología sistemática de la vida religiosa.* Madrid: Instituto vida religiosa, 1976. (Seg. ed., totalmente refundida y aumentada, Madrid: Instituto vida religiosa, 1979.)

————. "En busca de una nueva visión de la vida religiosa." *Vida relig.* 31 (1971): 332–338.

Haeffner, G. "Einige formale Vorüberlengungen zur Frage nach dem Sinn des Ordenslebens." *Erbe u. Auftrag* 51 (1975): 329–333.

Hinnebusch, P. *Salvation History and the Religious Life.* New York: Sheed and Ward, 1966.

————. *Signs of the Times and Religious Life.* New York: Sheed and Ward, 1967.

Holstein, H. "La vie religieuse, signe pour le monde d'aujourd'hui." *Vie comm. relig.* 28 (1970): 162–172.

————. "La vie religieuse en quête de son visage." *Vie comm. relig.* 29 (1971): 310–315.

Hostie, R. *Vie et mort des Ordres religieux: Approches psychosociologiques.* Paris: Desclée de Br., 1972.

Jacquemont, P. "Bulletin de Théologie: Recherches actuelles sur la théologie de la vie religieuse." *RESPT* 55 (1971): 283–326.

Keating, D. "Priorities in Religious Life: an Alternative View." *New Blackfriars* 55 (1974): 214–224.

Kooppenburg, B. "A doutrina do Vaticano II sobre a natureza da vida religiosa." *Rev. eccles. brasileira* 30 (1970): 59–70.

Koser, C. "Theology of Religious Life." *Sursum Corda* 34 (1972): 250–258.

————. "What Value Religious Life? Its Positive Value Today." *Sursum Corda* 35 (1973): 368–378.

Kuiters, R. *Le sens de la vie religieuse: Méditations théologiques.* Sherbrook: Editions Paulines, 1970.

Labourdette, M. M. "La vie religieuse aujourd'hui." *RT* 73 (1973): 257–272.

Lauter, H. J. "Der Ordensberuf in empirisch-theologischer Sicht." *GuL* 45 (1972): 116–129.

Leclercq, J. "La vie parfaite. Turnhout: Brepols, 1948.—Vers. Ital., *La Vita Perfetta.* Milano: Ancora, 1961.—Engl. tr., *Free Life of Perfection.* Collegeville: Liturg. Press, 1961.

Llamera, M. *"Crisis y reorganización de la vida religiosa."* *Teología Espiritual* 17 (1973): 7–70.

Lucier, P. "La vie religieuse: Nouveau questionnement." *Relations* (1973): 266–269.

Masterman, R. *Religious Life, a Mystery in Christ and the Church.* Staten Island: Alba House, 1975.

Matellán Vara, S. *"Los llamados a seguir a Cristo."* Madrid: Instituto Vida Religiosa, 1973.

————. *Hacia nuevas formas de vida religiosa.* Madrid: Inst. Vida Rel., 1974.

Matura, T. *Célibat et Communauté.* Paris, ²1967.—Vers. Ital.: *Celibato e Comunità.* Brescia: Queriniana, 1968.—Engl. tr., *Celibacy and Community.* Chicago: Franciscan Herald Press, 1968.

————. *La vie religieuse au tournant.* Paris: Cerf, 1971.—Engl. Vers., *The Crisis of Religious Life.* Chicago: Franciscan Herald Press, 1973.

————. "La vie religieuse dans un monde areligieux." NRT 99 (1977): 51–61.

Mellone, A. "La concezione della vita religiosa nel pensiero del Vaticano II." *Apollinaris* 42 (1969): 557–570.

Metz, J. B. *Zeit der Orden? Zur Mystik und Politik der Nachfolge.* Freiburg im Br: Herder, 1977.—Engl. tr., *Followers of Christ. Perspectives on Religious Life.* Burns and Oates-Paulist Press, 1978.—Vers. Ital., *Tempo di religiosi? Misticae e Politica della Sequela.* Brescia: Queriniana, 1978.

Murphy–O'Connor, J. *What Is Religious Life? A Critical Reappraisal.* Wilmington: M. Glazier, 1977.

Nau, P. "Sur la vie religieuse." EV 85 (1975): 568–575.

O'Meara, T. F. *Holiness and Radicalism in Religious Life.* New York: Herder and Herder, 1970.

O'Rourke, K. D. *Religious Life in the 70s.* Dubuque: Aquinas Institute.

Palmés, C. *Teología Bautismal y Vida Religiosa.* Bogotá: Clar., 1974.

Peter, W. L. A. "Religious Life, Buddhist and Christian." *Worldmission.* Summer 1974: 18–32.

Pikaza, X. *Esquema Teológico de la Vida Religiosa.* Salamanca: Sígueme, 1978.

Predovich, N. "Developments in the Theology of Religious Life." *Sister Formation Bulletin* Summer, 1970: 3–6.

Provera, P. *La vita consacrata* (2 vols.). Torino: Marietti, 1969.

Rahner, K. *The Religious Life Today.* New York: Seabury, 1976.

Régamey, P. R. *Redécouvrir la vie religieuse* (2 vols.). Paris: Cerf, 1971.

Regli, S. *Das Ordensleben als Zeichen in der Kirche des Gegenwart: Eine pastoraltheologische Untersuchung.* Fribourg: Universitätsverlag, 1970.

Renwart, L. "Théologie de la vie religieuse: Bulletin bibliographique." *Vie cons.* 42 (1970): 163–176; 43 (1971): 106–119; 44 (1972): 97–114; 45 (1973): 83–98; 46 (1974): 104–116; 47 (1975): 100–117; 48 (1976): 45–57; 49 (1977): 48–63.

Rosato, P. J. "Towards a Sacramental and Social Vision of Religious Life," *RRel* 36 (1977): 501–513.

Royo Marín, A. *La vida religiosa.* Madrid: BAC, 1965.

Schebera, R. "The Effects of Christology on Religious Life." *Sisters Today* 50 (1978): 226–230.

Schleck, C. A. "Religious Life Since Vatican II." *Cross and Crown* 25 (1973): 60–73.

Sebastián Aguilar, F. *La vida de perfección en la Iglesia.* Madrid: Coculsa, 1965².

————. *Vida evangélica.* Bilbao: Desclée de Br., 1966.—Vers. Ital., *Vita Evangelica.* Roma: Alma Roma, 1968.

————. *Renovación conciliar de la vida religiosa.* Bilbao: Desclée de Br., 1968.

Smith, R. "Subject Bibliography for Religious" (numerous sections: Theology, Authority, Celibacy, Charisms, Community, Obedience, Poverty, Vows, etc.). *Review for Religious* 29 (1970); 33 (1974): *passim.*

Spiazzi, R. *La vita religiosa in un mondo che cambia.* Napoli: Ed. Dehoniane, 1973.

Sudbrack, J. "Thesen zur Spiritualität religiöser Gemeinschaften." *Ordenskorrespondenz* 13 (1972): 125–133.

Tambasco, A. "The Vowed Life: Call, Response, Mission." *Review for Religious* (1973): 463–488.

Tillard, J. M. R. *Devant Dieu et pour le monde: Le projet de vie des religieux.* Paris: Cerf, 1974.

————. *Religieux. un chemin d'Evangile.* Bruxelles: Lumen Vitae, 1975.—Engl. tr., *A Gospel Path, Religious Life.* Bruxelles: Lumen Vitae, 1975.

————. "Pourquoi se faire religieux?" *Vie comm. relig.* 31 (1973): 48–54.

Ubaldo da Piave. *Vita consacrata, lo stato religioso nella Chiesa.* Padova: RDC, 1968.

Van Bavel, T. J. *De kern van het religieuze leven.* Tielt-Utrecht: Lannoo, 1973.

Van der Poel, C. J. *Religious Life, a Risk of Love: A Search for Meaning in Contemporary Religious Life.* Denville: Dimension Books, 1972.

————. "Theological Perspective in Religious Life." *Sister Formation Bulletin.* Spring 1970: 3–8.

VV.AA. *Per una Presenza viva dei Religiosi nella Chiesa.* Torino: Elle-Di-Ci, 1970.

VV.AA. *Il Rinnovamento della Vita Religiosa.* Firenze: Vallecchi, 1967.

VV.AA. *Los Religiosos en la Iglesia.* Madrid: Vida Religiosa, 1968.

VV.AA. *Verso una teologia della vita religiosa.* Roma: Ed. Paoline, 1971.

VV.AA. "What Is Religious Life?" *Supplement to Doctrine and Life,* (1974): 3–24.

Veilleux, A. "The Evolution of Religious Life in Its Historical Context." *Cist. Stud.* 6 (1971): 8–34.

————. "Points de vue sur la vie religieuse aujourd'hui." *Vie comm. relig.* 29 (1971): 194–207.

Viard, C. "Théologie de la vie religieuse: quelques réflexions." *Vocation* (1971): 179–190.

Voillaume, R. "Present Day Prospects in Religious Life." *Spode House Review,* (1970): 11–20.

————. *Concerning Religious Life: Retreat at Beni Abbes.* London: Darton, 1975.

Wiltgen, R. M. *The Religious Life Defined.* Techny: Divine Word, 1970.

Wulf, F. "Fenomenologia teologica della vita religiosa." In VV.AA., *Mysterium Salutis* 8. Brescia: Queriniana, 1975: 558–604.

2.1 Discipleship in the New Testament

Aerts, T. "Suivre Jésus. Evolution d'un thème biblique dans les Evangiles Synoptiques." TL 42 (1966): 476–512.

Agnew, F. "Vocatio primorum discipulorum in traditione synoptica." VD 46 (1968): 129–147.

Bassarak, G. "Die Wiederentdeckung der Nachfolge in biblischer Sicht." WzM 17 (1965): 425–434.

Best, E. "Discipleship in Mark: Mk. 8:22–10:52." SJTh 23 (1970): 323–337.

Betz, H. D. *Nachfolge und Nachahmung Jesu Christi im N.T.* Tübingen: 1967.

Bieder, W. *Die Berufung im N.T.* Zürich: 1961.

Bouwman, G. *Die Bijbel over volgen en navolgen.* Roermond en Maaseik: 1965.

———. *L'imitazione di Cristo nella Bibbia.* Bari: Paoline, 1968².

Brun, L. "Die Berufung der ersten Jünger Jesu in der evangelischen Tradition." *SQ* 11 (1932): 35–54.

Cothenet, E. "Imitation du Christ I, Dans l'Ecriture." *DSp* 7/2 (1971): 1536–1562.

Di Pinto, L. "Seguire Gesù secondo i vangeli sinottici." *Fondamenti Biblici della Teologia Morale: Atti della XXII settimana biblica.* Brescia, 1973: 187–251.

Donaldson, J. "Called to Follow: A Twofold Experience of Discipleship in Mark." *Biblical Theology Bulletin* 5 (1975): 67–77.

Dozzi, D. E. "Chi sono quelli attorno a lui di Mc.4:10?" *Mar* 36 (1974): 153–183.

Ernst, J. "Jüngerschaft und Nachfolge." *Anfänge der Christologie,* Stuttgart: 1972: 125–145.

Focant, C. *Les Disciples dans le second Evangile: Tradition et redaction.* Louvain: 1974.

Franzman, M. H. *Discipleship According to Saint Matthew.* Saint Louis: 1961.

Freyne, D. *The Twelve, Disciples and Apostles: A Study in the Theology of the First Three Gospels.* London: 1968.

Heinen, K. and Weiser, A. "Jüngernachfolge im Alten und Neuen Testament." *Lebzeug* 4 (1972): 7–21.

Hengel, M. *Nachfolge und Charisma: Eine exegetisch-religionsgeschichtliche Studie zu Mt. 8:21f., un Jesu Ruf in die Nachfolge.* Berlin: 1968.

Ittel, G. W. *Jesus und die Jünger.* Gütersloh: 1970.

Kingsbury, J. D. "The Verb *akolouthein* (to follow) as an Index of Matthew's View of His Community." *JBL* 87 (1978): 56–73.

Kittel, G. "Akoloutheo." *ThWNT* 1: 210–216.—Vers. It., *Grande Lessico NT* 1: 567–579.

Knoch, O. *Einer ist euer Meister: Jüngerschaft und Nachfolge.* Stuttgart: 1966.—Vers. It., *Uno è il vostro Maestro: Discepoli e Seguaci nel N.T.* Roma: 1969.

Lamarche, P. "L'appel à la conversion et à la foi: La vocation de Lévi (Mc. 2: 13–17)." *LV* 25 (1970): 125–136.

———. "L'appel de Lévi." Mc. 2:13–17", *Christus* 89 (1976): 106–118.

Larson, E. *Christus als Vorbild: Eine Untersuchung zu den paulinischen Taufund Eikontexten.* Uppsala: 1962.

Luz, U. "Die Jünger in Matthäusevangelium." *ZNW* 62 (1971): 141–171.

Merklein, H. "Der Jüngerkreis Jesu." In *Die Aktion Jesu und die Re-Aktion der Kirche,* K. H. Müller, ed. Würzbrug: 1972: 65–100.

Miyoshi, M. "Lk. 9:57–10:24: Die Nachfolge." In *Der Anfang des Reiseberichts: Lk. 9:51–10,24, Eine Redaktionsgeschichtliche Undersuchung.* Roma, 1974: 33–58.

Müller, G. "Nachfolge Christi als Zentralbegriff christlicher Ethik." *ZEE* 12 (1968): 321–333.

Neuhäusler, E. "Jüngerschaft: Ein biblischer Grundbegriff." *BiLe* 11 (1970): 67-72.

Pesch, R. "Berufung und Sendung, Nachfolge und Mission: Eine Studie zu Mk. 1: 16-20." *ZKTh* 91 (1969): 1-31.

Rengstorf, K. H. "Mathetés." *ThWNT* 4: 417-465.—Vers. It., *Grande Lessico N.T.* 6: 1121-1238.

Sabourin, L. "Essere discepolo." In *Il vangelo di Matteo: Teologia e esegesi* 1. Marino, 1975: 113-129.

Schelkle, K. H. *Jüngerschaft und Apostelamt.* Freiburg-Basel-Wien: 1965³.—Ital., *Discepoli e apostolato.* Roma: 1966.

Sheridan, M. "Disciples and Discipleship in Matthew and Luke." *Biblical Theology Bulletin* 3 (1973): 235-255.

Schmal, G. *Die Zwölf im Markusevangelium. Eine redaktionsgeschichtliche Untersuchung.* Trier: 1974.

Schneider, G. "Nachfolge Jesu heute?" In *Anfragen an das N.T.* Essen: 1971.

———. *Questioni Neotestamentarie.* Brescia, 1975: 119-132.

Schoeps, H. J. "Von der Imitatio Christi zur Nachfolge Christi." In *Aus frühchristlicher Zeit.* Tübingen, 1950: 286-301.

Schulz, A. *Nachfolgen und Nachahmen: Studien über des Verhältnis der neutestamentlichen Jüngerschaft zur urchristlichen Vorbildethik.* München: 1962.

Stock, K. *Boten aus dem Mit-Ihm-Sein: Das Verhältnis zwischen Jesus und den Zwölf nach Markus.* Roma: 1975.

Thysman, R. "L'éthique de l'imitation du Christ dans le N.T. Situation: Notations et variations du thème." *EThL* 42 (1966): 138-175.

Tinsley, E. J. "Some Principles for Reconstructing a Doctrine of the Imitation of Christ." *SJTh* 25 (1972): 45-57.

Tossato, G. "La sequela di Gesù nel racconto lucano della passione." In VV.AA., *Chiesa per il mondi, 1, saggi storico-biblici. Teologia Biblica* 19/1. Bologna, 1974: 73-96.

Turbessi, G. "Sequela ed imitazione di Cristo secondo il N.T." In *Gesù Cristo, mistero e presenza.* E. Ancilli, ed. Roma, 1971: 304-348.

———. "Il significato neotestamentario di sequela e di imitazione (Indagine esegetica su un aspetto centrale della Regola di San Benedetto)." *Ben* 19 (1972): 163-225.

van Iersel, B. "La vocation de Lévi (Mc. 2:13-17, Mt. 9:9-13, Lc. 5:27-32). In *Tradition et rédaction dans les Evangiles Synoptiques* 2. I. de la Potterie, ed. Gembloux, 1967: 212-232.

VV.AA. *Nachfolge. TBLNT* 2. Wuppertal, 1972³: 945-958.

———. "Seguire, discepolo." In *Dizionario dei concetti biblici del N.T.* Bologna, 1976: 1717-1732.

Vidal, M. "Seguimiento de Cristo y evangelización: Variación sobre un tema de moral neotestamentaria (Mt. 10:34-39). *Salm.* 18 (1971): 289-312.

Zimmermann, H. "Christus Nachfolgen: Eine Studie zu den Nachfolgeworten der synoptischen Evangelien." *ThGl* 53 (1963): 241-255.

2.2 Biblical Foundations of Religious Life

Albrecht, B. and Urs von Bathasar, H. *Nachfolge Jesu Christi mitten in dieser Welt.* Meitingen Freising: Kyrios, 1971. Ital., *Seguire Cristo Oggi.* Assisi: Cittadella, 1972.

Alonso, J. "Como se fundamenta hoy en el evangelio la vida religiosa." *SalTerr.* 58 (1970): 483-495.

Alonso, S. "Vida religiosa y misterio pascual." *Vida Rel.* 33 (1972): 107-112.

Bandera, A. "Radicalismo evangélico o pluralismo de la santidad?: Sobre el origen de la vida religiosa en la Iglesia. *Confer* 17 (1972): 7-60.

_____. "A ejemplo y en representación de Jesucristo: La consagración religiosa según Evangelica Testificatio." *Confer* 17 (1972): 179-204.

Burchill, J. P. "Biblical Basis of Religious Life." *RRel* 36 (1977): 900-923.

Chadwick, J. "The Scriptural Basis of Religious Life." *Mount Carmel* 17 (1969-1970): 193-203.

Cid, A. "Estado religioso o vida religiosa: Tiene su fundamento en el evangelio? Terminará supriméndose?" *Cultura Bíblica* (1971): 369-373.

Comblin, J. "A vida religiosa: Aprendizagem do evangelho." *Grande Sinal* 24 (1970): 753-760.

Cox, D. "New Testament Sources and the Religious Life." *Antonianum* 51 (1976): 377-760.

Denis, A. M. "Ascèse et vie chrétienne: Eléments concernant la vie religieuse dans le N.T." *RSPhTh* 47 (1963): 605-618.

Deseille, P. "Les origines de la vie religieuse dans le Christianisme." *Lumière et Vie* 19 (1970): 25-53.

De Bovis, A. "La vie religieuse est-elle essentiellement évangélique?." *VS* (1967): 697-710.

Espinel, J. L. "Fundamentos bíblicos de la vida religiosa." *CT* 62 (1972): 11-72.

Federici, G. C. "La vita evangelica: il radicalismo cristiano e la evoluzione delle sue espressioni nel mondo di oggi." *Vita cons.* 12 (1976): 520-535.

Heufelder, E. M. *Die Evangelische Räte: Die biblisch-theologischen Grundlagen des Ordenslebens im Blick aud eine Erneuerung in unserer Zeit.* Wien: 1963.

Hoornaert, E. "Origem da vida religiosa no cristianismo." *Teologica Perspectiva* (1971): 223-233.

Knoch, O. *Einer ist euer Meister: Jüngerschaft und Nachfolge.* Stuttgart: Kath. Bibelwerk, 1966. Ital., *Uno è il vostro Maestro: Discepoli e seguace nel Nuovo Testamento.* Roma: 1968.

Lamarche, P. "Les fondements scripturaires de la vie religieuse." *Vie cons.* 41 (1969): 321—327.

Larkin, E. L. "Scriptural-Theological Aspects of Religious Life." *RB* (StM) 27 (1968): 1013-1026.

Légasse, S. *L'appel du riche (Mc. 10:17-31 et parallèles).* Paris: Beauchesne, 1966.

McNamara, M. "The Biblical Basis for Religious Life." In *The Challenge to Religious Life,* C. O'Grady, ed. London, 1970: 73-117.

Mussner, F. "Die evangelischen Räte und das Evangelium." *Benedikt. Monatschrift* 30 (1954): 485-493.

Neumann, M. "Religious Life as a Profession of the Humanity of Christ." *Spirit Life* 20 (1974): 28–36.

O'Donoghue, N. D. "Vocation and Response." *IT*2 39 (1972): 130–149.

Pesch, W. "Zur biblischen Begründung des Ordenslebens." *Ordenskorrespondenz* 6 (1965): 31–46.

―――. "Ordensleben und Neues Testament: Grundlegende Feststellungen und konkrete Folgerungen." *Ordensnachrichten* 40 (1971): 1–8.

Schnackenburg, R. "Evangelische Räte. I. In der Schrift." *LThK* 3 (1959²): 1245–1246.

Schürmann, H. "Der Jungerkreis Jesu als Zeichen für Israel und als Urbild des christlichen Rätesstandes." In VV.AA., *Ursprung und Gestalt: Erörterungen und Besunnungen zum Neuen Testament*. Düsseldorf. Cf *GuL* 36 (1963): 21–34;—Vers. Fr., *Christus* 50 (1966): 184–209.—Engl., "Jesus' Disciples, Prototypes of Religious Life." *Ascent* (1970): 76–84.

Schwank, B. "Kann das Ordensleben biblisch begründet werden?" *Erbe und Auftrag* 44 (1968): 409–413.

Sebastián, F. "Origen de la vida religiosa." *Confer*. 16 (1971): 319–331.

Sicari, A. M. "L'origine evangelica della vita religiosa." In *Vita Religiosa, Bilancio e Prospettive*. E. Ancilli, ed. Collana Rivista di Vita Spirituale 11. Roma, 1976: 95–116.

Stanley, D. M. *Faith and Religious Life: A New Testament Perspective*. New York: Paulist, 1971.—Ital., *Fede e Vita Religiosa*. Milano: Ancora, 1976.

Sudbrack, J. "Letzten Norm des Ordenslebens ist die in Evangelium darlegegte Nachfolge Christi." *GuL* 40 (1967): 246–268.

Tillard, J. M. R. "Le fondement évangélique de la vie religieuse." *NRT* 95 (1969): 916–955.

―――. "Sequela Christi." *Spirit. Life* 18 (1972): 76–80.

―――. "Exigencias de la fe en la vida religiosa." *Vida Rel*. 36 (1974): 179–198.

Turbessi, G. "La sequela ed imitazione di Cristo nella vita religiosa." in *Vita Religiosa e Concilio Vaticano II*. Roma: Teresianum, 1968: 47–59.

van Cangh, J. M. "Fondement évangélique de la vie religieuse." *NRT* 95 (1973): 635–647.

von Severus, E. "Zu den biblischen Grundlagen des Mönchtums." *GuL* 26 (1953): 113–122.

3. Christian Vocations

Auman, J. "La vida religiosa, la Iglesia y el mundo." *Teología Espiritual* 13 (1969): 211–228.

Batany, J. "L'Eglise et le mépris du monde." *Annales* 20 (1965): 1006–1014.

Bataillon, J. L. "Le mépris du monde." *RSPT* 51 (1967): 23–38.

Bettini, O. "Secolarizzazione e vita consacrata." *Consacrazione e servizio* (1972): 19–27.

Bergeron, R. "La fonction eschatologique de la vie religieuse." *Vie comm. relig*. 28 (1970): 98–115.

Beyer, J. "Vie religieuse ou Institut séculier?" *NRT* 92 (1970): 505–535.

Boff, L. "Vida religiosa e secularização." *Rev. Eccles. Brasil.* 31 (1971): 561–580.

Bultot, R. *Christianisme et valeurs humaines: La doctrine du mépris du monde en Occident de Saint Ambroise à Innocent III.* Nauwelaert: 1963.

_____. "Un numéro de Revue sur la notion de mépris du monde." RHE 61 (1966): 512–528.

Cabielles de Cos, L. "Vocación universal a la santidad y superioridad de la vida religiosa en los Capítulos I y VI de la Const. Lumen Gentium." *Claretianum* XIX (1979): 5–96.

Daniélou, J. "Mépris du monde et valeurs terrestres d'après le Concile Vatican II." *RAM* 41 (1965): 421–428.

De Bovis, A. "Vie religieuse et sécularisation." *Vie cons.* 41 (1969): 257–279.

De Rosa, G. "La vita religiosa ha un senso in un mondo secularizzato?" *Civiltà Cattolica* 122/4 (1971): 438–452.

Dorsini, N. M. "The Contemporary Religious and the Authentic Christian Life." *Dimension* Spring, 1972: 28–34.

Escallada Tijero, A. "Primacía de la tensión escatológica en la vida religiosa." *CIT* 98 (1971): 457–530.

Frotz, A. and Linden, F. *Die Kirch und ihre Ämter und Stände.* Köln: 1960.

Grégoire, R. "Terrena despicere et amare coelestia." *Studia monast.* 7 (1965): 195 ff.

_____. "Introduction à une étude théologique du mépris du monde." *Studia monast.* 8 (1966): 91–07.

Gutiérrez, L. "La secularidad en la vida religiosa." *Confer* 15 (1970): 41–56.

Hortal, J. "Estado de vida consagrada Estado secular." *Teologica Perspectiva* (1971): 223–233.

Jolif, Y. J. "Signification du terme *monde.*" *Lumière et Vie* 73 (1965): 25–46.

Koser, C. "What is Sacred? Religious Life in the Process of Desacralisation." *Sursum Corda,* 35 (1975): 298–306.

Pérez Aguirre, L. *Esta hora de cambio: Teología Latinoamericana para la crisis de la vida religiosa.* Buenos Aires: Guadalupe, 1973.

Ramos-Regidor, G. "Secolarizzazione, desacralizazzione e cristianesimo." *Riv. Lit.* (1969): 473–565.

Schlosser, F. *Formes de vie chrétienne.* Mulhouse: Salvator, 1968.

Semmelroth, O. "Stände der Kirche." *LTK* IX ²1964: 1012–1023.

Süarez, G. G. "Vida religiosa y actitud ante el mundo en el magisterio contemporaneo de la Iglesia." *Confer.* 17 (1972): 283–294.

VV.AA. *La séparation du monde.* Paris: Cerf, 1961.

_____. *Le mépris du monde: La notion du mépris du monde dans la tradition spirituelle occidentale.* Paris: Cerf, 1965.

_____. *Accomplir l'Evangile dans le creuset du monde.* Paris: Fleurus, 1967.

_____. *Secularidad y vida consagrada.* Bilbao: Mensajero, 1968.

von Balthasar, H. U. Besondere Gnadengaben und die zwei Wege menschlichen Lebens: Kommentar zu S. Th. II-II q 171–182. DThA 23, Heidelberg, 1954: 251–464.

————. "Weltliche Frömmingkeit?": *Spiritus Creator, Skizzen zur Theologie III*, Einsiedeln: 1967.—Vers. Ital., Brescia: Morcelliana.

Wiederkehr, D. "La Chiesa come luogo di una multiforme esistenza cristiana." In VV.AA., *Mysterium Salutis VIII*. Brescia: Queriniana, 1975: 416–484.

Wulf, F. "Priestliche Frömmingkeit?": Ordensfrömmigkeit, Laienfrömmigkeit." *GuL* 29 (1956): 427–439.

————. "Priester, Leien: Wandlungen der kirchlichen Standeordnung." *GuL* 41 (1968): 60–62.

4. Dedication to God in the Church

Anastasio del SS. Rosario. *La vita religiosa nella Chiesa alla luce del Consilio Ecumenico Vaticano II*. Roma: USMI, 1966.

————. "La vita religiosa e Chiesa." *Riv. vita spir.* (1973): 244–251.

Balducci, E. "I religiosi nell'attuale problematica ecclesiale." *Studi Francescani* 67 (1970): 35–48.

Bamberg, C. "Ordensleben als kritische Diakonie." *GuL* 42 (1969): 17–34.

Bandera, A. "El misterio de la vida religiosa." *Teología Espiritual* 9 (1965): 439–486.

————. "La consacrazione a Dio per mezzo dei consigli evangelici." *Vita cons.* 7 (1971): 345–358; 431–441.

Barbariga, R. "La vita religiosa nel mistero della Chiesa." *Riv. vita spir.* 19 (1965): 61–92.

————. "Carattere ecclesiale dello stato religioso." *Vita Minorum* 8 (1966): 71–86.

Benson, R. L. *Vita consacrata e vita della Chiesa*. Francavilla a Mare: Paoline, 1967.

Bergh, E. "Les religieux dans l'Eglise de la charité." *Rev. comm. relig.* 36 (1964): 106–113.

Beyer, J. "La vie consacrée dans l'Eglise." *Greg.* 44 (1964): 32–61.

————. "I religiosi nella Chiesa." *Vita cons.* 12 (1976): 1–16.

Biffi, I. "Aspetti, implicazioni e problemi della 'Contemplatio' e della 'Vita contemplativa' nella *Summa Theologiae* di s. Tommaso d'Aquino" (II). *Scuola Cattolica* 97 (1969): 467–498.

Calati, B. "La vita religiosa 'segno' nella Chiesa e della Chiesa." *Studi Francescani* 67 (1970): 25–54.

Carmody, J. "Religious and Mystery." *RRel* 27 (1968): 1053–1063.

Comblin, J. "O religioso no papel da Igreja." *Grande Sinal* 24 (1970): 121–129.

Congar, Y. "La vie religieuse vue dans l'Eglise selon Vatican II." *Vie cons.* 43 (1971): 65–88.

Cusson, G. "La participation de la vie religieuse à la mission actuelle de l'Eglise." *Vie comm. relig.* (1972): 15–22.

Daniélou, J. "La place irremplaçable de la religieuse dans l'Eglise et dans la société." *Pensée Catholique* 151: 5–15.

Dantime, L. "La vie religieuse dans l'Eglise." *Rev. dioc. de Tournai* 20 (1965): 395–408.

De Bovis, A. "Le sens ecclésial de la vie religieuse." *VS* 114 (1966): 47–68.

De Guerra, I. "Aspectos eclesiales de la vida religiosa." *Verdad y vida* 23 (1965): 559–599.

Galot, J. *Les religieux dans l'Eglise. selon la constitution Lumen Gentium et le Décret sur la charge pastorale des évêques.* Paris: 1966.

Häring, B. "Ecclesialità della vita religiosa." *Studi Francescani* 67 (1970): 11–24.

Holtz, X. "Ordensleben als Zeichen des Endzustanden: Fragen zur Eschatologischen Bedeutung des Rätesstandes." *Ordenskorrespondenz* 9 (1968): 26–31.

Labourdette, M. M. "Signification de la vie religieuse dans l'Eglise." RT 71 (1971): 480–493.

Lafont, G. "L'institution religieuse dans l'institution de l'Eglise." VS Suppl. 20 (1967): 594–639.

Ligabue, G. *La testimonianza escatologica della vita religiosa.* Roma: PUL, 1968.

Mazzoli, E. "Le diverse forme di vita religiosa." *Studi Francescani* 67 (1970): 83–103.

Meinhold, P. "Les communautés religieuses, signe de l'Eglise." *Vita cons.* 40 (1968): 227–241.

Molinari, P. "Divino obsequio intimius consacratur." *Vita cons.* 7 (1971): 417–430.

Morlot, F. "Vocazione a un ministero, vocazione alla vita consacrata." *Vita cons.* 10 (1974): 428–441.

Nicolau, M. "Fundamento teológico de la vida religiosa." *Manresa* 37 (1965): 195–210.

Pesch, O. H. "Ordensleben und Verkundigung." *Ordenskorrespondenz* 9 (1965): 365–382.

Rodriguez, I. "Inserción de la vida religiosa en el misterio de Cristo y de la Iglesia." *Rev. Espiritualidad* (1972): 27–52.

Rondet, M. "Signification eschatologique de la vie religieuse." *Lumière et Vie* 19 (1970): 139–151.

Santaner, M. A. "Vie en Eglise, vie religieuse, vie en communauté." *Vie comm. relig.* 28 (1970): 86–96.

Schevenberg, R. "Inserção da vida religiosa na Igreja e sua irrdiação no mundo." *Grande sinal* 25 (1971): 354–364.

Schillebeeckx, E. "Het nieuwe mens-en Godsbeld in conflict met het religieuze leven." *Tijdschrift v. Theologie* 7 (1967): 1–27.

Schulte, R. "Das Ordensleben als Zeichnen." In Barauna, G. *La Chiesa del Vaticano II.* Firenze: Vallecchi, 19—.

VV.AA. *Le rôle de la religieuse dans l'Eglise.* Paris: Cerf, 1960,—Vers. Ital., *La missione della Religiosa nella Chiesa.* Alba: Paoline, 1962.

von Balthasar, H. U. "Une vie livrée a Dieu: sens de la vie selon les conseils." *Vie cons.* 43 (1971): 5–23.

Walz, "L'ideale religioso nella vita e nella dottrina de s. Tommaso d'Aquino." *Vita cons.* 10 (1974): 211–223.

Wulf, F. "Ordensleben und Welt. Theologische Neibesinnung und einige Folgerungen." *Ordenskorrespondenz* 5 (1964): 219-230.

————. "Gott allein: Zur Deutung eines christlichen Grundwortes." *GuL* 42 (1971): 161-169.

5.1 Charisms in General

Beni, A. "I carismi nella Chiesa e per la Chiesa." *Rivista clero italiano* (1972): 17-21.

Bettencourt, E. "Charisms." In *Sacramentum Mundi* I. Herder: 283-284.

Boschi, "I carismi nella s. Scrittura." *Sacra Doctrina* (1970): 357-382.

Brockhaus, U. *Charisma und Amt: Die paulinische Charismenlehre auf dem Hintergrund für frühchristliche Gemeindefunktionen.* Wuppertal: Brockhaus, 1972.

Cipriani, S. "Carismi ed istituzione nella Chiesa." *Consacrazione e servizio* (1972): 603-608.

Chenu, M. D. "Carismi e gruppi spontanei." *Sacra Doctrina* (1970): 431-446.

Conzelmann, H. Art., "Charisma." *TWNT* IX: 393-397—Engl. tr., *Theol. Dict. N.T.* IX: 402-406.

Cullman, O. "La notion biblique du charisme et l'oecumenisme." *RT* 71 (1971): 520-527.

De Haes, R. *Pour une théologie du prophétique.* Paris: Béatrice, 1974.

Dianich, S. "Carismi e ministeri in comunione d'amore." *Ut unum sint* (1971): 6-22.

Ducros, X. Art., "Charismes. *DSpir.*: 503-507.

Dumont, E. "La importancia de los carismas." *Rev. bíblica* 32 (1970): 35-39.

Flores, J. *Profecía y carisma,* Barcelona: Portavoz Evangelico, 1973.

Gewiess, J. and Rahner, K. "Charisma." *LTK* II: 1025-1030.Ghidelli, C. "I carismi nella Chiesa: Fondamenti biblici." *Presenza Pastorale* (1971): 647-660.

Hasenhütl, G. *Charisma, Ordnungsprinzip der Kirche.* Freiburg: 1969.

Küng, H. "Struttura carismatica della Chiesa." *Concilium* 1965/2: 15-37.

Lemonnier, M. "Riflessioni per una teologia dei carismi." *Riv. vita spir.* (1972): 3-34.

López, R. "Los carismas." *Christus* (Mexico) 40 (1975): 43-47.

Neuman, M. "The Gifts of the Holy Spirit: A Creativity Perspective." *RRel* 32 (1973): 298-312.

Piepcorn, A. C. "Charisma in the New Testament and the Apostolic Fathers." *Concordia Theological Monthly* 42 (1971): 369-389.

Pyfferoen, H. "Le charisme, unique structure fondamentale de l'Eglise." *Laurentianum* 12 (1971): 91-98.

Rahner, K. "Bemerkungen über das charismatische in der Kirche." *Schriften zur Theologie* IX. Einsiedeln, 1970: 415-431.

Robles, L. "Jerarquía y carismas en la Iglesia naciente." *RET* 29 (1969): 419-444.

Rodenas, A. "Teología biblica de los carismas." *Est. biblicos* 30 (1971): 345-360.

Ruaro, G. "Carismi e strutture nell'ecclesiologia del Concilio Vaticano II." *Presenza Pastorale* (1971): 673–686.

Turrado, L. "Carisma y ministerio en san Pablo." *Salmanticensis* (1972): 323–354.

VV.AA. *Charisms in the Church.* C. Duquoc, C. Seabury: 1978.

5.2 Charisms in Religious Life

Alvarez Gómez, J. "El profetismo de los Fundadores y el ministerio profético de sus discípulos." *RRel* 40 (1976): 131–144.

Anastasio del SS Rosario. "La vita religiosa é profezia." *Riv. Vita Spir.* (1973): 244–251.

Artigas, L. "El profetismo de Cristo, de la Iglesia y de los religiosos." *Vida Rel.* 40 (1976): 121–124.

Avo, N. "Variance in the Religious Vows: What Poverty, Why Chaste, Who Obey?" *RRel.* 31: (1972) 33–40.

Bandera, A. "Consigli evangelici e sacramenti." *Vita cons.* 9 (1973): 97–106.

_____. "La consacrazione a Dio per mezzo dei consigli evangelici." *Vita cons.* 7 (1971): 521–531; 609–613; 785–797.

Bergh, E. "Les conseils évangéliques d'après le Concile." *Rev. Comm. relig.* 37 (1965): 113–118.

Colorado, A. *Los consejos evangélicos a la luz de la teología actual.* Salamanca: Sígueme, 1965.

De Candido, L. M. "Carismi dei religiosi." *Servitium* 4 (1970): 807–817.

Deman, M. "Le spécifique de la vie religieuse." *Vocation* (1970): 93–100.

Doyle, S. C. "Religious Life: Prophetic Charism." *RRel* 36 (1977): 49–56.

Esnault, R. H. *Luther et le monachisme aujourd'hui.* Genève: Labor et Fides, 1964.

Gallen, J. F. "Function of the Evangelical Counsels." *RRel* 35 (1976): 735–739.

Gambari, E. "Elementi costitutivi e caratteristici della vita religiosa." *Vita rel.* 6 (1970): 98–106, 157–165.

Glaser, J. W. "Commands-Counsels: A Pauline Teaching?" *Theol. Stds.* 31 (1970): 275–287.

Gómez, I. "Verdadero y falso profetismo en la vida religiosa." *Vida Rel.* 40 (1976): 145–157.

Holstein, H. "Conseils et charisme." *Christus* 16 (1969): 173–175.

Lippert, P. "Die evangelische Räte. Grundprinzip oder Sonderform christlicher Spiritualität." In *Die Kirche im Wandel der Zeit,* Köln, 1971: 659–669.

Mennesier, A. Art., "Conseils Evangéliques." *DSpir.* II: 1592–1609.

Morta, A. *Los consejos evangélicos.* Madrid: Coculsa, 1968.

Nintemann, G. B. "Priestly Poverty, Prophetic Obedience, and Kingly Chastity." *Cross and Crown* 23 (1971): 320–336.

Rahner, K. "Über die evangelische Räte." *Schriften zur Theologie* VII, Einsiedeln, 1966: 404–434.—Engl. tr., "On the Evangelical Counsels." *Theological Investigations* VIII: 133–434.—Vers. Ital., "Sui consigli evangelici." *Nuovi Saggi.* Roma, 1968: 513–552.

Rambaldi, G. "Carisma ed istituzione nella vita religiosa." *Vita Cons.* 10 (1974) 401–413; 457–473.

Ranwez, E. "Trois conseils évangéliques?" *Concilium* 9 (1965): 63–71.

Sauvage, M. *Les fondements évangéliques de la vie religieuse.* Lasallianum 16. Roma: 1973.

Schlink, B. "Le plus beau chemin: Les conseils évangéliques et la réponse du chrétien aujourd'hui." *Vie cons.* 44 (1972): 168–177.

Schnackenburg, R. *Christliche Existenz nach dem Neuen Testament* I. München, 1967: 147–154; 131–155.—Ital., *L'esistenza cristiana secondo il Nuovo Testamento.* Modena: Paoline, 1971: 111–131.

Sebastián Aguilar, F. "Valoración teológica de los consejos evangélicos." *Confer* 7 (1965): 353–375.

Thomas, J. and Griolet, P. *Travail amour politique.* Paris: Mame, 1973.—Vers. Ital., *Lavoro Amore Politica:Lettura cristiana dell'esistenza.* Torino: Elle-Di-Ci, 1968.

Tillard, J. M. R. "Le fondement évangélique de la vie religieuse." NRT 95 (1969): 916–955.

———. "Consigli Evangelici." *Diz. Encicl. Istituti Perfezione.* Roma: Paoline II: 1630–1685.

Truhlar, K. V. "De theologia consiliorum hodierna animadversiones." ETL 38 (1962): 534–556.

———. "Laïcs et conseils." In *Laïcs et vie chrétienne parfaite,* Roma: Herder, 1963: 113–118.

Turrado, A. "Teología antropología y consejos evangélicos." *Rev. Agustiniana Espiritualidad* (1971):7–65.

Von Balthasar, H. U. "A Theology of the Evangelical Counsels." *Cross Currents,* 16 (1966):213–236; 324–337.

5.3 The Charism of a Religious Family.

Bouchard, C. E. "The Charism of the Community: Does it Really Make a difference?." *RRel* 37 (1978):350–356.

Brockman, N. "Directed Prayer and the Founding Charism." *RRel* 33 (1974):257–274.

Damizia, G. "Fondatore." *Enciclopedia Cattolica.* Vatican City: 1474–1475.

Efren de la Madre de Dios. "Carisma personal y carisma institucional: Contrastes." *Revista Espiritualidad* (1972):7–25.

Futrell, J. C. "Discovering the Founder's Charism." *Way* Suppl. 14 (1971):60.

George, F. E. "Founding Founderology." *RRel* 36 (1977):40–48.

Gilmont, J. F. Paternité et Médiation du Fondateur d'Ordre." *RAM* 40 (1964):395–426.

Juberías, F. "La paternidad de los fundadores." *Vida Rel* (1972):317–328.

Ledóchowska, T. *In Search of the Charism of the Institute,* Rome: Ursulines, s.a.

Lozano, J. M. *El Fundador y su Familia Religiosa.* Madrid: Instituto Vida Religiosa, 1978.

──────. "Founder and Community: Inspiration and Charism." *RRel* 37 (1978):214–236.

Murphy-O'Connor, J. "The Charism of the Founder." *Supplement to Doctrine and Life* (1974):10–18.

Oesterley, G. "Fundatores Ordinum et Congregationum quinam sint." *CpR* 27 (1948):72–75.

Olphe-Galliard, M. "Le charisme des Fondateurs Religieux." *Vie cons.* 39 (1967):338–352.

Seasoltz, R. K. "Monastic Autonomy and Exemption: Charism and Institution." *The Jurist* 34 (1974):316–355.

Tillard, J. M. R. *There are Charisms and Charisms.* Brussels: Lumen Vitae, 1977.

Wood, R. "The Vocation of a Community." *RRel* 36 (1977):412–420.

6. Celibacy

Adinolfi, M. "Il celibato di Gesú." BeO 13 (1971):145–158.

──────. "Il matrimonio nella libertà dell'etica escatologica di 1 Cor. 7." *Antonianum* 51 (1976):133–169.

Arnanz Villalta, E. "Virginidad y comunidad: Reflexión antropológica-teológica." *Vida Rel.* 40 (1976):67–71.

Audet, L. "Le célibat religieux comme temoignage et contestation." *Vie comm. relig.* 28 (1970): 240–248.

Balch, D. L. "Backgrounds of 1 Cor. 7: Sayings of the Lord in Q; Moses as an Ascetic, *Theios Aner* in 2 Cor. 3." *NTS* 18 (1972):351–364.

Balducelli, R. "The Decision for Celibacy." *TS* 36 (1975):219–242.

Bauer, J. B. "Entstehung des Zölibats." *Wort und Wahreheit* 25 (1970):493–506.

Blank, J. "Prophetische Ehelosigkeit und kultisches Sexualtabu." *Diakonia* 1 (1970):373–382.

Byrne, M. "Gift of Ourselves." *Sursum Corda* 33 (1971):307–315.

Ciappi, L. "Il voto di castitá." *Vita Rel.* 3 (1967):275–277.

Chapelle, A. "La maturation de la sexualité dans de célibat." *Vie cons.* 44 (1972):321–331; 45 (1973):5–27.

Cosgrave, W. "A Christian Understanding of Celibacy." *Doctrine and Life* 27 (1977):39–49.

Cothenet, E. "Les Apôtres étaient-ils mariés? *Esprit et vie* (1971):719–721.

Drago, A. "Speranza cristiana e castitá consacrata." *Vita cons* 9 (1973):480–491; 578–584.

Dubay, T. "Celibate Friendship: Illusion and Reality." *RRel* 36 (1977):833–843.

Ers, C. "Mariage et célibat dans la Première aux Corinthiens." *Vie cons.* 46 (1974):65–77.

Flich, M. "In quale senso il celibato sia un carisma." *Presenza Pastorale* 40 (1970):203–207.

Franquesa, P. "La virginidad en el Nuevo Testamento." *Vida Rel.* 40 (1976):7–30.

Futrell, J. C. "Living Consecrated Celibacy Today." *RRel* 31 (1972):931–936.

Galilea, S. "La impotencia como pobreza y actitud profética." *Servir* (1971):607–613.

Galot, J. "The Celibacy of Christ." *Emmanuel* 76 (1970):151–159.

————. "La motivazione evangelica del celibato." *Vita Cons.* 12 (1976):129–150.

Goergen, D. *The Sexual Celibate.* New York: Seabury, 1974.

Goggin, A. "Consecrated Celibacy." *Cath. Mind* 74 (1975):31–39.

Grabner-Haider, A. "Ehelosigkeit als Zeichen und Lebesform." *GuL* 47 (1974):213–227.

Gutiérrez Vega, L. "La virginidad en su dimensión de signo y de escatología." *Vida Rel.* 40 (1976):31–42.

Häring, B. "Sex and the Celibate." *New Cath. World* 220 (1977):272–275.

Harada, H. "A virgindade consagrada: o problema do celibato?." *Grande Sinal* 28 (1974):323–327.

Heisig, J. W. "Castità consacrata e mutilazione spirituale." *Vita cons.* 8 (1972):472–481.

Hinnebusch, P. "Religious Chastity, Its Divine Dimension." *Cross and Crown* 21 (1969):201–213.

Horan, H. "Chaste Love Among Celibates." *Cross and Crown* 21 (1969):85–92.

Kelly, J. "Consecrated Celibacy." *Sursum Corda* 36 (1974):78–84.

Kenel, M. and Callahan, R. "Human Sexuality and Religious Life." *Sisters Today* 47 (1976):257–265.

Ledure, Y. "Un célibat religieux pour notre temps." *Vie cons.* 43 (1971):325–341.

Léon-Dufour, E. "Mariage et virginité selon saint Paul." *Christus* 42 (1964):179–194.

Matura, T. Célibat et Communauté, Paris:²1967.—Vers. It., *Celibato e Comunitá.* Brescia: Queriniana, 1978.—Engl. tr., *Celibacy and Community.* Chicago: Franciscan Herald Press, 1968.

————. "Le célibat dans le Nouveau Testament d'après l'exégèse récente." *NRT* 97 (1975):481–500; 593–604.

Meany, J. O. "The Psychology of Celibacy: an In-Depth View." *Catholic Mind* (1971):11–20.

Moens, G. R. "Célibat religieux et amour humain." *Collect. Mechl.* 54 (1969):9–32.

Moioli, G. "Per una rinnovata riflessione sui rapporti tra matrimonio e virginità." *La Scuola Cattolica* 95 (1967):201–255.

Montini, I. "Il celibato tra sfruttamento e profezia." *Testimonianze* (1972):355–369.

Morta, A. *Dinamica della castità consacrata.* Roma: USMI, 1968.

Munster, L. *Virginità consacrata,* Roma: Paoline, 1965.

Nicolau, M. "Virginidad y continencia en la S. Escritura." *Manresa* 47 (1975):19–40.

Novak, M. "On Celibacy and Marriage." *Commonweal* July 27, 1973:398, 415; August 24, 1973:447, 463.

O'Connor, F. "Sexuality, Chastity, and Celibacy." *Doctrine and Life* 18 (1968):128-141.

Paradis, G. "La chasteté." *Vie cons.* 40 (1968):353-368.

Pauly, K. "Die Gnadengabe der Ehelosigkeit: Lebenserfullung und Lebensauftrag." *Dienender Glaube* (1974):193-197.

Phipps, W. E. *The Sexuality of Jesus: Theological and Literary Perspectives.* New York: Harper and Row, 1973.

Plé, A. *Vie affective et chasteté.* Paris: Cerf, 1967.

_____. "La vie affective du célibataire consacré." *VS Suppl.* 22 (1969):217-233.

Proietti, B. "La scelta celibataria alla luce della s. Scrittura." In VV.AA., *Il Celibato per il Regno*:7-75.

Ribando, W. "Celibacy: Gift for Loving." *Sisters Today* 49 (1977):227-230.

Riga, P. J. "The Kingdom and Celibacy." *Bible Today* 69 (1973):1378-1384.

Rigaux, B. "Le célibat et le radicalisme évangélique." NRT 94 (1972):157-170.

Rodriguez, E. M. "Problemática pastoral del celibato en la vida religiosa." *Servir* 7 (1971):77-90.

Santaner, M. A. "Célibat consacré et communauté fraternelle." *Vie comm. relig.* 32 (1974):10-23.

Schillebeeckx, E. Het ambts-celibat in de branding. Bilthoven: H. Nelissen, 1966.—Engl. tr., *Celibacy.* New York: Sheed and Ward, 1968.

Schrage, W. "Zur Frontstellung der paulinischen Ehebewertung in 1 Kor. 7; 1-7." ZNTW 67 (1976):214-234.

Schuler, F. E. "Ehelosigkeit im Neuen Testament." *Anzeiger fur die katholische Geistlichkeit* (1971):373-380.

Segalla, G. "Il testo più antico sul celibato: Mt. 19:11-12." *Studia Patavina* 17 (1970):121-137.

Shanley, K. "The Mystery of Celibate Love." *Pastoral Life* 22/8 (1973):11-16.

Thornton, T. C. G. "Jewish Bachelors in New Testament." *Journal of Theological Studies* 23 (1972):444-445.

Thüsing, W. "Die Intention Jesu und der Zölibat." *Diakonia* (1972):363-377.

Thornos, A. "La castidad religiosa: Renovación doctrinal y práctica." *Confer* 16 (1971):361-372.

VV.AA. *Consecrated Celibacy.* Ottawa: Canadian Relig. Conf., 1971.

Vidal, M. "Nueva comprensión de la sexualidad y sus incidencias en la vida religiosa." *Vida Rel.* 40 (1976):131-144.

Villatte, S. "Redonner sens au célibat religieux?" *Vie cons.* 43 (1971):129-155.

Wachter, M. de. "Celibacy in Man-Woman Relationships: A Case Study." *Louvain Studies* 3 (1970):83-98.

Wulf, F. "Zur Theologie der christlichen Ehelosigkeit und Jungfräulichkeit." *GuL* 36 (1963):341-362.

Zissis, T. N. *Techne parteneias: The Fathers' Arguments on Celibacy and Their Sources.* Bonn: Bouvier, 1973.

7. The Religious Profession of Christian Poverty

Andrés, D. "La pobreza de los religiosos en el magisterio de Pablo VI." *Vida rel.* 38 (1975):27–36.

Arnanz, E. "Pobre es el hombre fiel: Puntos para una revisión de los supuestos antropológicos de la pobreza." *Vida rel.* 38 (1975):19–16.

Batey, R. *Jesus and the Poor.* New York: Harper and Row, 1972.

Bernadicou, P. J. "Religious Poverty." *RRel* 23 (1964):770–778.

Böckmann, A. "Biblische Armut im Hinblick auf eine Renauerung der Armut im Ordensleben." *Ordenskorrespondez* 13 (1972):249–261.

Boff, L. "A pobreza no mistério do homem e de Cristo." *Grande Sinal* 28 (1974):162–183.

Bonaventura da Gangi. "La povertà evangelica oggi." *Palestra clero* (1973):1193–1205.

Byrne, M. "Gift of Ourselves: the Mystery of the Cross and Poverty." *Sursum Corda* 33 (1971):347–352.

Codina, V. "Notas para una teología de la pobreza religiosa." *Manresa* 40 (1968):125–136.

Conti, M. "Fondamenti biblici della povertà nel ministero apostolico" (Mt. 10:9–10). *Antonianum* 46 (1971):393–426.

————. "Povertà di Cristo e povertà della Chiesa." *Vita Cons.* 11 (1975):481–486.

Delanglade, J. "Travail et Pauvreté." *Vie cons.* 42 (1969):202–299.

De la Costa, H. "A More Authentic Poverty." *RRel* 35 (1976):191–204.

Demmer, K. "Zeugnis der Armut? Theologische Uberlegungen zur Gelübde der Armut." *ThGl* 61 (1971):413–443.

Domenach, J. M. "Pauvreté et societé de consommation." *Bible Vie chrét.* 98 (1971):54–77.

Doyle, M. "Religious Poverty and the Education of the poor." *Sisters Today* 48 (1977):7–10.

Drago, A. "La povertà come fede nell'esperienza della vita religiosa." *Vita Cons.* 11 (1975):551–569; 630–635.

Dupont, J. "La povertà religiosa alla luce della s. Scrittura." In VV.AA., *La Povertà Religiosa*:7–15.

————. "Renoncer à tous ses biens." Lc. 14:33." *NRT* 93 (1971):561–582.

Fabretti, N. "Pensieri sulla Povertà." *Servitium* 1 (1967):233–242.

Filipetti, B. "Elementi teologici della povertà evangelica." *Vita monastica* (1971):89–110.

Franquesa, P. "Reflexiones sobre el concepto bíblico de pobreza." *Vida rel.* 38 (1975):7–18.

Galot, J. "Le fondement évangélique du voeu religieux de pauvreté." *Gregor* 56 (1975):441–467.

————. "Il fondamento evangelico del voto religioso di povertà." *Vita Cons.* 12 (1976):17–38.

Gelin, A. "Les Pauvres de Yahvé." Paris: Cerf, [3]1953.—Eng. Transl., Collegeville: 1964.

Glowienka, E. "The Counsel of Poverty: Gospels Versus Acts." *RRel* 34 (1975):248–255.

Gomez Mier, V. "La pobreza de los institutos religiosos: Estructuras tradicionales y nuevas perspectivas." *Confer 17* (1972):551–564.

Granero, J. M. "Presupuestos para una renovación de la pobreza religiosa." *Manresa* 40 (1968):99–104.

Grosh, G. R. "On Commitment to the Poor." *RRel* 36 (1977):540–548.

Guerrero, J. M. "La pobreza evangélica." *Manresa* 43 (1971):327–334.

Häring, B. "Povertà personale e povertà comunitaria." In VV.AA., *La Povertà Religiosa:*55–65.

Heilbert, J. "A Note on Religious Poverty." *RRel* 34 (1975):380–389.

Hennaux, J. M. "Vers une pauvreté politique." *Vie cons.* 45 (1973):113–120.

Holstein, H. "La pauvreté religieuse aujourd'hui." *Vie comm. relig.* 29 (1971):44–55.

Hooreman, M. "Leben nach dem Evangelium: Die Innenseite der Armut." *Dienender Glaube* 46 (1970):228–232.

Hornung, A. "Verso una teologia della povertà." In VV.AA., *La Povertà Religiosa:*55–65.

Iturrioz, J. "Pobreza religiosa comunitaria." *Manresa* 48 (1976):41–50.

Kelleher, S. "Evangelical Poverty Today in the Context of Social Justice." *Word and Worship* (1974):1204–1205.

Kosar, C. "Pobres en un mundo dominado por la sociedad de consumo?" *Vida Rel* 33 (1972):131–140.

Kraus, H. "Aktuelle Aspekte der Ordensarmut." *GuL* 44 (1971):103–124.

La Croix, W. L. "The New Property and the Vow of Poverty." *RRel* 30 (1971):977–987.

Lapointe, R. "Pauvreté et messianisme." *Kerygma* 5 (1971):37–50.

Ledure, Y. "Pour une pauvreté religieuse au service des pauvres." *Vie cons.* (1973):99–113.

Légasse, S. "Les fondements évangéliques de la pauvreté religieuse." *Vie cons.* 42 (1970):257–283.

Lozano, J. M. "The Doctrine and Practice of Poverty in Early Monasticism." *Claretianum* 16 (1976):5–32.

Lucien M. de Saint Joseph. *Le mystère du Christ pauvre.* Paris: Desclée de Br., 1964.

Matura, M. C. *Povertà religiosa ed esigenze contemporanee.* Roma: Alma Roma, 1970.

Marlot, F. "Beati i poveri: beatitudine o consiglio?" *Vita Cons.* 11 (1975):46–55.

Mulhern, P. F. *Dedicated Poverty: Its History and Theology.* Staten Island: Alba House, 1973.

Optatus a Veghel. *Povertà Religiosa ed evangelizzazione dei poveri.* Brescia: Morcelliana, 1968.

Palacios, J. M. "Formación de la pobreza evangélica: Orientaciones psicopedagogicas." *Vida Rel* 30 (1971):8-14; 194-202.

Rahner, K. "Theologie der Armut." in *Schriften zur Theologie* VII: 435-478.
——Engl. Vers., "Theology of Poverty." *Theological Investigations* VIII: 168-214.—Vers. Ital., *Teologia della Povertà.* Roma: Paoline, 1968.

Régamey, P. *Pauvreté chrétienne et construction du monde.* Paris:1967.

————. "Poverty." In *New Catholic Encyclopedia* XI:648-651.

Riga, P. J. "Poverty as Theology." *World Justice* (1971):323-367.

————. "Christian Poverty in the Seventies." *Cross and Crown* 25 (1973):15-24.

————. "Poverty as Counsel and as Precept." *Bible Today* 65 (1973):1123-1128.

Rochais, G. "La communauté des biens dans l'Eglise primitive de Jérusalem." *Communauté chrétienne* (1972):372-383.

Rowe, M. "Poverty of Spirit: To Will One Thing." *Cross and Crown* 23 (1971):68-80.

Ruston, R. "Poverty and the Religious Community." *New Blackfriars* 55 (1974):254-264.

Tillard, J. M. R. "La pauvreté religieuse." *NRT* 92 (1970):806-848; 906-941.

————. "Le propos de pauvreté et l'exigence évangélique." *NRT* 100 (1978):207-232.

Trubac, E. "Poverty and a Common Living Standard." *Sisters Today* 49 (1976):278-283.

VV.AA. "Etudes sur la Pauvreté" (Symposium). *Missio* (1972):88-133.

VV.AA. *La Pauvreté Evangélique.* Paris: Cerf, 1971.

VV.AA. "La Pauvreté" (Symposium). *Vie cons.* 45 (1973):129-191.

VV.AA. "La Povertà Evangelica" (Symposium). *Servitium* 6 (1972):277-484.

VV.AA. *La Povertà Religiosa.* Roma: Instituto Vita Religiosa, 1975.

Voillaume, R. "Vie religieuse et pauvreté." *Vie comm. relig.* 28 (1970):66-85.

Wickham, J. F. "Actual Poverty Today." *RRel* 37 (1978):389-398.

Winstanley, M. T. "Jesus, Poverty, and the Kingdom." *RRel* 36 (1977):583-591.

Wulf, F. "Charismatiche Armut im Christentum: Geschichte und Gegenwart." *GuL* 44 (1971):16-31.

8. Community

Alaiz, A. *Los testigos de la fraternidad.* Madrid: Ed. Paulinas, 1973.

Alonso, S. M. "Comunidad y comunicación: Convivencia con los demás miembros del Instituto." *Vida Rel.* 40 (1976):303-315.

Aranguren, I. "La comunión cenobítica." *Cistercium* (1971):247-258.

Arrupe, P. "Communication sur les petites communautés." *Doc. Cath.* 73 (1976).

Asiain, M. A. "En búsqueda de la renovación de nuestra vida comunitaria." *Vida rel.* 38 (1975):405-420.

Banberg, C. "Wie kann in unseren Orden heute Gemeinschaft werden?" *GuL* 45 (1969):17-34.

Bandera, A. "Vida religiosa y comunidad eclesial." *CT* 97 (1970):177–217.

Barbaglio, G. "Linee di presentazione biblica della comunità cristiana." *Presenza Pastorale* 40 (1970):253–260.

Barosse, T. "Religious Community and the Primitive Church." *RRel* 25 (1966):971–986.

Beha, H. M. "Towards a Theology of Community." *RRel* 24 (1965):735–743.

Bertetto, D. "La comunità religiosa è comunità orante." *Vita Cons.* 11 (1975):514–520.

Bonhoeffer, D. *Gemeinsames Leben,* München: Kaiser, 1939.—Vers. Ital., *La Vita Comune.* Brescia: Queriniana, 1969.—Engl. tr., *Life Together.* New York: Harper, 1954.

Boyd, R. "The Prayer of the Community." *Way* 10 (1970):220–229.

Bracken, J. "Community and Religious Life: A Question of Interpretation." *RRel* 31 (1972):732–741.

Brooks, R. M. "Interpersonal Relationships in Religious Life." *RRel* 35 (1976):904–913.

Bruni, G. "La comunità nella prima lettera di Giovanni." *Servitium* (1973):883–892.

Butts, A. "The Modern Religious Community and Its Government." *RRel* 34 (1975):232–240.

Calasanz, F. J. "Visión de la fraternidad." *Naturaleza y Gracia* (1971):159–186.

Codina, P. "La pertenencia, factor de cohesión en la comunidad religiosa." *Vida Rel* 42 (1977):147–159.

Comblin, J. "O conceito de comunidades e a teologia." *Rev. Eccles. Brasileira* 30 (1970):568–589.

Conion, J. "The Contemplative in Communion." *Cist. Stud.* 11 (1976):24–59.

Delespesse, M. "Communauté et tradition." *Courrier communautaire international* Sept.–Oct. 1971:2–16.

Delplanque, B. "La vie en communion." *VS Supp.* 21 (1968):303–339; 495–542.

———. "La personne et la communauté." *Supplement* 24 (1971):263–302.

———. "Communauté et collectivité." *Cahiers St. Dominique.* Sept.–Oct. 1971:44–50.

De Lugo, A. "Vida común y perfección personal." *Confer* 14 (1970):93–97.

Demoustier, A. "Conversion et Communauté." *Christus* 23 (1976):79–91.

De Pierre, A. "Communion et institution." *Christus* 15 (1968):199–216.

De Ruiter, T. *Het Mysterie van de Kloostergemeenschap.* Melchen:[3]1964.—Vers. Ital., *Il mistero della vita comune.* Alba: Paoline, [2]1968.

Devaney, D. "Conflicting Values in Community Life." *Sisters Today* 44 (1972):620–627.

Dominian, J. "The Prophetic Community." *Spode House Review* May, 1974: 11–18.

Donnelly, J. "Small Group Living: Sharing a Vision." *RRel* 37 (1978):251–255.

Doppelfelt, B. "Das Kloster als Familie." *Erbe und Auftrag* (1974):5–20.

Driot, M. "Vie communautaire et vocation personnelle." *Supplement* 23 (1970):171–195.

Dubay, T. *Caring: A Biblical Theology of Community*. Denville: Dimension, 1973.

Dubois, G. "La communauté monastique dans l'Eglise." *Collectanea cisterciensia* (1972):295-330.

Ducharme, A. "De l'expérience spirituelle à l'expérience communautaire." *Vie comm. relig.* 29 (1971):271-283.

Duffrer, G. "Gemeinschaft und Gemeinde als Zeichen des gegenwartigen Christus." *Dienender Glaube* (1973):64-68.

Evans, M. "The Apostolic Religious Community." *Way* 16 (1976):30-38.

Faricy, R. J. "Religious Community." *Spiritual Life* 18 (1972):92-99.

Fichter, J. "Small or Large Communities?" *RRel* 35 (1976):757-765.

Fischer, G. D. "Zum Koinonia-Charakter christlicher Gemeinde." *ThGl* 61 (1971):39-46.

Fitzgerald, W. F. P. "Why Community?" *Supplement to Doctrine and Life* 8 (1970):19-25.

Futrell, J. C. "To be Together . . . in Spite of Everything." *RRel* 32 (1973):514-521.

García Paredes, J. C. R. "Pertenencia á la Iglesia, Pertenencia al Instituto." *Vida Rel.* 42 (1977):405-413.

Giallanza, J. "Witness Christ in Community Life." *RRel* 28 (1970):961-967.

Greeley, A. M. "The Risks of Community." *Critic* 28 (1970):18-26.

Gutiérrez, D. J. A. "La vida común religiosa." *Apollinaris* 50 (1977):119-148.

Hall, B. B. "La communautê chrétienne dans le livre des Actes: [Actes 6:1-17] et 10:1-11, 18." *Cahiers bibliques* May, 1971:146-156.

Haughton, R. "The New Communities." *Doctrine and Life* 27 (1977):53-64.

Heisig, J. "War and Peace in the Religious Community." *Cross and Crown* 23 (1971):435-441.

Julien, P. "Le groupe religieux, lieu de progrès." *Supplément* 25 (1972):5-22.

Kelly, A. "Intercession and Community Development." *RRel* 32 (1973):757-763.

Kirchner, L. "Oracão comunitaria, caminho a comunidade." *Grande Sinal* (1973):32-37.

Knight, D. "The Problem of Religious Community Today." *Sisters Today* 47 (1975):129-137.

Koser, C. "Small Communities." *RRel* 35 (1976):69-74.

Kosicki, G. W. "Steps Toward Christian Community." *RRel* 36 (1977):467-477.

Kratf, W. "Community Living." *RRel* 34 (1975):995-1003.

Légasse, S. "Saint Luc nous parle de la communauté." *Vie comm. rel.* 31 (1973):290-301.

Lindemann, K. "Toward a Definition of Community." *RRel* 29 (1970):833-842.

Linscott, M. "The Community Aspect of Covenant." USIC Bulletin 1973/3:6-9

Lopez-Olea, R. "La conversión como cambio de comunidad." *Manresa* 43 (1971):203-214.

Lozano, J. M. "La comunità religiosa nel suo sviluppo storico." In VV.AA., *Vita Comunitaria*. Milano: Ancora, 1979:10-41.

Molinari, P. "Comunidad: comunión en Cristo." *Vida Rel* 35 (1973):102–109.—Engl., "Community: Communion in Christ." *Sister Formation Bulletin* Winter, 1972:14–18.

Moloney, F. J. "Why Community." *Supplement to Doctrine and Life* (1974):19–31.

Moran, G. *The New Community*. New York: Herder and Herder, 1970.

Motte, A. *Un coeur et une âme en Dieu: La communauté religieuse*. Paris-Friburg: Ed. St. Paul, 1971.

Murphy, R. "Signs of Growth in the Local Community." *RRel* 36 (1977):746–752.

O'Donnell, D. "Group Dynamics and Community-Building." *Suppl. to Doctrine and Life* (1973):3–9.

Oraison, M. *Etre avec . . . La relation à autrui*. Paris: Le Centurion, 1967.—Engl. vers., *Being Together: Our Relations With Other People*. Tr. by Rosemary Sheed. Garden City: Doubleday, 1968.

O'Rourke, K. "Spirit, Law, and Community." *Cross and Crown* 21 (1969):5–14.

Parenteau, A. "Le défi de la fraternité évangélique." *Vie comm. relig.* 31 (1973):311–316.

Pastor, G. "Comunidades de base y grupos pequeños de vida religiosa." *Confer.* 17 (1972):261–282.

Pernos, P. "La notion de communauté dans les Actes de Vatican II: Un thème thélogique fondamental." *Maison-Dieu* 91 (1967):65–75.

Pin, E. "De l'Eglise comme manière d'être ensemble." *Christus* 15 (1968):166–178.

Régamey, P. R. "La comunità religiosa dallo psichico allo spirituale." *Vita Cons.* 10 (1974):266–278.

Rueda, B. *Apologie et démythisation de la vie commune*. Paris: Apostolat des Editions, 1972.

———. "La creatività nella preghiera comunitaria." *Vita Cons.* 10 (1974):334–345.

Salani, L. "Comunidad religiosa y vocación." *Vida en Fraternidad* 9 (1972):19–26.

Santaner, M. A. "Vie religieuse et vie de communauté." *VS* 115 (1966):154–167.

———. "Vie de communauté et mission." *Vie comm. relig.* 30 (1972):139–151.

———. "La vie fraternelle dans les communautés religieuses chrétiennes." *Vie comm. relig.* 32 (1974):130–148.

Schleck, C. "The Mystery and Holiness of Community Life." *RRel* 25 (1966):621–668.

Schlüter Rodés, A. M. "La amistad en la vida religiosa." *Vida Rel.* 40 (1976):73–79.

Schroth, R. A. "Living Together: The Religious Dilemma." *Commonweal* 96 (1972):258–260.

Sebastian Aguilar, F. "Attuazione comunitaria dei consigli evangelici." *Vita cons.* 8 (1971):545–556.

Secondin, B. "Comunità religiosa e comunione ecclesiale." In VV.AA., *Vita comunitaria*. Milano:Ancora, 1979.

Shaughnessy, E. J. "Reflections on the nature of Community." *RRel* 28 (1969):277-290.

Shehan, R. "Essential Factors in Creating Community." *Sisters Today* 43 (1971):192-199.

Silberer, R. "Die Einheit der Brüder: eine grosse apostolische Kraft." *Dienender Glaube* (1973):69-76.

Stenger, H. "Führung und Gemeinschaft: Zur Psychologie der vita communis." *Ordensnachrichten* (1972):1-10.

Steward, D. S. "Shaping Community: Learning to Live Beyond Ourselves." *Living Light* Winter, 1972:98-104.

Suárez, G. G. "La comunidad religiosa en el magisterio contemporáneo de la Iglesia." *Teol. Espir.* (1973):261-282.

Sullivan, J. "The Eucharist and the Local Community Living." *Sisters Today* 49 (1978):678-684.

Tiger, J. "La communauté, sacrement de communion." In *Religieuses aujourd'hui, demain.* Paris: Casterman 1970:125-131.

Tillard, J. M. R. "L'Eucharistie et la Fraternité." *NRT* 91 (1969):115-135.

———. "Le Mystère de la communauté." *Vie comm. relig.* 24 (1966):98-112.

———. "La comunità religiosa, segno della koinonia di carità." In *Il Rinnovamento della Vita Religiosa.* Firenze: Vallecchi, 1968:123-133.

———. "La communauté religieuse." *NRT* 94 (1972):488-519; (1973):150-187.

Urrutía, J. L. de. "Nuevas comunidades homogeneas de amistad." *Confer* 15 (1970):355-374.

Vaca, C. "La comunidad, escuela de perfección." *Rev. Agustiniana de Espiritualidad* 8 (1967):5-13.

van Molle, M. M. " Vie commune et obéissance d'après les institutions premières de Pachôme et Basile." *Supplement* 23 (1970):196-225.

VV.AA. "Prayer and Community." *Concilium* 52. New York: Herder and Herder, 1970.

VV.AA. "Los superiores generales ante la vida comunitaria" (Symposium). *Vida Religiosa* 32 (1972):427-500.

VV.AA. "Vivere la comunità" (Symposium). *Servitium* 6 (1972):513-687.

VV.AA. *Vita Comunitaria* (ed., Instituto Vita Religiosa, Roma). Milano: Ancora, 1979.

Wansborogh, H. "The Prophetic Community in Scripture." *Spode House Review* (1974):4-10.

Weakland, R. "Community: the Monastic Tradition." *ABenR* 26 (1975):233-250.

Whitson, R. E. *The Resurrection Christ: Community as Interperson.* Staten Island: Alba House, 1973.

Wilson, R. "Community and Loneliness." *RRel* 29 (1970):3-15.

9. Obedience

Alvarez Gómez, J. "Diversas formas de obediencia religiosa." *Vida Rel.* 42 (1977):422-434.

Alvarez Icaza, J. "Autoridad, obediencia y diálogo." *Servir* 6 (1970):33-54.

Amiet, P. "Exousia im Neuent Testament." *Internationale kirckliche Zeitschrift* (1971):233–242.

Aniz, C. "Concepto de obediencia perfecta." *GT* 83 (1956):305–336.

Artigas, L. "Sobre la obediencia del religioso apostolico." *Confer* 17 (1972):511–533.

Augé, M. "Autorità e obbedienza nella Vita Religiosa" (bibliography). *Claretianum* 18 (1978):5–34.

Bailly, G. "Autonomy and Authority in the Convent." *Cist. Stud.* 5 (1970):327–333.

Beha, H. M. "Gift of Ourselves: The Mystery of the Cross and Obedience." *Sursum Corda* 33 (1971):375–392.

Bergeron, R. "Le péché del l'homme et l'obéissance de Jésus." *Vie comm. relig.* 32 (1974):66–78.

Beyer, J. "Strutture di governo ed esigenze di partecipazione." *Vita cons.* 8 (1972):257–285.—Fr., "Structures de gouvernement et exigences de participation." *Supplement* 24 (1971):420–449.

Boado, F. "Obediencia y personalidad individual y comunitaria." *Manresa* 43 (1971):123–136.

Bock, D. C. and Clark, W. Neil, "Religious Belief as a Factor in Obedience to Destructive Commands." *Review of Religious Research* (1972):185–191.

Bonaventura da Gangi. "Oggetto del voto di ubbidienza." *Perfice Munus* 39 (1964):542–544.

———. "L'ubbidienza religiosa e i diritti della personalità." *Perfice Munus* 40 (1965):406–412.

Butler, C. "Authority and the Christian Conscience." *AmerBenR* 25 (1974):411–426.

Capelle, C. *Le voeu d'obéissance des origines au XII siecle.* Paris: 1959.

Casey, T. J. "The Democratization of Religious Life." *Cross and Crown* 22 (1970):290–305.

Chittister, J. "Religious Life: The Leadership That Is Needed." *Origins* 7 (1977):209.

Clancy, T. H. "Three Problems Concerning Obedience." *RRel* 33 (1974):844–860.

Murray, J. Courtney "Liberté, autorité, communauté." *Vie cons.* 39 (1967):321–337.

Cowburn, J. "The Analogy of Religious Authority and Obedience." *RRel* 27 (1968):604–612.

Crouzel, H. "Autorité et obéissance: un problème pratique." *NRT* 86 (1965):176–184.

Cusson, G. "Obéissance religieuse et maturité spirituelle." *Vie comm. relig.* 32 (1974):34–46.

Dennett, F. J. "Obedience." *Sursum Corda* 33 (1971):564–572.

Díez Presa, M. "Autoridad y obediencia un servicio a la libertad en favor del Reino." *Vida Rel.* 42 (1977):405–413.

Dominguez, O. "Reflexiones sobre la obediencia religiosa a la luz de la Evangelica Testificatio." *Confer* 16 (1971):641–664.

Donze, M. T. "Religious Obedience after Vatican II." *Homiletic and Pastoral Review* 74 (1974):63–68.

Dorff, F. "Reflection on the Renewal of Religious Obedience." *Spir. Life* 24 (1978):114–122.

Dubarle, D. "Un nouveau type d'obéissance." *Vs Suppl* 21 (1968):5–21.

Dubay, T. "A dialogue on mediated obedience." *RRel* 33 (1974):861–879.

Dubois, G. "Obedience: Evangelical and Monastic." *Cist Stud* 8 (1973):87–108.

Du Roy, O. "Obedience and Community Structures." *Cist Stud* 7 (1972):143–153.

Escallada, A. "Búsqueda de nuevas formas de relaciones entre autoridad y subitos en la Iglesia." *CT* 98 (1971):113–136.

Figuereido, F. A. "Autoridade e obediencia na Igreja." *Rev. Eccles. Brasileria* 34 (1974):586–599.

Fink, P. E. "Religious Obedience and the Holy Spirit." *RRel* 30 (1971):64–79.

Fanquesa, P. "Obediencia y Biblia." *Vida Rel.* 42 (1977):414–421.

Fuertes, J. B. "Auctoritas et servitium." *CpR* 49 (1968):203–214.

———. "Obedientia homini." *Ibid.*, 325–336.

García, C. "Conciencia y obediencia." *Revista Agustiniana Espiritualidad* 12 (1971):67–95.

Gau, J. V. "Discernment and the Vow of Obedience." *RRel* 32 (1973):569–574.

Giabbani, A. "Autorità. Aspetto Teologico." *Dizion. Istit. Perfez.* I (Roma: 1974):1003–1006.

Giovanna della Croce. "Autoridad y obediencia responsables." *Rev. Espiritualidad* (1972):172–182.

Goettermoeller, D. "Religious Government: a Reflection on Relationships; Structure of the Administration of the Religious Communities." *RRel* 34 (1975):70–79.

Goffi, T. *Di fronte all'autorità: Evangelo ed esperienza cristiana*. Brescia: Morcelliana, 1974.

———. "Obbedienza ed autoritá nella vita religiosa." *Riv. Vita Spir.* 30 (1976):486–501.

Goggin, A. and Knight, D. M. "Towards an Obedience of the Future." *RRel* 32 (1973):798–813.

Granado, C. "En torno al concepto de obediencia." *Manresa* 40 (1968):19–34.

———. "Autoridad y vida religiosa." *Ibid.*, 207–218.

Granero, J. M. "¿Mitos en la obediencia religiosa?" *Manresa* 45 (1973):229–240.

Guerrero, J. M. "El discernimiento comunitario." *Vida rel.* 38 (1975):271–292.

Gutiérrez Vega, L. "Renovación doctrinal y práctica de la obediencia religiosa." *Claretianum* 11 (1971):139–209.

———. "Misión fundamental del gobierno religioso." *Vida rel.* 34 (1973):97–111.

_____. *Autoridad y obediencia en la vida religiosa*. Madrid: Instituto Vida Religiosa, 1974.

_____. "Función de la autoridad en el discernimiento comunitario." *Vida rel.* 38 (1975):309–319.

_____. "La obediencia religiosa desde la teología de las mediaciones." *Vida Rel.* 42 (1977):453–473.

Hausherr, I. *L'Obéissance religieuse*. Toulouse: Prière et Vie, 1966.

Heyns, J. A. "A Theology of Obedience." *Reformed Theological Review* 32 (1973):37–47.

Hillmann, W. "Perfectio evangelica: Die Klosterliche Gehorsam in biblische-theologischer Sicht." *WiWei* 25 (1962):163–168.

Hughes, G. "Formation for Freedom." *Way* Suppl. 32 (1977):38–46.

Jacquemont, P. "Autorité et obéissance selon l'Ecriture." *Vs Suppl.* 21.

Justin, P. "Leadership in the Religious Life." *Cross and Crown* 24 (1972):12–18.

Kerr, F. "Authority in Religious Life." Supplement to *Doctrine and Life* (1973):87–92.

Kraus, H. "Der Gehorsam genenüber Menschen in den Ordenssatzungen: Reflexionen zu einer Zeitgemassen Anpassung des Ordensgehorsams." *GuL* 39 (1966):252–264.

Kunicic, J. "Oboedientia religiosae nova consideratii." *Divus Thomas* 69 (1966):199–212.

Kyne, M. "Religious Obedience." Suppl., *The Way* 19 (1973):118–125.

Langmaid, K. *The Blind Eye*. London: Jarrolds, 1972.

Lhoir, J. "Autorité et obéissance." *Collect Mechlinensia* 49 (1964):544–563.

Lumbreras, P. "La obediencia activa del Vaticano II." *Studium* 8 (1968):245–256.

Lyonnet, S. "Autorità ed obbedienza alla luce della s. Scrittura." In VV.AA., *Autoritá ed obbedienza nella vita religiosa*.

Magrini, E. "L'obbedienza nell'insegnamento del Concilio Vaticano II." *Studi Francescani* 72 (1975):83–119.

Marie Emmanuel, "Obedience Today." *Sisters Today* 47 (1976):284–288.

Martinez, M. "Condicionamientos psico-sociales del discernimiento comunitario." *Vida rel.* 38 (1975):293–308.

Melcon, A. "La obediencia y su formación." *CT* 95 (1968):461–482.

Mendizabal, I. "Riqueza eclesial y teológica de la vida religiosa." *Manresa* 36 (1964):283–302.

Müller, A. *El problema de la obediencia en la Iglesia*. Madrid: Taurus.

Mura, E. "Obbedienza religiosa e libertà dei figli di Dio." *Vita Religiosa* 5 (1969):209–215.

_____. "La pratica dell'obbedienza." *Ibid.*, 417–423.

_____. "L'autorità negli Istituti religiosi." *Ibid.*, 563–574.

_____. "L'esercizio dell'autorità." *Ibid.*, (1970):139–148.

O'Grady, D. "Authority Best When it Animates." *Nat. Cath. Rep.* 13 (1976):15.

Padilla, J. M. "La obediencia religiosa." *Cruz* 50 (1970):10–18; 43–49.

_____. "Los modelos de la obediencia religiosa." *Cruz* 50 (1970):79–89.

————. "La autoridad en la vida religiosa." *Cruz* 50 (1970):117–122; 155–160.

Paoli, A. "Obedience." *Cross Currents* 16 (1965):275–294.

Pasquier, J. "Models of leadership." *Tablet* 228 (1974):1203–1205.

Pozsagay, L. "Obedience of Judgment in Modern Context." *RRel* 27 (1968):822–837.

Rahner, K. "Le Christ modèle d'obéissance." In VV.AA., *Le Problème de l'Obéisance:*28–55.

————. "Eine ignatianische Grundhaltung." *Stimmen der Zeit* 158: (1955–1956):253–267.—Engl. tr., "A Basic Ignatian Concept: Some Reflections on Obedience." Woodstock Letters 86 (1957):291–310.

————. "Was heisst Ordensgehorsam? Überlegungen für eine heutige Theologie des Ordenslebens." *GuL* 46 (1973):115–125.

Ramírez, C. G. "El ejercicio de la autoridad religiosa concebida como servicio según el Concilio Vaticano II." *Franciscanum* 44 (1973):147–164.

Raus, J. B. *De sacrae oboedientiae virtute et voto secundum doctrinam Divi Thomae et Sancti Alphonsi: Tractatus canonico-moralis.* Lugduni-Lutetiae: 1923.

Recchia, P. "Nuovo volto dell'obbedienza religiosa." *Riv. Vita Spir* 26 (1972):541–554.

Renwart, L. "Réflexions sur l'obéissance." *Vie Cons.* 48 (1976):42–44.

Rongione, L. "Religious Obedience and the Apostolate." *Cross and Crown* 29 (1977):160–167.

Rothbluebber, F. B. "The Power of Decision in Religious Communities." *Studia Canonica* (1970):297–308.

Rubio, J. "Estructuras y libertad en la vida religiosa." *Revista Agustiniana de Espiritualidad* 11 (1970):385–407.

Rueda, B. *La Obediencia:* Circular a los Hermanos Maristas. Roma: 1975.

————. *Obedience,* Ottawa: Canadian Relig. Conf., 1977.

Saraggi, G. "L'obbedienza e l'autorità nella vita religiosa." *Palestra Clero* 50 (1971):987–911.

Sasseville, T. "Note sur l'obéissance religieuse et le monde actuel." *Vie comm. relig.* 29 (1971):127–130.

Sauras, J. "La Obediencia." *Confer* 7 (1965):476–491.

Schwager, R. "Gehorsam und Widerstand." *GuL* 47 (1974):202–213.

Singleton, M. W. F. "Changing Patterns of Obedience." *Clergy Review* 53 (1968):684–698.

Skudlarek, W. "Obedience to One Another." *AmerBenR* 21 (1970):484–495.

Spidlik, T. "L'obbedienza tra carisma ed istituzione." *Vita Monastica* 24 (1970):36–49.

Teresa Margaret, Sr. "Community and Authority: A Dialectical Tension." *Cross and Crown* 21 (1969):178–192.

Thalhammer, D. "Der religiöse Gehorsam." *Entschluss* (1971):229–232.

Tillard, J. M. R. "Aux sources de l'obéissance religieuse." *NRT* 98 (1976):592–626; 817–877.

———. "L'Obéissance religieuse, mystère de communion." *NRT* 87 (1965):377–394.

———. "Autorité et vie religieuse." *NRT* 88 (1966):786–806.

———. "Repenser le gouvernement des instituts." *Vie cons.* 42 (1970):163–170.

———. "Problemas en torno á la obediencia." *Vida Rel.* 42 (1977).

———. "Les chemins de l'obéissance." *Lumen Vitae* 31 (1976):141–173; 355–386.

VV.AA. *Autorità ed obbedienza nella vita religiosa,* Milano: Ancora, 1978 (ed. Istituto Vita Religiosa, Roma).

VV.AA. "A Discussion on Leadership and Authority." *Studies in the Spirituality of Jesuits* 4 (1972):53–81.

VV.AA. L'Obéissance (Symposium). *Vie cons.* 44 (1972):193–224.

VV.AA. *Le problème de l'obéissance,* Paris: Apostolat des Editions, 1969.

VV.AA. *L'Obéissance: problèmes de vie religieuse.* Paris: 1965.

Voillaume, R. "The Value and Practice of Obedience in the Religious and Apostolic Life of Today." *Spiritual Life* 17 (1971):123–134.

Voss, M. R. "The Superior's Role Within Obedience." *Woodstock Letters* 98 (1970):409–429.

Wulf, F. "Der biblische Sinn des Rates des Gehorsams." *GuL* 39 (1966):248–251.

Ziello, P. *Obedience and Authority in the Religious Life (in the light of the Vatican Council II),* India: Saint Paul Public., 1970.

10. The Religious Vow

Albrecht, B. "Man's Capacity for Final Commitment." *RRel* 37 (1978):203–213.

Alvaro Panqueva, P. "La consagración religiosa." *Vinculum* (1973):39–51.

Bandera, A. "La consacrazione a Dio per mezzo dei consigli evangelici." *Vita cons* 7 (1971):521–531; 609–613; 785–797.

———. "La consagración religiosa según Evangelica Testificatio." *Confer* 17 (1972):479–510.

Boisevert, L. "La consécration religieuse." *Vie comm. relig.* 25 (1967):280–286.

Boni, A. "Note storico-giuridiche sul concetto di consacrazione nell professione religiosa." *Vita cons* 8 (1972):666–682.

Brinkman, M. "The Vows: Historical and Psychological Perspective." *Sister Formation Bulletin* Spring, 1971:5–77; 11.

Campos, J. "El propósito monástico en la tradición patrística." *La Ciudad de Dios* 181 (1968):535–547.

Carpentier, R. "L'objet du triple voeu dans l'état de perfection." *Rev. comm. relig.* 29 (1967):60–67; 146–153.

Comblin, J. "Os votos e a vida religiosa." *Rev. ecles. Brasileira* 29 (1969):850–880.

———. "A vida religiosa como consagração." *Grande Sinal* 24 (1970):31–40.

Demmer, K. "Gelubde und Versprechen: Reflexionen über die Verplichtungskraft der Ordensgelübe." *ThGl* 61 (1971):297–320.

Dunne, E. "Vows, Promises: The Aim is Life-commitment." *Sursum Corda* 11 (1970):8–14.

Faller, A. "Decisione e lotta per Dio nella consacrazione." *Vita cons.* 8 (1972):633–642.

Farley, M. and Goettemoeller, D. "Commitment in a Changing World." *RRel* 34 (1975):75–92.

Forestier, M. D. "Baptême et vie religieuse." *VS* 115 (1966):143–153.

Fuertes, J. B. "Professio religiosa complementum baptismi." *CpR* 43 (1964):293–319.

Gallen, J. F. "Temporary Commitment to Religious Life." *RRel* 33 (1974):476–477.

Garvey, T. "Religious Life: A Commitment to Men." *RRel* 31 (1972):41–44.

Giardini, F. "Lo stato religioso come olocausto." *Angelicum* 38 (1961):187–199.

Isaac, J. *Réévaluer les voeux*. Paris: Cerf, 1973.

Kropf, R. "Radical commitment and fulfillment." *Spir. Life* 21 (1975):75–92.

Leclercq, J. "Genèse et évolution de la vie consacrée." *Rev. dioc. Tournai* 22 (1967):172–197.—Engl. tr., "Monastic Profession and the Sacraments." *Monastic Studies* 5 (1968):59–85.

————. "Evangile et culture dans l'histoire de l'engagement à la vie religieuse." *Vie comm. relig.* 32 (1974):79–93.

————. "Le caractère définitif de l'engagement religieux." *Vie comm. relig.* (1972):162–177.—Engl. tr., "The Definitive Character of Religious Commitment." *ABenR* 23 (1972):181–205.

Malone, P. "Vows and Witness." *Compass* 4 (1970):60–63.

McCool, G. A. "Commitment to One's Institute: A Contemporary Question." *RRel* 29 (1970):17–31.

Mendizabal, L. "La consagración y el sentido de los votos." *Manresa* 37 (1965):225–249.

Molinari, P. "Domino se peculariter devovet et divino obsequio intimius consecratur." *Vita cons.* 8 (1972):401–432.

Morlot, F. "Consécration sacerdotale et consécration par les conseils." *NRT* (1972):290–308.

Philippon, M. "Consécration sacerdotale et consécration religieuse." *Vocation* (1968):123–138.

Pousset, E. "Human Existence and the Three Vows." *RRel* 29 (1970):211–237.

Provera, P. *La consécration religieuse sous l'éclairage de Vatican II*. Paris: Apostolat des Editions, 1967.

Rahner, K. *Sulla professione religiosa*. Brescia: Queriniana, 1967.

Ramírez, E. "La profesión de los consejos evangélicos, expresión perfecta de la consagración bautismal." *Mysterium* 25 (1966):275–292.

Ranquet, J. G. *Consacrazione battesimale e consacrazione religiosa*. Alba: Ed. Paoline, 1968.

Régamey, P. R. "La consécration religieuse." *Vie cons.* 38 (1966):266–294; 339–359.

Rinaldi, G. "I voti religiosi." *Vita rel* 4 (1968):107–124.

Rocco, U. "Battesimo e professione religiosa." *Perfice munus* 40 (1965):157–162.

Sartori, L. M. "A consagração religiosa." *Grande Sinal* 26 (1972):171–182.

Secondin, B. "Battesimo e vita religiosa nel mistero della Chiesa." *Vita Rel* 3 (1967):203–214; 299–311.

Steidl-Meier, P. "Dynamic Aspects of the Traditional Vows: Hearing, Sharing, Indwelling." *RRel* 37 (1978):288–293.

Teresa Margaret, Sr. "Why take religious vows." *The Clergy Review* 53 (1968):806–811.

Troisfontaines, R. "Baptême et vie consacrée." *Rev. Dioc. Tournai* 22 (1967):236–259.

Indices

Index of Proper Names and Sources

Index of Scriptural Citations

Apocrypha